T0271688

Thomas Tooke and the Monetary Thought of Classical Economics

This study provides a comprehensive account and reconsideration of the contribution to political economy of Thomas Tooke (1774–1858), English classical economist and influential monetary historian and theorist. It clarifies Tooke's monetary thought and its legacy to modern economics. The study shows Tooke possessed a rich and extensive political economy, covering many aspects of economic activity relevant to key policy issues. Tooke's political economy is shown to be a unified and coherent body of intellectual thought in the classical tradition which, like most of his nineteenth-century contemporaries, was much influenced by Adam Smith's economics. More particularly, Tooke's monetary thought, especially his novel banking school theory, is shown to be theoretically coherent from the standpoint of nineteenth-century classical economics. It is also shown that, besides contributing towards a better understanding of the behaviour of monetary systems in general, key elements of Tooke's banking school theory make an important contribution to explaining distribution, growth and price inflation in modern economics.

In reconstructing Tooke's political economy the study provides insights into the conceptual properties of classical economics: into, for example, the approach to explaining market prices and their fluctuation, into explaining income distribution, the doctrine of free trade, the meaning of 'Say's Law' and explaining the fluctuation and trend movement in the general price level. The focus of the study is on reconstructing Tooke's monetary thought and, in doing so, to clarify the conceptual framework of monetary theory in classical economics. It is shown that Tooke's banking school theory contributes not only towards the construction of an 'endogenous money' theory as an alternative to the quantity theory of money approach, but that in the modern formulation of classical analysis it contributes towards a well-grounded conception of monetary forces, in particular, monetary policy, exerting a lasting influence on real economic variables such as income distribution, aggregate output and employment.

This book will be of interest to students and researchers of the history of economic thought and those interested in the foundations of the development of monetary thought and policy.

Matthew Smith is a Lecturer in Economics at the University of Sydney, Australia.

Routledge studies in the history of economics

Thomas Tooke and the Monetary Thought of Classical Economics

Matthew Smith

Routledge
Taylor & Francis Group

LONDON AND NEW YORK

First published 2011
by Routledge
2 Park Square, Milton Park, Abingdon, Oxon OX14 4RN

Simultaneously published in the USA and Canada
by Routledge
711 Third Avenue, New York, NY 10017

Routledge is an imprint of the Taylor & Francis Group, an informa business

British Library Cataloguing in Publication Data
A catalogue record for this book is available from the British Library

Library of Congress Cataloging in Publication Data
Smith, Matthew, 1959–
Thomas Tooke and the monetary thought of classical economics / Matthew Smith.
p. cm.
1. Tooke, Thomas, 1774-1858. 2. Economists–Great Britain. 3. Classical school of economics. 4. Money–Great Britain–History. 5. Prices–Great Britain–History. I. Title.
HB103.T53S65 2010
339.5'3–dc22
2010036863

ISBN: 978-0-415-58393-0 (hbk)
ISBN: 978-0-203-82970-7 (ebk)

Typeset in Times
by Wearset Ltd, Boldon, Tyne and Wear

To the memory of my father, Harold Smith (1932–2006), and good friend, Gordon White (1930–2007).

Contents

Appendices 232

Preface

This work has had a long gestation. It began nearly twenty years ago with research for a doctoral thesis on Thomas Tooke under the supervision of Peter Groenewegen at the University of Sydney, completed in 1999. While the present work bears a resemblance to that thesis, it represents a considerable expansion in the scope of the study and the development of the argument in consequence of ongoing research on Tooke and the monetary thought of nineteenth-century classical economics. Some of the key elements of the study have been published in journal articles and a book chapter in the past decade (see Acknowledgements). This book though has been designed with the larger purpose of bringing together all the elements into a unified study of Tooke in order to provide a rich, definitive exposition of his political economy.

My greatest debt is to Tony Aspromourgos, who provided valuable comment and advice on two chapters as well as on versions of much of the material for the book in draft and published form over the past ten years. I owe a great debt also to Peter Groenewegen who, similarly, has provided valuable comment on draft versions of most of the material for the book from its inception over the last fifteen years. I am further indebted to Massimo Pivetti, who first inspired me to study Tooke, for some helpful advice on key findings of the research. In addition, a special thank you is due to J. Jonnes and N. Fletcher for their translation of 'Tooke-Say' letters published in French. Others who I am grateful to, in various ways, for their time and knowledge, include R. Ciccone, G. de Vivo, P. Garegnani, C. Gehrke, R. Hirose-Smith, J. King, H.D. Kurz, M. Nearhos, R. O'Donnell, A. Palumbo, J. Pullen, A. Stirati and A. Trezzini. Furthermore, I am grateful to a number of anonymous referees over the years for their helpful comments on my various draft work on Tooke submitted for journal publication. Finally, I am indebted to the University of Sydney which has in a number of ways supported my research from its beginning. It needs hardly saying that I am solely responsible for the final product.

Matthew Smith
Sydney
August 2010

Acknowledgements

Acknowledgement is here given for permission to reproduce material from the author's following publications.

Chapter 3, not including sections 3.5 and 3.6, is a revised version of 'Tooke's Approach to Explaining Prices', *European Journal of the History of Economic Thought* (2002), 9(3), pp. 333–58, the copyright held by Taylor and Francis Group. Sections 3.6 and 4.4 of the book employ revised parts of 'Thomas Tooke on the Corn Laws', *History of Political Economy* (2009), 41(2), pp. 343–82, the copyright held by Duke University Press. Sections 5.5, 6.1 and 6.2.1 employ revised material from 'Thomas Tooke on the Bullionist Controversies', *European Journal of the History of Economic Thought* (2008), 15(1), pp. 49–84, the copyright held by Taylor and Francis Group.

Chapter 7, not including sections 7.4 and 7.5, employs revised material from 'Endogenous Money, Interest and Prices: Tooke's Monetary Thought Revisited', *Contributions to Political Economy* (2001), 20, pp. 31–55, the copyright held by Oxford University Press. Sections 7.4 and 7.5 of the book employ revised parts of 'On Central Banking "Rules": Tooke's Critique of the Bank Charter Act of 1844', *Journal of the History of Economic Thought* (2003) 25(1), pp. 39–61, copyright held by Cambridge University Press.

Chapter 8, not including section 8.3, and sections 6.3 and 7.3 of the book employs revised material from 'On Profits and Interest: Thomas Tooke's Major Legacy to Economics', *Contributions to Political Economy* (2006) 25(1), pp. 1–33, the copyright also held by Oxford University Press. These parts of the book as well as section 8.3 have also variously employed revised material from 'Thomas Tooke's Legacy to Monetary Economics', in *History and Political Economy: Essays in Honour of P.D. Groenewegen* (2004), edited by T. Aspromourgos and J. Lodewijks, London: Routledge, pp. 57–75, the copyright also held by Taylor and Francis Group.

Acknowledgement is also here given for permission by the British Library to quote and cite from following unpublished correspondence: 'Tooke to Charles Babbage', dated 28 June 1832, MS37186 f497; 'Tooke to Grenville', dated 19 and 24 November 1825, 'Grenville to Tooke', dated 23 November, *Grenville Papers*, Add 69082; 'Huskisson to Tooke', dated 8 December 1825, *Huskisson Papers*, Add 38747. In addition, the letter 'Tooke to Lord Monteagle', dated 30 September 1854, MS13401, is quoted and cited with the permission of the National Library of Ireland.

A note on citation practice

To best apprise the reader of the nature of historical lines of influence between the works of writers often referred to in this book, the year cited will be, as far as known, to the original year of publication of the reference work. In particular, this will be the case with reprints of published works and those works originally published in a non-English language with the English edition published some time afterward. Thus, for example, the year of citation for Wicksell's *Interest and Prices* is 1898, when originally published in German, with the first English edition published in 1936. In the case when *only* the second or later edition of a work in which a number of editions are published is cited and the content of the work referred to is originally published in its first edition, then the citation will consist of the year of the first edition followed in brackets by that of the later edition used. Thus, for example, the year of citation of J.S. Mill's *Essays on Some Unsettled Questions on Political Economy*, second edition, is (1844 [1874]) and of Adam Smith's *Wealth of Nations*, Glasgow edition, is (1776 [1976]). In the particular case of citations to Tooke's six-volume *History of Prices* (1838–1857), the citation will always be designated by the volume number in roman uppercase. Thus, for example, the citation to volume four of Tooke's *History of Prices* is (1848a, IV), even though this reference can be identified without designation of the volume number. Though William Newmarch was an important collaborator in the authorship of volumes V and VI of *History of Prices* (see section 2.2 below), for convenience they will sometimes be cited only by reference to Tooke.

A much-used reference source in this work is evidence given to British parliamentary committees by Tooke and others. This source is cited in the same way as published works by reference to the year of its publication and, in the case of parliamentary evidence given to two or more committees in the same year, then, in the same way as one of an author's multiple-cited publications of the same year, it is designated by alphabetical letters in lowercase. For example, Tooke's parliamentary evidence to the 1848 Commons Secret Committee on Commercial Distress is cited as Tooke (1848b) and his evidence to the 1848 Lords Secret Committee Appointed to Inquire into the Causes of the Commercial Distress is cited as Tooke (1848c). For those not familiar with references to minutes of evidence and reports of parliamentary committees (and appointed commissions), 'P.P.' refers to British parliamentary papers.

1 Introduction

The leading theorist of the banking school and author of the monumental six-volume *A History of Prices* (1838–1857) and the brilliant pamphlet, *An Inquiry into the Currency Principle* (1844), Thomas Tooke (1774–1858) can be rightfully counted among the most prominent figures in English nineteenth-century monetary thought. In addition to an impressive number of writings on money and prices, Tooke actively participated in the discussions of the Political Economy Club from its inception in 1821 until well into the mid-nineteenth century and gave evidence before no less than ten parliamentary committees between 1819 and 1848, most of them concerned with monetary issues and chiefly responsible for shaping Britain's banking policy in the nineteenth century. A number of eminent economists important to the development of monetary thought have closely studied Tooke's writings and, in various ways, have been influenced by his ideas. These include J.S. Mill, Marx, Knut Wicksell and Alfred Marshall, the latter two being pioneers of twentieth-century monetary thought whose theories, in their essentials, still dominate. But, despite Tooke's significant contribution, there has been relatively little literature in the history of economic thought devoted solely to a comprehensive study of his work and ideas. This neglect appears to have stemmed from a lack of interest borne of an underestimation of the constructive value of his contribution. The main theme in the commentary on Tooke is that, while he made valuable contributions with his large-scale empirical analyses, with his pragmatic arguments on policy issues and with his critically minded exposure of weaknesses in the quantity theory of money, the alternative monetary theory he developed has little positive value. This opinion is well represented by Wicksell:

> His [Tooke's] monetary contributions – no matter how highly one may regard them in other respects – are on the theoretical side purely critical in general outlook and negative in concept. It is quite impossible, I think, to construct out of them a positive theory of money.
>
> (1898: 43–4)

However, this opinion stems from interpreting Tooke's contributions through the looking glass of marginalist theory, which rose to dominance from the late nineteenth century. From the standpoint of marginalist economics, most of Tooke's key banking school ideas are not logically coherent and have thereby been judged to be of little constructive value. But Tooke developed his banking school ideas on the very different theoretical foundations of English classical economics which dominated the first half of the nineteenth century. These ideas would therefore have been seen by Tooke to only have constructive value when comprehended in terms of the theoretical foundations of classical economics from which they logically sprang. Why then should any scholar of Tooke who does not understand his ideas in terms of classical economics find constructive value in them? Like many of his classical contemporaries, a full understanding and hence appreciation of Tooke's contribution has become victim to the funda-mental change that has undertaken economic science since 1871. Fortunately, the rigorous reconstruction and revival of classical economics that occurred with Piero Sraffa's *Production of Commodities by Means of Commodities* (1960) has provided a clearer analytical perspective for better understanding the classical economists in general and, more particularly here, Tooke's economics. With this perspective, Tooke's banking school theory can be seen to make an enduring contribution to the theory of distribution, as well as monetary behaviour and the price level, relevant to modern capitalist society.

The purpose of this study is to provide a comprehensive account of the con-tribution of Tooke to economic science, with an evaluation of that contribu-tion. Though his contribution will be shown to be made principally in the field of monetary economics, it is not exclusively so. Indeed, an important aim of what follows is to show that in the tradition of classical economics Tooke pos-sessed a rich political economy encompassing explanations of various aspects of the economic system such as the fluctuation in activity and changes in income distribution as well as contributing to debate on a number of policy questions, usually as part of his wider historical analysis of price movements in England over the period 1792 to 1856. To this end, a concern of this study will be to discover Tooke's 'system' of political economy and what shaped it. An understanding of the unified nature of Tooke's economics will enable a more complete comprehension of his monetary thought, which is the main purpose of this study.

The chronology of this study is dictated by the manner in which Tooke developed his monetary thought over time, culminating in his banking school theory. In this regard, Tooke can be described as an 'inductive' thinker in the sense that he believed the robustness of economic principles could only be ver-ified by empirical findings. Tooke's scientific method basically consisted of establishing the concrete facts by exhaustive empirical analysis upon which explanations of general application could be formulated. This method did not preclude Tooke from employing existing economic theory in empirical analy-sis; indeed, it would be impossible to determine the scope of empirical inquiry or interpret its finding without theory for guidance. Rather, for Tooke, the development of economic theory proceeded from empirical analysis. Tooke's scientific method involved laborious analysis, the dismissal of theories which could not be empirically verified and the slow development of principles. In this manner Tooke slowly developed his own monetary thought from his empirical work. Therefore, before considering Tooke's monetary thought, this study will examine his empirically based explanation of price movements in England over the period 1792–1856. Moreover, in conjunction with other evidence, from Tooke's empirical analysis, it is possible to ascertain his method of analysis and theoretical approach to value and distribution as well as his theory-based arguments on a range of other relevant economic issues. In this way it is shown Tooke did possess a coherent theoretical framework as a necessary starting point to conduct his empirical analyses and upon which he subsequently built.

Chapters 3, 4 and 5 are concerned with these foundational elements of Tooke's work. In Chapter 3, the theoretical framework in classical economics that Tooke employed in his empirical analysis and upon which he developed his monetary thought is elucidated. Chapter 4 is concerned with Tooke's explanation of the movement in the price of agricultural commodities, consisting principally of corn, which was an important part of his explanation of the movement in the price level in general. In Chapter 5, Tooke's explanation of the movement in the general level of prices, consisting of the change in the prices of a range of products in addition to agricultural commodities, is considered. Having expounded the foundational elements, Tooke's monetary thought is comprehensively examined in Chapters 6 and 7. There is agreement among scholars who have closely studied Tooke's monetary thought that there are two main phases in its evolution (Gregory 1928: 16–17, 69–83; Arnon 1991: 2–3; Pivetti 1991: 75). Chapter 6 is concerned with the first phase, the pre-banking school phase, comprising Tooke's writings and parliamentary evidence from 1819 to 1838 when his monetary thought remained, albeit uneasily, within the bounds of the orthodox quantity theory approach of the classical economists. Chapter 7 is then concerned with the second phase, the banking school phase, comprising Tooke's writings and parliamentary evidence from 1840 to 1857, when he developed a novel set of principles more consistent with his empirical findings and in opposition to the classical economists' quantity theory of money. This set of principles formed the basis of Tooke's banking school theory. In these two chapters, consideration is given to the nature and causes of the transformation in Tooke's monetary thought. The last stage of this study is concerned with Tooke's legacy to economic science. By way of conclusion, Chapter 8 identifies the main lines of Tooke's influence on the development of monetary economics and the constructive value of his key ideas to contemporary economic theory.

Preliminary to undertaking the main part of this study, Chapter 2 provides an account of Tooke's life and his contributions to political economy, the latter consisting not only of his publications but also his evidence given to parliamentary committees. This survey will provide useful background to the study of Tooke's work undertaken in this book. Before this survey, an account of the commentary on Tooke is given in Section 1 of this chapter, followed in Section 2 by an exposition of the definition of classical economics employed in this study.

1.1 The commentary on Tooke

Most of the secondary literature on Tooke has consisted of brief accounts of his contributions in the context of wider historical studies of English nineteenth-century monetary economics that encompasses the currency–banking school debates of the 1840s. For a long time the most definitive account of Tooke's work was the 'Introduction' by T.E. Gregory to the 1928 reprint of *History of Prices*. It consists of a 120-page account of Tooke's writings, including a critical examination of his various views on major topics in monetary thought. While Gregory (1928) made a number of useful observations, he did not attempt an analytical exposition of Tooke's economics. Gregory believed Tooke was a 'magnificent controversialist' who stood not among the 'systematic writers of history, but among the Pamphleteers, the men with an intellectual axe to grind, who are the great glory of English economic literature – do they not include Defoe and Dudley North, Ricardo and Malthus, Jevons and Keynes?' (1928: 120). This praise masks the highly critical disposition of Gregory to Tooke's ideas (1928: 28–9, 82–91). As the French historian of monetary thought Charles Rist wrote: 'Professor Gregory finds more to criticise than to praise in [Tooke's] works' (1940: 182). There is no doubt that Gregory's interpretation of Tooke is heavily coloured by a strong attachment to the tradition of the quantity theory of money (see 1928: 22–3). It is not going too far to conclude that Gregory's (1928) introduction to Tooke's *History of Prices* ranks as one of the most unsympathetic introductions ever written for an author's re-published work in the history of economic thought.

The fullest study of Tooke so far undertaken is Arnon's book, *Thomas Tooke: Pioneer of Monetary Theory* (1991). In contrast to Gregory (1928), Tooke is given sympathetic treatment by Arnon, who considered 'Tooke's writing[s] to include a theoretical structure, which merits scholarly attention on several grounds' (1991: 1). For Arnon (1991), Tooke merits attention as the pioneer of the 'innovative' banking school theory. Arnon's book examines the evolution of Tooke's monetary thought from his emergence as a political economist and 'ally' of Ricardo to the development of his banking school views. According to Arnon (1991: 4, 74–7, 113–15), Tooke's lasting contribution to monetary thought consists of showing the important role of credit in explaining variations in economic activity and prices. However, Arnon (1991: 115) also considered Tooke's 'silence on the determination of the quantity of credit remains the weakest point in his analysis'. Notwithstanding a sympathetic treatment, it is apparent Arnon (1991) struggles to discover a coherent system of economic analysis in Tooke's work (particularly, see 113–16). This is reflected in the many gaps in Arnon's account of Tooke's contributions, especially of the latter's explanation of price movements and of his banking school theory, as well as his substantial influence on the development of monetary thought.

Another study exclusively devoted to Tooke's contribution is Laidler's essay, 'Thomas Tooke on Monetary Reform' (1975). This essay deals with Tooke's views on English banking policy in the currency–banking school debates of the

1840s. Though Laidler (1975) is predominantly concerned with practical issues of policy, the discussion considers, albeit briefly, some of the central ideas of Tooke's banking school theory. For the most part, Laidler is more sympathetic to Tooke's position on banking policy than that of the currency school, concluding that 'on the whole Tooke's programme is a more appealing one than that of the currency school' (1975: 223). However, with respect to Tooke's banking school theory, Laidler is critical, believing it not to be 'logically complete and rigorous ... where critical pieces of it are missing or badly set out, and where extraneous matters intrude unduly' (1975: 211).

Other secondary literature on Tooke has either accounted for his contributions as part of a wider study of monetary thought or been concerned with particular aspects of his monetary analysis. A lengthy account of Tooke's writings is given by Charles Rist in *History of Monetary and Credit Theory: From John Law to the Present Day* (1940). In chapter 4 of this book, Rist compared Tooke's views on a range of monetary issues with those of Ricardo, concluding that 'Tooke the Historian' is the superior counterpart to 'Ricardo the Logician' because '[H]is conclusions are always preceded by a detailed description and analysis of facts, and are so superior to and much more comprehensive than the Ricardian simplifications' (1940: 180). In chapter 5, Rist (1940: 202–38) examined Tooke's banking school theory, focusing on his distinction between money and credit and the important role he ascribed to credit in the operation of the monetary system. Rist (1940: 202–38) claimed Tooke to be the 'creator of the credit theory', anticipating the twentieth-century approach to monetary theory of Wicksell, Hawtrey and Keynes (a view shared by Spiegel 1971: 351–2, 592). Nearly waxing lyrical, Rist further wrote 'that his books are full of original and sound ideas' in which '[H]e illuminates every aspect of every problem which he discusses – the role of banks, the nature of bank-notes and cheques, the origin of crisis, the rate of interest' (1940: 181–2). But, while Rist had a high opinion of Tooke's writings, he did not believe them to contain a coherent monetary theory, commenting 'Tooke was no theorist' (1940: 191). A sympathetic account of Tooke's banking school views is also given in Green's (1992) historical study of theories of money, output and inflation in classical economics. However, Green (1992) is more concerned with examining the position of the banking school as a whole in the currency–banking school debates of the 1840s than with Tooke's position per se. Nevertheless, in relation to issues relevant to a 'fiduciary' and 'credit' system of money, Green (1992: 154–60, 171–2, 179–203) discusses many aspects of Tooke's banking school position. Essentially, Green argues that the banking school provided a more sophisticated analysis of the operation of a credit-based monetary system than Ricardo and the currency school, but that this 'progress' 'was gained at the expense of internal consistency; for, by accepting the Say's Law assumption of full capacity utilisation, they could explain concrete conditions only by going beyond the limits of existing classical doctrine' (1992: 182; on this issue, see Section 8.4: 219).

A highly critical account of Tooke and the banking school is given in Daugherty's (1942; 1943) twin articles on the currency–banking school controversy.

Daugherty believed that banking school theory largely consisted of a 'mass of obscure, disorderly, and often fallacious ideas' (1943: 251). Unable to discover any coherency in the 'doctrines' of the banking school, Daugherty (1942: 148–55; 1943: 246–7) provided only a brief and unsystematic discussion of them. Another highly critical interpretation of Tooke and the banking school is given by Mints (1945: 86–100, 121–2) who was particularly critical of the idea that the quantity of money was endogenously determined by the 'wants of trade' and, connectedly, of the law of reflux. However, Mints' unsympathetic account of banking school doctrine is piecemeal, being only a small part of a wider study of monetary thought.[1] By contrast, Morgan (1965: 120–43) provides a more balanced account of Tooke and the banking school in his discussion of the currency–banking schools controversy. However, Morgan (1965) gives little consideration to banking school theory, concentrating on the practical policy issues surrounding the Bank Charter Act of 1844. Morgan (1965) tends to emphasise the common ground of the two schools of thought. He believed the banking school made an important contribution toward understanding the operation of credit in the British monetary system and the motives for demanding gold, but was critical of their argument that the 'over-issue' of banknotes fully convertible into bullion was not possible.

A piecemeal account of Tooke and the banking school is also provided by Fetter (1965: 172–3, 187–94) in connection with the currency–banking school controversy. The main concern of Fetter (1965) is with the actual influence of these two schools on public debate and British banking policy. While believing Tooke to be inconsistent in some of his views, Fetter (1965: 173, 191–2, 204) nevertheless believed him to possess a better understanding of the practical operation of the monetary system than members of the currency school. Elsewhere, though, in a short biography of Tooke, Fetter (1968: 104) commented that Tooke 'had little ability to develop an organised monetary theory'. In Wood's (1939) study of nineteenth-century English theories of monetary policy, Tooke's views are not systematically dealt with, but are briefly considered in relation to specific issues under discussion (see 44–5, 49–50, 56–9, 140–3, 150–1, 179–80). Nevertheless, Wood (1939: 56–9) devotes particular attention to Tooke's denial of the Bank of England's influence on prices, concluding that 'Tooke really had *no* theory to explain how monetary causes were related to prices'. An account of the position of Tooke and the banking school is also given in Robbins' (1958: 121–43) study of Robert Torrens' contribution to classical economics. However, Robbins (1958) was concerned mainly with Torrens' criticisms of the banking school and, for the most part, provided an unsympathetic account of their views. In a concise assessment of his contributions, Schumpeter (1954: 520–1) praised Tooke for the empirical analysis of *History of Prices*, but was highly critical of him as a theorist. Indeed, Schumpeter referred to Tooke as a 'woolly thinker', lacking a 'theoretical edge to his thought' and 'deficient in command of economic theory' (1954: 520–1). Even more damning, Schumpeter wrote that Tooke 'had no notion of the logical relation between observation and analysis and never understood what facts may, and what facts may not, be adduced in verification or refutation of a theory' (1954: 709). Some aspects of Tooke's banking school theory were also critically examined in Marget's (1938: 189–205, 249–58, 311–27) book on twentieth-century monetary theory. For the most part, Marget (1938) presents Wicksell's original criticisms of Tooke's theory. In other historical studies of monetary economics by Viner (1937: 222–4, 233–8) and Feaveryear (1931 [1963]: 264–70), Tooke and the banking school receive very little serious attention.[2]

A small group of commentators have been more specifically concerned with Tooke's position on the relationship between the determination of the rate of interest, rate of profit and prices. In his article 'The Theory of Interest in the Classical Economists', Caminati (1981: 98–101) examines Tooke's theory of interest and, in particular, compares it to that of J.S. Mill and Marx. A more thorough examination of Tooke's monetary analysis in connection with interest-rate determination is provided in Panico's book, *Interest and Profit in the Theories of Value and Distribution* (1988: 21–45). In this book Panico (1988: 37–8) shows how Tooke's position on interest and profit could form the basis of a theory of distribution in classical economics. The latter subject is also taken up by Pivetti (1991: 38–9, 74–86; 1998),[3] who is mainly concerned with showing that Tooke's position on the relationship between the rate of interest and prices provides the foundation for an explanation of distribution relevant to a modern capitalist economy. In connection to this subject matter, Pivetti (1991: 75–81) examines some aspects of Tooke's banking school theory, especially the conception of endogenous money. An appreciation of Tooke's banking school theory has also been shown by Moore (1988: 5) and Wray (1990: xiii, 102–10), contemporary advocates of theories of endogenous money. Unlike most of the commentary surveyed above, these commentators have a positive opinion of Tooke as a monetary theorist, believing his banking school ideas provide a valuable contribution to contemporary monetary analysis but not in the quantity theory tradition (see Sections 8.4 and 8.5).

This survey supports the point made earlier that, with some notable exceptions, most commentators in the literature have formed a negative opinion of the constructive value of Tooke's contributions. While they have valued the historical content of Tooke's empirical analysis and been sympathetic to his practical views on banking policy, they have been largely dismissive of his banking school theory. This opinion largely stems from an inability to discover a coherent economic analysis in Tooke. It perhaps best explains why there have been few attempts to provide a comprehensive exposition of Tooke's political economy in the literature. Economic science would therefore benefit from a comprehensive study of this neglected economist able to discover the coherency in his political economy from its theoretical roots in nineteenth-century classical economics.

1.2 Tooke and classical economics

Tooke is commonly characterised as a classical economist. However, there is not general agreement on what 'classical economics' or, the equivalent term, 'classical political economy', is. There are indeed various definitions of classical economics to be found in the literature, although the most commonly accepted ones *date it* from Adam Smith through Ricardo to J.S. Mill (Blaug 1987). In this respect there is certainly considerable agreement as to who the classical economists are, notwithstanding differences in what classical economics is. Hence, as a contemporary of Ricardo and a much younger J.S. Mill, Tooke has been largely regarded as a classical economist of second-order importance, along with James Mill, Torrens and McCulloch but in ranking of contribution, below Malthus, Say and Senior. While one could disagree about Tooke's relative importance, it could not be denied that Tooke is a classical economist in the sense that his intellectual bearings come from a framework largely shaped directly by Adam Smith and Ricardo. But the question remains: what is classical economics which somehow defines coherently the intellectual framework within which Tooke's economics operated?

Classical economics is most usefully defined by the central unifying concept that characterises its analytical approach to economic problems. This central unifying concept is 'social surplus' on the grounds that it lies at the heart of the analytical structure of classical economics. Social surplus is conceived of as that part of the annual gross product of an economic system that remains after deducting that which is necessary for its reproduction, consisting of the replacement of the means of production and the subsistence of employed workers. The social surplus is therefore the residual part of the annual product that can be freely disposed of by society without affecting the reproduction of the existing annual product. It is this concept of social surplus that gives coherency to classical economics as a body of economic thought. Accordingly, classical economists most responsible for the development of this body of economic thought have employed what is referred to as the 'surplus approach' to value and distribution. This surplus approach had its beginnings with William Petty in the seventeenth century, was progressively developed by eighteenth-century writers, Cantillon, Quesnay (leader of the French physiocrats), Turgot, James Steuart and Adam Smith, and, then, in the nineteenth century, by Ricardo and Marx, before being rehabilitated in the twentieth century by Piero Sraffa.[4]

From the beginning, classical economists believed that a social surplus was a necessary but not sufficient condition for the economic development of society. The expansion in productive capacity (or 'wealth') of society rather depended on the manner of disposal of the surplus which, in turn, required examination of those factors governing its distribution among the social classes into which society divided. Hence, the determination of the size of the social surplus and its distribution among social classes has been a central focus of classical economics around which its basic theoretical structure developed. This basic theoretical structure can be outlined by consideration of the datum necessary to determine the social surplus (see also Kurz and Salvadori 1998c: 162–3):

1   the size and composition of the social product (or, alternatively, the annual gross outputs of products);

2 the *social* real wage consisting of the quantities of the several commodities making up the wage rate as minimally required by the standards and conventions of society;

3 the surplus real wage, being the *ruling* real wage rates in excess of the social real wage or, alternatively, the normal rate of profits;

4 the dominant technique of production;

5 the quantities of different qualities of land available for use and the known stocks of depletable resources, such as mineral deposits.

The maximum social surplus available for distribution is determined on the basis of (1), (2), (4) and (5), while its distribution between wages and profits (and rent) will depend also on (3).[5] As Sraffa (1960) showed, on the basis of this datum, relative prices can be determined (in terms of a numeraire) simultaneously with the distribution of income at which a uniform net rate of profit on capital is established by competition.[6]

The surplus approach adopted by classical economists has a number of distinctive features. First, all the datum above used to determine prices and distribution is objective in the sense that it is observable, and measurable or calculable (Kurz and Salvadori 1998c: 162). Second, classical economists adopted the 'long period method', whereby they focused on identifying the persistence forces determining the normal or natural values of economic variables. These normal values are conceived to be centres of gravitation of actual observable or market values established at long period positions of the economic system. Under conditions of 'free competition' these long period positions are, in particular, characterised by a uniform net rate of profit on capital employed in the production process. Hence, the surplus approach to value and distribution is primarily concerned with explaining the normal prices of products and the normal distribution of income between wages and profits (and rents). On the basis of their long period theories of normal values, classical economists developed short-period analyses to explain market values determined by temporary forces operating in the economic system (more on this in Section 3.1). Third, distribution is determined in this approach on the basis of either the real wage or the rate of profit being taken as exogenous so that the other distributive variable is residually determined, along with prices for a given technique. In turn, rent on the intra-marginal value of natural resources employed in production is then determined (for a substantial treatment, see Kurz and Salvadori 1995: 277–311, 351–74). Hence, in classical economics, the distributive variables are determined *sequentially* in which distribution is explained by reference to socio-economic, political and institutional factors that determine the exogenous distributive variable. Classical economists traditionally took the real wage to be the exogenous distributive variable.

A fourth feature of classical economics is the *separability* between the analysis of the determination of the social product (i.e. level of output) and its composition on the one hand and the analysis of the determination of distribution and prices on the other hand. As shown above, the determination of (relative) prices and income distribution is at the core of the classical theoretical structure, requiring the *prior* determination of its data: output (and its composition), the technique of production and either the real wage or general rate of profit. In this theoretical structure, as clearly articulated by Garegnani (1984; 1990a), these data lie outside the core, each determined by a separate analysis. Whereas at the core prices and distribution are conceived to be determined by precise quantitative relations, outside the core gross outputs, the exogenous distributive variable (either the real wage or profit rate) and the technique of production are conceived to be determined by socio-economic, political and institutional factors less conducive to representation by quantitative relations.[7] This separability means that just like distribution the level of social output is open to various explanations. After Adam Smith, classical economists supposed that the output of each commodity was determined by its effec-tual demand while explaining the determination of aggregate output by reference to the 'stage of accumulation' of the economy (see Section 3.1). Notably, the clas-sical economists did not consider competitive forces operated so that the aggregate level of output determined at long period positions corresponded with the full employment of labour.

The surplus approach of classical economics is very different to the 'supply-and-demand approach' of marginalist economics. This is most evident in the dif-ferent data required to determine prices and distribution. In marginalist economics the data required to determine prices and distribution in general equi-librium theory are (1) consumer preferences (including in relation to saving–consumption decisions), (2) the technical conditions of production and (3) the endowments of resources, including labour and capital, available for production and distributed among agents in the economic system. The main difference with the classical approach and which essentially defines the marginal 'optimisation' method is data (3) which impose the market-clearing condition that equilibrium in the system is characterised by the full-employment of labour, capital and other inputs.[8] Datum (3) is the basis in marginalist economics for conceiving that equi-librium prices, including factor prices, are determined by conditions of scarcity. Another important difference that follows from this approach is that prices and distribution in equilibrium are determined *simultaneously* with the outputs and the fully employed quantities of inputs used to produce the outputs. Hence, unlike classical economics, in marginalist economics the analysis of the determi-nation of the level of output and of its distribution is inseparable. Furthermore, the monotonic functional relationship between quantities and prices supposed by the demand and supply functions for products and inputs which, conceptually, underpins the stability of competitive equilibrium in marginalist economics, cannot be logically derived in classical economics.

In its seminal development the pioneers of marginalist economics, notably Marshall and Wicksell, adopted the long-period method employed by the classi-cal economists so that competitive equilibrium was characterised by uniform rates of remuneration on inputs of the same kind. However, since the Second World War, this method has been gradually abandoned in marginalist economics with the formulation of temporary and inter-temporal general equilibrium theory,

based on specifying not only the aggregate value but also the physical composition of endowed resources in which competitive equilibria determined are characterised by market-clearing corresponding to non-uniform net rates of return on
capital (Garegnani 1983b; 1987: 44–60; Kurz and Salvadori 1995: 20–33,
455–67; Petri 2004: 136–65).

Following Marshall's 'continuity thesis', a common interpretation of the
history of economic thought is that classical economics is an embryonic forerunner to marginalist economics in the seamless development of economic science.
Given the fundamental theoretical differences between them, this continuity
thesis rests heavily on the contention that marginalist economics is scientifically
superior to classical economics in explaining economic phenomena. However,
this contention is undermined by the capital debates of the 1950s and 1960s
which demonstrated the impossibility of logically quantifying an aggregate value
of capital independent of distribution and, consequently, of defining well-
behaved demand functions for inputs, in a generalised economic system that produces heterogenous commodities by means of heterogenous commodities.[9] This
critique strikes at the very heart of the marginalist approach to value and distribution, invalidating the scientific basis of its determination of stable competitive
equilibria relevant to a decentralised capitalist society.

In Sraffa's (1960) important contribution to these debates, the critique of the
marginalist approach was intricately connected with the rehabilitation of classical economics by the formulation of a general solution to the problem of determining the rate of profit and relative prices which had been left unsolved by
classical economists, in particular Ricardo and Marx, and which had been a
major cause for the decline of classical economics. By re-discovering the surplus
approach of the classical economists and reconstructing its analytical formulation, Sraffa (1951; 1960) revived classical economics.[10] With this revival there
have been two particular lines of theoretical development that are pertinent to
what later follows in this book. The first consists of explaining the level of social
output and its growth by reference to Keynes's principle of effective demand. As
shown above (pp. 9–10), in the theoretical structure of classical economics the
level of social output is open to explanation, which allows its determination and
its growth to be explained by Keynesian demand-led theory (Garegnani 1983a:
61–3). The other particular line of theoretical development is explaining distribution by taking the rate of profit rather than the real wage as the independent
distributive variable. This explanation, elaborated in Section 8.4, is considered
more relevant to modern capitalist society. It also has significant implications for
monetary theory in classical economics. The body of economic theory that has
developed with the revival of the analytical approach of the classical economists
we shall refer to as 'modern classical economics'.

Any definition of classical economics is bound to be a generalisation given
the heterogeneity of contributions by those identified as classical economists
(Steedman 1998: 117–20). As will be shown in what follows in this book,
Tooke's work is mainly concerned with monetary behaviour and makes no direct
contribution to the core theory of value and distribution. Nonetheless, the surplus

approach to value and distribution that took different forms in the writings of Adam Smith and Ricardo provided the theoretical basis for Tooke and other nineteenth-century classical writers to conduct studies in more specific fields of analysis. The definition of classical economics employed here is therefore wide enough to capture most but not all writers of significance on political economy before the ascendency of marginalist economics in the 1870s.[11] According to our definition, from its inception by William Petty in the 1660s, historically, classical economics dominated economic science for over 200 years before marginalist economics took over and came to dominate. Classical economics did not end in the 1870s but was submerged until rediscovered, chiefly by Sraffa, and revived from the 1950s onwards.[12] The outlook of this book then is that classical economics is not just of archaeological interest but is a living body of theory which today represents a genuine alternative long-period theory to the supply-and-demand approach of marginalist economics. From this perspective, the contributions of the classical economists of which Tooke is one warrant close study not just in order to understand the history of economic ideas but because they are capable of advancing contemporary economic science.

2 Tooke's contributions

On Tooke's death in 1858, the Royal Statistical Society honoured his contributions 'to economic science and statistics' by the foundation of a 'Tooke Memorial' with an endowment for the establishment in 1859 of a 'Tooke Professorship in Economics Science and Statistics' at Kings College, London.[1] The Tooke Chair, long since transferred to the London School of Economics, has in its 150-year-old history been held by eleven eminent scholars, including Edgeworth and Hayek, and remains today a reminder of Tooke's contributions to economics. Indeed, Tooke's achievements are considerable. They consist, most prominently, of an historical analysis of economic fluctuations and price movements in England over the period 1792–1856 as based on an exhaustive investigation of facts deduced from a compilation of available statistical information; of informed contributions to all the major policy debates whose outcomes greatly shaped British economic life in the first half of the nineteenth century; and of the development of an original though controversial theory of monetary behaviour with a far-sighted position on the role and conduct of monetary policy. These achievements were the result of unrelenting activity by an energetic man. In his lifetime, Tooke published five volumes of books, two in collaboration with William Newmarch, five pamphlets and gave evidence to numerous parliamentary committees. He also chaired a commission appointed by Parliament to draw up recommendations for social legislation. Through the Political Economy Club, Tooke made regular contact with other prominent political economists of his generation, including Ricardo, Malthus, Torrens, McCulloch, Senior and J.S. Mill. In addition, Tooke was well connected with men of influence in commerce and government which he often exploited to advance his views on economic policy. In particular, Tooke was a strong advocate for free trade and argued for measured reforms to the English banking system. Like Ricardo, Tooke had a strong commercial background. Before becoming involved in political economy, Tooke was a well-established London merchant with an expertise in international commodity trade and in commercial finance. His commercial background helps explain the pragmatic approach that Tooke brought to political economy, with his desire for effective policy an important motivation for many of his writings. These are the bare bones of Tooke's public life and contributions that is elaborated in what follows. A short biography of Tooke in Section 2.1 precedes a chronological account of his contributions to political economy in Section 2.2, covering his pre-banking school phase 1819–1838 and, then, in Section 2.3, covering his banking school phase 1840–1857.

2.1 Life and activities

Thomas Tooke was born at Kronstadt, Russia, on 29 February 1774, the eldest son of three children to the Reverend William Tooke (1744–1820) and Elizabeth Eyton (b. 1750), who married in 1771. At the time of his birth, Tooke's father was chaplain to the British trading post in Kronstadt. He had been appointed in 1771 after receiving letters of ordination both as deacon and priest from Bishop Terrick of London. In 1777, on the invitation of resident merchants, Reverend William Tooke took up the position of chaplain of the English church at St Petersburg, then capital of Russia. It was in the close English merchant-based society of St Petersburg that the young Thomas grew up. In this small expatriate society, his father was a prominent intellectual figure, being a Fellow of the Royal Society elected in 1783 and a member of the Imperial Academy of Sciences and Free Economical Society of St Petersburg. He was acquainted with Russian nobility in the court of Catherine II (the 'Great') as well as men of letters and science of various European nationalities.[2] These connections and his access to the imperial library allowed Reverend Tooke to embark at his own leisure on a large-scale study of Russian history during his eighteen-year residence in St Petersburg. This resulted in his publication of several works on Russian history, most notably his three-volume opus, *View of the Russian Empire During the Reign of Catherine II and to the Close of the Present Century* (1799), among many other literary works.[3] The intellectual disposition and strong literary interest of Reverend Tooke could not have failed to leave an impression on Thomas as well as his younger brother William, who was to follow in his father's footsteps and become a distinguished man of arts and literature.[4] However, Tooke, unlike his father, took up a career in commerce. At age fifteen, he began work in Russian trading with an English merchant house in St Petersburg.

There is little historical information on Tooke's early life and his career as a merchant in the Russian trade. Given that his father was an intellectual who valued education, it seems likely Tooke received a formal education at least until the age of fifteen, when he entered the Russian trading business. No doubt the success of his career as a merchant led to an interest in political economy. We know Tooke had returned to England by 1795 and became a partner in the London firm of Stephen Thornton & Co., reputedly one of the largest Russian merchant houses (Tooke 1819a: 125; 1822: 351).[5] We also know that in 1802 Tooke married Priscilla Combe (b. 1781), with whom he had two sons. By 1826 he was a senior partner of the Russian trading firm, Astell, Tooke & Thornton. It is clear that by this time he had become well-established as a business leader in the City of London with very good connections to bankers and statesmen. As a mark of his recognised organising skills and leadership in City commerce, Tooke was elected Chairman of the St. Katherine Dock Co., a joint-stock company formed in 1825 with a capital of over £3,200,000 to construct and commercially operate 'additional convenient wet dock and bonding accommodation near the seat of business in the port of London' on a scale 'nearly equal in extent to the London Dock' with the capacity to accommodate annually 'about 1,400 merchant ships' (*The Times*, 2 July 1825).[6] It is perhaps indicative of Tooke's standing at this time that the directors of the company included two prominent Members of Parliament, James Alexander and Pascoe Grenfell, the City banker, William Glynn, and the director and future Governor of the Bank of England, John Horsely Palmer (*The Times*, 2 July 1825). Prior to this commercial project, Tooke was involved with other prominent businessmen in the establishment by Act of British Parliament of the Australian Agricultural Company in 1824, a company still in existence today (Gregson 1907: 1–14).[7] An original stock holder, Tooke was an inaugural and longstanding director of the company (Tooke 1848b: (Q 5301) 410). He was also a director of the London and Birmingham Railway Company which was authorised by Parliament in 1833 to build a 122-mile railway line linking London to Birmingham, completed in 1837 with a share capital of £2.5 million (Francis 1851: 181; Reed 1975: 136). Hence, Tooke had first-hand knowledge of the British railway boom of the 1830s and 1840s of which he variously wrote about in his published works.[8]

After his retirement from Russian trading business in 1836, Tooke was elected Governor of the Royal Exchange Assurance Corporation in 1840 and held this powerful commercial position until 1852, over which time he implemented lasting changes to its organisation (Tooke 1848b: (Q 5301) 410; 1848c: (Q 2975–6) 333; also Supple 1970: 350–9).[9] Hence, from his long experience in the world of commerce, Tooke acquired considerable expertise in the operation of the London financial and commodity markets as well as in international trade, especially Russian trade. Indeed, Tooke immodestly made this point about himself in the following evidence to the 1848 Lords Committee on Commercial Distress:

Q 2977 In your Capacity of Governor of the Royal Exchange Insurance Company does it form Part of your practical Business to invest Monies from Time to Time? – Tooke: Yes, it does, to a considerable Extent.

Q 2978 And on that Account, independently of the Attention which you have given to the Question of Currency and of Circulation as a Matter of scientific Research, have you been led to consider it in its practical Bearings? – Tooke: I have, constantly; and few Persons, I conceive, are better situated than I am for judging of the State of commercial Matters.

Q 2979 On what Ground? – Tooke: From being constantly in attendance during at least Two to Three Hours a Day at the Royal Exchange Assurance, and likewise once a Week and sometimes twice a Week at the St. Katherine Docks; and having not only for the Royal Exchange Assurance, but for the

St. Katherine Dock Company occasionally, to manage considerable financial Operations.

(1848c: 333)

Much earlier, in evidence to the 1820 Lords Committee on the means of extending and securing the Foreign Trade of the Country, Tooke showed his expertise on Russian trade that came, as he said, from being involved in it for 'about thirty years altogether' (1820: 25). He also showed an expertise in shipping costs and, as a part-owner as well as an experienced charterer of ships, of the cargo shipping business in general, in evidence given to three parliamentary committees on the foreign trade of the country in the early 1820s.

Tooke's entry into the public arena of economic debate began with his evidence to the committees of both the Commons and Lords Houses of Parliament on the resumption of cash payments by the Bank of England in 1819 (Tooke 1819a; 1819b). For the most part, Tooke's evidence lent support to Ricardo's position to uphold the principles of the Bullion Committee of 1810 and to return to the gold standard (Hilton 1977: 43; Smith 2008: 51–8). However, it was authorship of the 'Merchants Petition', advocating free trade and presented on behalf of London merchants to the House of Commons by Alexander Baring on 8 May 1820, that first brought Tooke to prominence among leading lights of political economy and public policy. Tooke (1857, VI: 335–44) later acknowledged that he was encouraged in this campaign by the Liverpool Government. His strenuous efforts to advance the cause of free trade probably explain Tooke's election as a Fellow of the Royal Society by member economists in March 1821, given that he had not yet published anything of scientific substance.[10] It was also instrumental in the inception of the Political Economy Club. The Club was founded in April 1821 with the main purpose of advancing the principles of the Merchants Petition. Tooke was in fact the 'prime mover' in its foundation (Higgs 1921: x–xi).[11] The Club's 1860 historical volume names Tooke as the 'moving spirit' in its formation. While Tooke was most certainly the main organiser, the idea of the Club probably came 'from the eagerness of David Ricardo to enjoy the society of the economists of his time' and from the desire by Tooke and others for a 'more neutral arena for debate' away from Ricardo's breakfast table (Higgs 1921: viii–x). Tooke became its most active member and a dominant figure in the discussions of the Political Economy Club, regularly attending meetings until the end of his life.[12] As the Club's recorded minutes of questions sponsored for discussion show, Tooke used this forum to clarify his own ideas on political economy arising out of his inquiries and which he was endeavouring to address in his writings (Higgs 1921: 9–66, 449–51). The Political Economy Club, with a membership that included prominent City businessmen and politicians, including Cabinet ministers, was also a forum by which Tooke could by force of argument exert insider influence over government policy-making.[13]

Initially, Tooke's reputation as a political economist was built on his expertise of the causes of price movements, especially the movement of agricultural prices. Tooke first revealed this expertise in evidence before the Commons Select Committee on Agricultural Distress in 1821. Tooke was its 'star' witness and its 'Final Report' drew heavily on his evidence for its conclusions (see P.P. 1821 (668), IX: 8–9). Ricardo, as a member of the committee, was in fact instrumental in summoning Tooke to give evidence before it (see Ricardo 1819–1821: 373–4). As Tooke later explained:

> I was summoned to give evidence before that Committee [on agricultural distress] at the instance of Mr. David Ricardo, who was a member of it. The purport of my evidence was to state reasons for believing that the Low Price of Corn, and the consequent distress of the agricultural interests, were sufficiently accounted for by the Abundance of the supply, both from the unusually large produce of the proceeding harvest, and from the surplus of the extraordinary importations of Foreign Corn.
>
> (1857, V: 66–7)

Tooke's evidence was valued by Ricardo, not least because, coming from someone with a reputed expertise, it showed that an excess supply of corn was the main cause of depressed agricultural prices and not the resumption of cash payments by the Bank of England in 1821. At the time, resumption, and Ricardo, as its chief parliamentary defender, had come under some heavy criticism from the 'landed interest' for the depressed state of agriculture (Arnon 1991: 44–6; Smith 2008: 56). The Liverpool Government, intent on resisting calls by agriculturalists for more protective Corn Laws, also welcomed Tooke's evidence showing that the operation of the 1815 Corn Law had failed to prevent the depression in corn prices (Hilton 1977: 98–126). Essentially, Tooke (1821a: 229–30, 237–8) argued that in absence of an export bounty which could encourage the export of corn when highly productive harvests in Britain depressed corn prices, as occurred in 1820, the 1815 Corn Law could not effectively protect domestic agriculture during periods of abundance. Tooke's evidence to the 1821 Committee on Agricultural Distress so impressed Ricardo that the latter cited it heavily in support of arguments against the Corn Laws in his 1822 pamphlet, 'On Protection of Agriculture' (Ricardo 1822: 221, 228, 231, 259).

The debate in Britain over the steep decline in prices that accompanied a general depression in economic activity in the period after the French Wars largely motivated Tooke to write his first book on political economy, *Thoughts and Details of High and Low Prices of the Last Thirty Years*, published in 1823. The book was well received, confirming Tooke's growing reputation as a political economist 'remarkable for his range of knowledge and sound judgement' (Higgs 1921: xiii). His prominence as a major political economist was further enhanced by the publication in 1826 of *Considerations on the State of the Currency*, an influential pamphlet on banking policy. This was followed by two substantial pamphlets on currency issues and the Corn Laws, his two *Letter[s] to Lord Grenville*, published in 1829. After 1829 and until the mid-1830s, Tooke ceased writing on political economy, probably as a result of poor health and a depressed state of mind brought on by the tragic suicide of his eldest son, William Eyton Tooke, in 1830. In a letter to Babbage in 1832, Tooke wrote:

> I will not pursue the subject of prices further than to observe that a con-
> nected view of them and of the causes by which they have been influenced
> in the 10 years which have been elapsed since the period embraced by my
> treatise on high and low prices is a dedication. I have been urged to under-
> take it but am doubtful whether I should have leisure or spirit or health for
> the task.
>
> (28 June, British Library, MS 37186, f.497)

Nevertheless, during this interregnum, Tooke remained otherwise active, promoting discussion in the Political Economy Club and giving evidence before the
parliamentary committee for Renewing the Charter of the Bank of England in
1832. The years 1832 and 1833 saw Tooke much occupied as chairman of the
Factory Inquiry Commission appointed to collect 'Information of Children in
Factories and to report on the Propriety and Means of Curtailing the Hours of
their Labour'. As chairman of the Commission, Tooke was involved in the
onerous task of organising the collection of a mass of evidence, obtained from
various manufacturing districts, and then evaluating this information in order to
draw up recommendations for a parliamentary report.[14] From its inception the
Commission was surrounded by controversy, accused by reformers of being a
government device to delay legislation and bring recommendations to Parliament favourable to factory owners (Inglis 1972: 340–68). In addition, it was met
with hostility from the 'Ten Hour Movement'.[15] With the able assistance of
liberal parliamentarians Edwin Chadwick and Thomas Southwood Smith, Tooke
overcame these difficulties and brought forward a prompt report that one historian has said 'marks a decisive point in the evolution of factory legislation'
(Thomas 1948: 60). To the Commission's credit, its report led to the passage of
more effective legislation for policing the restriction of factory employment by
children and in the provision of parish education for them.[16]

Tooke resumed writing on political economy in the mid-1830s, publishing
volumes I and II of *A History of Prices and of the State of the Circulation from
1793 to 1837*, in 1838. This work marked the beginning of his most productive
writing period. Motivated by debates over Bank of England policy and the currency school's plans for institutional change embodied in its Charter due for
renewal in 1844, Tooke formulated his most original ideas on money and prices,
which became the basis of the banking school theory. In 1840 Tooke published
volume III of *History of Prices*, followed by his best-known pamphlet, *An
Inquiry into the Currency Principle* in 1844, and then produced volume IV of
History in 1848. In this period he also gave evidence to the 1840 Select Committee on *Banks of Issue*, whose report cleared the way for the Bank Charter Act of
1844, and the 1847–1848 Commons and Lords Committees on the 'Causes of
Commercial Distress' which, among other things, was concerned with inquiring
into the causes for the Bank of England suspending regulations under its 1844

Charter in October 1847. Although much of the heat had gone out of the currency–banking school debates by the end of the 1840s, Tooke continued to work on issues in monetary thought up to the end of his life. In 1856 Tooke published the pamphlet *On the Bank Charter Act of 1844, its Principles and Operation*, and then in collaboration with William Newmarch, published his final work, the fifth and sixth volumes of *History* in 1857, thereby completing an historical analysis of prices in England covering a sixty-five-year period from 1792 to 1856.

On the morning of Friday, 26 February 1858, Tooke died at his residence, 31 Spring Gardens, London, a few days short of eighty-four years of age.[17] He was buried in the family vault at Kensal-Green Cemetery. In the obituary published in the *Economist* the following tribute was paid to him:

> The long career of Mr. Tooke has been one which invites and will repay scrutiny. He united in an eminent degree the sagacity and penetration of mind which enabled him to be a guide and discoverer in new paths, and the practical wisdom and soundness of judgement which qualified him to occupy a conspicuous place in the active business of life. In Mr. Tooke's case, the combination of the speculative with the practical faculty was exceedingly remarkable. Few men could be found more ardent in their pursuit of new truths, or more ready to adopt and maintain them when he had once satisfied himself that the discovery was a real one; but, at the same time, he may be classed among that small number of persons whose judgement is so clear and unbiased, that the cases are exceedingly rare in which their deliberate advice is not fully justified by the event.
>
> (6 March 1858: 255)

As well as the perpetual 'Tooke Memorial' established by the Royal Statistical Society on his death, Tooke had been honoured in the last years of his life with the distinction of being elected 'Corresponding Member to the French Academy of Moral and Political Sciences' in 1853. These honours well reflect the high regard felt for Tooke by his peers.

2.2 Pre-banking school contributions, 1819–1838

Prior to Tooke's first publication he appeared as a witness before six parliamentary committees. Besides the Commons and Lords 1819 committees on the resumption of cash payments by the Bank of England and the 1821 committee on agricultural distress, Tooke gave evidence to three parliamentary committees in the years 1820, 1821 and 1822 concerned with the means by which to maintain and improve Britain's foreign trade. In his appearances before all these committees, Tooke showed himself to be a strong supporter for the restoration of the gold standard and an effective campaigner for free trade, including noted critic of the Corn Laws. However, among peers, Tooke largely obtained eminence as a political economist from his first book, *Thoughts and Details of High and Low Prices of the Last Thirty Years* published in 1823. As already mentioned in

Section 2.1, Tooke was motivated to write the book by the depression in prices after the French Wars (1793–1815). He was much encouraged in this project by Ricardo, who believed Tooke would be able to contribute to a better understanding in political economy of how the interaction between supply and demand determined market prices.[18]

Tooke embarked on the writing of *High and Low Prices* 'in the latter part of 1822 and the beginning of 1823' with the object to 'account for the fluctuations of prices during the thirty years ending in 1822' (Tooke 1824: iv). The book was published in two editions. The first edition consisted of four parts with Part I devoted to the effect on the price level of an inconvertible system of currency which prevailed during the restriction period of 1797–1821; Part II concerned the effect on the price level of the French Wars; Part III the effect on the price level of climatic conditions affecting agricultural output; and Part IV contained price series of various commodities with some 'General Remarks'.[19] Part I was published in January 1823, in a separate volume to Parts II, III and IV, published together, in July 1823. The second edition, published as a whole in May 1824, included an extension to Part II, the addition of a supplementary section and a re-organisation of Part IV.[20] *High and Low Prices* provides considerable statistical evidence in support of the argument, with tables of data provided in the appendices accompanying each of the four Parts. The book was well received by his peers. In his review in the *Quarterly Review*, Malthus wrote effusively. '[W]e look upon this work of Mr. Tooke as a very valuable contribution to the science of political economy' because it 'adduces a large and interesting collection of facts' which is 'more particularly required at the present moment, when it must be acknowledged that some of our ablest writers in this science have been deficient in that constant reference to facts and experience' (1823: 214). It was also praised by Torrens, who, in the preface to the third edition of *An Essay on the External Corn Trade* (February 1826), described the work as 'one of the most valuable contributions which have of late years been made to the science' and 'excellent in its kind' (1829: ix, xii).[21]

Tooke's next work, the pamphlet, *Considerations on the State of the Currency* (1826), was sparked by the collapse of the London financial market in late-1825. This financial crisis was accompanied by bank collapses, widespread bankruptcy and, most significantly, an internal drain of bullion reserves which nearly forced the Bank of England to suspend cash payments on demand, only four-and-a-half years after resumption had been accomplished in 1821. The crisis was to be the beginning of a severe economic downturn which persisted throughout 1826 and early 1827. It took many by surprise because it came at a time of apparent prosperity and healthy economic activity. No major event could be identified as the catalyst for the crisis. However, Tooke (1826: 48–9) had a clear understanding of its origins. He believed the crisis was the result of an unsustainable boom in the stock market which had all the hallmarks of the speculative mania of the famous 1720 South Sea Bubble. Indeed, Tooke was among those who foresaw the dangers of the speculative boom and fully anticipated financial disaster.[22] Thus, when in late-1825 the financial system went into crisis and the economy was heading for a severe downturn, Tooke set himself the task of explaining the causes of the crisis and the lessons for banking policy. His motivation for writing the *Considerations* was therefore to influence policy debate and to procure overdue reform of the English banking system at a politically opportune time. With the encouragement of Lord Grenville, former Prime Minister and influential parliamentarian, and William Huskisson, President of the Board of Trade,[23] Tooke hurriedly wrote the pamphlet over the winter of 1825–1826 in readiness for public debate on the crisis at the parliamentary session beginning in early February 1826.

It appears that initially Tooke had in mind a substantial 'scientific' work. This is supported by a draft plan for a published work submitted to Lord Grenville and Huskisson for comment (see Tooke–Grenville Letter, 19 November 1925, *Grenville Papers*, British Library, Add. 69082; Smith 1996a: xix–xx; Tooke 1996: Appendix G, 135–8). It is also supported by the 'Advertisement' to the first edition of the *Considerations* (1826: 1) in which Tooke strongly suggested that originally he had intended to update his history of prices with a sequel (from 1822) consisting of a more detailed monetary analysis. In this connection it is evident by questions Tooke sponsored at meetings of the Political Economy Club in 1824 and 1825 that he had given much thought to the theoretical side of many of the monetary issues that the *Considerations* dealt with.[24] Thus, while Tooke abandoned his original plan and settled on a less ambitious pamphlet designed to influence upcoming debate, the *Considerations* contained well-thought-out arguments. The pamphlet was highly successful with two editions published within a month of each other. The first edition is dated 28 January, the second, 22 February 1826. The second edition was prepared by Tooke in conjunction with the progress of parliamentary debate and proposed legislative reforms to the English banking system by the Liverpool Government. It added 'explanatory notes' to the first edition and a long 'Postscript', extending the discussion on banking policy to account for 'measures which are in progress, as likewise on those which are supposed to be in contemplation with reference to the currency' (Tooke 1826: 2). These legislative measures were in large part anticipated by Tooke in the first edition, suggesting he had access to the top levels of government policy-making. In particular, Tooke seems to have had a fairly close relationship with Huskisson, the political economist's minister, which probably developed out of consultations over the Merchant's Petition of 1820.[25] In the Postscript to the second edition, Tooke gave support to the legislative reforms introduced into and passed by Parliament. They essentially consisted of measures to suppress small country banknotes in circulation and to admit joint-stock banking in provincial England. The *Considerations* was Tooke's most influential pamphlet, with its explanation of the 1825 crisis gaining wide acceptance and with the main thrust of its recommendations for reform of the English banking system implemented by Parliament (on its role in the public debate on the crisis and legislative reform, see Smith 1996a: xxii–xxvii).

Tooke re-entered public debate in 1829 with his two pamphlets, *Letter*[s] to Lord Grenville.[26] The first, *A Letter to Lord Grenville on the Effects Ascribed to the Resumption of Cash Payments on the Value of the Currency*, was published on 26 January 1829. It was motivated by renewed criticism of the resumption of cash payments for restricting the quantity of notes in circulation and, thereby, having a depressing effect on trade and prices. The criticism was led by Member of Parliament and author of the pamphlet *Corn and Currency* (1826), Sir James Graham, in a parliamentary debate on the restriction of small notes in circulation in 1828.[27] The stated object of the first *Letter* was to demonstrate

> that a contraction of the Currency was not a necessary consequence of, nor, in point of fact, produced by, Mr. Peel's Bill ... that, without any reference whatever to that Bill, or to any anterior preparation, the circulation of the Bank of England notes and coin together, could have been neither more nor less than it actually has been.
>
> (Tooke 1829a: 4)

As a follow-up to the first, the second pamphlet, *A Second Letter to Lord Grenville: On the Currency in connection with the Corn Trade and on the Corn Laws*, aimed to show that 'the fall of prices *does* admit of being explained by circumstances affecting the supply of commodities relatively to the demand for them, independently of any alteration in the amount of the Bank circulation' (Tooke 1829b: 1–2).[28] Tooke had already dealt with this question in *High and Low Prices*, 'but I have been enabled to bring forward some fresh proofs and illustrations in support of my conclusions' which 'serve to throw no inconsiderable degree of fresh light on the actual state and prospects of the corn trade' (Tooke 1829b: 3).

The second *Letter*, published 14 May 1829, also contained a strong criticism of the Corn Laws as well as a postscript, 'On the Present Commercial Stagnation', which repudiated the view that economic stagnation in 1828–1829 was attributable to resumption and the withdrawal since 1826 of small banknotes from circulation. These pamphlets were essentially intended to defend, against the criticism of some prominent parliamentary figures,[29] modifications to the banking system wrought by resumption in 1821 and by the suppression of small notes. As it turned out, Tooke's position on monetary policy prevailed. Tooke again argued for institutional reforms of the English banking system in evidence given to the Bank Charter committee in 1832. In particular, Tooke (1832) advocated for greater public accountability by the Bank of England and other note-issuing banks, the move towards monopoly control by the Bank of England over the issuance of banknotes and the repeal of the usury laws (see Section 6.4).

In the mid-1830s, Tooke began preparing his largest single work, volumes I and II of *History of Prices*, published in 1838. Covering the period 1792 to 1837, this two-volume work extended Tooke's historical analysis of prices begun with *High and Low Prices* (1823). Like the earlier work, *History* (1838) consisted of four parts, though arranged differently, so that the 'more general causes' of price variations preceded rather than followed the more detailed historical analysis of prices presented in chronological order: Part I, 'On the

Effect of the Seasons'; Part II, 'On the Effect of War'; Part III, 'On the Currency'; and Part IV, 'Historical Sketch of Prices, and of the State of the Circulation, from 1792 to 1837'. The work incorporated various aspects from previous writings but, as Tooke stated in the preface, 'with the exception of a very small part, the whole of that which is now submitted to the public, has been written afresh' (1838, I: iv). It is evident *History* (1838) was intended by Tooke to be a scholarly work of lasting value rather than as a contribution to monetary debates which were then going on.[30]

2.3 Banking school contributions, 1840–1857

At the end of the 1830s monetary debate was dominated by the proposals of the currency school for altering the Bank of England's management of the currency. Tooke entered this debate with the publication of volume III of *History* in 1840, providing an analysis of prices in 1838 and 1839. Much of this volume dealt with criticisms made of the Bank of England and reviewed various proposals for altering the system of monetary management (Tooke 1840a, III: 1–2).[31] It contained Tooke's first criticisms of the policy proposals of the currency school and set down the beginnings of his banking school position. However, the battle lines between Tooke and the currency school became more sharply defined in parliamentary hearings of the Select Committee of Banks of Issue in 1840. The main protagonists in those hearings was Lord Overstone (Samuel Jones Loyd), leading advocate of the 'currency principle' and Tooke, champion of the contrary view, the 'banking principle'.[32] These parliamentary hearings were the opening salvos in the heated monetary debates between the currency school and banking school of the 1840s and 1850s. The central contributors to these debates on the side of the currency school were Overstone (1837, 1840a, 1844), Torrens (1837, 1840, 1844, 1848, 1858) and Norman (1838, 1841) and, on the side of the banking school, were Tooke, its leader, Fullarton (1845) and James Wilson (1847).

In many respects the debates were a 120-year forerunner to the Monetarist–Keynesian debates of the 1960s and 1970s: with controversy over the issues of rules versus discretion in the conduct of monetary policy, the role and definitions of money, 'exogenous' versus 'endogenous' money and, connectedly, the transmission process of monetary policy actions onto economic activity and prices. When it was clear the Peel government was going to embody the currency school's plan in legislation for the renewal of the Bank of England's Charter in 1844, Tooke published his most outstanding work, *An Inquiry into the Currency Principle, the Connection of the Currency with Prices and the Expediency of a Separation of Issue from Banking*. In this pamphlet Tooke provided the most coherent exposition of his newly developed monetary analysis which was the foundation of the banking school position. The object of the *Inquiry* was to advance this alternative position in opposition to the currency school and their policy proposals to be given effect by the Bank Charter Act of 1844.

The *Inquiry* went through two editions. The first edition was published in March and the second in May 1844. The second edition included some minor alterations to the text and the addition of a 'Supplementary Chapter' which gave a critical review of Prime Minister Peel's parliamentary speech to the Commons given on 6 May 1844, in recommendation of the bill for the renewal of the Bank Charter. While Tooke had spent some time developing and writing down the ideas in the *Inquiry*, its publication was timed to influence debate against Peel's 1844 Bank Charter Act. In the preface to the first edition, Tooke gives the distinct impression that he thought publication in 1844 of his innovative ideas in the *Inquiry* was premature:

> Some part of the following pages was written immediately after the appearance of the reports of the committee of the House of Commons on Banks of Issue, and the greater part has since been put together without any definite view to publication. The reason which has determined me in now publishing them is, that whether the views here presented be assented to or not, they are such, I think, as ought not to be wholly overlooked in the consideration of the measures which the government has announced its intention of proposing to Parliament in the course of the present session, with a view to placing the banking system of the United Kingdom on an improved and permanent footing.
>
> (1844: iv)

To use the words of McCulloch, the *Inquiry* was '[D]ecidedly the ablest tract in opposition to the recent measures' (1845: 184). Its main influence during the currency–banking school debates was on fellow members of the banking school, Fullarton (1845) and Wilson (1847), and also on J.S. Mill (1844 [1874], 1848 [1909], Bk. III). However, the *Inquiry* had no immediate effect on English banking policy, failing altogether to prevent the enactment by Parliament of Peel's Bank Charter Act of 1844.

Tooke's next opportunity to rejoin the debate came with the severe financial crisis of 1847, causing the government to temporarily suspend the 1844 Act in order to relieve intense liquidity pressures on the Bank of England (Fetter 1965: 201–14). The episode revived controversy over the Act with both Houses of Parliament appointing committees in 1847 to inquire into the causes of commercial distress. Tooke gave evidence to both these committees against the operation of the 1844 Act. In February 1848, and prior to his appearance before these committees (in March and May), Tooke published the fourth volume of *History* in anticipation of parliamentary debate on the financial crisis:

> if my forebodings of commercial discredit, combined with what I considered was likely to be the operation of the banking act, should be realised, it was in the highest degree probable that the new parliament, on its meeting, would have it attention drawn to the general state of commercial credit, in connection with the act of 1844. This consideration rendered it important that whatever I might determine to publish should be completed by, or soon after, the meeting of parliament, at the usual time of its assembling.
>
> (Tooke 1848a, IV: vii)

Tooke began writing in mid-August 1847, and with the able assistance of statisticians J.T. Danson and William Newmarch completed the volume in less than six months.[33] The work updated his historical analysis of prices from 1840 to 1847, a period in which Tooke (1848a, IV: vi) believed 'great alterations' in the Corn Laws and the banking system demanded an 'historical record'. However, the overwhelming bulk of its contents consisted of an elaboration of his banking school position and a restatement of his arguments against the 'currency principle'.[34] In particular, Tooke further developed his conception of endogenous money relevant to a fiat-based monetary system and, in this context, further articulated the problems in the transmission process of the classical economists' quantity theory of money. The work also contained a revealing insight into Tooke's banking-school-informed view of nineteenth-century English monetary thought, including criticisms of Thornton, Ricardo and fellow Bullionists. There is little doubt that with commercial distress prevalent in industry, Tooke's criticisms of the 1844 Act, as re-stated in *History* (1848a, IV), carried more weight in 1848 than in 1844. Indeed, reflecting public opinion, the Lords Committee of 1848 on the Causes of Commercial Distress concluded that the financial panic in late-1847 was 'materially aggravated' by the operation of the 1844 Act and recommended its amendment (P.P. 1847–1848 (565) VIII: xx). Nevertheless, the 1844 Act survived intact a lively parliamentary debate.

In 1856 Tooke produced another pamphlet, *On the Bank Charter Act of 1844, its Principles and Operations; with Suggestions for an Improved Administration of the Bank of England*, being a critical discourse on the practical effects of the 1844 Act over the period 1844–1855. It also contained Tooke's recommendations for greater institutional independence of the Bank of England and for a more professional system of management of its monetary policy. The material in the pamphlet was prepared as part of and incorporated into Tooke's last work, produced in collaboration with William Newmarch (1820–1882), the fifth and sixth volumes of *History*, published in 1857.[35] Tooke published the pamphlet in anticipation of parliamentary debate in early 1856 on the laws governing the Bank of England. It also served as an 'advertisement' for his upcoming volumes of *History*, which were well in hand. As early as 1852, when 'the marvels of the gold discoveries were bursting upon us and other important events in connection with prices were attracting general attention' (Letter to Lord Monteagle, 30 September 1854, National Library of Ireland, MS. 13401), Tooke had it in mind to complete his historical analysis with a fifth volume comprising a 'copious' index covering all volumes of *History*. With the assistance of Newmarch, 'advantageously known as the writer of a paper on gold discoveries' (Letter to Lord Monteagle, 30 September 1854, National Library of Ireland, MS. 13401), *The New Supplies of Gold* (1853), Tooke began preparations in the summer of 1854 with the aim of publishing in the following spring of 1855. However, not long after work began, 'it became apparent that the plan so sketched was too circumscribed to admit of doing full justice to several topics' which have 'an important bearing upon the general subject proposed for narration and discussion' (Tooke 1857, V: iii–iv). These topics notably included progress in the railway system, progress in free trade, banking in France and the new discoveries of gold, all of which were treated in separate parts of an enlarged two-volume work.[36]

As well as updating the historical analysis of prices from 1847 to 1856, the two-volume work comprehensively covered the above topics, provided an expansive discussion of monetary policy and presented a massive amount of statistical information in the appendices. Newmarch was in fact the main contributor to *History* (1857, V and VI), writing five of its seven parts: Part II, on the course of prices and trade for commodities other than corn in the period, 1848–1856; Part III, on the progress of railway construction in the United Kingdom and foreign countries; Part IV, on the progressive application of free trade from 1820 to 1856; Part VI, on commercial and financial policy in France since 1848;[37] and Part VII, on the new supplies of gold from California and Australia in the period 1848–1856. By contrast, Tooke drafted only two of the seven parts of *History* (1857, V and VI): Part I, 'On the Prices of Corn from 1847 to 1856'; and Part V, 'On the Management and Policy of the Bank of England during the Period, 1847–56, with Special Reference to the Operation of the Bank Charter Act of 1844'. In addition, Newmarch was mainly responsible for compiling the statistical and other information in Appendices I–XXXIII of volume VI of History. The statistician J.T. Danson assisted in the preparation of the table of prices in Appendix VII and Mr Wheatley, Librarian of the Royal Medical Institution, in the preparation of the index to the whole six volumes of *History* enclosed in the sixth volume (Tooke 1857, V: xi; VI: 489). Notwithstanding Newmarch's immense contribution, in the preface to the work, Tooke (1857, V: ix) makes it clear that he supervised the research and was responsible for overseeing the whole manuscript through to publication so that it accorded with his position. In this regard, Newmarch was very much Tooke's protégé. With its completion, Tooke and Newmarch's six volume *History of Prices* (1838–1857) provided economic science with what Jevons (1865: 119) proclaimed 'a unique work, of which we can hardly overestimate the value'.

3 Tooke's approach to value and distribution

The main focus of Tooke's writings was to explain the actual movement in prices and, connectedly, variations in the price level and economic activity, in England, by an exhaustive empirical analysis. It was out of this empirical study that Tooke formulated his views on monetary questions that arose from consideration of the influence of monetary forces on prices and which led him to eventually develop his own monetary principles. In this regard, Tooke's empirical study was the *concrete* foundation upon which he built his monetary thought and formulated his policy positions. As would be expected of a systematic thinker, Tooke adopted a scientific method to conduct his empirical analysis. Tooke also possessed a theory of value and distribution necessary to logically underpin his empirically based explanation of price movements. But, unlike other political economists of his day, most notably, Ricardo and Malthus, Tooke does not set out a formal statement of his method of analysis and his theory of value and distribution. Nevertheless, Tooke's methodological and theoretical approach to explaining prices and distribution is inherent in his empirical analysis as well as in the arguments he advances on economic policy issues. This approach is firmly grounded in the science of the classical economists from whom the origins for the development of his own system of political economy is owed and to whom he most wished to persuade of the scientific merit of his findings. The purpose of what follows in this chapter is to illuminate Tooke's approach to value and distribution, which lies at the heart of his system of political economy. By this illumination Tooke's explanation of prices, his monetary thought and, indeed, his position on a range of economic policy issues, which are subsequently examined in this study, will become more comprehensible.

In the first section below the method of analysis employed by Tooke in explaining prices is shown to be based on the 'long period method' articulated by Adam Smith in the *Wealth of Nations* (1776) congruent with a role for competition in a capitalist economic system. This long period method was in fact adopted by most of Tooke's classical contemporaries. Distinctive to Tooke's economics, though, this method is employed in empirical analysis as well as in theoretical specification. In connection to theoretical content, Tooke adopted what has been called an 'adding-up' theory of value and distribution. Section 3.2 is concerned with examining the precise form of this theory adopted by Tooke.

This enables us in Section 3.3 to then examine Tooke's position on the determination of normal prices and distribution. Directly important to Tooke's empirical analysis for explaining actual prices is his conception of the determination of market prices. In Section 3.4 it is shown that, in accordance with the long period method of the classical economists, Tooke's approach to explaining short-run prices is based on the conception that market prices are determined by the interaction between the demand for and supply of commodities brought to market. Most of Tooke's empirical analysis covers a period in which Britain's monetary system was based on a metallic standard, a de facto gold standard in the years prior to 1797 and an official gold standard after 1821. Because monetary values were tied to gold, the value of the metallic standard had an important bearing on the long-run general price level in Britain during this period. Section 3.5 concerns Tooke's standpoint on the determination of the normal value of the metallic standard, being gold, considered by reference to the theoretical positions of Ricardo and Senior, who appear to have exerted a considerable influence on his own conception. Another consideration in explaining prices is the role played by trade protection since, by directly affecting the prices of tradable commodities, it can affect prices in general. Section 3.6 concerns Tooke's argument for free trade considered in the light of his views on the implications for long run prices as well as for economic development of trade protection.

3.1 Method of analysis

In Tooke's empirical study the explanation of actual price movements in England was based on the collection and interpretive analysis of all available qualitative and statistical information. Besides the enormous amount of statistical data, especially price data, he collected and arranged into series, Tooke heavily employed trade circulars and reports on market conditions in his study. It was through the establishment of the relevant factual situation that Tooke arrived at his explanation of price movements. He also disputed alternative explanations by reference to an interpretation of the facts. Tooke employed a method of analysis in his approach to explaining prices based on the long period method, as articulated by Adam Smith in the *Wealth of Nations* (1776) in relation to a decentralised capitalist economic system and, which was afterwards followed by other classical economists.[1]

In classical economics the long period method is best understood in the distinction made between natural price (or normal price or necessary price) and market price: whereby natural price is the result of systematic (or regular) behaviour of markets and is determined by permanent forces, and market price results from more complex behaviour of markets, including specific or irregular causes, and whose deviation from the former is attributed to temporary forces. In the famous Chapter VII, 'Of the Natural and Market Price', Book I of the *Wealth of Nations*, Adam Smith developed the conception of competition in a capitalist society with decentralised markets that linked the establishment of natural price with a uniform net rate of profit on capital.[2] According to Smith (1776 [1976]: 72–81), the natural price of commodities was first, associated with natural or 'ordinary' rates of rent, wages and profits, and, second, associated with the deployment of land, labour and the capital stock in the economy to ensure that the quantity of commodities produced and brought to market satisfied 'effectual demand'. Hence, at a position of equilibrium, the establishment of natural (or normal) prices was associated with the determination of the normal distribution of income between social classes.

In Smith's conception, natural prices, established by the systematic operation of competitive forces, are centres of gravity around which market prices fluctuate according to supply and demand conditions in the market. Any inequality in the demand for and supply of commodities would cause a deviation of market price from natural price, associated, most particularly, with a non-uniform net rate of profit. When, in any industry, the supply of a commodity brought to market exceeded effectual demand, its market price would be relatively lower than the natural price, associated with a rate of profit relatively lower than effective in other industries; and, when supply fell short of effectual demand, vice versa. However, deviations between market and natural price would be only temporary as the process of competition tended to restore market equilibrium (Smith 1776 [1976]: 75). In this respect, for Adam Smith 'free competition' essentially consisted of capital and labour mobility so that, in response to unequal rates of remuneration, the capital stock and labour would be re-deployed in a manner that adjusted supply to effectual demand and caused prices to adjust towards their natural values consistent with the restoration of uniform rates of remuneration. This method was adopted in Tooke's empirical economic studies.

In Tooke's analysis a clear distinction is made between short-run and long-run price movements (for example, Tooke 1838, I: 174–373; II: 346–7). Whereas short-run price fluctuations are seen to be the result of disparities between the demand for and supply of commodities brought to market, long-run price movements are attributable to changes in the average cost of producing and bringing to market an average supply of commodities. This average supply corresponds to the average technical conditions in which commodities are produced in their tendency towards (if not actual) equality with the average effectual demand. Thus, in a discussion of the question of the fluctuation of market prices, Tooke states in his very first work, *High and Low Prices*:

> although the cost of production must regulate the price of all commodities on the average of a certain number of years, the immediate cause of fluctuations in the market value at particular intervals is to be found in the variations of the relative proportion of supply and demand ... the demand for and supply of any particular commodity may be said to be balanced, and prices to be on a fair level, when the stock for sale is sufficient to cover the consumption at its estimated rate, till the reproduction or importation at the usual time, provided there be no alteration in the cost of production or of importation, or in the state of the seasons or of political relations, leading to the anticipation of an alteration in the amount of future supply.
>
> (1823, iv: 5–6; also 1824, iv: 330)

In Tooke, 'market value' corresponded with the observed price that is the immediate object of explanation. When the market value is at its 'fair level' demand and supply are in balance. The centre of gravity for market price is the 'cost of production', which is equivalent to what Smith called natural price and whose statistical counterpart is average price under average conditions of production.[3] Thus, in Tooke, the long-run movement of prices is statistically verified by the average price over a sufficient number of years to rule out the operation of temporary and accidental forces which cause imbalance between market demands and supplies. According to Tooke, an explanation of the long-run movement of prices is based on the identification of those persistent factors that influenced the cost of production of commodities *independent* of demand and supply. The number of years upon which Tooke calculated 'average' prices for the purpose of statistical inference varied according to the *systematic* nature of the economic forces which he believed was relevant to fully explaining the underlying course of movement in prices.

The short-run fluctuation of prices is explained in Tooke's analysis by reference to those temporary and specific factors that caused an inequality between the demand for and supply of commodities. Hence, in reference to causes of fluctuation in the prices of 'raw produce', Tooke and Newmarch (1857, V: 84–5) listed a number of 'accidental circumstances' altering the balance between supply and demand in the market. Tooke clearly conceived of these fluctuations in prices as deviations from their normal values to which they were attracted by the gravitational pull of persistent regular forces:

> The word 'fluctuation' is itself derived from the analogy which variations of price incidental to all Markets bear to undulations of the surface of the water. And the variations of price within moderate limits are as harmless as the waves which are caused by slight and varying breezes; while the fluctuations on an extensive scale may be likened to gales and hurricanes in the physical world, causing wreck and ruin to the property exposed to their violence.
>
> (1857, V: 84–5)

Hence, for historical perspective Tooke always developed his explanation of price fluctuations in the context of their underlying trend movement. He frequently referred to average prices (over various periods of time) in order to ascertain the amplitude of short-run price fluctuations as well as making comparisons between price changes over different periods of time for the purpose of establishing their historical context. As the passage on page 29 above indicates, Tooke was fully aware in framing his explanations of the error of equating average price with any concept of natural price (or cost of production) because of the unequal fluctuation of prices over time: the average statistical price could in fact be higher or lower than the natural price because of the preponderance of excess demand or excess supply conditions in the market, thereby corresponding with a high or low fair level of market-clearing prices. However, the main point is that Tooke's method of establishing the complexion of short-run price fluctuations at different times, which are to be then explained by reference to the interaction between demand and supply forces in the market, is entirely consistent with the classical approach of explaining market prices in terms of a deviation from the natural price.

The approach then taken by Tooke in his empirical analysis was to identify the *general* and *persistent* factors determining the average costs of production of commodities and then go to the *specific* and *fitful* factors influencing the interaction between demand and supply to *also* explain market prices. The approach is entirely consistent with the long period method in the *theory* of prices developed by Adam Smith.

3.2 The 'adding-up' theory

An interpretation of Tooke found in the literature is that he did not possess a coherent theory of prices and only developed a partial one after 1838 when he propounded an 'income theory of prices' (see Gregory 1928: 21–2; Marget 1938: 311–17; Arnon 1991: 70–2, 110–11).[4] This interpretation supposes implausibly that Tooke conducted most of his empirical analysis of prices without a theory of their determination. What is more, those advancing this interpretation have failed to show how Tooke believed this income theory of prices of his was supposed to work. In fact, from the very beginning Tooke had a coherent theoretical conception of price determination as a frame of reference for his applied work. But, unlike other leading economists of his day, Tooke did not set out a formal statement of his own position on value theory. Instead, Tooke's position can be distilled from his voluminous writings and parliamentary evidence, especially from his approach to explaining actual prices and from various propositions which underlie aspects of his monetary thought. In what follows it is shown that Tooke adopted a modified version of Adam Smith's theory of prices in the classical tradition.

An insight into Tooke's position on value theory is provided by his extant correspondence with J.B. Say in the years 1825, 1826 and 1828.[5] This correspondence shows clearly that Tooke rejected Ricardo's labour theory of value in favour of a less abstract theory of the origin of value.[6] Consistent with his writings, this correspondence also shows that Tooke adopted what can be called the 'adding-up theory' to natural price. It could also be called a 'cost of production' theory. Common among classical economists of Tooke's day, it was derived from Adam Smith's (1776 [1976]: 65–72) theory of value and distribution in which the natural price of products is resolved into the remunerations on capital, labour and land (as well as other scarce resources) used in their production, consisting of profits, wages and rent.[7] The corollary of Adam Smith's (1776 [1976]: 69–70) conception is that the 'revenue' of society is resolved into these three distributive variables.[8] The adding-up theory consists of explaining the natural price of products (and also 'revenue') by reference to profits, wages and rent for a given technique of production.

The distinctive feature of the adding-up theory is that the distributive variables are explained as if they are determined independently of each other for a given technique of production. Indeed, Ricardo (1821: 46, 307–9) was critical of Smith's adding-up theory precisely because normal prices and distribution were explained free of the analytical constraint posed by the interdependent determination of the distributive variables.[9] By contrast, the core of Ricardo's theory of value and distribution was that normal prices are determined on the basis of *interdependence* between the rate of profit and the real wage for a *given* technique of production.[10] However, as shown by De Vivo (1984: 46–73) and Bharadwaj (1989: 47–60), by the end of the 1820s the core of Ricardo's theory had been largely abandoned by 'Ricardians' in the face of criticism by Malthus (1820; 1824), Torrens (1829) and Bailey (1825). Having rejected or failed to comprehend Ricardo's core theory, most classical economists of Tooke's generation, notably Say (1821: 284–367), Malthus (1836: esp. 77–9) and Senior (1836: 101–3, 128–99), adopted the less analytically coherent adding-up theory to distribution and prices. The most significant difference between this theory and Adam Smith's theory was that following Ricardo's theory of differential rent, most economists, including Tooke, treated rent as *determined by* price according to the marginal cost associated with the diminishing productivity of scarce resources (i.e. land) used in production. This meant that the scope of the adding-up theory to prices was reduced essentially to explaining only the profit and wage components of what was called 'cost of production', which was equivalent to natural price when rent was zero (on marginal land).

Evidence that Tooke adopted this theory of natural prices is provided in the following passage taken from a letter to J.B. Say in which he criticises Ricardo's theory:

> Concerning the doctrine of wages, Ricardo's school affirms in a much categorical manner, and without having taken the true facts into account, that any rise in relation to *wages* takes place at a cost to *profits*, and *vice versa*. This is based on the supposition that capital and industry always produce a fixed and limited product, and that as a result of this, there would always be a set quantity that wages and profit would have to distribute among themselves; whereas, on the contrary, it is a fact that a larger demand which raises prices, wages and profits can frequently operate in the same way. To reply to this objection, the supporters of the doctrine in question say that the adjective *proportional* must always be taken as being included in their word *wages*. But nothing justifies this claim which, moreover, clarifies nothing; it does not lead to the explanation of any phenomenon and up until now, I do not find that this school has given a clear definition of the point which truly separates wages from profit. What is more, I have already publicly expressed my full approval of everything you say on wages in your chapter on *industrial revenues*.
>
> (Say 1848: 529–30 [Tooke to J.B. Say, 12 March 1826, as translated by N. Fletcher and J. Jonnes])

The passage shows clearly Tooke believed wages and profits could be explained without reference to any interdependence between them à la Ricardo.[11] Elsewhere in the letter Tooke wrote, 'I share your ideas on the principles which are developed so well in your *Treatise*' (Say 1848: 529–30). Given that in the *Treatise of Political Economy*, Say (1821, II: 21–32, 69–229) adopted an adding-up theory to price determination, Tooke's approval of the 'principles' of this work provides strong evidence that he adopted this common theory.

Perhaps the strongest direct evidence for Tooke's adoption of the adding-up theory is the analytical basis of his 'principle of limitation' which was a crucial part of his banking school monetary analysis. This principle maintained that in a monetary system in which the currency was convertible into gold (or specie) the short-run fluctuation in the price level was limited upwards by social income and downwards by 'cost of production'. The analytical basis of this principle was the 'dual-circulation' framework that Tooke derived from Adam Smith (1776 [1976]: 322). This analytical framework and its important role in Tooke's banking school monetary thought is elaborated in detail in Section 7.1. Our present concern is only with the essential conceptual basis of this framework for monetary circulation. Dual-circulation refers to the conception that monetary circulation in an economic system is divided into two branches: monetary circulation between what Tooke called 'dealers and dealers', who were associated with the intermediate stages of production and distribution of products, and monetary circulation between 'dealers and consumers' associated with income payments and consumption expenditure on final output. The conceptual basis of Smith's framework is that the value of the goods in the intermediate stages of production and distribution which are exchanged between 'dealers and dealers' could not be greater than the value of the final goods ultimately sold by 'dealers' to 'consumers' (see Smith quotation in Section 7.1: 164).[12] As Marx (1861–3, I: 125, 251–2; 1885: 479–81; 1894: 842–3) well indicated, Tooke's conception was based on Adam Smith's method of resolving natural price into wages, profits and rent in an economy with only circulating capital such that the 'valued added' in the intermediate processes of production and distribution could not be systematically larger than the total value of final output, what Smith called 'neat revenue'.[13] On this basis Tooke argued that

> [I]n a convertible state of the currency, given the actual and contingent supply of commodities, the greater or less demand will depend, not upon the total quantity of money in circulation, but upon the quantity of money constituting the revenues, valued in gold, of the different orders of the state under the head of rents, profits, salaries and wages, destined for current expenditure.
>
> (1844: 74–5)

Through its determination of aggregate consumption expenditure, Tooke (1844: 71–2) contended that the gold value of social income (which was equivalent to what he called 'revenue'), especially wage income, constituted a limitation on short-run upward movements in the general level of prices. He also contended that a short-run downturn in the price level would be limited by the normal cost of production of commodities since it would not be profitable for producers to supply at prices below it for very long. This principle of limitation was most clearly explained by Tooke when he wrote:

> It is the quantity of money constituting the revenue of the different orders of the state, under the head of rents, salaries, and wages, destined for current expenditure, according to the wants and habits of the several classes, that alone forms the limiting principle of the *aggregate of money prices*, – the only prices that can properly come under the designation of *general prices*. As the cost of production is the limiting principle of supply, so the aggregate of money income devoted to expenditure for consumption is the limiting principle of demand for commodities.
>
> (1840a, III: 276)

Tooke's principle was about giving effect to the notion that market prices fluctuated around normal money prices fixed to a gold standard (also see Tooke 1848a, IV: 195).[14] The relevant point here is that the analytical framework of Tooke's principle of limitation is based on an adding-up theory of prices, with its corollary that revenue resolves itself into rent, profit and wages. Further strong evidence of Tooke's adoption of an adding-up theory is his conception, elaborated in Section 7.3, that the long-run average rate of interest (and, thereby, normal rate of profit) constitutes a cost of production of commodities such that he believed lasting changes in the rate of interest was a major contributing cause of long-run price movements. Hence, as will be further developed below, it is argued that Tooke adopted an adding-up theory as a theoretical frame of reference for explaining price behaviour.[15]

Although the adding-up theory did not constitute an altogether coherent theory of value and distribution, it did provide a sound basis for Tooke's empirical study. Paradoxically, it allowed Tooke to develop empirically based arguments on the causes of price movements which would have been otherwise ruled out a priori from the standpoint of Ricardo's more theoretically coherent approach. In particular, as is indicated in Sections 4.4 and 5.7 below, it led Tooke to develop a position on the distribution of income between social classes in nineteenth-century England, different to, and more plausible than the position held by Ricardo. In Tooke's analysis interdependence between the shares of income going to landowners, capitalists and labour emerged in the context of long-run *changes* in money prices. With regard to the theoretical content of Tooke's conception of price determination, in accordance with the adding-up theory it is best examined by reference to his empirically based views about the determination of wages, profits and rent as 'component parts' of natural price.

3.2.1 Rent

Tooke adopted Ricardo's differential theory of rent. A sign of this is first provided in the following answers Tooke gave in parliamentary evidence to the Agriculture Committee of 1821:

> Does a high rent produce any effect on the price of corn, or is a high rent the effect of a high price of corn? – Tooke: I conceive the high rent is the effect of a high price of corn.
>
> (1821a: 292)

> If the landlord were to give the whole of his rent to the farmer, do you think corn would be more plentiful or cheaper? – Tooke: No, I do not imagine that the corn would be either more plentiful or cheaper; I think if corn is more plentiful and cheaper, it may not leave so much rent to the landlord.
>
> (1821a: 293)

The proposition that higher rent on land causally contributes to a higher price of agriculture accords with Adam Smith's conception of rent as the cost of employing land in agricultural production which, thereby, contributes to the determination of its natural price. By contrast, the proposition that a higher rent on land will causally result from a higher price of agriculture accords with Ricardo's theory that rent on land is a residual of the profit of farmers which, for a given technique, is determined on the basis of the natural price of agriculture.

As is well known, the rent on land in Ricardo's theory is determined by the incremental cost associated with the diminishing productivity of land employed in agricultural production and which is calculated by the difference between the natural price determined on the least productive land brought into use and the relatively lower cost of production on lands of higher productivity. Hence, in this theory, given the presence of diminishing returns to land in agriculture, an increase in the natural price of agriculture caused by less productive land brought into production would increase the rent going to landowners. In accord with this theory, Tooke clearly believed it was the price of agriculture that played the leading role in determining the extent to which land of lesser productivity was profitably employed and, therefore, the amount of rent. This is well shown in another answer he gave to the 1821 Agricultural Committee:

> Is it your opinion, that the price of corn in this country has been raised by bringing inferior soils into cultivation within these twenty years? – Tooke: I should rather conceive that cause and effect as there stated, might be reversed, and that the high prices have induced inferior land to be taken into cultivation.
>
> (1821a: 287)

Tooke (1821a: 287–8) well understood that the adjustment of agricultural production to demand required a higher (lower) price which, by making farming

more (less) profitable, induced an increase (decrease) in the amount of less productive land brought into production that raised (lowered) differential rent. Furthermore, it is evident Tooke (1821a: 233–6) conceived that when this
adjustment process came to end a uniformity in the rate of profit of all lands of
different quality employed in agriculture was established.

Tooke's adherence to Ricardo's theory of rent is also shown in his analysis of
the large increase in income that went to 'farmers and landlords' as a result of
the high price of corn in England over the period 1792 to 1812.[16] The 'succession of crops more or less deficient' saw 'rents, upon the expiration of leases'
being 'advanced in full proportion to the high range of prices of produce; and, in
several instances, they were raised to treble of what they had been in 1792'
(Tooke 1824, iii: 311; also see 1838, I: 186, 312–13). Tooke (1824, iii: 301–12,
317–18; 1838, I: 326) linked the rise (fall) in rent directly to the extension
(reduction) in the amount of land that came under cultivation, which he factually
ascertained by annual statistics of the number of bills of enclosure granted. Elsewhere, in connection with a discussion of the effect of a bounty on the price of
corn, Tooke declared openly his assent with Ricardo's theory of rent in the following way:

> The ultimate effect of a bounty on the exportation of corn may, I think, be
> clearly proved to be that of raising the price to the consumer at home, by
> eventually inducing resort to land of inferior quality, and thereby increasing
> the cost of production. On this point, as on most others involving any
> important principle in political economy, I have the advantage of agreeing
> with Mr. Ricardo, who, page 368, Principles of Political Economy, 3rd
> edition [i.e. Ricardo 1821: 312], after observing that the 'natural price of
> corn is not so fixed as the natural price of commodities, because with any
> great additional demand for corn, land of worse quality must be taken into
> cultivation, on which more labour will be required to produce a given quan-
> tity, and the natural price of corn will be raised,' adds, 'by a continued
> bounty, therefore, on the exportation of corn, there would be created a tend-
> ency to a permanent rise in the price of corn'.
>
> (1824, iii: 244–5n.)

There should be little surprise in Tooke adopting Ricardo's differential theory of
rent given that it had been invented at the same time also by Malthus (1815) and
Edward West (1815), and then widely adopted by his classical contemporaries.[17]
It is notable though that Tooke reportedly defended Ricardo's theory of rent
against attack by Torrens at a Political Economy Club meeting in 1831.[18] While
Tooke (1857, V: 185–95) was fully aware that capital applied to land would
increase its productivity (i.e. enclosures, drainage), in his analysis he did not
clearly distinguish between rent on the *intensive* from the *extensive* margin. On
the one hand, Tooke (1821a: 233–4) saw increased applications of capital to
agriculture a result of persistently higher prices that raised the prospect of higher
profits to farmers and, thereby, of higher rent going to landlords. On the other

hand, he also believed that a lowering of the price of agriculture could induce greater applications of capital to improve productivity and lower production costs as a way of preventing a significant reduction in profits and rent. In this latter regard Tooke (1821a: 233–4, 287) clearly believed greater capital intensity would tend to lower the normal price of agriculture by increasing the productivity of existing employed land. The important point is that, following Ricardo, Tooke adhered to the view that, for a given technique, including given normal climatic conditions, rent *depends* on the price of agricultural products (corn) and not vice versa.

3.2.2 Wages

The various discussions of wages in Tooke's writings show that he adhered to the general position among classical economists that the real wage was determined by a complex set of socio-economic, institutional and technical factors. Thus, on wage determination, Tooke makes reference to 'custom', 'habit', 'style of living', employment conditions, international competitiveness and the pace of capital accumulation in relation to population growth. His position appears to accord with Adam Smith's approach to explaining natural wages. In this regard, it is significant that there is no hint in Tooke's writings of adherence to the Malthusian population theory that Ricardo (1821: 99–109) adopted as a mechanism for the gravitation of the wage to its natural level. Instead, Tooke seems to have believed that the normal wage would alter according to the state of economic development associated with technical progress.

A particularly distinctive feature of Tooke's position is the notion of a socially determined minimum subsistence wage below which the real wage does not fall. In this regard Tooke believed the real wage in England was normally above subsistence such that social norms tended to play an indirect role in the determination of the normal real wage through their determination of the minimum subsistence wage. Interestingly, Smith (1776 [1976]: 85–6) had earlier maintained that there was a 'certain rate below which it seems impossible to reduce, for any considerable time, the ordinary wages of the lowest species of labour', this minimum wage being 'the lowest consistent with common humanity'. Tooke essentially proposed that in England this social minimum was fixed by parish allowances provided under the Poor Laws. He believed that in both England and France social welfare was particularly important in giving relief to the 'lowest classes' at times when crop failures induced very high food (corn) prices:

> in France ... it is a part of the general policy of the government to provide by the purchase of corn, in times of dearth, for the subsistence of the lowest classes, and particularly for that of the inhabitants of Paris; and in this country, where the poor laws create funds for the maintenance of the lowest classes, at the expense of all the classes above them; where, moreover, the voluntary contributions of richer individuals swell that fund.
>
> (Tooke 1838, I: 14)

Tooke (1838, I: 72n., 185–6, 227; also see 1857, V: 80) argued that the English Poor Laws, made more benevolent by government sanction of the 'Speenhamland System' in 1795, played an important role in supporting living standards in the face of high price inflation during the French Wars. It was ascertained by Tooke that the real wage of most classes of labour declined during this period because of the persistent increase in the price of 'provisions' not matched by a commensurate increase in money wages.

It was in the context of workers obtaining higher money wages in response to the permanent increase in the cost of living that Tooke (1824, i: 54–6n.; 1838, I: 225–7, 313, 329–31) discussed factors determining the real wage:

> I am disposed to admit, that the rise of wages, extending over such numerous classes of labourers, may be looked upon to be the general rule ... the advance is fully accounted for, by the rise in the price of necessaries during the period referred to: for, it is clear, that if the accumulation of capital keeps pace with the population, there must be a rise of wages in some proportion to the rise, if this be of any considerable duration, in the price of provisions and other necessaries of the labourer.
>
> (1824, i: 54–5n.)

> The wages of agricultural labourers and artisans had been doubled, or nearly so. Salaries from the lowest clerks up to the highest functionaries, as well as professional fees, had been considerably raised on the plea of the greatly increased expenses of living; the expense of living having been increased, not only by the increased price of necessaries, but by a higher scale of general expenditure, or style of living, incidental to the progress of wealth and civilisation (1838, I: 330–1).

The state of employment was also seen as a factor influencing (relative) wages, at least in the short run. Thus, for example, in 1838–1839 when food prices were high, Tooke (1840a, III: 52–3) noticed that while wage increases had been granted to agricultural labourers, the wages of manufacturing labourers tended to fall because of economic recession and weak employment conditions. It was also ascertained by Tooke (1838, II: 70–1, 248–9) that in the twenty-year period after the French Wars the secular decline in the price of provisions outweighed any decline in the money wage, with the effect of permanently raising the real wage.

That Tooke believed social norms played a role in the determination of the real wage is confirmed by J.L. Mallet's diary account of the reasons advanced by Tooke for the permanent rise in the real wage of skilled labour over the twenty-year period after 1813 at the Political Economy Club meeting of 9 February 1833. Tooke had sponsored the following question for this meeting: 'Have Wages fallen in money value in proportion to the money price of other commodities; and if not, how is the difference?' (Higgs 1921: 451). As recorded by Mallet, Tooke argued that money wages remained relatively constant despite 'the fall in the price of the necessaries of life, such as bread, potatoes, beer, sugar, candles, soap, salt, house rent and all commodities in the manufacture of which machinery is concerned, such as cottons and hardware' (Higgs 1921: 246). On the reasons for the resulting higher real wages:

> Mr. Tooke thought it was chiefly to be resolved into moral causes inducing such combinations, activity, determination of purpose, limitation of apprentices in trade and so forth on the part of artisans, whose wants and comforts having been enlarged would not suffer a reduction of their acquired advantages, and also from the greater weight of public opinion and popular feeling which supported them against the capitalist.
>
> (Higgs 1921: 246–7)

This quote indicates that, similar to the positions of Ricardo (1821: 96–7) and Torrens (1815: 62–5), Tooke believed that once wage-earners became accustomed to a certain standard of living afforded by their occupation, they could effectively resist any reduction below it on the basis of a change in social norms. It also indicates that Tooke (1857, V: 284–5, 290–7) recognised that 'combinations' strengthened the bargaining position of workers in obtaining higher wages. However, Tooke believed that wage outcomes ultimately depended on the state of trade in industry. Taking up arguments by J.S. Mill (1848 [1909]: 609–10, 622–5) and Senior (1830: 1–35), Tooke (1857, VI: 204–11) later maintained that permanent increases in the real wage of English workers (relative to those in other countries) during the 1850s stemmed from their 'superior skill' in industries producing 'better and more attractive commodities for the general markets of the world'. Hence, Tooke's position on wages was similar to Adam Smith's notion that natural wages would vary according to the progress of accumulation and state of economic prosperity. In Tooke's picture this was connected with the technological conditions of production, which he believed exerted the *decisive* influence on the normal real wage by its systematic effect on prices in relation to the money wage.

3.2.3 Rate of profit

Tooke's position on the determination of the normal rate of profit does not clearly emerge until the first two volumes of *History* in 1838. Prior to this date the only reference made by Tooke (1826: 10–11) to its determination is when he states rather obscurely that as the 'sources of production' and 'the degree of their productiveness' increase, the 'returns to mercantile and other professional skill' rise. This only suggests Tooke believed the rate of profit was generally determined by conditions of production. From 1838 onwards Tooke (1838, II: 355–6) conceived that the normal rate of profit is the aggregate of two independently determined component parts: the average rate of interest on 'monied capital' of the 'best security' and the remuneration for the 'risk', 'trouble' and 'professional skill' of the productive employment of capital. From this standpoint and in contrast to the commonly held view, Tooke essentially proposed that the normal rate of profit was *governed by* the rate of interest determined *in* the financial market. This interpretation follows from Tooke's argument that in the long-run the rate of interest and thereby, implicitly, the rate of profit, entered into the cost of production of commodities (see Section 7.3). In order for persistent changes in the profit rate (via the rate of interest) to so affect long-run prices, as Tooke argued, then he must have assumed that there would be no counteracting reduction in the cost of production as a result of a simultaneous reduction in the real wage for given rates of productivity growth. Hence, Tooke's argument, though incomplete, is entirely consistent with and, in fact, provides strong evidence of his adherence to the adding-up theory of price determination.[19] In Tooke's picture, then, an explanation of the normal rate of profit turned on the manner of determination of the average rate of interest. A fuller account of Tooke's explanation of the latter is provided in Section 6.3. In short, Tooke conceived that the average rate of interest was determined by politico-institutional factors regulating the supply of and demand for 'monied capital'.

A comment is warranted on the imprecise nature of Tooke's explanation of the rate of profit in relation to theory contemporary of his day. The rate of profit in Tooke is determined exogenously without explicit reference to the social and technological constraints of the production system that determines the size of social surplus from which profits can be appropriated. From the standpoint of a surplus approach to value and distribution, the viability of Tooke's explanation depends on assuming that the rate of profit so determined does not exceed the socio-technical limit given by the maximum profits which can be appropriated by capitalists from the surplus of society as a ratio of the capital stock employed in production. In Tooke's time an understanding of this viability condition involved at least an appreciation of Ricardo's theory that the rate of profit was determined by the subsistence real wage for a *given* technique of production and on the assumption that capital consisted entirely of wages advanced. That Tooke may have been aware of the socio-technical limit on the rate of profit in Ricardo's theory is hinted at in the following question he sponsored at a Political Economy Club meeting in 1825:

> When it is said that the *rate of Profit depends on wages*, is the term *Wages confined to necessaries of the most common labourers*, or does it include the higher remuneration for the various gradations of skilled labour?
>
> (Higgs 1921: 25; emphasis added)

However, there is no firm textual evidence to support an interpretation that for a given technique of production Tooke believed the socio-technical maximum rate of profit was determined by reference to his socially determined minimum subsistence wage that was discussed above (p. 37). Aside from Ricardo's followers and J.S. Mill (1844 [1874]), other contemporaries of Tooke, most notably Say (1821), Malthus (1836) and Senior (1836), failed to account at all for this socio-technical constraint, thereby leaving their theories of the rate of profit open to indeterminacy.[20] Hence, on purely analytical grounds, Tooke's explanation had as much validity as those of the leading (non-Ricardian) economists who, also adhering to an adding-up (or cost of production) theory of value and distribution, failed to develop a coherent theory showing how real forces in the system of production determined the (maximum) normal rate of profit.

3.3 Normal prices and distribution

In the adding-up theory of Tooke, for a given technique of production, normal price depends on the rate of profit and the wage into which the cost of production of commodities is resolved. As shown in the previous section, Tooke, following Ricardo's theory, saw rent as a residual part of profit which, thereby, depended on price. On this basis, Tooke believed the normal rent on land was ultimately regulated by long-run conditions of supply, which he believed played the major role in determining the normal price of agricultural commodities (e.g. corn). Thus, Tooke (1838, II: 21–85, 346–7) identified factors that systematically affected the productivity of land used in agriculture, principally long-run average climatic conditions, as being the main determinant of agricultural prices and, thereby, the rent going to English landlords (see Section 4.1). The share of non-wage income going to landlords was dependent on how these factors determined the cost of production on the least productive (i.e. no-rent) land profitable for farmers to employ in agricultural production. In connection with wages and profits, it may be inferred from the discussion above that Tooke believed they were determined independently of each other. However, in relation to his explanation of the long-run movement of prices, Tooke's view about the determination of the real wage and profit rate does provide an explanation of distribution that takes account of interdependence between these two distributive variables.

The key to Tooke's apparent position on distribution is that his analysis of prices is conducted in terms of *money values*, which, under a gold standard, consisted of measuring commodities in gold commanded at its official mint price (Laidler 1975: 218). As is shown in Section 3.5, Tooke (1844: 9–14, 136) adhered to Ricardo's theory that the normal value of gold (or silver) was in the long run determined as a scarce commodity by its cost of production at the marginal (or no-rent) mine. In accord with this theory Tooke (1857, VI: 216–18, 225–6) evidently believed that the value of gold only changed slowly with a change in the productivity of the marginal mine. He therefore considered gold to be a stable standard for long-run money values. On this basis, the real wage in Tooke depended on the relative change of the money wage in relation to the money prices of provisions. In Tooke's analysis, the long-run movement in prices was predominantly due to factors that affected the cost of producing and bringing commodities other than gold to market. Most of these constituted (or were equivalent to) a change, either progressive or regressive, in the technique of production. An important exception was the rate of interest on capital, which, as already mentioned above, Tooke treated as a cost of production. It was listed by Tooke (1838, II: 347, 349) as a major cause of the long-run movement in prices (see Section 5.7: 122). By contrast, the money wages of labour was *not* listed by Tooke as a major cause of price movements.[21] The reason for this is that Tooke believed changes in money wages were nearly always in response to and lagged well behind prior changes in the price of provisions. Thus, Tooke maintained that historical experience indicated 'the little tendency which exists in wages to follow a fall or rise in the prices of provisions *except at long inter-vals, and then only in a degree far short of such fall or rise*' (1840a, III: 52; emphasis added). This meant that, subject to a lower social limit set by parish allowances, the real wage in Tooke largely depended on factors which deter-mined the price of provisions in relation to a given money wage.

In Tooke's analysis, then, the rate of interest and, by implication, the rate of profit, having a causal influence on price, appear to have been treated as the independent distributive variable and the real wage, causally dependent on price for a given money wage, was treated as the residual one. It is interesting to note that on the 'question of a measure of value' Tooke considered 'that the money price of common day labourer is a better criterion than corn, of the value of the precious metals' (1838, I: 56). This suggests Tooke was well aware of measur-ing the money value of commodities in terms of money wages (i.e. price–wage ratios). On this basis, it is possible to attribute to him a notion of an exogenous rate of profit which, for a given technique of production (and therefore all mater-ial input costs), governs distribution by influencing money prices in relation to the money wage (Panico 1988: 36–8). While Tooke certainly does not give a clear explanation along these lines, the outlook of his position on price determi-nation is consistent with it.

Tooke's position on distribution emerges in connection with his analysis of the effect of permanent changes in the technical conditions of production on the prices of provisions that enter into the real wage of workers. This position is best appreciated by recognising that for a given rate of profit and money wage, a per-sistent increase (decrease) in money prices from a reduction (rise) in productiv-ity will tend to lower (raise) the real wage and redistribute income from (toward) wages to (from) profits. Given Tooke's position that technical and other extrane-ous factors (influencing productivity) exerted by far the most important influence on long-run prices, persistent price inflation in his analysis tended to bring about a reduction in the real wage associated with a redistribution of (a smaller real) income from wages to profits; while persistent price deflation, vice versa. Hence, during the inflationary period of the French Wars from 1793 to 1814, which Tooke (1838, I: 81–5, 114–17, 328–30; II: 346–7) largely attributed to a long-run climatic-induced deterioration in agricultural productivity and war-induced disruptions to foreign supplies, he believed the real wage declined and his analy-sis indicates that he believed the income of the 'landed interest' increased at the expense of the 'labouring class'. Identifying a period of persistent price deflation from 1815 to 1837 which, with the cessation of the above-mentioned factors, Tooke (1838, II: 13, 248–9, 348–9) mainly attributed to technical progression, his analysis indicates that he believed it brought about a higher real wage, asso-ciated with a redistribution of income away from the 'landed interest' to other classes. This position on distribution which comes to light in the context of

Tooke's analysis of a long-run change in prices is in fact consistent with an add-ing-up theory because the interdependence between wages and profits (non-wage income) so posited is associated with a *change* in money (real) income that is accompanied by a change in the technical conditions of production and the price level.

3.4 Market prices

In accordance with the position of most classical economists after Smith (1776 [1976]: 72–81), Tooke believed commodity outputs tended to adjust to their effectual demands. To explain short-run fluctuations in market prices, Tooke therefore focused on identifying causes of disruption to the actual process of adjustment of supply to the effectual level of demand. In the short run, Tooke found demand conditions to be generally more stable than supply conditions. In this regard, he believed the demand for particular commodities was liable to change only slowly in the longer run. Hence, Tooke considered supply distur-bances to be the main source of commodity price fluctuations. Tooke did not completely rule out the influence of short-run variations in demand, which he mainly attributed to speculative activity of traders in the market. However, Tooke believed that, aside from credit conditions, speculative activity was largely explained by reference to trader's expectations about prospective con-ditions of supply.

An important aspect of Tooke's analysis was to ascertain the extent to which disturbances to the balance of supply and demand in the market, mainly originat-ing with conditions of supply, caused fluctuations in the price of commodities. With most commodities, Tooke (1824, iii: 283–4; iv: 328–9) contended that the rise or fall in prices would be in a ratio greater than the quantity of excess demand or excess supply which caused these respective fluctuations in prices. The degree to which prices varied in response to shortages or surpluses in the market depended on the nature of the commodity:

> according as they come more or less under the description of necessaries – according as they are more or less perishable – more or less bulky and expensive to keep in proportion to their value – and according as a differ-ence in price may extend or limit the consumption.
>
> (Tooke 1824, iii: 284)

Tooke was aware that in the case of excess supply in the market, the ability to stock the commodity and its cost of storage had an important bearing on the degree to which the price would fall. For excess demand, the degree of potential price rises depended heavily on the extent to which the particular commodity was part of the necessary consumption of society or was substitutable by other commodities. Upon this reasoning Tooke (1824, iii: 283–300; 1838, I: 10–20) explained why the market prices of agricultural commodities tended to vary in a ratio well beyond any difference existing between their supply and demand.

Tooke believed corn to be the agricultural commodity whose price was most subject to extensive variation in response to market disequilibria.

Most of Tooke's discussion of the variation in market price centres on corn. In the case of a deficiency in the supply of corn compared with the 'average rate of consumption', Tooke deferred to the 'King–Davenant Law', which represented an attempt 'to deduce a strict rule of proportion between a given defect of the harvest, and the probable rise of price' (1824, iii: 285; also 1838, I: 12). This arithmetic rule is presented by Tooke (1824, 1838) in Table 3.1 taken from Davenant (1699: 224).

While Tooke made it clear 'that no such strict rule can be deduced', nevertheless, on empirical grounds, 'there is some ground for supposing that the estimate is not very wide of the truth, from observation of the repeated occurrence of the fact' (1824, iii: 285–6; also 1838, I: 12–13).[22] Tooke attributed this phenomenon to the fact that the demand for corn was highly unresponsive to a change in its price because, as the main subsistence commodity of necessary consumption, there was very little scope for substitution. In this explanation, Tooke, similar to Malthus's position in *An Investigation of the Cause of the Present High Price of Provisions* (1800),[23] attached considerable importance to the role of social policy in England and France in the maintenance of subsistence living for the lowest income classes. On this matter it is worth quoting Tooke in full:

> The process in which the rise beyond the proportion of defect takes place, is the struggle of every one to get his accustomed share of that which is necessary for his subsistence, and of which there is not enough or so much as usual for all. Supposing a given deficiency, the degree in which the money price may rise, will depend upon the extent of the pecuniary means of the lowest classes of the community. In countries where the pecuniary means of the lowest classes are limited to the power of obtaining a bare subsistence in ordinary times, as in Ireland, and on many parts of the Continent, and where neither the government, as in France, nor the poor laws and contributions by wealthy individuals, as in England, come in aid of those means, a proportion of the population, according to the degree of scarcity, must perish or suffer diseases incidental to an insufficient supply of food, or to a substitution of inferior and unwholesome diet. And the increased competition of purchasers being thus limited to the classes above the lowest, the rise in price may not

Table 3.1

Defect		Above the common rate
1 tenth		3 tenths
2 tenths		8 tenths
3 tenths	raises the price by	1.6 tenths
4 tenths		2.8 tenths
5 tenths		4.5 tenths

be very considerably beyond the defect of quantity. But in France, where it is a part of the general policy of the government to provide by the purchase of corn in times of dearth, for the subsistence of the lowest classes, and particularly for that of the inhabitants of Paris; and in this country, where the poor laws create a fund for the maintenance of the lowest classes, at the expense of all the classes above them; where, moreover, the voluntary contributions of richer individuals swell that fund; it is clear the competition of purchasers would be greatly increased, while the supply being limited, the price would rise very considerably beyond the ratio of deficiency. The final effect ... is to limit consumption and to apportion the privations resulting from scarcity over a larger part of the population; thus diminishing the severity of pressure upon the lowest class, and preventing or tending to prevent any part of it from perishing, as it might otherwise do, from actual want of food.

(1824, iii: 286–7; also 1838, I: 13–14)

In the case of an excess supply of corn on the market, Tooke (1821a: 240; 1857, VI: 68–9) argued that the price would tend to fall sharply because with the population 'adequately fed' its lowering provided little inducement to higher consumption. But, while an excess supply was generally 'attended with a fall of price much beyond the ratio of the excess', Tooke contended that it 'is not calculated to be in the same ratio as that of deficiency in raising price' (1838, I: 20n.). The reason given for this difference was that in the case of excess production, corn could be stocked by farmers and therefore surpluses withheld from coming onto the market and depressing the price. However, this depended on the financial position of the farmer and the existing level of accumulated grain stocks (Tooke 1857, V: 168–71). Should there be a series of abundant harvests which caused farmers to accumulate stocks to the point at which they are 'manifestly and inconveniently large, the subsequent depression [in the price of corn] would be the greater, in proportion to the previous resistance to a fall, and the only remedy would be an exportation at ruinously low rates' (1838, I: 20n.).

Tooke was clear that the operation of the above principle of the 'general effects of quantity on price' are 'subject to various modifications arising from the great and almost infinite variety of circumstances which may affect the relations of supply and demand, as far as concerns the market value of a particular commodity' (1824, iv: 329). It was precisely the task of the analyst to identify and weigh the various influences operating in the market at any particular time by reference to the facts. But in doing so Tooke pointed to the importance of accounting for 'expectations' which can affect the behaviour of buyers and sellers in the commodity market. In this connection he distinguished between 'actual' and 'prospective' want on the demand side and between 'actual' and 'contingent' quantity on the supply side. It is on the basis of expectations of 'prospective' flow demand and 'contingent' flow supply that traders calculated future prices in relation to current prices and determined the most profitable stock levels. Tooke (1824, iv: 330–2) pointed out that whenever 'actual' demand

and supply varied from what is widely anticipated, traders will often drastically adjust their stock levels with considerable repercussions to the market price. Moreover, it can often appear that the actual price moves in a direction contrary to the quantities of the commodity in stock; for example, lower prices with stock-building, because the adjustment process lags behind 'actual' flow demands and supplies. Tooke illustrated this point by way of an historical example in which supply well exceeded what dealers anticipated. The subsequent reduction in price was necessary to induce 'successive dealers to increase their stock' (1824, iv: 331) on the expectation that lower prices will induce a higher future demand by consumers and that future sales will occur at relatively higher prices which bring a revenue that more than offsets the loss sustained by the current depreciation in the value of their previously accumulated stock. However, consistent with Tooke's view about the relative stability of demand compared to supply, he emphasised that in these circumstances the dealers will often be in a vulnerable position because the 'increase of consumption' of 'articles in general use is a slow process, compared with the possible increase of supply' (1824, iv: 331). Thus, if there is a further unanticipated increase in supply, then:

> every person who has bought with a view to future resale, will lose in proportion to the degree in which he has extended his stock; and the consumers, (among whom, when speaking of raw materials, manufacturers are usually classed) most of whom have been tempted by cheapness to anticipate their probable consumption, by extending their stocks, will find that they would have done better if they had postponed demand.
>
> (Tooke 1824, iii: 331)

As a lagged response to the actual situation, traders will rundown their stocks to low levels simultaneously with a sharp decline in the price until the actual excess is eliminated. In this way Tooke pointed out that an unanticipated glut of this kind will aggravate the downturn in price such that the lowest price will coincide with the smallest stocks on hand. This same reasoning is employed to explain the process in reverse in the case of an unanticipated shortage in the market leading to a sharp rise in the price associated with large and growing stock levels.[24]

In Tooke's analysis ascertaining the opinion of the market with respect to 'contingent' supply and 'prospective' demand is therefore important in explaining short-run price fluctuations. This is because the degree of fluctuation in the price of commodities will depend heavily on the extent to which the opinion of traders is 'well or ill founded'. From his observation of market behaviour, Tooke maintained that the less accurately traders anticipated actual excess demand and excess supply in the market and the longer it took for them to adjust their stock position accordingly, the greater will usually be the fluctuation in commodity prices to correct the disequilibria in the market.[25] This notion is important in relation to Tooke's view of the part played by speculative activity in commodity markets in explaining price fluctuations.

3.5 Value of the 'metallic standard' and the price level

In the eighteenth and nineteenth centuries monetary values in Britain and other Western European nations were usually fixed to a designated metallic standard in peacetime, consisting of either gold or a silver standard, according to the official mint price per unit of quantity. Hence, classical economists conceived that on the basis of the given monetary standard, the normal money prices of commodities were determined by their exchange (or relative) value to the designated precious metal; that is, by the metallic (gold or silver) price of commodities. This meant that in the long run the general price level, however it was calculated as a theoretical construct, depended heavily on factors which determined the value of the 'metallic standard'. This was well understood by Tooke from the beginning of his studies.[26] However, Tooke's theoretical position on the determination of the metallic standard only fully comes to light in his banking school writings from the early-1840s and afterwards.

In his writings Tooke does not provide a clear account of his theoretical position on the determination of the value of the metallic standard which, in post-1821 Britain, was officially gold. Nevertheless, it is apparent Tooke adhered to the positions of Ricardo (1821) and Senior (1840) that the normal value of gold (or silver) was in the long run determined as a scarce commodity by its cost of production. In deference to the position of 'Mr. Senior, in one of his lectures on the value of money' Tooke wrote: 'it is the cost of production of the precious metals, and not their quantity, which constitutes their values, and determines the prices of commodities with reference to the cost of production of the latter measured in metallic value' (Tooke 1844: 136).

It was the first of Senior's *Three Lectures on the Value of Money*, delivered at the University of Oxford in 1829 and subsequently published in 1840, which Tooke was referring to above. In these lectures Senior developed on Ricardo's theory of the determination of the value of gold (and silver) as a scarce commodity in order to examine the factors that regulated the value of money in an economy in which money values are normalised by a gold (or a silver) standard.

Senior (1840: 30) showed that the value of gold (or silver) money 'does not depend *permanently* on the quantity of it possessed by a given community, or on the rapidity of its circulation' but rather depends on '*the cost of its production*' as measured in labour commanded. To illustrate this position Senior (1840: 32–40) set out a model in which it was assumed that there was a spectrum of mines all of different natural fertility which were available for exploitation and in which labour was the only input employed in equal quantities in these mines. In equilibrium, when a uniform net rate of profit was earned on capital and a uniform wage was paid to labour, the value of scarce gold (or silver) was determined by its cost of production at the least productive (no-rent) mine brought into use. In accordance with Ricardo's theory, rent went to those producers using mines whose productivity was higher relative to the least productive mine commanding a zero rent. The value of rent per mine (measured either in terms of gold, silver or in labour commanded) was determined by the difference between the cost of producing gold (or silver) at each mine and the cost of production at the no-rent (or marginal) mine. Highest at the most productive mine, rent was progressively lower at successively less-productive mines down to the least productive mine employed in gold (or silver) production.

On this basis, Senior came to the same conclusion as Ricardo that providing the cost of production at the marginal mine remained unchanged, the value of gold (or silver) would be invariable to changes in output to satisfy its demand. This was consistent with the longstanding conception in classical economics that in the *long run* the quantity of gold used as money was endogenously determined by its value for a given level of aggregate output and a given velocity of circulation at the competitive equilibrium position of the economy (see Green 1992: 14–15; also see Section 7.6). The following two passages from Ricardo and Senior convey this conception:

> Gold and silver, like all other commodities, are valuable only in proportion to the quantity of labour necessary to produce them, and bring them to market. Gold is about fifteen times dearer than silver, not because there is a greater demand for it, nor because the supply of silver is fifteen times greater than that of gold, but solely because fifteen times the quantity of labour is necessary to procure a given quantity of it.... The quantity of money that can be employed in a country must depend on its value: if gold alone were employed for the circulation of commodities, a quantity would be required, one fifteenth only of what would be necessary, if silver were made use of for the same purpose.
>
> (Ricardo 1821: 352)

> The quantity wanted [for money] would depend partly on the cost of producing gold, and partly on the rapidity of circulation. The rapidity of circulation being given, it would depend on the cost of production. It is obvious that twice as much money would be required to effect every exchange, if a day's labour could obtain from [mining] 34 grains of gold, as would be necessary if a day's labour could obtain only 17. And the cost of production being given, the quantity of money would depend on the rapidity of its circulation.
>
> (Senior 1840: 21)

Senior (1840) took the analysis a step further than Ricardo (1821) in examining how, on the one side, changes in the permanent demand for gold (or silver) and, on the other side, changes in the productivity of mines which could be profitably utilised, affected its cost of production and, thereby, the value of money. What, in particular, Senior (1840: 76–7) showed is that the stability of the value of gold (or silver) and, thereby, given other things, the price level, depended largely on a gradual change in the productivity of mines. This was consistent with the position of Ricardo (1821: 14, 86–7), who believed that the relative stability in the value of the precious metals stemmed from their scarcity in the sense that new mining deposits were difficult to find. These two writers clearly believed that variability in their value arose from factors which substantially altered productivity in the gold (or silver) mining industry: mainly consisting of the discovery of new and more fertile deposits, the introduction of improved methods of production and the resort to less fertile mines with the exhaustion of deposits at the best ones.

The opening quotation of this section by Tooke indicates he largely adopted the position of Senior (1840) that the value of the gold standard depended on its conditions of production in conjunction with its demand as a scarce commodity. It also indicates that Tooke adopted Senior's conception that through its influence on the demand for gold as money, the cost of production of gold exerted a systematic effect on the determination of the quantity of gold (coin) in monetary circulation. Further evidence of Tooke's adoption of this position is evident in the discussion in Chapter II of the *Inquiry* (1844) on the causal relationship between the general prices of commodities and the quantity of metallic money in circulation. Tooke begins this discussion by supposing that: 'the value of gold in the commercial world is assumed to be constant, i.e. that the cost of production and the general demand are unvaried' (1844: 9).

This indicates Tooke well understood the conditions set out by Senior (1840) for the stability of the value of the precious metals. Tooke (1844: 10–11) also embraced Senior's argument that the use-value of the precious metals primarily stemmed from their non-monetary use as material in the production of luxury commodities out of which their use as money stemmed. He contended that a large proportion of the world's stock of gold was in fact used for non-monetary purposes:

> As this country is not only a large consumer of the precious metals for purposes other than money, but is also an entrepôt for receiving from the mines, and distributing the greater portion of the quantity applicable to the consumption of other countries, the bullion trade, totally independently of supplying currency, must of necessity be very considerable.
>
> (Tooke 1844: 12–13)

Besides the demand for such non-monetary purposes, Tooke contended that a 'very considerable amount of the precious metals' (1844: 13–14) was held as bullion reserves by central banks for the purpose of meeting international debt payments. The function of the precious metals as a means of settling international payments was seen to spring from their 'universal demand' as commodities, which Tooke linked to their being 'less liable to fluctuations in market value than any other[s]' (1844: 13).

Hence, at least by the time of his banking school phase, Tooke had adopted the theoretical position of Senior as well as Ricardo on the determination of the normal value of gold (or silver). Indeed, Senior's analysis is likely to have helped Tooke clarify his banking school monetary thought. However, later writings on the subject are not altogether consistent with this analysis. This is particularly so in Part VII of *History* (1857, VI) devoted to a study of the effect of the mid-nineteenth-century gold discoveries in California and the East Australian colonies on prices over the period, 1848–1856. Though this Part of the book was written by Newmarch, it must be assumed Tooke endorsed its arguments. As considered in more detail in Section 5.6, Tooke rejected the possibility that the employment of the newly discovered gold mines contributed to higher money prices on the grounds that they were no more productive than existing ones:

> It may be said that whatever may be the facts as concerns a fall in the Value of Gold, by reason of augmented *quantity*; there can at least be no question as to a fall in the value of Gold by means of a diminished *cost* of production of that metal; meaning by diminished Cost of Production, that since 1850, a larger amount of Gold than previously has been procured by the expenditure of the *same* amount of Labour and Capital.
>
> (1857, VI: 225)

This amounted to arguing that the gold discoveries led to an increased production of gold without any accompanying rise in the productivity at the marginal mine.

The difficulty with Tooke and Newmarch's argument arises from how there can be an increased production of gold in absence of a systematic reduction in its cost of production which would induce an increase in its normal demand. The only plausible basis for consistency in this argument with the classical theory of the determination of the normal value of gold (or silver) outlined above, is that Tooke believed the demand for gold to be unresponsive to changes in its value so that, despite there being no reduction in its cost of production, nearly all available mines (both existing and new ones) are profitably brought into production. That Tooke adopted this assumption may well be inferred from his view that '[G]old is an object in such universal demand, or in other words so universally marketable' that it 'may always command a market' (Tooke 1844: 10; also 1857, VI: 216–18).[27] It means that providing there is no change in the productivity of the marginal (no-rent) mine, new gold discoveries or the exhaustion of existing mines will have no lasting effect on the value of the gold standard, and thereby, on the general level of money prices. Any associated change in the productive capacity of the gold industry, either its augmentation with the discovery of new mining deposits or its contraction with the exhaustion of existing deposits, will result in a corresponding adjustment in the demand for its production. This was perhaps the implicit basis upon which Tooke and Newmarch (1857, VI: 225–6) dismissed the possibility that the discovery and exploitation of the Californian and the East Australian gold fields lowered the cost of production of gold. Indeed, this seems to be the position adopted by Tooke for precluding from his historical analysis factors which *directly* affected the conditions of production and the value of the precious metals from exerting a significant influence on the long-run level of money prices.

3.6 On free trade

In Tooke's picture, an institutional factor that persistently influenced prices was trade protection. When asked by the Parliamentary Committee on the Depressed State of Agriculture in 1821 of the effects of restrictions on trade Tooke answered as follows:

> the ultimate effect is, that all the classes of the community have either worse or dearer commodities; inferior in quality, or less in quantity, than they would under a general freedom of foreign as well as of internal trade.
>
> (1821a: 234)

Hence, in a nutshell, Tooke was a fervent advocate of free trade because prices would tend to be lower, the quality of commodities produced better and the quantity of them consumed greater. In common with most of his classical contemporaries, Tooke's advocacy for free trade was heavily based on principles articulated in Adam Smith's *Wealth of Nations*.[28] He employed two main arguments in support of free trade which are deeply rooted in the post-Smith classical tradition.

First, Tooke argued that free trade ensures the most productive allocation of capital and labour toward the greater development of an economic system. Thus, in the merchant's petition of 1820, Tooke wrote:

> That the prevailing prejudices in favour of the Protective or Restrictive System, may be traced to the erroneous supposition that every importation of foreign commodities occasions a diminution or discouragement of our own productions to the same extent: whereas it may be clearly shown, that although the particular description of production which could stand against unrestrained foreign competition would be discouraged, yet as no Importation could be continued for any length of time without Exportation, direct or indirect, there would be encouragement, for the purpose of that exportation, of some other production to which our situation might be better suited: thus affording at least an equal, and probably a greater, and certainly a more beneficial, employment to our own Capital and Labour.
>
> (1857, VI: 333)

In this regard free trade was conceived generally by classical economists to foster a technically efficient allocation of capital and labour that would enlarge economic surplus which, in the dynamic process of capital accumulation, would promote stronger growth. Second, Tooke argued that free trade would enlarge the market for exports. This is consistent with Adam Smith's (1776 [1976]: 31–6) well-known conception that the extension of a nation's market will tend to promote technical advancement of its industry. These arguments were largely articulated by Tooke in connection with his opposition to the Corn Laws which, from 1815 until their repeal in 1846, were the most controversial legislative restrictions on trade in Britain.

Tooke's opposition to the English Corn Laws was first expressed publicly in evidence given to the afore-mentioned Commons Select Committee on the Depressed State of Agriculture in 1821. Questioned on the 'effect on the interests of the public at large' of the 1815 Corn Law, Tooke answered:

> I conceive, that without being beneficial to the farmer or the landlord, it is highly injurious to all other branches of the community, by disturbing the proper application of capital and industry; by keeping a considerable part of our manufactures on hand which would be exported, if the foreign consumer had the means of paying for them in his corn. There appears to be at this moment, a quantity of corn on one side of an impenetrable barrier, and a quantity of manufactures on the other, which would naturally be interchanged, if it were not for the artificial hindrance occasioned by the present system.
>
> (1821a: 230)

This passage reflects Tooke's main argument against the Corn Laws and, indeed, any trade restrictions, that they distort the allocation of capital, labour and land from otherwise producing commodities of superior quality and at the lowest technically possible prices consistent with the structure of demand. In particular, Tooke conceived that the resulting misallocation of capital would reduce the national wealth that would have been otherwise created. Thus, in the scenario of a 'repeal of the corn law, and unrestricted importation of corn' which permanently lowered the price of corn, Tooke gave the following opinion:

> Would not the country be enriched by the amount of commodities, which the capital withdrawn from the land, would be made to produce? – Tooke: The capital so saved would clearly be the means of creating so much additional wealth.
>
> (1821a: 233)

At least implicitly, Tooke's free trade argument relies on a Say's Law notion in which demand is not a constraint to the alternative employment of capital increasing production of Britain's manufacturing exports. In this connection he believed the removal of Britain's trade restrictions would tend to induce a higher demand for its manufacturing largely through the higher export income earned by those foreign countries gaining greater access to Britain's freer market. Indeed, this was a major argument employed by Tooke in advocating the removal of the Corn Laws. He also believed that domestic demand for manufacturing products would, in the long run, not be reduced by the decline in those industries in Britain, mainly agricultural-based industries, which became uncompetitive with the removal of trade protection. Thus, Tooke (1821a: 235–6, 293–4) rejected the proposition propagated by Malthus that, by maintaining their income, the Corn Laws enabled 'the agricultural classes in England to consume larger quantities of manufactures' and 'thereby stimulate their production'.[29]

Tooke reasoned that the income enjoyed by the 'landed interest' came at the expense of the income of 'other classes' who also formed an important part of the demand of the 'home market' for manufactures. Removal of the Corn Laws would therefore simply redistribute income from the landed interest to other classes in society without reducing purchasing power in aggregate. Indeed, like most classical economists, Tooke conceived that freer trade would in the long run lead to a higher level of global income and employment for trading nations corresponding, in Britain's case, with a permanently higher demand for domestically produced as well as for foreign products.

Tooke clearly believed that protection of agriculture had an adverse effect on Britain's manufacturing industry. There were two aspects to his position. In the first place, the Corn Laws caused capital and labour to be re-allocated from manufacturing (and other non-protected agricultural) 'trades' towards the relatively more profitable cultivation of corn. This re-allocation process is outlined by Tooke (1821a: 234) in response to a hypothetical example posed by the 1821 Agricultural Committee:

> In consequence of the first exception mentioned, of a freedom of trade in favour of the clothier, would he have a higher permanent rate of profit than any other capitalist? – Tooke: He would not have a higher rate of permanent profits, supposing the trade left open to competition within the country; supposing the protection to extend only against foreign competition.
>
> If he [the clothier] got higher profits than were got in other trades, would not an increased quantity of capital be attracted to his trade, and his profits thereby reduced to the general level? – Tooke: Yes.
>
> The Committee then understand you to say, that the clothier is a sufferer in common with all other consumers of cloth by a rise in its price, in consequence of the protection to his trade, without receiving any permanent compensation in increased profits? – Tooke: His profits would be reduced to the common level, as soon as a full competition from capital withdrawn from other occupations could take place.

Trade protection would therefore accommodate a temporary increase in the profit rate of the favoured industry before internal competition operated in the long run to drive it down to the general rate of profit. The important aspect of this adjustment is the re-allocation of capital. In relation to agricultural protection provided by the Corn Laws, Tooke conceived that the re-allocation process would involve capital being withdrawn from manufacturing to be employed in the extension of cultivation to 'inferior land' (1821a: 233–4). The resulting expansion in corn production would therefore come at the expense of otherwise potential expansion in the manufacturing industry denied capital and labour (and land). Hence, Tooke was in general agreement with Ricardo that trade protection of agriculture would be disadvantageous to the manufacturing industry, of which Britain had a considerable competitive advantage in the international market.

Second, Tooke agreed with Ricardo's argument that by raising the price of the 'necessaries of life' the Corn Law *tended* to increase the 'nominal price of labour' and, thereby, to raise the costs of production of manufacturers. This is expressed by Tooke in the following evidence to the 1821 Committee on Agricultural Distress:

> Is not the price of labour, in your opinion, in this country, raised by the higher price of commodities, besides corn, which are protected by duties, and are necessary to the labourer? – Tooke: Our system of duties, partly from taxation and partly from our protective regulations, does make the money price of the necessaries of life higher, and consequently does so far effect the nominal price of labour.
>
> (1821a: 288)

> I cannot conceive how the manufacturers can be gainers by an increased price, given only in consequence of the high price of corn; the manufacturer would have to pay at least as much for himself and for his labourers in the advanced price of corn, as the increased price that he obtained for his manufactures.
>
> (1821a: 293)[30]

However, Tooke did not share Ricardo's view that the money wage would fully adjust to an increase in the price of necessaries such as to sustain the real wage at its pre-existing natural level. Instead, as shown in Section 3.3, Tooke believed that, in response to a permanent rise in the price of wage goods, the (gold) money wage would adjust with a long lag so that the living standard of workers declined though associated with some increase in the labour cost of production to manufacturers. While Tooke clearly believed the Corn Laws acted to raise labour costs in general, unlike Ricardo, he did not believe this necessarily meant a significant diminution in the profit rate of Britain's manufacturing industry. Moreover, it is evident that, because of the technical superiority of Britain's manufacturing industry relative to the rest of the world, Tooke (1821a: 290) did not believe its exports were much affected by the higher input costs resulting from the Corn Laws and other trade protection.

According to Tooke, the Corn Laws, like other trade protection, inhibited Britain's manufacturing exports by denying an income to foreign consumers that would otherwise facilitate their demand. In evidence given before the Select Committee on Extending and Securing the Foreign Trade of the Country (Relative to Timber) in 1820, Tooke (1820: 27–31) argued that duties on Russian imports, including corn, inhibited British trade with the country. He maintained that a reduction in this protection would, through an increase in Russian imports, finance an increased Russian demand for British manufactures: 'I think any increase of demand for Russian produce would have a tendency to increase the exportation of British manufactures' (1820: 31). Upon this reasoning Tooke (1821a: 290) argued that a free trade in corn would expand Britain's manufacturing exports to those countries from which foreign corn was supplied. Indeed, he advocated a unilateral policy of trade liberalisation because it would extend Britain's international trade with the benefit of an expansion in manufacturing exports:

> Would it be good policy in England, to establish a free trade, although all other countries should support the restrictive system? – Tooke: Undoubtedly; if that were the only thing in contemplation.
>
> (1821a: 290)

Perhaps naively, Tooke believed that a policy of trade liberalisation by Britain would induce its trading partners to adopt a more liberal policy that would open up foreign markets for its manufacturing exports.

Although Tooke was a strong supporter of free trade, his position was qualified by the imperative to impose taxes and duties on commodities for the purpose of raising public revenue and to service Britain's national debt which had grown enormously during the French Wars. Tooke (1821a: 290) therefore advocated free trade 'as far as consistent with preserving an existing revenue' of the state. With regard to the Corn Laws, the ostensible policy objective was to protect the 'landed interest' and British agriculture and not to raise public revenue.[31] However, based on principles set out by Adam Smith (1776 [1976]: 465–7), Tooke (1821a: 238) accepted that the imposition of duties with the object of protecting domestic industries was appropriate to the extent of counteracting the discriminatory effect of taxes (and duties) imposed for the purpose of raising public revenue (see Section 5.3). Tooke's position was that trade protection should only be applied to ensure that foreign commodities were subject to the 'peculiar duties' imposed on domestically produced commodities (1821a: 293). Therefore, the only kind of protection for agriculture that Tooke considered warranted was that which would compensate it for a higher taxation burden relative to that imposed on other branches of production: 'To the extent of the amount of taxation which falls *exclusively* on the production of corn, a countervailing duty on importation would be justifiable' (Tooke 1829b: 88).

Tooke believed that largely because of the poor rates on land, agriculture did carry a higher tax burden than manufacturing, thereby qualifying it for some trade protection until the late-1830s when he evidently believed that reform to the Poor Laws had eliminated this tax discrimination.[32] To compensate for the estimated tax burden falling exclusively on agriculture, Tooke advocated in 1829 a (fixed) duty on corn of no more than 10s. per Imperial quarter (equivalent to 12.7 kilograms) when the price was usually between 50s. to 70s.[33] However, evidently believing that reform to the Poor Laws in 1834 had nearly eliminated all this tax discrimination, Tooke proposed in 1840 an impractical duty of 1s. per quarter that 'would amply answer the justice of the case' (1840a, III: 48). He also advocated the removal of any (contingent) prohibition on imported corn that characterised the Corn Laws of 1815 and 1822 but not those of 1828 and 1842 (for an explanation of these Corn Laws, see Section 4.4; Chapter 4, n.14). Hence, while Tooke supported a fixed duty on corn until 1840, he advocated a trade in corn free of import prohibitions. From 1840 onwards it is evident Tooke (1840a, III: 49–53) supported the repeal of the Corn Laws altogether.

Tooke's position on free trade provides an insight into the analytical considerations of the classical economists on trade policy issues. Following in the footsteps of Adam Smith, they generally favoured free trade not only because they considered it led to a more technically superior allocation of existing inputs, including land, that would increase global output of the trading nations, but that it would over time promote technological advancement itself, chiefly in manufacturing, through the 'division of labour' afforded by an extension of the market.[34] As was discussed above (pp. 52–3), this argument relied heavily on a Say's Law conception in which demand is not a constraint to an expansion in the global output of trading nations; indeed, that chiefly through the income effects arising from an expansion in trade as well as an eventual lowering in the prices of freely traded products, global demand would expand.

It should be emphasised that these grounds for favouring free trade are different from those proposed today within marginalist theory. In marginalist theory free trade is conceived to produce the most efficient global allocation of *given* quantities of available inputs consistent with their full employment in equilibrium. In this theory demand constraints are not an issue because, through the adjustment in the relative price of internationally traded products and in the price of inputs employed, the demand of the trading countries would alter to facilitate the change in the structure of their output caused by the adoption of free trade measures consistent with a full-employment position. However, no such price mechanisms to adjust the demand for products to their outputs and the demand for inputs to their supply logically exist in classical economics.[35] Hence, the classical economists never conceived that a technically productive allocation of inputs was associated with their full employment. On the contrary, consistent with Say's Law, they conceived equilibrium output was associated with unemployed labour observable as a normal phenomenon (see also Section 5.4). Moreover, since classical economists after Adam Smith conceived that the equilibrium output of industries was determined by their effectual demands, their argument in favour of free trade was problematic to the extent that the changes in the structure of the international demand for tradable products may not necessarily entail an increase in global demand. Certainly Tooke was well aware of the possibility of such a demand constraint but rejected it largely on the ground that free trade would bring about a mutual expansion in the income of the trading countries.[36] Hence, from this classical standpoint, Tooke maintained that trade restrictions caused an inefficient allocation of capital and labour which resulted in less global output, higher prices and the production of lower-quality products. With respect to the specific effect of the Corn Laws, Tooke believed they would tend to allocate capital and land from the manufacturing industry to agriculture, to be much employed in bringing inferior quality land into cultivation. Hence, any resulting expansion in Britain's agriculture would come at the expense of its manufacturing industry, in which it had a clear competitive advantage. An important part of

Tooke's argument was that, by denying income to foreign producers of corn, the Corn Laws retarded the foreign demand for Britain's manufacturing exports, so limiting the growth of its market. In this way it acted to inhibit Britain's economic development.

Nevertheless, consistent with principles laid down by Adam Smith, Tooke conceded that a countervailing duty on corn was appropriate to compensate agriculture for the imposition of discriminatory taxes in the form of poor rates. Until 1840, after the reform of the Poor Laws, he advocated a fixed duty on freely traded corn. However, it is curious that Tooke made this concession without any reference to his own argument that, during periods of scarcity, which followed unproductive harvests, the Poor Laws tended to heighten the rise in corn prices and, thereby, to increase the income going to the 'landed interest'. As previously explained in Section 3.4, a central proposition of Tooke's analysis of the effect of shortages on the market price of corn was that its demand in England was unresponsive to higher prices because social welfare under the Poor Laws ensured a greater minimal purchasing power for subsistence food. Hence, the agricultural sector was already being compensated to some extent for the extra tax burden of poor rates through the systematic effect of the Poor Laws in raising the average price of corn. Surely this argument of Tooke's weakened the claim for a countervailing duty, but it does not seem to have occurred to him.

4 On Tooke's explanation of agricultural price movements

A substantial part of Tooke's historical study of prices is devoted to agricultural commodities, principally on explaining the price of corn. With wheat being the dominant grain produced in England and most of Northern Europe, corn represented wheat in Tooke's analysis. The price of corn (or wheat) is considered by Tooke to be central to ascertaining the movement in the general price level relevant to the cost of living in England. This is based on the reasoning that the price of corn was, at least from the early eighteenth century, the most essential of foodstuff provisions entering into 'necessary' consumption of the English population. Moreover, the price of corn is seen by Tooke to be an index of the price of agricultural commodities in general which, besides entering into food consumption, also constituted a significant part of the raw materials that entered into manufacturing production. Being input costs to manufacture, the price of raw materials was therefore important in explaining the movement in a general price level that encompassed manufacturing products. This reasoning is implicit in the following part of an answer Tooke gave in evidence to the Agricultural Committee of 1821:

> if the fall of the raw materials be accounted for, the same reasoning will apply to the manufactures into the composition of which such raw materials enter. During a long continued fall in the price of raw materials, the manufactured articles must, by the law of competition, follow the same course, or nearly so ...
>
> (1821a: 352)

In the case of corn, it was a major raw material that entered both as a material input and, through labour cost, directly and indirectly into the cost of production of all manufacturing as well as agricultural commodities in general. It was shown in Section 3.6 that Tooke believed the price of corn could, by affecting living costs, exert a long-run influence on the money wage and, thereby, labour costs (see quoted passage, p. 54). But its predominant influence on general prices was seen by Tooke to occur through its effect on the cost of material inputs to the production of food, predominantly of bread. Thus, for Tooke, as an index of agricultural prices, the price of corn was important because it

greatly impacted on living standards. Indeed, the price of corn was traditionally seen by classical economists to be the most reliable indicator of the cost of
living with a crucial bearing on the real wage of workers. For this reason classical economists often measured wages in terms of corn in their theoretical
constructs. The best example of this is provided by Ricardo's 'corn model'
presented in 'Essay on the Influence of a Low Price of Corn on the Profits of
Stock' (1815). In this model corn is the only basic commodity which, as the
sole constituent of wages, enters indirectly into the production of other (non-
basic) commodities according to their labour requirements.[1] While obviously
Tooke understood that wages composed of a variety of commodities, including
manufactured ones, he believed that changes in the price of corn was the most
important in explaining variations in the cost of 'provisions' of English
workers and, thereby, their real wage.

This chapter is concerned with examining Tooke's explanation of the movement in the price of agricultural commodities, centring on the price of corn.
Section 4.1 examines the important role attributed by Tooke to long-run 'seasonal conditions' in explaining the secular movement in the price of corn and the
prices of other agricultural commodities. Following it, Section 4.2 examines in
some detail Tooke's approach to explaining short-run fluctuations in the price of
corn and other agricultural commodities. The conceptional basis underlying
Tooke's explanation of agricultural prices is considered in Section 4.3, providing
some insights into the method of analysis he generally employed in his empirical
study of prices. Section 4.4 then considers Tooke's argument on the effect of the
English Corn Laws on the price of corn from 1815 until their repeal in 1846. It
also considers Tooke's position on the effect of the Corn Laws on the distribution of income between wages, profit and rent.

4.1 'Seasonal conditions' and secular price movements

In Tooke's empirical analysis, the main factor that systematically influenced the
price of agricultural commodities, in particular corn, was 'seasonal conditions':
that is, climatic conditions that affected agricultural productivity. Tooke referred
to this factor as a 'natural' factor. While it is evident seasonal conditions must
have played an important role in explaining price movements in pre-1850
England, when it was at a relatively early though rapidly developing stage of
industrialisation, Tooke believed it was a considerably underrated explanatory
factor. This is made clear in the opening paragraph to Part I, 'On the Effect of
the Seasons', in volume I of *History of Prices*:

> Nothing has struck me as being more strange in all discussions and rea-
> sonings upon the subject of the high and low prices of the period under
> consideration, than the little importance which has been attached to the
> effects which a difference in the character of the seasons is calculated to
> occasion.

(1838, I: 7)

Tooke argued that seasonal conditions were important not only for explaining short-run price fluctuations but were also important for explaining long-run price trends in the price of agricultural commodities.

Tooke first advanced this viewpoint as a witness before the 1821 Parliamentary Committee on the Depressed State of Agriculture ostensibly to warn it against instituting higher trade protection for agriculture in response to what was likely to be only a temporary depression in agricultural prices. In his evidence before the committee, Tooke 'lay[ed] considerable stress upon the prevalence of favourable or unfavourable seasons for a longer continuance than has been usually taken into consideration' (1821a: 355), appealing to Adam Smith and Edmund Burke for support for this approach to explaining agricultural prices. The following are key passages from quotations of these two authorities read by Tooke to the committee:

> The seasons, for these ten or twelve years past, have been unfavourable through the greater part of Europe, and the disorders of Poland have very much increased the scarcity in all those countries which in dear years used to be supplied from that market; so long a course of bad seasons, though not a very common event, is by no means a singular one; and whoever has inquired much into the history of the prices of corn in former times, will be at no loss to recollect several other examples of the same kind.
> (1821a: 355; as quoted from Smith 1776 [1976]: 217)

> years of scarcity or plenty do not come alternately or at short intervals, but in pretty long cycles and irregularly; and consequently that we cannot assure ourselves, if we take a wrong measure from the necessities of one season, but that the next and probably more, will drive us to the continuance of it.
> (1821a: 355; as quoted from Burke 1795 [1887]: 156])[2]

In order to demonstrate the correctness of this 'long' approach to explaining corn prices by reference to climatic conditions, Tooke presented evidence in *High and Low Prices* (1823, iii; also 1824, iii) and, then, in *History* (1838, I: 21–85), showing the prevalence of 'favourable or unfavourable' seasons over long periods from the early seventieth century until 1792. Tooke (1838, I: 21–85) ascertained four such long periods. The first was the twenty-three-year period 1692–1715, characterised by a preponderance of unproductive seasons with 'deficient' harvests (in at least eleven of the years) and, thereby, a relatively high range of corn prices. The second was the 'long interval' of 1716–1765, in which a preponderance of abundant seasons (with only five of 'marked deficiency') induced low historical 'prices of provisions' in England. The third was the ten-year period 1766–1775, consisting of a 'recurrence of seasons of scarcity in this country' and 'on the continent of Europe' resulting in comparatively high and rising corn prices. The fourth was the sixteen-year period 1776–1792, which, though characterised by a preponderance of 'irregular' and 'scanty' seasons, nevertheless saw a lower range of prices due to improved methods of farming.

Other historical comparisons between different long periods are also made by Tooke to show the important role of seasons in determining price trends.[3] In particular, Tooke compared the preponderance of abundant seasons in the first sixty-five years of the eighteenth century with the relative deficiency of seasons in the last thirty-five years 'with the effect of raising the average price [of corn] of the entire century to a level with the average price of the whole of the 17th century' (1838, I: 82).

It is significant that Tooke's historical survey covered similar ground to that which Adam Smith covered in his famous 'Digression concerning the Variations in the Value of Silver during the course of the Four last Centuries', in the *Wealth of Nations* (1776 [1976]: 195–275). However, Tooke challenged Adam Smith on two points. First, he criticised Smith for claiming that the export bounty (instituted in 1688) prevented the price of corn falling to otherwise lower levels during the 'golden era' of English agriculture, 1716–1765 (and, more specifically, 1741–1750). Tooke (1838, I: 45–6n., 52–3) contended that with consistently productive seasonal conditions, the export bounty, by preventing prices in the short run from collapsing during periods of excess domestic production, encouraged a greater extension of cultivation than would have otherwise occurred, which had the effect of maintaining low prices over the long run. Second, Tooke criticised Smith for underrating the systematic influence of seasonal conditions on the movement of corn prices. In particular, Tooke (1838, I: 54–6) disputed Smith's view that, in the first half of the eighteenth century, the decline in the price of corn was attributable mainly to an increase in the value of silver and that the concurrent rise in money wages was the result of an 'increased demand for labour'. Instead, Tooke contended that the 'marked fall in the price of provisions' was due mainly to a long succession of favourable seasons which, on the supposition that the 'money price of common day labour is a better criterion than corn, of the value of the precious metals' (1838, I: 56), was so powerful as to offset the mild inflationary effect of a depreciation in silver.[4]

In challenging an important authority like Adam Smith on these questions, Tooke's short historical survey of the seventeenth and eighteenth centuries was concerned with showing that the primary influence on agricultural price trends over periods 'extending as far as 50 and 60 years' was seasonal conditions affecting productivity in agriculture; while showing that other major factors identified in the literature, namely variations in the value of silver (money), wars (i.e. the English civil war of the 1640s and the American War of Independence of the 1770s) and export bounties on corn were of secondary importance. According to Tooke, his survey showed

> that there is nothing therefore at variance with the experience derived from former periods of our history, in the assignment of a greater proportion of unfavourable seasons in the interval between 1792 and 1819, than in an equal interval anterior or subsequent to that period.
>
> (1838, I: 84–5)

This 'long' approach is applied by Tooke to explain the secular movement in corn (or agricultural) prices in the period 1792–1856.

In explaining the trend movement in corn prices in the years 1792–1856, Tooke identified three main phases in which there were alternations in long-run seasonal conditions in England. These phases are graphically represented in Figure A1.1 (p. 232). The first phase is from 1792 to 1817 when Tooke ascertained that '[T]he frequent recurrence of seasons of an unfavourable character, there having in that interval been no fewer than eleven seasons in which the general produce of corn, but more especially of wheat, was deficient' (1838, II: 346–7).[5] Of those deficient seasons, 1799, 1804, 1809 and 1816 were especially unproductive, coinciding with unproductive seasons over much of continental Europe. It was the long-run deterioration in climatic conditions inducing a decline in agricultural productivity in England (and Ireland) which Tooke attributed to be the *main*, though not sole, cause of the upward trend in the price of corn in this phase. The second phase was from 1818 to 1837 when Tooke ascertained a downward trend in the price of corn which he attributed to:

> A succession of more favourable seasons, there having been in the last twenty years, namely, from 1818 to the present time, only five seasons in which the produce of wheat was decidedly deficient; and in none of them was the inclemency of the season, or the scarcity resulting there from, at all comparable to some of those which occurred during the war; nor was there any one of them that extended over Europe. This prevalence of favourable seasons, and the total exemption from such desolating seasons as 1816, and some previous ones, have developed the effects of an extended and improved cultivation in this country, and in many other parts of the commercial world.
>
> (1838, II: 348)[6]

The last phase dated from 1838 to 1856 when Tooke ascertained a long-run deterioration in climatic conditions and productivity associated with a greater irregularity in seasons. Tooke (1840a, III: 3–13; 1848a, IV: 3–37; 1857, V: 55–6) finds thirteen of the nineteen seasons were deficient and only three very abundant.[7] While there was a strong upward trend in the price of corn until 1846, thereafter it levelled out largely because of the

> unusually large Importations from abroad in aid of the produce of the crops in this country; those Importations being the direct and specific result of the Repeal of our Corn Laws in 1846: and apart from the effects of that Repeal, it is certain that the series of deficient seasons, from 1847 to 1852, would have subjected this country to great privations and great peril.
>
> (1857, V: 223)

4.2 Short-run price fluctuations

In agriculture, mainly cultivation, seasonal conditions affecting productivity occur in an annual cycle according to their impact on the annual process of production which, in England and Northern Europe in general, basically consisted of seed sowing in autumn and winter then, with the assistance of fertiliser, the growth stage to maturity and then, finally, in late summer, harvesting. It follows that the 'character' of annual seasons affecting the size of the agricultural harvest is shaped by reference to its influence on these various stages of the annual production process. This is reflected in Tooke's empirical analysis of short-run fluctuations in the market price of agricultural commodities, most specifically of corn, in England over the period 1792 to 1856 inclusive, in which he assiduously ascertains the character of seasons by reference to their effect on the annual production process in determining the yearly output of agriculture (corn) and its quality. It is well illustrated in the following passage:

> a rise of [corn] prices was inevitable, and they advanced accordingly, with the aid of dry and very severely cold weather in the progress of the spring, to average of 50s. 4d. for the imperial quarter of wheat, in May, and to 51s. 1d. in the first week of June. But seasonable rains came on in the early part of June, and the weather from that time till the harvest was favourable to the growing crops; and as the harvest approached, it became manifest that they had not sustained any essential injury. The markets therefore declined; and as the harvest-time in the home counties was favourable, so that the wheats were mostly secured by the third week in August, in fair condition, and reportedly favourably of as the yield, prices gave way, and ranged at about 47s. to 48s. for some weeks. But the further fall, which seemed otherwise inevitable, was arrested by the unfavourable accounts of the weather, and the state of the crops, in the northern division of the island.
>
> (Tooke 1838, II: 258)

In accord with his general approach to explaining market prices discussed in Section 3.4, Tooke ascertained that climatic conditions was the primary exogenous factor, the natural factor, which determined the supply of corn in relation to its demand and, thereby, its market price. Its central role in Tooke's explanation of the fluctuation in corn prices is best considered in terms of his general method of analysing the interaction between supply and demand in the corn market which can be distilled from his large empirical study.

There are four elements, mainly on the supply-side, which are systematically considered in Tooke's analysis of the corn market. The following will examine the manner by which Tooke explained the short-run fluctuation in the price of corn by reference to each of these elements.

The first and most important element in Tooke's (1848a, IV: 33; 1857, V: 16, 25, 33, 41) analysis was the effect of the 'vicissitudes of the seasons' on the supply of corn, by altering the productiveness of land cultivated, as measured by 'yield per acre'. The impact of climatic conditions on the supply of corn brought to market was considered by Tooke to primarily depend on two factors: on the quality of the harvest and, for a given technique, on the existing amount of land under cultivation. With regard to the first factor, in ascertaining the availability of corn 'fit' for the market, Tooke systematically accounted for the quality (or 'condition') of each yearly harvest. Tooke (1838, II: 85, 197–8; 1848a, IV: 8–9, 15, 27) held that in a direct way the quality of corn brought to market affected its price; with, for example, a harvest of an 'inferior' quality obtaining a lower price than one secured in 'fine' condition, *ceteris paribus*. Other aspects of corn (i.e. wheat) quality are discussed below (pp. 66–7).

The second factor, land under cultivation, is crucial to determining the output of corn for any season. Much of Tooke's analysis is therefore concerned with ascertaining the extension (or reduction) of land brought under cultivation and, to a lesser extent, changes in the intensity of cultivation. For this purpose Tooke relied mainly on qualitative information in the form of various agriculturalist reports and evidence given before parliamentary committees, as well as on available statistics on the annual number of enclosure bills (of the latter for the years 1795–1808, see Tooke 1838, I: 257n., 326n.). Tooke identified two particular circumstances affecting the amount of land cultivated. The first was weather conditions during the crucial period of 'sowing' in autumn and winter which could affect how much of the land purposely set aside by farmers for cultivation would actually turn out to be used for crop-growing in a given season. Thus, Tooke contended that due to '[E]xtensive floods in most parts of the country' (1857, V: 31) the 'quantity of land sown' in the 1852–1853 season 'was less by from one-fifth to one-fourth than in the previous years' (1857, V: 31, 33; also see 1848a, IV: 6, 26; 1857, V: 13, 51–2). The second circumstance consisted of the amount of land purposely set aside by farmers for cultivation on the expectation of higher profitability. Accounting for this cause is an important aspect of Tooke's analysis because it links changes in supply with changes in the (relative) price of corn.

The amount of land (as well as capital) applied to cultivation will according to Tooke depend on whether or not the average price of corn prevailing in the market in a 'course of years' have, for a given technique, afforded farmers on marginal lands with the ordinary rate of profit on their investment. For Tooke, what determines whether there is an expansion or contraction in the amount of land under cultivation (and capital applied) is the relation of *this* average market price with the cost of production to farmers 'who are, in point of soil, and climate, and distance from markets, the least favourably situated' (1857, V: 175–7). When this average market price exceeds the cost of production so as to earn farmers a higher than normal rate of return, there will be an expansion in cultivation, and when it is below the cost of production 'for any extended period' so as to be 'unremunerative' to marginal farmers, there will tend to be a contraction in the amount of land cultivated. As a theoretical concept, Tooke's cost of production is essentially a centre of gravity for market prices which, therefore, cannot be empirically determined. This is because it must be based on an average or normal season determined over a 'course of years' upon which farmers would calculate the normal productivity of their land and determine the amount of land they will cultivate (and the degree of intensive farming to be adopted) in order to earn a normal rate of profit (1857, V: 175–7).[8] It was on this basis that, for example, Tooke attributed the 'extension of tillage, and the application of fresh capital to land already in cultivation' (1838, I: 326) to a sustained period of high corn prices over the period 1805–1812 (also see 1838, I: 237; II: 2–3; 1840a, III: 16–17; 1857, V: 38, 41).

It is chiefly through the adjustment of the amount of land under cultivation by farmers that supply tended to adjust to demand in the markets for corn and other 'raw produce'. Tooke recognised that this adjustment process involved changes in the allocation of land (or the substitution of land use by farmers) to the production of different raw produce according to their relative prices and, hence, profitable opportunities.[9] However, in Tooke this adjustment process is seen to operate relatively slowly and, in terms of its 'immediate' effect on supply conditions and thereby on market prices, is subordinate to climatic conditions. Tooke contended that, often, changes in the amount of land undergoing cultivation by farmers in response to a range of market prices in relation to the cost of production of previous seasons can, in the event of a drastic change in climatic conditions, compound any resulting supply and demand imbalance in the immediate market and, thereby, exacerbate the fluctuation in the price of corn. Thus, for example, in reference to evidence of the highly abundant harvest of 1820 in England which 'proved to be decisive of a great impending fall of prices', Tooke (1838, II: 82) estimated

> the produce was *at least* one fourth above an average per acre: and it is highly probable, at the same time, from the great encouragement of the recent high prices, that the number of acres under cultivation must have been considerably extended.

Similarly, in reference to the inferior corn harvest of 1835, Tooke ascertained 'that much less wheat had been sown in the autumn of 1835' with 'the short sowing to be to the extent of from one fifth to one fourth' (1838, II: 257), which followed the 'fall of the prices of corn, from the harvest of 1832 to the close of 1835, [which] was the necessary consequence of a succession of abundant crops' (1838, II: 342). Moreover, Tooke (1840a, III: 4–7) contended that after the deficient harvests of 1835 and 1836 the resulting 'higher range of the price of wheat in 1836 and 1837 had a tendency to restore the ordinary relative proportions of sowing in the autumn of 1837' which partially offset the effect on output of an unproductive season. In this way, Tooke accounted for the dynamic interaction between supply and prices in its role in the fluctuation of the market price of corn. His analysis showed that any instability in the fluctuation of corn prices tended to be reinforced by the supply responses of farmers; in other words, price stability tended to ensure a more orderly adjustment process in the markets for raw produce which, over time, begets continued price stability. In this way

Tooke argued that the predominant determinate of the short-run fluctuation of corn prices was climatic variations.

The second element that Tooke systematically considered was the available grain stocks which could be released onto the market. Most stocks of domestically produced corn were held by suppliers, consisting of dealers (i.e. corn merchants) and (large-sized) farmers. Under the operation of the 1815 and 1822 Corn Laws, there were also stock holdings of imported corn held in bond by the authorities on behalf of merchants. Smaller stocks were held on the demand-side of the market by final users of grain, consisting mainly of millers, bakers, malt beer brewers and distillers involved in the production of provisions and, to a lesser extent, farmers who (in winter) grain-fed their livestock. In Tooke's analysis, stock holdings have a stabilising effect on corn prices (see, in particular, Tooke 1857, V: 173). Thus, for example, Tooke (1838, II: 21) contended that 'after so bad a harvest as that of 1816' the 'surplus of the old stock' accumulated from former seasons had 'prevented prices from rising so much as, upon such a scarcity, they otherwise would have done'. The 'stock on hand' does not depend simply on the accumulation of surplus quantities from earlier seasons, but also on the quality of corn harvested. In particular, if the crop secured was 'damp' or suffering from 'mildew' such that it 'was not generally fit for immediate use', there would tend to be an involuntary increase in stocks with the 'immediate' requirements of the market being supplied by 'old stock', often as an 'admixture' of 'damp' new with old 'dry' wheat (Tooke 1838, II: 14–15, 238; 1848a, IV: 23). This would tend to be associated with a rise in prices (see, for example, Tooke 1848a, IV: 4–5; 1857, V: 43–4). On the other hand, the reverse would tend to occur in the event of a crop of higher quality as dealers attempted to immediately sell off their inferior 'old stock' (Tooke 1838, II: 85). These tendencies are of course contingent on there being no immediate shortfall in the market. Hence, when after a deficient harvest a shortfall emerges in the market, a rundown of stocks will occur with higher than usual prices obtained for inferior quality corn (1838, II: 258–9). The level of stocks also depended greatly on speculative activity by traders in the corn market as based on expectations about future prices. It is mainly in connection with stocks that Tooke accounted for the role of expectations in explaining the short-term (i.e. monthly and/or quarterly) fluctuation in the price of corn (1848a, IV: 4–5; 1857, V: 43–4). When the prevailing expectation in the market was that the price of corn would increase in the future, stock levels tended to rise because it was more profitable for traders to withhold supply from the 'immediate' market in order to sell at a later date. This tended to immediately raise its price. In contrast, the price of corn tended to immediately decline when, instead, market expectations favoured a decline in future prices, causing traders to rundown their stocks by an immediate increase in sales in an attempt to reduce any (potential) losses arising from a devaluation of old stock.

Much of Tooke's analysis was therefore concerned with ascertaining the 'opinion' of the corn market with respect to the future direction of prices. This market opinion is seen by Tooke (1848a, IV: 10–11) to be based on the prospects for supply satisfying (yearly) average consumption requirements. There are two key elements in the formulation of an opinion by the corn market about prospective supply: first, the existing levels (and quality) of stock on hand and, second, the expected output (and quality) of the next domestic crop harvested (in late summer). According to Tooke (1840a, III: 154), speculative activity by dealers and merchants was a normal part of the operation of the corn market. He argued that it primarily centred on the progress of seasonal conditions and, as garnered from the reports of farmers (and inspectors), its anticipated impact on the upcoming harvest. When a shortage of domestic supply was anticipated by traders in the corn market, then, usually leading up to the harvest, speculative activity would turn on the circumstances surrounding foreign supply, in particular, until 1846, on the rules of importation under the operation of the English Corn Laws. Thus, Tooke believed the moving cause of speculative activity in the corn market was actual and anticipated conditions of supply; with monetary conditions having a secondary influence, dampening such activity in times of stringency and facilitating it in 'easy' times (1838, I: 204–5; II: 120–40, 199–201; 1840a, III: 152–3; and on how liquidity conditions influenced holdings of grain stocks by farmers, see 1857, V: 167–74). It was through its effect on stock holdings by dealers and merchants that speculative activity was seen by Tooke to be transmitted to corn prices. In his analysis, the extent to which the opinion of the market about prospective supply, upon which the stock levels of dealers was based, is 'well' or 'ill' founded had an important bearing on the fluctuation of prices. The more this opinion deviated from actuality such that dealers and merchants were faced with a greater adjustment of stocks in order to either eliminate undesired holdings or acquire additional holdings, the greater the magnitude of correction in the corn price. It therefore followed that the more unstable were seasonal conditions, and thereby the conditions of supply to the corn market, the greater was the propensity for stocks levels to be based on ill founded opinion and, ultimately, the greater the instability in the price of corn.

The third element accounted for in Tooke's analysis was changes in the consumption of corn. As was shown in Section 3.4, Tooke argued that, because it was the basic constituent of English food the consumption of corn (and, more generally, provisions) was relatively stable in the short run, changing slowly over the longer run with population, the state of employment in 'manufactures and trade' and with wages. Hence, in Tooke's analysis, generally consumption played a subsidiary role to supply conditions in the determination of the market price of corn (1838, I: 18–20). Nevertheless, on occasions, Tooke found changes in the consumption of corn to be significant in explaining its short-run price fluctuations. In this connection, short-run variations in the consumption of corn were attributed by Tooke to two main causes. The first was 'profitable employment among the labouring classes' which varied with economic activity and was usually accompanied by sympathetic changes in money wages (Tooke 1838, II: 238, 255–6; 1848a, IV: 23). The second and major cause was extensive changes in the (relative) price of corn (i.e. wheat) brought about by alterations in the conditions of supply of provisions in general; with the consumption of corn, on the one hand, 'restricted' by a high relative price, and on the other hand, 'increased' by a low relative price (Tooke 1838, I: 293–4; II: 263; 1840a, III: 4). These variations usually involved substitution between corn and other raw produce destined for consumption as 'human food' and livestock feed. Thus, for example, Tooke (1838, II: 239) maintained that the 'extra consumption of wheat, so notorious in 1834 and 1835', was associated with its substitution for barley and oats in malting and distilling and in livestock feeding. This was the result of the 'disproportionate cheapness of wheat' which 'was in part occasioned by some degree of deficiency of the crops of barley and oat, and beans and peas' (1838, II: 239).[10] But, despite the 'enormous extra consumption', Tooke (1838, II: 239, 257–60) argued that it made little impression on the price of wheat until (excess) supply was reduced by the unproductive season of 1836.

In contrast, the substitution in social consumption associated with the 'potato famine' of the mid-1840s was shown to have a dramatic effect on corn prices. The widespread failure of potato crops from disease in Ireland, parts of England and Scotland and 'a great part of continental Europe' led to a 'large extra demand' for corn on the international market. Tooke (1848a, IV: 24–32) argued that, together with ordinary harvests and declining stocks, this caused the price of corn to rise markedly in the period 1845–1847.[11] On the outlook for corn prices, Tooke contended:

> [I]f the potato disease should continue, although in a mitigated form, it will exercise more or less influence on the prices of corn by the extra consumption thus thrown on wheat and other breadstuffs, and thus counteract, possibly for some time, the tendency to cheapness which may be anticipated from more propitious seasons, combined with the improved and extended cultivation to which recent high prices will have offered an inducement.
>
> (1848a, IV: 38)

However, Tooke believed there was a lower limit to these variations in consumption which, according to the importance of corn as human food, was fixed by the minimum necessary subsistence requirements of the population as determined by social policy in England (see Section 3.4). It is therefore only in situations (as discussed above) in which domestic consumption varies at levels above this minimum that Tooke finds it significant in explaining the fluctuation of corn prices.

The fourth element systematically considered by Tooke was the conditions of foreign supply at those times when the importation of corn into England was necessary to meet demand. Tooke identified three historical factors that greatly influenced the conditions of England's foreign supply over the period 1792–1856. The first was the operation of the English Corn Laws in the period from 1815 until their repeal in 1846, which is dealt with in Section 4.4. The second was 'obstructions' to shipping (or 'navigation') and trade arising out of war: consisting of the French Wars 1793–1801 and 1803–1815, the short-lived American War 1812–1814 and the Crimean War 1854–1856 (Tooke 1838, I:

181–2, 218, 237, 253, 267–8; 1857, V: 44–5). As is elaborated in Section 5.2, Tooke believed corn was among a wide range of imported commodities whose prices were affected by war-induced obstructions to foreign supply.

The third and most ever-present factor was climatic conditions affecting the corn production of foreign countries. In this connection Tooke's analysis focused on seasonal production in Northern Europe, mainly France and Germany, rather than in the major export regions of Russia, Southern Europe and North America. This suggests Tooke believed the net demand for wheat by Britain and other Northern European countries (and competition between them) exerted a predominant influence on the international corn market. Tooke (1838, I: 53, 331) ascertained that, although subject to 'considerable exceptions', there was a 'prevalence of a general similarity of seasons' between the British Isles and (Northern) Continental Europe.[12] Hence, domestic corn prices usually reflected those in the international market. Tooke (1838, I: 182n., 331–9; II: 15–17, 57, 86–93; 1857, V: 34–7) showed, for example, that the unproductive seasons in the British Isles in the years 1795, 1810–1812, 1816–1817, 1853 and the productive seasons in 1818–1821 coincided with those in Continental Europe. On those few occasions when, as in 1808 and 1809, Tooke ascertained that the seasons had 'been more productive on the Continent of Europe, and in France especially, than in this country' (1838, I: 331), relief was afforded to the domestic market and the rise in corn prices somewhat moderated (also 1838, II: 196; 1848a, IV: 31; 1857, V: 55–6). However, Tooke (1857, V: 56–66) maintained that it was not until after the repeal of the Corn Laws in 1846 that the relief afforded by the coincidence of divergent seasons between England and foreign countries could exert a stabilising influence on domestic corn prices. Tooke believed all these factors affecting the conditions of foreign supply were the subject of speculative activity in the corn market when a domestic shortage in stocks was widely anticipated. Thus, Tooke (1848a, IV: 20, 30–32; 1857, V: 34) noticed that, when domestic seasonal conditions appeared unfavourable, speculation by corn dealers and importers turned on 'reports' about the progress of seasonal conditions and harvest yields in European countries.

4.3 Tooke's conceptual framework for explaining agricultural prices

What emerges in Tooke's empirical analysis is a conceptual framework appropriate for explaining agricultural prices which throws further light on the long period method of the classical economists. Three types of conceptual prices of corn can be identified in Tooke's analysis, where corn is representative of agricultural commodities in general.

The first is the long-run secular price associated with technical conditions of production established by the systematic operation of natural, political and other forces. This secular price corresponds with an average technique (as defined by yield per acre) over a long period (or era) as determined by average seasonal conditions for the given quality of (marginal) land utilised and capital applied to

cultivation. It also corresponds with the permanent state of commercial interchange, conditions of transport and navigation as well as trade prohibitions (i.e.
Corn Laws) which determine the average cost of freight, insurance and duty on
imported corn. In addition, it is apparent that the secular price of corn accords
with its average supply, consisting of domestically produced and imported corn,
which satisfies demand in the long run. In Tooke this long run consists of eras,
consisting of an unspecified number of years, characterised by long-lasting
changes in natural and political factors that determine the trend movement in the
price of corn. Hence, as indicated above, the period 1792–1817 is an era characterised by a series of unproductive seasonal conditions that Tooke attributed to
be the main cause of a strong upward trend in the price of corn. This era was
therefore associated with a historically high secular price of corn.

The second price is the cost of production or normal price corresponding with
equilibrium between supply and demand at which a normal rate of profit is
earned in the production of corn. The establishment of a normal price involves
the (tendency of) adjustment of supply to demand through alterations in the
quantity of land under cultivation and the amount of capital employed for *given*
seasonal conditions in response to variations in the rate of return for producing
corn in relation to other branches of production, including other kinds of
farming. It also depends on the normal costs of freight and duty of imported
corn. In this way the normal price is an attractor for market prices and corresponds with Tooke's conception of the cost of production 'as the regulator of the
Minimum price below which the market price cannot fall for any extended
period' (1857, V: 179). Tooke explained this conception in the following way:

> The only mode on which the Cost of Production operates on the prices of
> Corn is, that if in a course of years Prices are unremunerative to those
> growers both at home and abroad, who are, in point of soil, and climate, and
> distance from markets, the least favourably situated, the cultivation will, as
> far as these are concerned, be discontinued. And according to the proportion
> they furnish of the total supply, will be the greater or less consequent influ-
> ence on the ultimate level or average of prices.... It is only in this general
> and very indistinct point of view that the Cost of Production can be said to
> have any influence on the price of Corn; and the same remark is applicable
> to most other descriptions of Raw Produce.
>
> (1857, V: 176–7)

It was because of the overwhelming influence of natural forces (i.e. climatic conditions) that Tooke believed the cost of production has only a 'general' and
'indistinct' influence on the market prices of agricultural commodities through
adjustments in farming practice.

The third price is the market price determined by supply and demand conditions in the market. Its empirical counterpart is actual (or 'immediate') prices
which was the main object of Tooke's study. As shown in Section 4.2, in
Tooke's system variations in the market price of raw produce are seen to be

overwhelmingly due to changes in supply rather than in demand. Short-run variations in supply are, in turn, due predominantly to the vicissitudes of the seasons affecting productivity (or yield) for a *given* quantity of land and capital applied to production. According to Tooke, it is 'from this cause alone [that] there is an inevitable liability by a natural law to an occasional great rise or great fall, or, in other words, to a great fluctuation in price' which is confined not only to 'the character of the seasons in this country, but the abundance or deficiency of the harvests abroad, that operates on prices here' (1857, V: 84). Aside from climatic conditions, supply from foreign sources was seen by Tooke to 'operate powerfully on the Markets for Corn', mainly consisting of 'the discovery and opening of new, or the exhaustion or interruption of former, sources of foreign supply', the latter arising, in particular, from 'the occurrence of a war (like that with Russia) with a heretofore largely exporting country' (1857, V: 84). In addition, Tooke ascertained 'that restrictions on the Importation of Corn were a fertile source of fluctuation' as well as 'changes in the legislation of Foreign States in regard to the admission of external supplies' (1857, V: 84). But, while in Tooke 'variations of *consumption* are on a much smaller scale than those of supply' nevertheless, 'the *demand* on the Markets may occasionally have a considerable temporary influence on prices' (1857, V: 89).[13] Tooke also identified numerous other specific causes for 'minor' fluctuations in the market price of corn (and other 'raw produce'):

> the varying wants and necessities of buyers and sellers; speculations also on the weather as affecting the prospects of the harvests; the difference in quality and condition of the samples brought to market in one week compared with another: casual obstructions to internal communication by frost and snow at one time, and by floods at another: and casual interruptions of demand by mills standing still for lack of wind or water. Foreign supplies also may at one time be kept out by adverse winds, and so cause a temporary scarcity; and then, by a sudden change, arrive in fleets so large as to cause more than a usual pressure of sellers.
>
> (1857, V: 85)

It is evident in Tooke's framework that fluctuations in market prices are closely associated with adjustments in corn stocks resulting from immediate imbalances between supply brought to market and demand on the market.

4.4 Effect of the Corn Laws

In his historical analysis Tooke systematically accounted for the influence of the English Corn Laws operating from 1815 until their repeal in 1846 on conditions in the corn market and on the price of corn. Changes to the regime of agricultural protection over this period were instituted by four different Corn Laws: the 1815, the inoperative 1822, the 'permanent' 1828 and the 'mitigated' 1842 Corn Law. Except for the 1822 Corn Law, which never came into operation, each of these regimes operated in a different way and, thereby, exerted its influence on the English corn market in a different way. The fundamental difference was that the 1815 (and 1822) Corn Law instituted a contingent prohibition on corn imports at a pivotal price point, whereas the 1828 and 1842 Corn Laws permitted trade without any prohibition but with a full sliding scale of import duties.[14] Tooke's analysis provides a valuable account of precisely how these Corn Laws, in their different way, affected the operation of the corn market and the price of corn. With regard to their general effect, Tooke argued that the Corn Laws exacerbated the short-run fluctuation in corn prices caused fundamentally by the vicissitudes of the seasons without providing effective protection to English agriculture.

A major policy objective of the Corn Laws was to bring about steady prices that would encourage corn production in the British Isles and, thereby, in absence of reliable foreign supplies, contribute towards more moderate prices in the long term. Tooke argued that in fact they had the opposite effect of destabilising grain prices. To begin with, when a shortage in the domestic market emerged as a result of unproductive seasons, Tooke argued that the Corn Laws tended to encourage speculative activity which induced a sharp rise in the price of corn until it reached a certain level, at which point a large quantity of imported corn would suddenly flood onto the home market, causing recoil in price. In particular, the 1815 Corn Law, with its high prohibition prices, had this effect. Tooke (1840a, III: 37) supported this view by reference to the sharp fluctuation in corn prices which followed the very unproductive season of 1816. With rapidly declining stocks, the price of corn rose sharply to well above the prohibition price of 80s. from Autumn (harvest time) 1816 to late 1817. However, because of the system of calculating the 'quarterly average' price to determine when the 'ports would open', the relief from exorbitant prices which would have been afforded by imported corn was much delayed. When, in late-1817 and in 1818, a large importation of corn arrived, the 'urgency of the want was over' and, especially after the propitious season of 1818, there emerged a large 'surplus' which pressed down on prices in subsequent years (see Tooke 1829b: 45–6; 1838, II: 13–23). Along similar lines, Tooke (1829b: 58–71; 1838, II: 139; 1840a, III: 37) argued that, had not the government rendered the 1822 Corn Law inoperative by ordering the release of bonded corn onto the market below the prohibition price in 1825, 1826 and 1827, unpropitious seasons would have led to otherwise wider price fluctuations. According to Tooke, upside fluctuations in prices had the propensity to be more regular but less violent under the 'sliding scale' regime of the 1828 Corn Law (and the 'mitigated one' of 1842).[15] Tooke contended that under the 1828 Corn Law, when a domestic shortfall emerged, the sharp descending scale of duties that corresponded with a more gradual rise in the price of corn tended to encourage speculative activity in the market which advanced the price to the highest range at which the duty is at its minimum and inducing a large quantity of imported grain to flood the domestic market at the 'highest protecting' price, subsequently resulting in a sharp decline in the price of corn (Tooke 1840a, III: 27–8, 30–1, 37–8; 1848a, IV: 12–13).[16] Tooke

(1829b: 77–8; 1838, II: 200–1; 1840a, III: 41) believed the recoil in price was more violent the more ill founded the opinion of traders in the market that a foreign supply was required.

Associated with their tendency to heighten prices, Tooke argued that the Corn Laws operated to 'aggravate in a peculiar degree the evil of visitations' (1840a, III: 39) of deficient seasons and domestic shortages. Their 'tendency to cause an exhaustion of our home stock before any resort is made to foreign supply' (1840a, III: 39) led to unnecessarily large shortages in the home market with considerable hardships for consumers. The delayed flood of imports which then followed led to surpluses which often left corn dealers with excess stocks.[17] Tooke (1829b: 74–5) also contended that at times of great scarcity the urgency for foreign supplies often led to the importation of poor quality wheat which, thereby, degraded the quality of subsistence food (i.e. bread). Furthermore, Tooke argued that, because of the urgency of obtaining imported grain quickly at these times, the Corn Laws confined the foreign sources 'from which our supply is habitually drawn in ordinary seasons' (1840a, III: 39) to regions of Continental Europe that usually shared similar climatic conditions with the British Isles. They therefore prevented an 'extension of the radius of our habitual supply' to 'parts of Asia bordering on the Black Sea and the Mediterranean, to Egypt, and above all, to the United States of America' (1840a, III: 39) where climatic conditions usually differed considerably from Europe at any one time. Hence, a key criticism of Tooke was that the Corn Laws tended to prevent the possibility of obtaining cheaper imported corn afforded by diverse sources of foreign supply.

In the opposite situation, when highly productive harvests caused excess supply to emerge in the domestic market, Tooke argued the Corn Laws failed to prevent prices falling to unprofitably low levels. Since low prices could not induce absorption by domestic consumption, he held that the only way Britain's excess supply could be expelled in the short-term was by exportation. However, in absence of an export bounty this could occur only in exceptional circumstances because seasonal conditions and, thereby, the movement in corn prices in the British Isles usually coincided with those on the European Continent (Tooke 1821a: 232; 1840a, III: 39). Hence, a domestic surplus and low corn prices usually corresponded with even lower European corn prices. Tooke's point was that, under a protective regime of 'contingent prohibition' and/or import duties, seasonal swings from unproductive to productive harvests would, through the belated arrival of foreign supplies, tend to induce an excess supply in the market which, without an export duty, cause a sharp recoil from a high to a low price of corn. Moreover, the price would remain depressed until the reoccurrence of unproductive harvests. For this reason, Tooke (1821a: 230–1; 1840a, III: 44–7) argued that whenever an import duty (or prohibition) is implemented, it should be matched by an equal export bounty in order to ensure steadier prices.

A key argument of Tooke's was that the Corn Laws failed to provide effective protection to British agriculture because they did not secure a 'higher average price' for corn (1821a: 230; 1840a, III: 20–30). The problem was that they did not provide protection to farmers when they most needed it, during those times when abundant seasons depressed domestic corn prices. In evidence to the 1821 Agricultural Committee, Tooke gave the following opinion:

> In what way do you think the present corn law operates to the disadvantage of the farmer? – Tooke: In rendering hopeless his state, in the event of two or three abundant seasons, inasmuch as he is precluded from the chance of any exportation, except at prices lower than those prevailing on the continent.
>
> (1821a: 229)

His view was based on the fundamental notion of the 'effects of quantity on price' examined in section 3.4 above, which supposed that in the short run the income of farmers in aggregate tended to vary with prices rather than output so that productive harvests and low corn prices would be accompanied by a reduction in agricultural income (Tooke 1821a: 240; 1824, iii: 283–300; 1838, I: 10–20). Hence, Tooke (1838, II: 85–6; 1840a, III: 21–2, 30–1, 37, 40–2) showed, in particular, that the Corn Laws were impotent in arresting the depression in English agriculture during the periods 1818 to 1822 and 1832 to 1836 when, as a result of a sequence of productive seasons, low prices persisted.[18] He argued that without an export bounty to induce the exportation of corn when excess supply emerged in the home market, the Corn Laws failed to prevent agricultural distress in these situations (Tooke 1821a: 229; 1829b: 88; 1840a, III: 45).

Underlying Tooke's argument above that the Corn Laws tended to increase the short-run fluctuation of corn prices as well as lowering its average price, was 'the supposition that we grow, on the average of seasons, enough for our own consumption' (1821a: 287). He admitted that if domestic production of corn was 'on average' not able to keep up with domestic demand, protection consisting of only an import duty 'may keep prices steadier' with adjustments in the market tending to fall on the quantity imported (1821a: 288). It seems that Tooke did not believe Britain had become a persistent net importer of grain until the late-1830s.[19] He believed the Corn Laws in fact undermined the capacity of British agriculture to keep pace with a 'rate of consumption' consistent with the country's increasing population. By aggravating the amplitude of fluctuation in corn prices, which is basically attributable to the vicissitudes of the seasons, Tooke (1840a, III: 35–8) contended that the Corn Laws inhibited the long-term expansion of domestic agricultural production. They therefore utterly failed to achieve 'the objects proposed by the promoters and supporters', to secure to the farmer 'a constantly remunerating price' afforded by a 'steady price' for grain (1840a, III: 21–30). This perhaps explains why, faced with a landed interest which had the political power to obtain protection, Tooke emphasised the need for an export bounty to at least ensure price stability.[20] Of course, according to Tooke, whether Britain was a net importer or not, the first best solution was a free trade in corn. Thus, after the repeal of the Corn Laws in 1846, he claimed that corn prices had become 'remarkable for [their] steadiness, or absence of Fluctuations' (Tooke and Newmarch 1857, V: 81).

Tooke's argument that the Corn Laws did not afford effective protection until the late 1830s appears to rest on the view that corn produced in Northern Europe was not cheap as to pose a genuine threat to British agricultural producers. In evidence given to the Agricultural Committee of 1821, Tooke stated that 'I believe we have an exaggerated view of the cheapness of corn upon the continent, from casual and temporary circumstances' (1821a: 232), and, repeating his opinion 'that there is no such disproportion, or anything approaching to it, between our power of producing corn for our consumption, and the power of the Continent of supplying us, as is assumed in the question' (1821a: 288).[21] Tooke's reasoning for this belief was two-fold. First, he argued that much of the difference in price could be attributed to the transportation cost and, in Northern Europe, where corn was usually the cheapest on the Continent, to its inferior quality. To demonstrate this point, Tooke prepared 'accounts' for the committee, giving a breakdown of the 'cost on board', freight, shipping insurance and storage costs of Russian wheat (per quarter) imported from the Baltic ports of St Petersburg, Archangel and Riga for the years 1814 to 1820. These accounts showed that the peacetime cost of bringing this foreign wheat to the British market was 10*s*. to 13*s*. per quarter, representing between 15 to 25 per cent of its final market value.[22] Tooke (1821a: 226–7) indicated that after accounting for these transport and storage costs, and also having regard for the inferior quality of these various Russian grains, their price was not significantly cheaper than domestically produced corn. Indeed, in comparison to manufacturing commodities for export, Tooke (1821a: 290) stated that 'the growers [of corn] here have the protection of the freight upon an infinitely more bulky commodity' more expensive to ship. Second, Tooke (1821a: 226–8, 237) contended that, by its exclusion from the British market, the Corn Laws tended to depress European corn prices. He argued that a free trade in corn would, through the effect of a higher British demand for foreign supplies, raise the price of European corn towards the English price:

> Supposing a free trade in corn was to be established, would the prices on the Continent in your opinion, rise generally, or those here fall? – Tooke: I think that both effects would follow, that ours would be somewhat lower than the present range; and those on the Continent very decidedly higher.
>
> (1821a: 287)

Hence, with regard to Northern Europe, Tooke contended that an increased foreign supply to meet domestic shortages would only come forth by raising prices to those in England somewhat lowered by a free trade.[23] In this connection Tooke (1821a: 239) believed the Corn Laws discouraged the long-term development of corn production in Northern Europe.

The claim by Tooke in 1821 that under a free trade Northern Europe did not represent a serious competitive threat to British agriculture and, connectedly, his argument that until the late-1830s the Corn Laws failed to effectively protect it, is not supported by the historical evidence. The historian Susan Fairlie (1965: 574; 1969: 92–3) has shown that in the period from 1815 to the repeal of the Corn Laws in 1846, corn prices in Europe were systematically lower than English prices by a margin that would well account for the transport costs of imported corn that were estimated, for example, by Tooke (1821a: 224–6) for the period 1814–1820.[24] Notwithstanding Tooke's argument that a free trade in corn would have raised European prices, there seems little doubt that it would also have ensured that prices in England remained systematically lower than they actually were under the Corn Laws. Furthermore, the evidence indicates that the average price difference narrowed over the period 1815 to 1846, mainly because of a trend rise in European prices, while Britain's dependence on foreign supplies of corn increased, something which was partially masked by the prevalence of productive harvests, especially in the mid-1830s. This evidence considerably undermines Tooke's argument that a moderate export bounty could have effectively stabilised corn prices. As previously indicated, Tooke (1821a: 288) conceded that the effectiveness of his bounty depended on Britain not being a net importer of corn. While in 1821 Britain's importation of corn under the 1815 Corn Law appears to have been small, the evidence suggests that, by the late-1820s, it had become significant and was growing in size. In any case, given the similarity of climatic conditions of the British Isles and Northern Europe, something Tooke much emphasised, it is unlikely that a bounty would ever have come into effect given that corn prices in Europe were nearly always significantly lower than in Britain.

Although Tooke's argument on the ineffectiveness of the Corn Laws to protect British agriculture is unconvincing, he was certainly correct in contending that they exacerbated the fluctuation in corn prices compared to a free trade in corn. Hence, Tooke clearly saw that a welfare gain from free trade was more stable prices. Moreover, given the mounting inability of Britain's agriculture to meet the demand for food of a fast-growing population at a moderate price, Tooke had long identified the key problem with the Corn Laws was that they discouraged the long-term development of a reliable supply of foreign grain from regions whose climatic conditions were different from that shared by Northern Europe and the British Isles. It was Britain's significant dependence on foreign supplies, so evident from the late-1830s, that caused Tooke and others to believe the repeal of the Corn Laws was urgent in alleviating the hardships imposed on the population by artificially higher food prices. Indeed, it is evident in his writings from 1829 onwards that Tooke's fundamental objection to the Corn Laws was that at times of scarcity they operated to raise food prices to higher levels than they would have otherwise reached, with particularly adverse effects on the welfare of the 'working classes'. He argued that during periods in which there were a series of unproductive harvests and domestic shortages of corn, specifically 1828 to 1831 and 1838 to 1842, the Corn Laws operated to aggravate the increase in the price of provisions and, given the money wage, considerably worsen the condition of the working classes (Tooke 1829b: 76–82;

1840a, III: 51–3; Tooke and Newmarch 1857, V: 73, 76). In particular, Tooke observed that in 1839–1840 much of the working population of the 'manufacturing districts' suffered 'cruelly' with the depression of industry actually causing a reduction in money wages at a time when the prices of their 'provisions' rose considerably as a result of the domestic shortages.[25] Indeed, he pointed out that during these times of scarcity famine occurred and 'the state of public feeling' sometimes led to civil disturbances and food rioting.[26] As the following quote shows, for Tooke this infliction of misery on the working population was the foremost reason for opposing the Corn Laws:

> *the substantial and enduring ground of objection is* … it artificially raises the price of food to the community, who suffer a loss by it, much greater in amount than the utmost gain derived from the monopoly by the classes in whose favour, and by whose preponderance in the legislature, it is inflicted.
>
> (1840a, III: 51; emphasis added)

As Tooke became aware of Britain's significant growing dependence on foreign supplies, he became concerned the Corn Laws would inflict considerable misery on working people by magnifying the increase in the price of provisions when domestic shortages emerged and the more urgent he saw the need to adopt a free trade in corn (Tooke and Newmarch 1857, V: 49–81, 180–5, 422–31).

Tooke's fundamental objection to the Corn Laws on the grounds that they lowered the living standards of the greater population is entirely consistent with his viewpoint about their effect on income distribution. To the extent the Corn Laws effectively kept the price of corn persistently higher than would otherwise occur under free trade, which he ascertained had occurred by the late-1830s, Tooke (1821a: 233–4, 287–8) believed they would distribute income in favour of landlords. This argument is based on Ricardo's theory of land rent adopted by Tooke, in which the Corn Laws, by keeping up a higher price of corn that made it profitable to cultivate lands of inferior fertility, thereby increased the rent on intra-marginal lands. But while Tooke agreed with Ricardo that the Corn Laws tended to increase the rent going to landlords, he held the very different position that this redistribution of income occurred mostly at the expense of the working class rather than the capitalist class.

As is well-known, in his 'Essay on the Influence of a Low Price of Corn on the Profits of Stock', Ricardo (1815) argued that by artificially raising the natural price of corn, the Corn Laws tended to increase rent at the expense of profits of industry. Ricardo (1815; 1821: 156–9, 203) contended that because the Corn Laws would, for *given* real wages (in corn) of labour, lead to the adoption of more costly techniques of production, the rate of profit on capital would decline. This is associated, first, with a decline in non-wage income and, second, with the redistribution of the smaller non-wage income in favour of landlords. In accord with his view of the importance of distribution, Ricardo argued that the permanent reduction in the general rate of profit would inhibit the accumulation of capital and the development of the British economy. By contrast, in Tooke's picture, it is the real wage rather than the rate of profit that declines as a consequence of Corn Laws which artificially raise the average price of corn and increase the rent on land.[27] This difference stems from Tooke's different approach to distribution and prices explained in Section 3.3, in which he treats the rate of profit as the exogenously *given* distributive variable so that for a given technique, the real wage is residually determined to a limit of the social minimum established under the Poor Laws. For Tooke, then, the Corn Laws tended in the long run to redistribute income to the landlord class largely at the expense of the working class rather than the capitalist class (including farmers). Hence, besides causing a technically inferior allocation of inputs, Tooke's opposition to trade protection on British agriculture was based on its adverse effect on the working class rather than on the capitalists of industry.

5 An explanation of general price movements

In explaining the movement in the general level of prices in England over the period 1792–1856, the price of agricultural commodities was an important but only one aspect of Tooke's empirical study. His study encompassed a broad range of commodities besides agriculture for which it was possible to collect price information. Aside from corn, in *High and Low Prices* (1823, 1824) and *History of Prices* (1838–1857) Tooke compiled price series data for up to thirty-four different categories of commodities, consisting mostly of raw materials used in manufacturing. On this basis Tooke was able to ascertain with some precision changes in the general level of prices and to better identify its causes. In particular, Tooke was concerned with accurately determining changes in the general price level for the purposes of correlating it with changes in monetary aggregates, especially of Bank of England notes, in order to ascertain the causal role of monetary policy in relation to changes in economic activity. He was also concerned with ascertaining changes in the cost of living and, thereby, the real wage, which was seen to be affected not only by changes in the prices of agricultural commodities produced domestically but also by imported food items and manufactured products. In addition, ascertaining the prices of those commodities which contributed most to movements in the general price level enabled Tooke to better identify the main causes of the latter and explain it. For Tooke, the degree to which movements in prices of commodities were *general* was important in determining the causes of their general movement. Indeed, changes in the structure of prices that accompanied their general movement were often cited by Tooke in support of his own explanation.

A feature of Tooke's empirical analysis is that it considers comprehensively the contributing causes of price movements. It was shown in the previous chapter that Tooke contended that natural factors was a major cause of the movement in the prices of agriculture and, therefore 'provisions', in England over the period 1792–1856. They were also important in explaining the change in prices of a large range of raw materials imported into England. Political factors affecting the supply conditions of commodities were equally important in Tooke's explanation of price level movements. As will be shown in this chapter, Tooke contended in his history of English prices that political factors consisting of war-induced interruptions to international trade, the imposition of protection by the government against foreign trade, an alteration in the monetary system and the government's long-term fiscal strategy, was a major contributor to significant movements in the general level of prices. Technical progress was also considered by Tooke to be an important factor in explaining long-run secular price movements. Factors affecting the effectual demand for commodities also figure in Tooke's analysis, though, for the most part, they are seen to play a secondary role. In this connection, monetary policy in Tooke's analysis plays a secondary role in the short-run movement of the general price level. In all, Tooke sought to account for the overall circumstances shaping market conditions and determining price movements.

This chapter examines all the contributing factors that Tooke identified in his explanation of the movement of the general level of money prices. It is also concerned with Tooke's arguments against other competing explanations of price movements. Section 5.1 considers Tooke's analysis of commodities other than corn in connection with his conception of a general price level and the basis for ascertaining its movement. Section 5.2 then examines Tooke's argument that the effect of war on prices largely depended on the manner and extent to which it obstructed British commercial trade, considered in particular reference to the French Wars. In Section 5.3, Tooke's position on the effect of taxes and duties on prices is examined. It is followed in Section 5.4 by consideration of Tooke's position on the effect of government expenditure on prices in particular connection to the policy adopted for financing Britain's war with France over the period 1793–1815. Section 5.5 then deals with Tooke's view on the effect on prices of the institutional change in England's monetary system which occurred with the restriction of cash payments on demand by the Bank of England in 1797 and its effective resumption at a fixed gold standard in 1821. Much of this discussion concerns Tooke's view on the role played by monetary policy in contributing to price inflation during the period of 'currency restriction'. In Section 5.6, Tooke (and Newmarch's) position on the effect of the mid-nineteenth-century gold discoveries in California and the East Australian colonies on the price level is examined. Finally, Section 5.7 of this chapter provides an exposition of Tooke's overall explanation for the secular movement in the general level of money prices in Britain over the period 1792–1856.

5.1 Explaining general price movements

Tooke clearly conceived that the real wage of English workers consisted of a composition of wage goods of some complexity. Certainly wheat, used in making bread, was considered a primary constituent of the 'necessaries' (or 'provisions') of English life. It was also an input in the production of other food items, in particular beer and spirits, which could too be regarded as necessaries. Besides these basic foodstuffs, Tooke considered meats and vegetables to be 'provisions' within the reach of those with income higher than the lowest classes. Tooke also believed wholly foreign produced and imported food items, such as sugar, coffee, tea and tobacco, to be significant provisions entering into the real wage. In the hierarchy of needs, these items were regarded by Tooke to be 'the most necessary articles of food' (1848a, IV: 69) whose prices had a significant bearing on the cost of living. In addition, Tooke believed there were 'articles of secondary necessity' (1848a, IV: 69) which consisted mainly of manufactured consumer products; in particular, woollen and cotton clothing whose prices entered into the cost of living of workers.

Aside from commodities that entered directly into provisions, Tooke's analysis of prices consisted of a wide range of raw material inputs into the production of manufacturing products, both 'consumables' and fixed capital (machinery and infrastructure). The commodities other than corn for which price series data were compiled are divided by Tooke and Newmarch (1857, VI: 490–1) into three major groups: first, 'Colonial and Tropical Produce (food); and Provisions'; second, 'Raw Materials of Manufacture'; and, third, 'Metals'.[1] Along with grains and vegetables, the first group comprised food products entering into the basic real wage. On the supposition that the prices of cotton and wool are indexes of the cost of clothing, then taken together with the above food group, this array of commodities captured the cost of living (excluding cost of housing). Hence, when variously explaining the prices of these commodities, Tooke reflects on factors influencing the cost of living in English society. By also taking into account the prices of the above-mentioned second and third groups, Tooke's analysis captured a price level with a wider economic meaning. On the grounds that material input prices are an indicator of the cost of manufacturing products then, altogether, the prices of all the commodities variously covered by Tooke come best to reflecting what is understood in modern parlance as a producer price index.

In contrast to his treatment of corn, Tooke does not systematically provide a comprehensive historical explanation of the movement in the 'prices of produce other than corn' in his empirical study. Instead, Tooke explained the movement in the prices of these commodities when they were seen to be significant in explaining the general movement of prices. Thus, iron and other metal products became prominent in Tooke's analysis of prices when, during the railway investment boom of the 1840s, they were in strong demand for use in railway construction (1848a, IV: 68). For the most part, Tooke's analysis tended to concentrate on those commodities whose prices significantly changed during the historical period under consideration. Tooke was fully aware that there could be significant differences in the variation of prices between commodities according to the different circumstances that specifically determined their conditions of production and the supply brought to market and their demand. This follows from the fact that most of the commodities other than corn in his study consisted of raw produce imported into Britain from different regions of the world (see Table A2.1, p. 233). Hence, Tooke often found disparate movements in the prices of different commodities which sometimes made it difficult to ascertain any definite change in the general level of money prices. As an example, Tooke (1848a, IV: 44) ascertained that in the years 1838 to 1840 the prices of the 'principal articles of produce other than corn' showed 'a considerable diversity of movement', with hemp, tea, coffee, sugar and rum having risen, cotton and indigo fallen, while timber, tallow, raw silk and wool remaining 'nearly the same'. According to Tooke, the 'enormous increase' in the price of sugar in late-1839 was the result of the 'failure of the supply in the West Indies' (1848a, IV: 44); while, independently, the high price of tea was the result of speculative buying induced by the disruption to supply from China which was only brought to an end in 1841 with 'Captain Elliot's preliminary arrangement with the Chinese authorities at Canton, promising a speedy and satisfactory conclusion of hostilities' (1848a, IV: 45–6).

Many other examples can be found in Tooke's (1838, II: 212–13, 250–7; 1840a, III: 54–67; 1848a, IV: 43–62) analysis showing that specific circumstances influenced the conditions of supply of foreign produced commodities independently of each other. They, in turn, were entirely separate to circumstances that affected the supply conditions of domestically produced commodities. Thus, the high price of English beef which persisted in the three years up to 1842 is attributed by Tooke to 'the disease which had prevailed among cattle in this country' (1848a, IV: 53). Variations in the movement of prices of different commodities could also arise from changes in the structure of demand. For example, Tooke (1838, I: 254) pointed to the increase in the 'prices of naval and military stores' caused by their greatly increased demand during the French Wars. In connection with these wars, Tooke (1838, I: 273) argued that an increase in the demand for metal by a rapidly expanding shipbuilding industry resulted in a substantial increase in metals prices, especially of copper, in the period 1804–1808. Similarly, Tooke and Newmarch (1857, V: 299) ascertained that the increase in the prices of 'Copper, Iron, Tin, Timber, Oil, and Logwood' in 1853 is 'explained by the greatly increased demand for manufactures and shipbuilding' in preparation for war in the Crimea. In addition, Tooke also referred occasionally to the effect of changes in foreign demand on the prices of British re-exports, consisting mainly of 'colonial produce' (e.g. coffee and sugar) destined for European markets. Hence, Tooke attributed the 'ruinously low range of prices' for 'Sugar and coffee, and some other articles of Colonial produce' in the years 1806 to 1812 to the exclusion from markets on the Continent by Napoleon's blockade which narrowed 'the channels for export' (1838, I: 272–3). In another dramatic example, Tooke and Newmarch (1857, V: 235) referred to the adverse effects on the prices of 'raw materials and manufactured goods' of the 'cessation of demand' caused by the 'political disturbances on the Continent' which occurred during the social revolution of 1848. Overall, then, in determining the general movement in prices, Tooke accounted for variations in the prices of different (groups of) commodities attributable to separate factors operating on demand and supply conditions in their respective markets. Indeed, Tooke used evidence of changes in the prices of commodities which were contrary to the direction of change in the general level of money prices to support his own explanation against that of the classical quantity theorists.

In accord with Tooke's analytical approach factors affecting supply conditions were pre-eminent in his explanation of the prices of commodities other than corn. However, Tooke gave more prominence to demand in explaining the short-run fluctuation in the prices of these commodities than he did for corn. It is apparent Tooke progressively gave greater weight to the general conditions of demand which were associated with variations in economic activity to explain the short-run movement in the general level of money prices. A greater emphasis on the role of demand is evident in the analysis in Part II of both volume IV (1848a: 42–80) and volume V (1857: 228–347) of *History of Prices*. The main way 'general demand' influenced the price level in Tooke's analysis, particularly in his pre-banking school writings, was through widespread speculative activity in commodity markets by traders. The resulting rise in prices inevitably led to overstocking and a subsequent collapse in prices. Thus, Tooke (1838, I: 272–9, 300–16; II: 5–13, 140–7, 154–7) ascertained that widespread commodity specu-lation was the cause of a general increase in prices (other than for corn) in 1808, in 1813–1814 and 1824–1825, followed by collapses in 1809–1811, 1815–1816 and 1825–1826, respectively. While 'apprehensions' by traders about shortages in (foreign) supply were important, the prospects of an opening in foreign markets for re-exports was considered by Tooke to have played a key role in the latter two speculative booms.

The influence of regular variations in economic activity on the price level is further shown by Tooke (1838, II: 209–14) in his explanation of the 'stagnation of trade and depression of prices' in the period 1828–1831. Following the com-monly held doctrine of other classical economists, Tooke (1829b: 104–7) acknowledged that 'overproduction' by domestic manufacturers was a major cause of this economic downturn. In relation to iron, Tooke (1838, II: 212) argued that its overproduction in this period was largely the result of 'the appli-cation of increased powers of machinery' which caused 'an augmentation of supply' to 'outrun an increasing rate of consumption'. However, on the grounds that the supply of raw materials used in manufacturing is the 'necessary limit to the application of machinery', Tooke (1829b: 105, 107) traced the economic downturn 'to an increase of supply of raw produce (food excepted) beyond the previous rate of consumption'. In 1829 Tooke believed the loss of foreign markets 'contributed to diminish the demand' such as to 'add to the depression of manufactures' (1829b: 107). Tooke (1840a, III: 63) also ascertained that over-production in the cotton industry led to a decline in the prices of cotton goods in 1839.[2]

Importantly, in this analysis Tooke developed a conception of cyclical changes in activity and prices in a peacetime economy, involving the alternation between excess aggregate supply and excess aggregate demand. This conception was outlined by Tooke in reference to the afore-mentioned economic downturn in the period 1828–1832 and its subsequent recovery in the period 1832–1835:

> as a state of rising markets, and eventually a high range of them, in con-sequence of supplies having for some length of time fallen short of expecta-tion, or of the estimated rate of consumption, is usually followed by a reduction of stocks, while the consumption is extended; so a long course of

falling markets is eventually followed by a reduction of stocks, while the consumption is extended; and this state of things is the precursor of improved markets, and of a period of prosperity in the branches of trade to which the previous distress from low prices had applied. Accordingly the fall and low range of prices observable through a great part of the interval now under consideration, laid the foundation for the activity and generally prosperous state which, as we shall have occasion to see, prevailed among the manufacturing, and mining, and trading classes, in the three years following the present epoch.

(1838, II: 214)

In Tooke, this cyclical behaviour in the economy was conceived essentially in terms of the interaction between production (supply) and consumption (demand); whereby production was driven by the profit motive and consumption was increased by lower prices. Hence, Tooke regarded overproduction in the economy as a temporary phenomenon associated with 'a diminution of profit, if not loss to producers' and '[W]hen prices have fallen to the point which extends the consumption in proportion to the increased supply, profits are restored to their ordinary level' (1829b: 106–7).[3]

Tooke's outlook on the economic development of Britain conformed to that commonly held by classical economists after Adam Smith. This consisted of the view that the driving force of economic development was technical progress that promoted an improvement in the methods of production of industry which, through its lowering of the price of superior-quality manufactured goods (or processed re-exports), progressively enlarged both its domestic and foreign markets. The enlargement of its markets, in turn, supported industrial expansion. In consideration of the question, '[W]hence does the increase in production arise?' Tooke wrote:

In the great majority of cases, the increase of production may, unless where it is merely the effect of difference of seasons, be referred to some, one or other of the following causes: extended and improved cultivation; a resort to fresh soils; new sources of supply; cheaper substitutes for more expensive materials; a more skilled application of manual labour; and, above all, the application and progressive improvement of machinery.

(1829b: 106)

There appears to be two *potential* interrelated constraints to the growth of production in Tooke's thinking. The first potential constraint is a persistent shortage in the supply of raw materials to manufacturing industry which, considered by Tooke in relation to Britain's economy, would occur if there were permanent obstacles to the importation of those available only from foreign sources. Hence, in relation to the 'great rise' in the price of imported silk which occurred in the period 1808 to 1811 as a result of obstructions to trade, Tooke argued that '[I]f those obstacles had been permanent, it must be obvious that that trade [i.e. silk trade] would have been destroyed' but happily, these instances have 'been rare, of any permanent diminution of supply of the staple article of our manufactures' (1829b: 107n.). The second potential constraint to the growth in production is a lack of sufficient demand. As discussed above (p. 83), Tooke (1829b: 107–8) believed that the diminution of demand in Britain's foreign markets contributed to the economic downturn in early 1829. He also believed a decline in domestic demand contributed to the economic depression that occurred after the end of the French Wars in 1816–1818 (see Section 5.3). However, it is evident in these cases that Tooke considered 'general demand' to be a constraint on aggregate production in the short run but not in the long run. As shown in relation to our consideration of Tooke's position on free trade in Section 3.5, and which is elaborated in more detail in Section 5.3, Tooke adopted Say's Law so that in the long run demand was not seen to be a substantial constraint to the accumulation process. Potentially, though, in Tooke's political economy, as derived principally from Adam Smith (1776 [1976]), a lack of growth in demand can be a constraint to the accumulation process in the particular sense that an inability to persistently extend the size of the economy's market, mainly its foreign market, would limit the scope for technical progress and expansion in production.[4] For Tooke this potential demand constraint is interrelated to the afore-mentioned potential supply constraint of a persistent shortage of foreign-only produced raw materials by reason that they jointly depend on extending the nation's access to global markets.

In connection to explaining short-run price fluctuations, 'general demand' was considered by Tooke to usually play a secondary role. But, as previously mentioned, Tooke began to give more prominence to demand in his analysis of prices in the 1840s and onwards. Thus, Tooke maintained that 'a brisk and increasing demand for manufactured produce, at home and abroad' (1848a, IV: 54) was a major cause of the general rise in prices of raw materials in 1844. While Tooke believed that in this instance the opening up of new markets and the expansion in export trade was an important stimulus, he attached more importance to an increase in domestic demand. Interestingly, Tooke linked this increase in domestic demand for 'consumable commodities' to the 'prevalence of full employment in every branch of industry' and to the

> amount of capital currently devoted to the payment of wages, and thence conveyed through the hands of retail dealers in payment for supplies of food, clothing, household furniture, &c, the demand for which had been reduced much below the ordinary level during the previous years of depression.
>
> (1848a, IV: 54–5)

Though still primitive in form, a closer link between 'general demand' and income was made by Tooke and Newmarch (1857, V: 367–70) in the analysis of the influence of railway investment on expenditure over the period 1846–1850. This period covered a spectacular boom and then collapse in railway shares. It was estimated by Tooke and Newmarch (1857, V: 352–3, 367) that £150 million was expended on 'Railway Works' over the period. This analysis related both the employment of labour from railway investment and changes in wealth connected with railway shares to expenditure in the economy.

On the one hand, the large employment created by railway construction and its service operations contributed towards higher expenditure by the 'working classes'. Tooke and Newmarch (1857, V: 368) estimated

> during the two years 1847 and 1848, not less than One Million persons were dependent on Wages provided by Railway Expenditure; and on the average of the five years, 1846 to 1850, both inclusive, it is not permissible to state the number of persons dependent on such wages at less than 600,000.

Interestingly, this estimation was made on the basis of what in today's economic language is called a 'multiplier effect' of railway expenditure. Thus, in the peak years of railway expenditure in 1847 and 1848, besides the 188,000 workers employed directly in construction and operations, Tooke and Newmarch (1857, V: 357) estimated that at least another 300,000 were indirectly employed as

> artisans, scattered over the different workshops of the country, engaged in preparing the iron rails; the materials for the stations; in building locomotives, carriages, and wagons; in cutting and preparing timber for sleepers; and other processes, all indispensable to the completion of the work.

Their estimate of one million persons deriving a livelihood from railway expenditure was then based on accounting for the family dependents (i.e. 'men, women, and children') of these workers.

On the other hand, Tooke and Newmarch (1857, V: 368–70) ascertained that the multiplier effect of increased railway expenditure was outweighed by a reduction in the expenditure by 'Middle and Wealthier classes' whose wealth was diminished by the collapse in railway share prices in 1847 and 1848. This overall decline in expenditure 'contributed to the low range of general prices which prevailed' during the years of commercial distress in 1847–1850 (1857, V: 370).[5] In another example of the role of 'general demand' in explaining short-run price fluctuations, Tooke and Newmarch (1857, V: 282) largely attributed the general increase in prices in 1853 to 'the vast consumption of every description of manufactured and imported articles' as a result of a substantial advance in 'the wages of nearly all kinds of labour' which raised 'the weekly income of millions of the population'. However, as will be shown in much of what follows in this chapter, despite the greater prominence progressively given to 'general demand' in Tooke's writings, supply conditions were seen to be the primary cause of short- and long-run movements in the general level of money prices.

While Tooke was clearly concerned with explaining the general movement of prices, as Gregory (1928: 14–15) has pointed out, Tooke did not 'introduce the device of index-numbers' in aid of his analysis despite its employment by contemporaries, Lowe (1823) and Porter (1838: 236–7). There are two issues connected with this omission. First, Tooke was well aware of the concept of a statistical scale to measure relative changes of variables over time. Gregory (1928: 14–15) argued that the concept was well-known to Tooke from its employment during the controversies over the restriction of cash payments.[6] This knowledge is particularly manifest in the inclusion in Tooke and Newmarch (1857, V: 103) of a table constructed by Jacob (1828) containing a scale of annual wheat output in Great Britain over the period 1816–1827. It is equally demonstrated by the inclusion in Tooke and Newmarch (1857, VI: 389–92) of several statistical tables constructed by Arthur Young (1812) which employed a scale (of twenty) to historically compare the wages of agricultural labour and the prices of various items. Given that much of Tooke's analysis consisted of making historical comparisons, it therefore remains a mystery why he did not construct price indices to a base year for *single* commodities (e.g. wheat) which Newmarch later did for *The Economist*'s annual 'Commercial History' series begun in 1863. As Porter (1838: 227–8) argued, a major advantage of such indices was that price changes of different commodities, whose prices are given by reference to heterogeneous measures of weight and quantity, could be more transparently compared in determining the main contributions to changes in the general price level.

Second, Tooke was aware of the problem of weighting a composition of commodities to construct a general price index.[7] Tooke expressed his opinion on this issue to the Commons Committee on Banks of Issue in 1840 when invited to comment on a price index composed of fifty equally weighted commodities constructed by Porter (1838: 236–7):

> Q 3615. Have you seen a table contained in a work published by Mr. Porter, called 'The Progress of the Nation', showing the comparative prices of fifty articles at different times during the years 1833–4–5–6, and 7, and also showing the amount of the Bank of England and country circulation during that period; and can you give any opinion as to its correctness? – Tooke: Yes; I have seen the table, I am aware of the manner in which it has been constructed. The prices of fifty articles of merchandise have been taken monthly, for each month from January 1833 to the close of 1837; but the construction of the table is such, that in my opinion, it can give no correct information of the kind which it professes to give. In forming this table, no reference is made to the *relative value* of the articles contained in it; therefore, if the object of judging of the value of the currency, by comparison of the prices of all or any of the articles contained in the list, were desirable or obtainable, it could not be done by this method. The comparisons are made, and the result drawn, without any reference whatever to the value of the articles compared.
>
> (1840b: 337; also quoted in 1848a, IV: 464; emphasis added)

Having gone on in his answer to illustrate the need for different weights to be apportioned to the various commodities,[8] Tooke maintained that the unreported indices of individual commodities calculated by Porter to construct his unweighted general price index would be of 'value to any body wanting to see the fluctuations in any particular article' (1840b: 337).

The likely reason why Tooke did not attempt to construct a general price index along the lines suggested in the quote above was that he saw no accurate means by which to statistically determine the weights. There simply was no reliable statistical data of the quantity of commodities consumed in Britain or of their output in Tooke's day, or indeed, throughout the nineteenth century, to estimate social expenditure patterns necessary to calculate an accurate general price index (see also Arnon 1990: 4–6).[9] Nevertheless, as mentioned in Appendix 2, we found a high degree of correlation between an unweighted price index and an estimated weighted average price index calculated from Tooke's price data for up to twenty-two commodities, indicating that by removing insignificant commodities, an unweighted index could be useful in measuring general price movements. It appears Tooke did not think such price indices would add very much to his empirical analysis.

As has been argued by Arnon (1990: 10–18), Tooke had a sound comprehension of the movement of the general price level without the benefit of index numbers. This came from an exhaustive study of the statistical and qualitative information available on prices. It also came from a detailed knowledge of the relative importance of various commodities entering consumption, usually via a manufacturing process, which gave Tooke a 'feel' for the general movement of prices. From his research, Tooke attained a comprehensive understanding of the circumstances under which different commodities were demanded, produced and brought to market. Often Tooke referred to a change in the structure of demand associated with a change in the (relative) prices of commodities that affected the relevant price level. Thus, for example, Tooke (1838, I: 91, 189, 211, 273–4; 1857, V: 316–37) pointed to the increase in the prices of war materials (e.g. flax, hemp, tallow and timber) caused by their increased demand during the French Wars and the Crimean War. Similarly, Tooke (1838, II: 238–9, 257; 1848a, IV: 25, 38) showed an awareness of changes in social consumption induced by a change in the relative prices of provisions. Overall, from his detailed study of prices, encompassing the range of commodities for which statistical information was available, Tooke acquired a sound understanding of the general movement of prices.

5.2 On the effect of war on prices

In Tooke's empirical study, much consideration is given to the effect of war on prices. This was because of the powerful impact that the long-running French Wars of 1793–1801 and 1803–1815 had on the behaviour of prices. It was the major political factor in Tooke's explanation of persistent inflation in 'general prices' in England over the period 1792–1814. According to Tooke, war raised prices by its tendency to 'diminish supply' in two possible ways: '1st., by a diminution of reproduction, and 2ndly, by [an] increased cost of production, and by impediments to commercial communication' (1838, I: 114).

With regard to the first cause, Tooke acknowledged war would 'abstract a portion of capital and labour' (1838, I: 114) from its employment in the 'reproduction' of civilian commodities to its use in military operations. In addition, 'diminished production' would occur if 'military operations' or 'arbitrary government exactions' caused an 'insecurity of property' (1838, I: 114). Tooke was referring to countries in which military conflict was taking place, involving the invasion and occupation by foreign armies of its territory. He contended that during the course of the French Wars, a reduction in production, in particular in the cultivation of agricultural produce, occurred in those states of Continental Europe which were subjected to 'extensive military operations'.[10] Tooke believed that this effect did not operate strongly when military conflict had ceased, even in those countries occupied by foreign armies as, indeed, many European states were, by French forces during the wars.

Spared French invasion, the British economy was not directly damaged by any military operations. Instead, Tooke believed that the tendency for the French Wars to adversely affect the British economy came from the re-allocation of capital and labour from civilian production to 'unproductive' military operations. However, Tooke argued that this tendency was outweighed by the following circumstances:

1　Increased activity, industry and intelligence, in the mass of the population, so that the portion remaining, after the abstraction of labourers for the purposes of war, may be able and willing to produce as much, or even more than, was previously produced.
2　Increased disposition on the part of individuals to accumulate capital, so as to compensate for the war expenditure, without any diminution of the funds applicable to reproduction.
3　Improvements in agriculture and machinery, tending to increase reproduction with the same or less capital and labour.
4　Greater security of property relatively to other countries, thus inducing an influx of capital from abroad.

All these circumstances concurred in this country, during the whole of the last war, and the consequence was an increase of production and population *in spite of the opposite tendency arising out of a state of war.*

(1838, I: 115–16)

Tooke therefore maintained that the French Wars had little impact on the supply of Britain's domestically produced commodities. For this reason Tooke (1838, I: 7–9; II: 346–7) believed seasonal conditions remained the primary factor in determining agricultural prices during the course of the wars. Instead, Tooke argued that the French Wars adversely affected the British economy by obstructing foreign trade and causing an increase in the costs of production of a large range of imported commodities. He identified two sets of circumstances that induced a persistent increase in the cost of production of commodities: those connected with war finance and the accumulation of government debt and those connected with obstructions to the supply of foreign produced commodities to British markets (Tooke 1838, I: 115). The former circumstance is discussed in Section 5.4 and, connectively, Section 6.3. The remainder of this section is concerned with the latter circumstance in the wider context of the 'extraordinary' disruptions to international trade that Tooke believed characterised the French Wars.

According to Tooke (1838, I: 116–17), the French Wars 'operated most powerfully' to increase prices in England because, unlike 'former wars', they had an 'anti-commercial character':

> It is, in fact, only with reference to the nature and degree of the impediments to commercial communications, that the last war, as far as relates to prices, is to be distinguished from former wars ... the extraordinary nature of the contest should be more especially borne in mind, as a caution against drawing any inference from average prices during [the] last war. The prices were regulated by the increase, which was enormous, of the cost of production arising from the obstructions to commercial intercourse, which were peculiar to the last war, and not, in all human probability, likely ever again to occur.
>
> (1838, I: 116–17)

The 'obstructions to commercial intercourse' mainly consisted of the continental blockade imposed by Emperor Napoleon of France as an integral part of his strategy to weaken Britain's economic capacity to prosecute war.[11] It also referred to wartime obstructions to British shipping routes and the loss of access to European markets for export as well as to trade disputes and war with the United States. These obstructions to British trade are pivotal to Tooke's explanation of the behaviour of prices over the course of these wars.

In the first place, Tooke held that, by raising the rates of freight and insurance of naval transport, obstructions to supply increased the cost of production of imported commodities over 'the whole period of the war' and particularly 'in the last six years of it amounted to an enormous charge on all importations from the continent of Europe' (1838, I: 115). While the resulting increase in transport charges was 'greatest' for foreign trade, Tooke ascertained that they also increased considerably for coastal trade, 'forming no inconsiderable item in the cost of all commodities, the more bulky ones especially, such as corn, coals, building materials, &c. conveyed coast-wise' (1838, I: 115). Aside from the additional risks of naval transport that particularly raised insurance premiums on shipped goods, Tooke (1838, I: 106, 309–11, 353) argued that freights were increased by the resort to 'circuitous routes' to elude the enemy, by more expensive methods of conveyance and by the reduction in shipping available for carrying on mercantile trade as a result of its appropriation for 'transports' in the conduct of naval war.[12] Later, Tooke (1857, V: 318–22) likewise attributed the sharp rise in freights in 1853 and 1854 to an increased demand for 'transports' in military service during the short-lived Crimean War. Another cause for increased freights during the long-running French Wars which Tooke (1838, I: 310–11n., 313) identified, was the higher cost of shipbuilding, largely the result of an increase in the price of imported building materials, especially timber. To justify the higher price of merchant ships, owners naturally required an increased rate of return obtained through higher freight charges. Thus, Tooke believed that high naval transport costs contributed considerably to persistent price inflation in England over the course of the French Wars.

Second, wartime obstructions to supplies of imported commodities as well the export of commodities to foreign, principally European markets, are prominent in Tooke's explanation of price fluctuations during the French Wars and, to a lesser extent, during the Crimean War. Anti-commercial measures that disrupted Britain's foreign trade were considered by Tooke to affect general prices over the course of the French Wars by, on the one hand, inducing shortages of imported commodities that the country was 'in need of' and, on the other hand, inducing gluts of export (or re-export) commodities deprived of foreign demand. In Tooke's explanation, the wartime effects on supply clearly predominated in contributing to price inflation. Thus, Tooke (1838, I: 188–91, 224–5, 235–6) ascertained that the prices of commodities from Northern Europe, especially hemp, flax, iron and timber which constituted 'naval stores', rose over the period 1796–1801, largely as a result of competing war demand by France and Britain, an 'embargo by Russia' and threats to shipping routes by a hostile Denmark. Tooke (1838, I: 236–8) held that, as a result of the Peace of Amiens, these obstructions to supply were temporarily removed, thereby facilitating a decline in the prices of these imports over the period 1801–1803.[13] However, according to Tooke (1838, I: 290), the most acute and sustained constriction on the supply of raw material imports occurred with the effective imposition of Napoleon's continental system of prohibition under the Berlin and Milan decrees of 1806 and 1807, respectively, compounded by trade disputes with the United States. Having been 'excluded from direct commercial intercourse with every country in Europe, Sweden excepted' Tooke (1838, I: 273) maintained that shortages led to considerable increases in the prices of 'every article of European produce, required as raw materials for our manufactures, or as naval stores' from 1807 to early 1809. He showed that in the same years growing trade disputes with the United States led to hikes in the prices of tobacco and cotton imports (1838, I: 275).

Tooke (1838, I: 300–1) argued that in subsequent years European traders, in connivance with their state authorities and assisted by the British government, were induced to circumvent Napoleon's blockade by the 'enormous high range of prices' that could be gotten for their products in England. In this argument Tooke (1838, I: 339–40) revealed a strong appreciation of the need for prices to rise well in excess of those prevailing in European markets to cover the exorbitant costs (and risks) of illegal naval transport. The resulting supply of foreign commodities, especially from northern Europe, relieved the domestic market and led to a 'very great fall in price' in the years 1809 to 1811. This was followed by a return to shortages and high prices of European imports from late-1811 to late-1812, which Tooke (1838, I: 340–1) attributed to the 'cutting off' of supplies from Northern Europe by the French occupation of Prussia and 'preparations' for the invasion of Russia. The subsequent decline in their prices in 1813 and 1814 was attributed by Tooke (1838, I: 343–4, 374–5) to the 'opening up of the ports' in Europe which, following Napoleon's military defeat in Russia, marked the breakdown of the continental blockade. In contrast, Tooke (1838, I: 343; II: 9) pointed to the high range of prices for American imports, in particular, cotton, during the 1812–1814 war with the United States. Hence, political events that affected the supply of imported commodities from Europe and across the Atlantic from America and the West Indies featured prominently in Tooke's analysis of prices over the period of the French Wars. In a similar way, Tooke held that the 'stoppage of trade with Russia raised the price of several important Raw Materials of manufacture' (1857, V: 308) during the Crimean War of the 1850s.

In relation to his explanation of the general price level, Tooke's view of the effect on corn prices of war-induced obstructions to foreign supplies was critical. For Tooke, their effect depended on seasonal conditions which determined whether or not England became reliant on imported corn. Therefore, Tooke maintained that obstructions to supply only came to the fore in raising corn prices during the French Wars when unproductive seasons at home 'made us dependent on other countries for an adequate supply of food' (1838, I: 117). Over the course of the French Wars, Tooke (1838, I: 180–3, 213–19, 265–72, 293–300, 319–28) identified 1795–1796,[14] 1799–1801 and 1808–1812 as years of scarcity in which political obstructions to foreign supplies, principally from northern Europe, caused extraordinary rises in corn prices. According to Tooke (1838, I: 117), it was because of the 'succession of unfavourable seasons' in British agriculture that these obstructions led to a very high range of prices of corn (and provisions generally) over the period of the French Wars. Tooke's position accords with the view that Napoleon's continental blockade provided effective agricultural protection to the landed interest of England and Ireland (Hilton 1977: 3–4).

On the demand side, Tooke believed wartime obstructions that closed off foreign markets to Britain induced downturns in the price of manufacturing exports and raw material re-exports. Tooke (1838, I: 273) maintained that 'by narrowing the channels for export' the continental blockade had brought about 'a ruinously low range of prices' for these tradable commodities. Having been denied their European markets, Tooke ascertained that in 1806 and 1807 there occurred an 'extreme' depression in the prices of '[S]ugar and coffee, and some other articles of Colonial produce' (1838, I: 272–3). The prices of these commodities recovered somewhat in 1808 when, as Tooke put it, 'the virtual emancipation of the colonies of Spain from the control of the mother country, opened the trade of a great part of South America' (1838, I: 276). Tooke (1838, I: 316–17) ascertained that with the subsequent reduction of foreign demand from this source, the prices of exports again declined from 1809 to late-1811. He also ascertained that the loss of traditional markets in the United States as a result of war with that country exerted a depressing effect on the prices of exports in 1811 and 1812 (1838, I: 345–6). According to Tooke (1838, I: 317, 345–8), it was with the breakdown of the continental blockade and a renewal of trade with Europe that the prices of export commodities permanently recovered in 1813 and 1814.

Faced with inflated prices for raw materials and an uncertain export market for their products, Tooke's analysis embraced the view that during the French Wars obstructions to foreign trade had an adverse influence on much of the manufacturing industry not connected with military and naval supply. Aside from the French Wars, fundamental changes in the 'state of politics' which affected foreign demand was taken account of by Tooke. Thus, in explaining the upturn in the price of tradable products in 1824 and 1825, Tooke (1826: 42–3; 1838, II: 140–54) emphasised the importance of the opening up of new markets for export in South America after the independence of many of its states from Spanish colonial rule. Similarly, as already mentioned, Tooke (1857, V: 230–7) believed the disruption to export trade caused by European revolution contributed significantly to a depression in the price of manufacturing products (and foreign produced re-exports) in 1848 and 1849.

There are two important aspects in the role assigned by Tooke to political obstructions to foreign trade in explaining the fluctuation in the price level. First, these obstructions became the subject of speculative activity by traders in commodity markets. In relation to wartime obstructions to supply discussed above, Tooke (1838, I: 272–5, 339–41) maintained that the 'prospect of scarcity' usually 'excited' a 'spirit of speculation', which caused sharp rises in the prices of imported commodities so affected. Hence, Tooke argued that, after the Milan decree in 1807, which tightened the continental blockade against Britain:

> The prospect of scarcity [of European produce] thus held out, naturally excited a spirit of speculation; and in proportion as that prospect became realised, was the speculative demand extended through different periods in 1808, and the early part of 1809, when the obstructions to importation, from the political causes, nearly reached their height.
>
> (1838, I: 273–4)

Tooke (1838, I: 276–7, 344–8) pointed out that speculative increases in prices also occurred when there was a prospect that foreign markets would be re-opened for export by the removal of wartime obstructions. In particular, Tooke (1838, II: 5–7) argued that the spectacular rise in prices of 'exportable produce and manufactures' in 1813 and 1814 was the result of speculation 'founded upon the most unwarranted expectations of demand *in consequence of the peace*, and of the renewal of commercial intercourse with the Continent'. For Tooke, speculative activity of this kind usually spread across a wide range of commodities, causing a general upturn in prices, but which was inevitably followed by 'overstocking' and a collapse in the markets. It was because political obstructions were conducive to speculative activity by traders in commodity markets that Tooke believed they tended to induce price instability.

Second, associated with the general movement in prices, there were significant changes in the relative prices of commodities according to the nature of the political obstructions to foreign trade. This is evident in much of Tooke's analysis of the effect of obstructions on prices over the course of the French Wars. The best example of this is provided in his following explanation of the diversity in movement of prices in 1813:

> As a still further illustration of the manner in which the anti-commercial character of the war and of the Continental system had operated on prices, it may be observed, that while corn and other European raw produce were falling, all articles of export, viz. West Indies, and generally all transatlantic, produce began to rise coincidently with the first tendency of the former to fall. The lowest point of depression of West India produce, and of other commodities, including manufactures, calculated from the markets of the Continent of Europe, and the United States, occurred at the close of 1811, and in the early part of 1812. All these articles experienced a moderate degree of improvement towards the close of 1812, with the exception of such descriptions as were exclusively or chiefly calculated were much depressed by the war which then broke.
>
> (Tooke 1838, I: 344–5)

Tooke's analysis shows that as a result of Napoleon's continental blockade and other disruptions to trade, there occurred a permanent rise in the prices of corn and other raw materials, especially non-substitutes necessary for military and naval stores produced in Europe, relative to all other commodities. It also shows that the prices of 'colonial produce', mainly from the West Indies, rose in relation to manufacturing exports. Thus, Tooke's analysis shows that persistent inflation in the general level of money prices during the French Wars corresponded with an unfavourable change in the terms-of-trade for British manufacturers of civilian goods, with the price of their exports declining in relation to the price of their raw material inputs.

5.3 On the effect of taxes and duties on prices

Over the twenty-year period of the French Wars there was a massive increase in British government expenditure. This was in part financed by heavy increases in taxation on income, on land and on a range of consumer items, including significant rises in custom duties on imported commodities.[15] In addition, an increase in unemployment and poverty led to a considerable rise in poor rates and tithes over this economically difficult period.[16] Moreover, as a legacy of the huge amount of government debt accumulated during the French Wars, successive governments were required in the following decades to maintain an enlarged system of taxes and duties in order to raise sufficient revenue to service this debt. For this reason, Tooke deals, albeit briefly, with the effect of taxes on general prices. Unfortunately, nowhere does he provide an explicit account of the

principles of taxation which underlie his position.[17] The following will endeav-
our to distil those principles from his writings and by reference to the analysis of
tax incidence by those classical writers which are likely to have had the most
influence on him.

From the outset, Tooke made the obvious point that the 'effects of taxation on
prices are liable to vary according to the mode in which the taxes are imposed'
(1824, ii: 146; also 1838, I: 87). With regard to 'income or property tax', Tooke
(1838, I: 87) asserted that providing they were 'equally levied upon all classes'
of society, these taxes would not tend to raise prices in general. This proposition
implied that when equally applied to wages, profit and rent, the burden of these
taxes fell directly on incomes without any significant change in general prices.
The most likely origin for this position was Adam Smith's treatment of *direct*
taxes in the *Wealth of Nations*. In relation to property taxes, Smith (1776 [1976]:
858–64) argued that they would fall unambiguously on its owners. However,
Tooke's position on income taxes will only accord with Smith (1776 [1976]:
864) on the assumption that 'wages of the inferior classes of workmen' are
largely excluded from its incidence. Adam Smith (1776 [1976]: 847–8, 869–71,
887–8) argued that while income tax on rent would fall on rent and, on profit,
would fall on the 'interest of money', on wages (applied directly or via a tax on
the 'necessaries' of workers), it would instead tend to raise money wages such
that it ultimately fell upon the 'superior ranks of people'. According to Smith
(1776 [1976]: 864–5), the resulting rise in money wages would in the case of
agricultural labour lead to a reduction in the rent of land and in the case of manufacturing labour lead to a rise in the price of 'consumable commodities'.[18]
Therefore, Smith conceived that in the case of manufacturing workers, a *direct*
tax on their wages would in the long run induce an increase in the price of manufactured commodities, by which its incidence was ultimately shifted onto other
classes.[19] In contrast, consistent with his tendency to treat the real wage as the
residual distributive variable, Tooke appears to have taken the view that a direct
tax on wages falls largely on wages. It then follows from Tooke's approach to
distribution examined in Section 3.3 that the application of income tax on wages
would tend to lower the real wage of workers, but with the proviso that the
lowest classes would be protected by the poor rates, involving some shift in tax
incidence predominantly onto landlords.

A more important consideration was the effect on prices of *indirect* taxes
levied on commodities, consisting of excise and custom duties. Tooke (1824, ii:
146; 1838, I: 87) contended that when levied 'upon particular commodities'
these taxes will have the 'effect of raising the price of those commodities' with
the price of 'manufactured articles' rising 'in some proportion to whatever tax
may be imposed on the raw materials' used in their production. Furthermore,
Tooke was perfectly aware that according to the complexity of input–output
relations of the production system, taxes on commodities which were the 'ingre-
dients or instruments of production' would 'have an indirect or circuitous effect
in raising the price of untaxed commodities' (1824, ii: 146; 1838, I: 87). He held
that the tax incidence would not apply equally to commodities, implying a

change in relative prices. The central proposition underlying Tooke's position was that new or additional indirect taxes would only increase the prices of those particular commodities whose costs of production were raised relative to other commodities. The prices of these commodities would be raised by magnitudes necessary to ensure that its producers obtained 'a profit equal to that derived from other productions' (1838, I: 88). In absence of an increase in prices to restore their rates of profit to the general rate, Tooke contended that producers of commodities upon which an unequal burden of indirect tax fell would reduce their levels of output. Tooke therefore maintained that a compensating rise in price was a condition for their continued supply. If the affected producers did not so directly raise prices, they would have been raised indirectly as a result of their 'diminished supply'. However, Tooke maintained that if taxes were applied 'nearly' equally to all industries there would be little effect on prices:

> if taxes on the instruments of production, as on corn, or other necessaries of the labourer, or on the materials composing machinery and the implements of husbandry, apply equally, or nearly equally, to all branches of industry, they cannot have the effect of raising the price of the produce to which they are applied; for, provided the power of reproducing in general be not impaired, there will be no inducement to withdraw capital from one occupation and to transfer it to another. An advance of price is not, under such circumstances, a condition of continued supply.
>
> (1824, ii: 147; also 1838, I: 88)

The implication of this position is that an increase in taxes on commodities will only raise the general level of money prices to the extent that they impose an unequal burden on producers. This position was first expressed by Tooke in his evidence before the Agricultural Committee of 1821. Asked by the committee for an opinion of the effect of taxes on the price of corn, Tooke stated 'that taxes, in as far as they are general, operate rather as a diminution of income, than as a condition of prices' (1821a: 292). Providing taxes were equally applied, Tooke argued that they would not lead to a general rise in prices such as to impair the international competitiveness of a country.[20] Therefore, for the purposes of raising government revenue, Tooke (1821a: 291) believed the system of custom and excise duties should aim to equalise the burden of taxation on industry. Consistent with his principles of free trade, Tooke (1821a: 291–3) advocated that protective duties should be imposed on tradable commodities in a way that would compensate for any disproportionate burden of taxation necessary to provide 'existing' government revenue.[21] Moreover, it is apparent that by tax equalisation Tooke is referring not only to indirect taxes, but to income taxes and all other taxes that compose the taxation system as a whole. This raises some puzzling questions about the principles of tax incidence which lay behind Tooke's position.

The notion mentioned above that, providing they are equally applied, taxes on commodities will fall on the profits of producers without any rise in prices, gains little justification from the writings of influential classical economists. It is probable that Tooke developed the notion from a misunderstanding of Adam Smith's distinction between the incidence of a 'general' and a 'particular' tax on the profits of industry. Whereas Smith (1776 [1976]: 855–8) maintained that a general tax on profit would fall on interest, a tax 'imposed on the profits of stock in a particular branch of trade' would in the case of manufacturers result in a rise in the price of their goods so that the impost would be passed onto consumers and, in the case of farmers, it would be passed onto landlords in the form of lower rent. With respect to manufacturers, Smith argued that in response to a 'particular' tax there would be a withdrawal of 'stock' and a reduction in supply until prices rose to levels that would restore their rates of profit to pre-existing levels. However, with respect to agriculture, Adam Smith argued that farmers, tied by leasehold to a fixed quantity of land, had no interest in diminishing their production to raise prices and hence, were only able to restore their profits by paying less rent to landlords. It appears Tooke agreed with Smith that, unlike manufacturers, farmers had no capacity for price-setting to pass on tax incidence, but mainly on the grounds that agricultural prices were largely determined by natural forces (see Sections 4.1–4.3).

Importantly, Tooke seems to have applied these principles generally to all kinds of taxes. Yet Smith was clearly referring here to a direct tax on profits and *not* an indirect tax on 'consumable commodities'. In relation to the latter, Smith (1776 [1976]: 869–906) contended that it would raise the price of manufactured goods irrespective of whether or not it was generally applied. Moreover, Smith indicated that as a result of the 'real necessaries of life' being so taxed, there was likely to be a series of price–wage increases with the burden ultimately passed from workers and manufacturers to landlords and 'rich consumers'. Only in the case of agricultural commodities would the indirect tax be passed backwards to landlords in lower rent. Hence, in contrast to Tooke's apparent position, Adam Smith believed that a generally applied increase in indirect taxes would cause an incalculable rise in general prices. It is only on the unrealistic assumption that all 'necessaries' so taxed are agricultural commodities that, consistent with Smith's principles, Tooke could claim their incidence would not raise prices. However, this is hardly consistent with Tooke's argument in the passage quoted above. Furthermore, as Ricardo (1821: 156–72) clearly showed in contradiction to Smith, an indirect tax on 'raw produce' would in the first instance be passed forward onto consumers by farmers in higher natural prices.[22] In all, Tooke's implausible position points to an unsatisfactory treatment of tax incidence and reflects his weakness in the analysis of distribution (for a contemporaneous criticism of Tooke's position, see Blake 1823: 40–2). The confused nature of his position on tax incidence is flagged by his own empirically based conclusions on the effect of increases in taxation on the general price level in Britain during the French Wars.

On the grounds that the increase in taxes raised by the British government during the French Wars were applied nearly equally to 'all branches of industry' in England, Tooke (1824, ii: 147; 1838, I: 88) contended that they did not

operate to raise prices in general. Since this contention could not be easily verified, Tooke fell back on another argument. He claimed that, even if there was
some rise in prices as a result of the unequal imposition of taxes during the
French Wars, the continuation of this tax burden in peacetime from 1815 to
1822, a period when the general level of prices in England significantly declined,
was evidence of its weak explanatory force (Tooke 1824, ii: 147–8; 1838, I:
88–9).[23] But, in contradiction to this argument, Tooke (1838, II: 225) identified
as a cause of the 'dearness of many articles of general consumption' in the
wartime period of 1799 to 1801, the 'heavy duties of excise' imposed on a broad
range of 'necessaries'. Tooke's contention above is also contradicted in his later
analysis of the systematic effect on prices of the removal of taxes largely connected with the free-trade reforms of the 1840s and 1850s:

> The effects produced by Free Trade on the general range of the Prices of
> nearly all Commodities in this country have extended much farther than the
> cheapening of the cost to the Consumer by the mere amount of the Customs
> or Excise Duty abated or repealed. The Consumer has not only had the full
> benefit of the reduced or abandoned duty, but he has, year by year, in an
> accelerating ratio, the greater benefit arising from the operation, on the
> largest scale, of the new and powerful influence of Production, of certainty
> on the part of Producers that no intricate, obsolete, oppressive, or fluctuating
> fiscal policy, stood between them and the great body of customers upon
> whom they relied for a remunerative market.
>
> (Tooke and Newmarch 1857, V: 391–2)

Hence, in this instance, Tooke and Newmarch (1857, V: 449–51) held that by
inducing a lowering in the prices of articles of consumption, a general reduction
in custom duties and excise, raised the real incomes of the working classes as
well as the 'general community'. He argued that this led to an increased consumption of 'articles of comfort and luxury', consisting mainly of imports, associated with an expansion in the country's trade. It was for this reason Tooke and
Newmarch (1857, V: 452–7) believed there was an increase in government
revenue following this reduction in the scale of taxes. In addition, as shown in
Section 4.4, Tooke maintained that with Britain having become dependent on
imported grain, the repeal of the Corn Laws in 1846 contributed thereafter to a
permanent lowering in the price of provisions. Hence, the shortcomings of
Tooke's apparent position on the effect of taxes on the general level of prices are
exposed by his own empirical findings.

5.4 On the effect of government expenditure and war finance on prices

The enormous increase in British government expenditure during the French
Wars placed a considerable strain on public finances. It has been estimated that
over £1,500 million had to be raised in taxes and loans to finance Britain's

long-running war effort against France.[24] In particular, public debt increased by an unprecedented £500 million over the period 1793 to 1815 to reach a level of £745 million, imposing a lasting burden on fiscal policy. Indeed, until the mid-nineteenth century, the annual charges on public debt accounted for over 50 per cent of British government revenue.[25] The British government was enabled in its fund-raising only by the continued expansion in the economy throughout the wars. Viewed in conjunction with the post-war depression that extended from 1816 until 1822, the comparative buoyancy of the wartime economy provided a priori evidence to some political economists that high government expenditure actually helped to sustain economic activity and, through its generation of demand pressures, contributed significantly to price inflation during the wars.

Of these political economists, the 'ablest advocate' of the 'doctrine of the great influence of a government expenditure defrayed by loans, on general prices' (Tooke 1824, ii: 163n.) was William Blake in his pamphlet, *Observations of the Effects produced by the Expenditure of Government during the Restriction of Cash Payments*, published in 1823.[26] No doubt influenced by Malthus's position that aggregate production depended on demand, Blake (1823) set out the most comprehensive argument for attributing the wartime rise in the price level largely to an 'extra demand' induced by the 'enormous' increase in debt-financed government expenditure. In a new section added to the second edition of *High and Low Prices* (1824) titled 'Examination of the Effect of the Stimulus or Excitement supposed to have been occasioned by the Government Expenditure during the late War', Tooke (1824, ii: 183–5) critically appraised Blake's argument. He also replied to some criticisms made by Malthus (1823) that were supportive of Blake's position in a review of the first edition of *High and Low Prices* (1823).

Tooke (1823, ii: 7–8; 1824, ii: 149–50; 1838, I: 90–2) began his examination by outlining what he regarded were the essential elements of the argument that high government expenditures during wars created an 'extra demand' which, in the process of stimulating additional aggregate production, induced an increase in 'general prices'. First, government expenditure for 'naval and military purposes' created a 'new source of demand' that directly raised the prices of naval and army 'stores'. Second, the prices of corn and other necessaries were raised by the 'additional consumption' of 'men composing the fleets and armies'. Third, the increased demand for labour, not only for 'seamen and soldiers', but also for workers employed in military supply industries and indirectly, for other civilian industries, induced a persistent advance in 'wages in general', increased the population and, thereby, increased the consumption of the 'labouring classes'. In this way, war expenditure by the government would 'vivify every branch of industry' and 'stimulate' a 'general increase of production'. With peace and the withdrawal of 'extra demand' this process was seen to operate in reverse, inducing depressed prices, a reduction in aggregate production (and consumption) and 'distress among the producing classes'. Tooke set out to rebut this argument essentially on the basis of 'Say's Law' ('Mr. Mill's Principle') to which he clearly declared his adherence:[27]

I fully concur in the doctrine laid down by Mr. Mill, who, in his Chapter on Interchange (Elements of Political Economy) proves with great clearness and force of reasoning that *aggregate* of demand must always be equal to the *aggregate* of supply.

(1823, iv: 5n.)

The equality between aggregate supply and aggregate demand is conceived by Tooke to correspond with equilibrium conditions in which the supplies of all commodities are adjusted to their effectual demands such that the 'cost of production must regulate the price of all commodities on the average of a certain number of years' (1823, iv: 5n.). This conception lay behind the following criticism by Tooke of the doctrine that war-demand raises prices in general:

The fallacy of this doctrine, which represents a general elevation of prices, both of commodities and labour, to be a necessary consequence of a state of war, proceeds (and cannot otherwise than so proceed) on the supposition that the money expended by the government consists of funds distinct from and over and above any that before existed; whereas, it is perfectly demonstrable, that any expenditure by government, whether defrayed by immediate taxes to the whole amount, or by loan on the anticipation of taxes to be levied, is nothing but a change in the mode of laying out the same sum of money; and that what is expended by government would and must have been laid out by individuals upon objects of consumption, productive or unproductive.

(1823, ii: 8–9; also 1824, ii: 150–1 and 1838, I: 92)

Tooke was mainly concerned to apply this argument to increased government expenditure financed by public debt rather than by taxes, since it was 'perfectly clear' that, with respect to the latter, 'whatever is expended by government must be exactly so much abstracted from what would otherwise have been the expenditure by individuals' (1823, ii: 10–11; also 1824, ii: 152; 1838, I: 94). For the purposes of argument, Tooke also ruled out an increase in government expenditure financed by an increase in the quantity of paper money which, implicitly, he acknowledged could induce 'extra demand'.[28]

Foreshadowing a point made by Blake (1823: 54), Tooke (1823, ii: 9; 1824, ii: 151; 1838, I: 92) fully acknowledged that any wartime expenditure by the government which used existing 'hoards' of 'treasure' would add to demand. However, he ruled out this possibility for practical purposes by supposing that the 'habit of hoarding' was not very extensive. Moreover, Tooke (1823, ii: 12; 1824, ii: 152–3; 1838, I: 95) intimated that, if anything, the expenditure of funds by the government unproductively on war which could have otherwise been laid out 'reproductively', adversely affected the 'quantum of production'. In accordance with the conventional position of classical economists, Tooke maintained that supposing 'aggregate supply to be undiminished by war' (1823, ii: 12; also 1824, ii: 153; 1838, I: 95), the increase in government expenditure 'would not and could not' increase 'the sum total of demand' (1823, ii: 9; also 1824, ii: 151; 1838, I: 93). Instead, it would alter the structure of demand causing a 'disturbance of the proportion of the prices of commodities, relatively to each other, and relatively also to the price of labour' (1838, I: 93). The price of those 'articles' needed for the purposes of prosecuting war 'which might suddenly be the objects of government demand would rise' while 'those articles which would, but for the war, have been purchased by individuals, from the fund which is withdrawn from them, would experience an equivalent fall' (1823, ii: 9–10; also 1824, ii: 151; 1838, I: 93). Therefore, Tooke (1823, ii: 12–13; 1824, ii: 152–3; 1838, I: 94–6) maintained that this change in relative prices caused by the increase in debt-financed government expenditure did not entail any significant increase in the general price level.

To support his position, Tooke (1823, ii: 13–21; 1824, ii: 153–61; 1838, I: 96–100) appealed to evidence of price movements in 'former wars'. By reference to the prices of wheat, meat and other provisions, he showed that, historically, from 1688 to 1792, there is 'no observable coincidence of a rise of price during the war, and a fall during peace' (Tooke 1824, ii: 153; also 1838, I: 97). He also provided historical evidence that showed that there was no tendency for war to raise the wages of labour in general (Tooke 1823, ii: 19–20; 1824, ii: 160; 1838, I: 98–9). However, in the French Wars, both prices and money wages in general rose. Invoking the arguments of Say's Law, as previously defined, Tooke denied this was due to any 'extra' aggregate demand. As indicated above, Tooke (1823, ii: 22–4; 1824, ii: 162–4; 1838, I: 100–2) maintained that there was a fundamental change in the structure of demand, consisting of a shift from private to public expenditures, which brought about a corresponding alteration in the composition of output (or supply) away from the production of civilian commodities towards the production of war provisions. In the short run, the lagged adjustment of supply to a 'sudden' additional demand may well cause the price of war provisions to rise considerably, contributing to inflationary pressures. The effect on the general price level largely depended on the offsetting reduction in the prices of civilian 'consumables' whose effectual demands declined in relation to their pre-existing supplies.

According to Tooke (1823, ii: 28–39; 1824, ii: 168–73; 1838, I: 103–4), in the long run, when supply adjusted itself to the new structure of effectual demand, the sustained increase in government expenditures during the French Wars had little effect on the general level of prices. Instead, as shown in Section 5.2, Tooke believed the main cause of the persistent price inflation was the war-induced obstructions to foreign supply, especially for those military provisions whose demand by the British government had permanently increased. Entirely consistent with this line of argument, Tooke (1838, I: 98–9n.) also denied there was any additional demand for labour as a whole which induced a rise in the 'general price of labour' during the French Wars. He appears to have agreed with McCulloch (1830: 489), whom he quotes approvingly, that the increased demand for workers arising from government expenditure during the wars represented a '*substitution* only for the demand which would otherwise have existed by individual employers' (1830: 489). Hence, while aggregate employment was unaffected by the wars, its composition shifted from civilian industries to those of the government. This is consistent with Tooke's view that, due to the strong demand for labour, the money wages of workers employed in the military effort rose relatively to the wages of other workers employed in the civilian industries which were in relative decline throughout the French Wars.

Tooke's arguments accorded with the orthodox position articulated best by Ricardo (1821: 290) that 'demand is only limited by production' and stood against Malthus's (1820: 351–75) alternative position that production could be checked by a want of effective demand. However, as indicated above, Tooke invoked Say's Law as a long-period position which therefore encompassed persistent conditions in the economy consistent with the operation of competition. Tooke therefore did not rule out the possibility of an excess in aggregate demand or a general glut *in the short-run*. The point is that this phenomenon was seen by Tooke to be only temporary, associated with disequilibria in the economy when *market* prices deviated from normal values. Hence, Tooke (1823, ii: 29–30) conceded that, with the 'breaking out' of the French Wars, the 'suddenness' of the increase in demand for war materials in relation to supply could induce a temporary upturn in general prices. Tooke (1824, ii: 205) appears also to have believed that, with the transition from war to peace, there occurred a short-lived 'glut' of commodities in 1815 and 1816. But Tooke objected strongly to the 'inference' by Blake (1823: 91) that due to the 'cessation of war demand' a general excess supply could persist from 1815 until 1822: 'Now I will venture to say that a glut of ten, or even of nine years continuance, is wholly at variance with all mercantile experience' (1824, ii: 204).[29] It follows that Tooke rejected the notion that capital accumulation could be limited in the *long run* by a deficiency of demand. This was the notion lying behind Blake's position.

Blake (1823) attacked the orthodox position that Tooke stood by on the grounds that it logically failed to explain England's 'prosperity and wealth' during the French Wars. Given that war expenditures involved the consumption (or 'destruction') of capital, Blake (1823: 43–54) begged the following question: How was it possible for a given fund of capital to be successively diverted from productive to unproductive employment without leading to a serious slowdown in the nation's accumulation of capital over the long period of the French Wars? It led Blake to conclude that 'savings were actually accumulating simultaneously with the [increased] expenditure of government' (1823: 55). He argued that as a result of the increase in aggregate demand generated by debt-financed government expenditure, capital that had remained unutilised in peacetime was fully employed in reproduction during the wars.[30] Moreover, Blake (1823: 68–70) contended that this process was associated with an increased demand for workers and, thereby, fuller employment of the population, which, inducing higher wages, contributed to a stronger 'effective demand' for consumer products.

According to Blake, government expenditure, through the stimulus of demand, enabled the fuller utilisation of capital in reproduction, increasing the 'progress' of capital accumulation and generating additional savings that more than offset its debt funding requirements. This is very similar to Malthus's argument that 'owing to the union of great powers of production with great consumption and demand, the prodigious destruction of capital by the government was much more than recovered' (1820: 493). However, distinct from Malthus, Blake (1823: 42–78) believed that in the civilian sphere of production, the increase in wartime demand induced a greater shift in the employment of capital from 'unproductive' purposes to 'reproduction', thereby contributing to the capital accumulation process.[31] In comparison, Tooke (1823, ii: 48–9; 1824, ii: 209; 1838, I: 115–16) contended that the wartime growth in the British economy during the French Wars was largely attributable to productivity growth and an increased propensity to save by the community sufficient to offset the capital funds consumed by the government. Given that saving was conceived by all these economists to be identical to investment, the difference between Malthus and Blake, on the one side, and Tooke, on the other side, rested on whether an increase in savings involved a reduction in consumption as a proportion of 'revenue' (net income) or an increase in 'revenue' in proportion to the capital stock from which higher savings could be drawn. Whereas the orthodox position of Tooke involved an increase in saving through a proportionate reduction in consumption out of 'revenue', the position of Blake and Malthus involved an increase in 'revenue' and, thereby, savings, in proportion to the capital stock, achieved through increased effective demand.

In consideration of these debates concerning Say's Law, it should be kept in mind that the classical economists in common did not distinguish between decisions to invest and decisions to save, which is a necessary basis for a substantive theory of aggregate output. Indeed, as Garegnani (1983a: 24–8) has shown, the Say's Law of classical economists was the result of a lack of any investment-saving analysis and theory of output (see also Milgate 1982: 46–57). Say's Law represented the truism to classical economists, including Tooke, that at long period equilibrium positions in which natural prices were established by competition, aggregate demand was equal to aggregate production, corresponding to a given stage of accumulation of the economy. This followed from the equality between the demand for and supply of commodities in all markets when prices are conceived to conform to their natural values at long period equilibrium.

This notion of Say's Law of the classical economists is very different to that connected with marginalist economics in which demand can play no logical role in the determination of aggregate output in long-period equilibrium.[32] First, in marginalist economics there is a coherent theory of output, based as it is on the aggregate production function, which incorporates an investment-saving analysis. As is well-known, in this theory investment adjusts to saving through changes in the rate of interest. Second, through adjustment in the real wage as well as in the rate of interest, the equilibrium level of output determined in the marginalist theory is characterised by the full-employment of labour as well as of capital. Hence, whereas Say's Law in marginalist economics is firmly based on a coherent theory of output which excludes demand from having any significant long-run role, Say's Law in classical economics stems from the absence of any coherent theory of output. In addition, as previously indicated in Section 3.6, for the classical economists, with their very different theoretical approach, adopting Say's Law did not imply a belief that the rate of accumulation would be such that at long period equilibrium positions a full-employment level of output would be routinely established. Indeed, they considered unemployment to be a normal social phenomenon, though varying according to the rate of accumulation that generated the growth in labour demand. Furthermore, the Say's Law adopted by the classical economists did not rule out a significant role for demand in the accumulation process. To begin with, the output of individual commodities is conceived by the classical economists to be determined by the level of their effectual demand (see Section 3.1). More important still, as explained in our discussion on free trade (in Section 3.6), after Adam Smith, classical economists did believe that demand played a significant role in promoting the accumulation process, chiefly through the expansion in the global market. This belief derived from Adam Smith's well-accepted notion that the 'extension of the market' facilitates greater specialisation and, thereby, productivity growth (Aspromourgos 2009: 138–40). Notwithstanding that this notion does not by any means constitute a substantive theory, it does show that there is no reason why from the standpoint of classical economics demand cannot be supposed to play a leading role in explaining economic growth.

The problem for Malthus and Blake, who argued that demand was a constraint to growth, is that they did not have a coherent theory of output to substantiate their argument. Their arguments therefore ultimately relied on empirical verification which was highly contestable ground. It was largely to explain the stagnation in the British economy that followed the French Wars that Malthus (1820: 490–522) and Blake (1823) formulated their argument that the reduction in government expenditure from its high wartime levels caused the 'stagnation in effectual demand' which induced a slowdown in capital accumulation and persistent unemployment of labour. A major contention of their argument was that the rate of increase of population, production and consumption was greater during the French Wars than in the post-war period from 1815 to 1822. Tooke vehemently objected to this empirical contention and was particularly concerned to answer Malthus (1823), who had taken issue with him in the first edition of *High and Low Prices* (1823) on these grounds. In the second edition of this work, Tooke (1824, ii: 185–203) presented statistical evidence showing that the growth rates of population, production and consumption were significantly greater in peacetime than during the French Wars.[33] He acknowledged that by causing 'the loss of capital, [the] disturbance of the ordinary channels of industry, and the uncertainty as to the eventual subsidence of prices' (1824, ii: 205), the transition from war to peace resulted in a temporary depression of the economy in 1815 and 1816. However, Tooke attributed the persistence of low prices over the following six years instead to improved conditions of domestic production and the absence of political obstructions to foreign supply. Afterwards, with the benefit of more history, Tooke (1838, I: 111–12) argued that, in comparison to the long period of the French Wars, there was considerable evidence to show that there was much greater progression in the 'prosperity and wealth' of the country in the twenty-two-year period of peace that followed.[34] Tooke (1823, ii: 27–8; 1824, ii: 166–7; 1838, I: 103–4) maintained that 'but for the war' the prosperity of the country, especially of its 'labouring classes', would have been greater. To believe otherwise, would, according to Tooke, lead to the 'monstrous' conclusion 'that perpetual war would be attended with perpetual prosperity' (1826: 9).

Although Tooke rejected the doctrine of war-demand, he nevertheless believed debt-financed government expenditure exerted a persistent influence on the general level of prices during and after the French Wars through an altogether different route. As will be shown in Section 6.3, in Tooke's theory of interest, the rate of interest will be higher the greater the proportion of 'monied capital' which is allocated to 'unproductive' borrowers such as the government. Tooke therefore attributed the high levels of interest that persisted throughout the French Wars and afterwards to the war finance policy of the British government. In conjunction with the conception that the rate of interest constitutes a cost of production of commodities, Tooke contended that the war-finance policy contributed towards higher price inflation. Hence, Tooke (1838, II: 347) argued that 'in consequence of the absorption by the war loans of a considerable proportion of the savings of individuals' there was a 'higher rate of interest' which, 'constituting an increased cost of production', contributed to higher 'general prices'.

5.5 On the effect of alterations in the system of currency on prices

The restriction of cash payments by the Bank of England from 1797 until resumption in 1821, the 'restriction period', gave rise to the bullionist controversies over the causes of the depreciation of the value of the currency (on these debates, see Viner 1937: 119–217; Fetter 1965: 26–63; Morgan 1965: 23–74). Closely connected to the depreciation of the pound sterling, the controversies were concerned also with the causes of price inflation in Britain which, at times, exceed 20 per cent per annum. An important factor underlying the controversies was that the currency depreciations and bouts of high price inflation coincided with the period of the French Wars, 1793–1801 and 1803–1815. The bullionist writers, led by Thornton (1811: 325–35) and Ricardo (1811a; 1811b: 214–21, 236–44),[35] argued that the price inflation and the depreciation of the paper currency were predominantly the result of an excess issue of paper money (i.e. banknotes) made possible only by its inconvertibility into specie. They attributed this excess issue of paper money to the Bank of England, contending that its accommodating monetary policy facilitated an expansion of banknotes by country banks (Thornton 1802: 208–29; 1811: 328–30; Wheatley 1803: 204–30; Huskisson 1810: 26–40, 106–8; Mushet 1811: 21–7, 33–6; Ricardo 1811a: 86–8; 1811b: 227–35; and also the Bullion Report 1810; Cannan 1925: 16–17, 36–9, 61–7).

The bullionists pointed to the premium of the market price of gold over its official mint price as evidence of the extent of the depreciation of paper currency to what it would otherwise have been under a system of strict convertibility at the 1797 metallic standard. There were differences among the bullionists that chiefly revolved around the extent to which real disturbances to the balance of payments and the foreign exchanges such as government remittances abroad or wartime disruptions to trade could contribute towards the depreciation of the currency. The most uncompromising were Wheatley (1803: 89–91; 1807: 175–82, 227–59) and Ricardo (1811a: 59–64), who minimised the influence of these real disturbances and maintained that any such effects could occur only as a result of an accommodating monetary policy.[36] A more moderate position was taken by Thornton (1802: 143–5, 151–60), Huskisson (1810: 139–41), Malthus (1811: 342–5) and most other bullionists, who acknowledged that in wartime these real disturbances could depress the foreign exchanges which no monetary policy action could counteract. Some moderate bullionists, especially Thornton (1802: 197–229), accepted that the quantity of country banknotes and credit instruments could in the short run be influenced by demand according to prices and economic activity. Nevertheless, under restriction they believed that in the long run the Bank of England, through the regulation of its issue of banknotes, could exogenously determine the quantity of paper money in circulation.[37]

The anti-bullionists tended to be defenders of the Bank of England and the war finance policy of the government. They included Boase (1804; 1811), Bosanquet (1810), Trotter (1810), Herries (1811), Hill (1810) and the parliamentary speeches of long-time Chancellor of the Exchequer, Nicholas Vansittart (1811).[38] These writers generally argued that the depreciation in the currency was attributable to an adverse balance of payments, due especially to government payments (mainly in gold) abroad in prosecution of the French Wars and to large imports of corn after unproductive domestic harvests (Boase 1804: 19–23; Bosanquet 1810: 22–3, 38–48, 97–102; Trotter 1810: 46–56; Hill 1810: 40–9; Herries 1811: 41–53). In answer to the bullionists' claim that the premium on gold was clear evidence of a persistent depreciation of the paper currency, anti-bullionists argued that in fact it was the international value of gold (and silver) that had increased with the rise in its wartime demand (Boase 1804: 24–6; Bosanquet 1810: 19–32; Trotter 1810: 44–51; Herries 1811).

Furthermore, the anti-bullionists denied the Bank of England could issue an excess amount of banknotes, arguing that they were issued by way of loans according to their demand. They contended that any unwanted banknotes in circulation would return to the Bank of England and other note-issuing banks. Although not well articulated, in this manner anti-bullionists such as Bosanquet (1810: 50–60), Trotter (1810: 10–22) and Boase (1804: 6–11; 1811: 57–61) groped towards a concept of endogenous money with a notion of reflux that was to be later developed by the banking school.[39] However, they did not successfully break from the entrenched view that the amount of paper currency on issue was exogenously determined by the discretionary policy of the Bank of England. Hence, when in evidence to the Bullion Committee of 1810, the directors of the

Bank of England invoked the so-called 'real bills' doctrine to deny that their monetary policy led to an excess issue of paper money and its depreciation, they invited considerable criticism from the bullionists.[40]

The debate shifted decisively in favour of the bullionist position with the Bullion Report of 1810, which recommended the resumption of cash payments within two years. At the end of the French Wars, policy-makers moved steadily towards bringing about a resumption of cash payments. By the time of resumption in 1821, the bullionist position had become dominant, especially among political economists. While there were ongoing criticisms of the establishment of a gold standard that went on for years afterwards, this was largely based on the ground that it had a depressing effect on prices and industry rather than on any anti-bullionist position. Tooke's own contribution to these monetary debates was belated, consisting only of his parliamentary evidence before the Resumption Committees of 1819 (see Section 6.1). Nevertheless, the main issues at dispute in those important debates figure prominently in Tooke's writings devoted to explaining prices during the restriction period.

Tooke was concerned with dealing with what he regarded was the commonly held view that the alteration in the system of currency that accompanied the restriction and then resumption of cash payments by the Bank of England was the *primary* cause of price movements in England over the period 1797 to 1837. Thus, in *High and Low Prices*, Tooke wrote:

> An opinion has arisen of late, and has been countenanced and spread by no mean authorities, that the paper was depreciated, not merely to the degree indicated by the rise of gold above the mint price, but to a much greater and almost indefinite extent; that, in fact, although other causes may have concurred in producing the elevation of general prices in this country between 1797 and 1814, and the decline since that period; such other causes, whether in detail or collectively, sunk into utter insignificance, compared with the alterations in the currency.
>
> (1823, i: 6–7; also 1824, i: 5)

And, then in the introduction to volume I of *History*:

> The preponderant, and almost exclusive theory, is that which refers all the phenomena of high prices from 1792 till 1819, and of the comparative low prices since 1819, to alterations in the system of our currency, holding all other circumstances that can have had any influence to be so subordinate as not to be worth mentioning.
>
> (1838, I: 2)

Tooke argued that alterations in the currency system were instead only a secondary cause of the movement in the general level of money prices. He contended that restriction of cash payments could only explain part of the price inflation occurring between 1797 and 1814, which was due to a depreciation of paper currency equal to the premium on the market price of gold over its mint price. According to the same reasoning, Tooke argued that the resumption of cash payments could only explain that part of the price deflation after 1821 which was associated with the official restoration of the value of paper currency to the pre-1797 gold standard.

In a methodical approach to the issues, Tooke set out criteria by which to determine and measure the causes of depreciation in the value of paper money that occurred during the restriction period. First, Tooke defined 'depreciation of money' to mean an 'increased *price* of all objects measured in money' which is caused by

> an increase of the quantity of money, and to be confined to an alteration, exclusively on the side of money; while the cost of production, and the supply relatively to the rate of consumption of commodities, are considered to be unaltered.
>
> (1838, I: 119)

This definition was conceived by Tooke to broadly encompass factors connected to the system of currency operating directly to lower the exchange value of money as distinct from 'real' factors operating directly to raise the exchange value of commodities in relation to the gold (and silver) standard. Thus, Tooke maintained that when applied to the 'world at large', the term 'depreciation of money' was 'synonymous with a diminished value of gold and silver among all countries, which are in communication by international exchanges' (1838, I: 120). In this connection, Tooke made reference to the 'discovery of the American mines' which had since 'diminished' the value of money 'throughout the commercial world' (1838, I: 120). Tooke also maintained that 'depreciation of money' equally applied to a 'particular country or state' in which the value of local currencies was depreciated by a 'diminished value of the precious metals, or by a degradation of the standard, or by an excessive issue of paper' (1838, I: 120). It was these three monetary causes of depreciation of the value of the pound sterling that Tooke was concerned to separately identify.

Second, and to this end, Tooke defined 'depreciation of the currency' to mean a state in which the 'coin is of less value in the market than, by the mint regulations, it purports to be' or in which 'the paper [currency], if compulsory current, is of less value than the coin in which it promises to be payable' (1838, I: 120). With respect to coin, Tooke contended that it would be depreciated and lead to higher money prices if the coinage was debased or if it was subject to seigniorage and 'not accompanied by a principle of limitation' which fixed the quantity of coin and paper in circulation.[41] Providing the coin was in a 'perfect state' and not subject to seigniorage, Tooke (1838, I: 122–3) maintained that in a free market for bullion where 'the exportation and melting of [coin] be allowed', it was not possible for the value of coin to fall below the mint price of gold. It followed then that in a convertible system of currency in which these conditions were satisfied, if the market price of gold was above its mint price the 'whole of the difference would constitute the exact measure of the depreciation of the paper'. However, this would not be the case if the export or melting of gold coin was prohibited by law, as it was during the restriction of cash payments. In this case, consistent with arbitrage, Tooke (1838, I: 122–3) held that the price of bullion could rise above the mint price by a magnitude that covered 'the risk of the penalty on the [illegal] export or melting' of coin.[42] He inferred that this magnitude could be no more than 1 per cent of the mint price.[43] On this basis, Tooke (1838, I: 123–4) contended that, after deducting this small magnitude, an 'excess of the market price above the mint price of gold' would 'exactly' measure the depreciation in the paper currency during the period of restriction.

Third, Tooke defined 'alterations in the value of the currency' to be 'variations in the combined value of bullion, and coin and paper, or, in other words, of the standard as well as of the coin and paper' (1838, I: 123–4). This definition is meant by Tooke to refer to a change in the purchasing power of paper currency (or coin) over commodities *other than* gold (and silver) as the standard, which may occur under the restriction of cash payments compared to the case under a convertible system of currency. Tooke's reasoning is as follows. Whereas under a convertible system of currency in which the value of paper is tied invariably to the gold standard and there is no debasement of the coin, a sustained depreciation of the currency could only arise from a reduction in the exchange value of gold (i.e. the 'standard'), under restriction it could *also* arise separately from an excess circulation of paper that reduced its value in relation to the mint price of gold. Given that for significant periods during restriction the market price of gold was above its mint price, the problem was determining whether this translated into a reduction in the above defined purchasing power of the currency. This depended on the extent to which there was any excess circulation of paper currency, on the one hand, and the direction and degree to which there was any simultaneous change in the exchange value of gold (with other commodities), on the other hand. The problem is illustrated by Tooke in the following example:

> For instance, if, while the market price of gold should be 10 per cent. above the mint price, indicating a depreciation of the paper, or coin, or both, to that extent, gold, or in other words, the standard itself, should from a great diminution of the produce of the mines, or from extended functions, (as for military purposes or hoarding, or for a circulation retarded by want of confidence and credit, or for a very general substitution of gold for paper,) become more valuable by 10 per cent., then although the currency would, according to the definition, be depreciated to that extent, i.e. be less in price than it ought legally to be, yet, the standard itself being increased in value in the same degree, there would be no alteration in the *value of the currency*. On the other hand, if ... the standard itself *gold* were, whether from increased produce or diminished functions, reduced in value likewise 10 per cent., I should say that the alteration in the *value* of the currency generally was to the extent of 20 per cent.
>
> (1838, I: 124–5)

Thus, only 'if the metal of which the standard is composed were assumed to be of a uniform value' was it possible to measure the depreciation in the value of the currency by the magnitude of an excess in the market price of gold over its mint price. However, since there was 'no infallible criterion' for measuring variations in the value of gold and therefore the 'bullion prices of commodities and labour', Tooke (1838, I: 125) argued that it could only be ascertained by appealing to circumstances that influenced the money prices of commodities and money wages 'independently of the supposition of any alteration in the quantity or rate of circulation of the currency'. In this way, Tooke distinguished clearly between those factors that affected the value of gold in relation to other commodities and those which affected the value of currency, principally paper currency, in relation to the gold standard. This distinction had been at the heart of the bullionist debates. It was the basis upon which Tooke proceeded to examine the various propositions supporting the argument that the value of the currency was depreciated by restriction and appreciated by the resumption of cash payments in a degree greater than the difference between the market price and the mint price of gold.

There were essentially three propositions that Tooke examined. The first consisted of the argument that as a result of the withdrawal and exportation of metals ('gold principally') from the internal circulation of England, the restriction induced a considerable reduction in the value of gold and silver on the international market. It was held that, with resumption, the absorption of metals from the international market into the internal circulation of the country subsequently raised their value (Tooke 1838, I: 130). Tooke first addressed this question in relation to the resumption of cash payments in evidence before the Agricultural Committee of 1821. Asked how much the value of gold had been raised since 1819 by 'preparations' by the Bank of England for the resumption of cash payments in 1821, Tooke (1821a: 296) replied, 'about six per cent' as measured in silver. However, Tooke made it clear that this estimate was based on the supposition that the increase in the relative price of gold to silver was not the result of a fall in the value of the latter. At the time he had no grounds for believing silver had varied in value.[44] However, shortly afterwards in *High and Low Prices* (1823, i: 36–42), Tooke revised his opinion. Based on new evidence of a considerable increase in the supply of silver to Europe from the East, he believed that the value of silver had in fact declined rather than gold having risen. Whereas prior to 1820 the trade balance was such that there was a net flow of silver from Europe to the East Indies and China, Tooke (1823, i: 37–9; 1838, I: 139–40) established that after 1820 there was a reversal in this trade balance and, thereby, in the flow of silver. Tooke believed that this variation in the value of silver relative to gold was a temporary phenomenon that accompanied cyclical changes in the balance of trade between Europe and the East and could not therefore be attributed to the permanent effect of alterations in Britain's system of currency. Thus Tooke ruled out changes in the value of gold relative to silver as evidence of the effect of alterations in the system of currency.

Tooke (1823, i: 35) proceeded in his inquiry to examine the influence of various factors connected with the alterations in the system of currency that had a persistent effect on the 'aggregate value' of gold and silver (i.e. precious metals). With reference to available evidence and influential opinion, Tooke (1823, i: 21–35; 1838, I: 130–6) argued that the quantity of precious metals which was added to the 'circulation of the rest of the commercial world' under restriction and then withdrawn under resumption had an insignificant effect on their value. He estimated that, after accounting for domestic hoarding, the amount of precious metals that was actually expelled from England during the restriction and returned with resumption was a 'sum of from twelve to fifteen millions' (1823, i: 25; 1838, I: 134) which, 'other things remaining the same', made 'little more than 1 per cent., and certainly not 2 per cent., difference in their value' (1823, i: 27; 1838, I: 135). However, Tooke argued that 'other things were not the same', and, in particular, during restriction there was 'a great and unusual demand for the precious metals' as a 'consequence of the wars on the Continent' (1838, I: 138). Tooke believed a large amount of specie was absorbed by the 'military chests and the treasuries of the belligerent powers' as well as by the 'very extensive practice of hoarding which prevailed among the inhabitants of those states of the Continent which were either the seat of war, or which had issued paper to excess' (1838, I: 138). In particular, Tooke ascertained that there was an intense demand for gold as a means of international debt settlement in the

> interval 1808 and 1813, when by the violent anti-commercial decrees and regulations of the French government, there was great difficulty and danger attending the transmission of bills of exchange, and when, in fact, commercial operations, depending on credit, were nearly suspended.
>
> (1823, i: 28)

Overall, Tooke (1838, I: 139; 1823, i: 27–30) appears to have agreed with those witnesses before the Bullion Committee of 1810, who argued that the large demand for specie, principally on the Continent, more than offset the 'utmost quantity spared from circulation as coin in this country' and the 'utmost rate of annual increase from the mines' to have caused an increased value of precious metals during the French Wars. According to Tooke (1838, I: 143), it followed 'by parity of reasoning' that with the reduction in the demand for precious metals for military purposes and for hoarding on the Continent which occurred after the wars, the domestic re-absorption of specie under resumption induced no greater effect in lowering the value of gold (and silver) than restriction had of raising it. Tooke thereby rejected the argument that restriction contributed to a permanent reduction in the value of gold (and silver) relative to commodities and that resumption had the inverse effect. As further elaborated below in this section (pp. 113–15), Tooke believed that it was events connected with the French Wars that had a significant effect on the value of gold rather than alterations in Britain's system of currency in the period 1797 to 1821.

The second proposition was that currency restriction induced both an increase in the 'economised use' of money and accommodated an expansion in credit facilities which, by supporting inflationary expenditures in the economy, contributed to the diminution in the value of the currency 'beyond the degree indicated by the difference between paper and gold'. The economisation of money was associated by Tooke (1823, i: 43–50) with a 'heightening' in the velocity of circulation of a *given* amount of money. The argument that it contributed to the depreciation of the currency was attributed by Tooke to the authors of the Report of the Bullion Committee of 1810, 'to account, consistently with their view, for the striking and rather puzzling fact of the very small numerical increase of Bank notes to which they ascribed such depreciating effects' (1838, I: 144n.). By way of examining this argument, Tooke identified two motives for the economised use of money. The first was the convenience of simplifying payments, a motive that Tooke claimed 'must exist more strongly in proportion as the currency consists in great part of coin' (1823, i: 44). The second motive was a high rate of interest that Tooke (1823, i: 46–7) believed, in particular, caused London bankers during the restriction period to adopt the 'practice' of borrowing banknotes from one another for 'only a few hours'. However, contrary to common opinion, Tooke believed the improved economisation of money during restriction was a reaction to conditions of scarcity (and, thereby, high bill rates) in the money market. Moreover, Tooke believed that the process of economising was an ongoing one which, irrespective of the system of currency, accompanied institutional improvements in the monetary system. Hence, Tooke (1838, I: 144–5) argued that for the economising of money to have contributed significantly to a depreciation of the currency during the restriction period, it would have to be shown that the process regressed upon resumption of cash payments.

In 1838, some seventeen years after resumption, Tooke (1838, I: 144–5) maintained that, in contrast, there had been a continual progress in 'economising practices' which accompanied further institutional improvements in the financial system.[45] He therefore dismissed the proposition that the economising of the currency contributed to a 'diminution' in its value under restriction and a 'subsequent increase' under resumption. With respect to an expansion in credit facilities, Tooke (1823, i: 50–4; 1838, I: 146–7) associated it with the 'substitution of credit for currency' which resulted in a 'multiplication of the circulating medium'. This was the basis of the argument that under restriction the system of currency accommodated an excessive issue of inconvertible banknotes by country banks which, thereby, depreciated the value of the currency. Tooke (1823, i: 54) held that this argument largely rested on the 'supposition that an excessive issue of country bank paper must of necessity have been an invariable concomitant of the excessive issue of Bank of England'. Tooke (1823, i: 60–1) disputed that country bankers were afforded additional facility of discount by London bankers and 'perpetual security' to lend funds under restriction. Tooke (1823, i: 61–2; 1838, I: 148–52) also disputed that restriction induced an expansion in credit in relation to the quantity of Bank of England notes in circulation as to cause a depreciation in paper currency beyond the difference between the market and mint price of gold.

The third proposition, which was central to the bullionist controversies, was that under restriction the currency was depreciated by a 'constant' excess issue of inconvertible paper money which could not have otherwise occurred under a 'convertible state of the currency'. Tooke (1838, I: 153–4) agreed with the bullionists that under currency restriction the Bank of England's monetary policy accommodated a depreciation in the value of inconvertible paper which could not have otherwise occurred under a convertible system of currency. The evidence for this was the premium of the market price of gold over its mint price for significant periods of time during restriction. In evidence to the Agricultural Committee of 1821, Tooke (1821a: 296) gave some indication of the degree to which he believed the paper currency was then depreciated in value when, based on the above test, he estimated that, on resumption, the restoration of the mint price of gold at the pre-1797 standard led to an appreciation in paper currency of 'somewhat above four per cent'.[46] However, Tooke disputed that any of the depreciation was caused by an excess quantity of banknotes in circulation. Instead, Tooke argued that the cause of the depreciation were those real disturbances adversely affecting Britain's balance of payments which were identified by the anti-bullionists. In particular, Tooke contended that the depreciation of the currency stemmed from the frequent depreciations in the rate of foreign exchange that were primarily the result of 'extraordinary foreign payments' of the British government in prosecution of the French Wars. In support of this contention Tooke pointed to evidence showing that '*the exchanges upon every pause from the pressure of extraordinary foreign payments tended to a recovery*, and when the pressure had entirely ceased, the exchanges and the price of gold were restored to par' (1838, I: 157–8) in absence of any contraction in the amount of money in circulation.[47] Moreover, Tooke upheld the views of the anti-bullionists, arguing that because 'extraordinary foreign payments' were usually paid in gold, 'it was the gold that, by increased demand departed from the paper, and not the paper by increased quantity from the gold' (1838, I: 158) which, operating to depress the foreign exchanges, induced the accompanying depreciations in the value of paper currency. Furthermore, Tooke (1838, I: 168–9; II: 347) argued that the frequent depreciations in the rate of foreign exchange exerted an inflationary influence on money prices by increasing the cost of imports.

In absence of the convertibility of the currency, Tooke maintained that only by a sharp tightening in monetary policy could the Bank of England have countered the depressing influence of these real disturbances on the foreign exchanges and prevented depreciations of the currency. But Tooke (1848a, IV: 118–23) believed such a policy response would have unnecessarily imposed a highly depressing influence on commercial activity and contributed to internal financial instability. In comments that would strike a familiar chord with a modern central banker, Tooke wrote:

> the alternative in the regulation of the Bank issues, presented by the extraordinary state of things which prevailed at particular periods of the war, but

more especially during the closing years of it, was that of causing great and rapid changes in the quantity of money, with corresponding violent alterations in the rate of interest and in the state of credit, both commercial and financial, *or*, of preserving a greater degree of uniformity in the amount of circulation and in the rate of interest, at the expense of very great fluctuations of the exchanges, and their enormous attendant and *preponderating* evils.

(1838, I: 164)

Hence, Tooke (1838, I: 168, 172, 242, 350; II: 28–34; 1848a, IV: 129–42) concluded that during the restriction period, in order to ensure internal financial stability, which would have been important to the main policy objective of defeating Napoleonic France, the Bank of England adopted a more accommodating monetary policy than required to counter the pressure on the exchanges of an unfavourable balance of foreign payments.

Tooke's explanation of price movements and the depreciation of the paper currency during the restriction period largely supported the position of the anti-bullionists in general. As discussed above (p. 113), he agreed that the cause of the depreciations in the paper currency were real disturbances, mainly British government 'extraordinary foreign payments', which adversely affected the balance of payments and depressed the rate of foreign exchange. He also agreed that when depreciations occurred it was the value of gold that rose in relation to the paper currency rather than paper falling against gold. The only concession Tooke made to the bullionists was that currency restriction enabled the Bank of England to accommodate currency depreciations in preference to depressing economic activity. But in this regard, Tooke disagreed with the bullionists' fundamental view that monetary policy ought to have been mainly guided by the state of the foreign exchanges and the price of gold in the particular wartime circumstances of the currency restriction. This was indeed a key point of the 1810 Bullion Report (see Cannan 1925: 32–45). Whereas most bullionists attributed price inflation under restriction predominantly to the Bank of England's accommodation of an excessive expansion in the quantity of paper money, Tooke attributed it wholly to natural and political factors connected to the events of the French Wars. Moreover, Tooke (1838, I: 158–9; 1848, IV: 118–29) argued that in the circumstances the Bank of England conducted, if unwittingly, a sound policy during restriction, maintaining a discount rate at not less than 5 per cent on short-term bills of exchange and, for the most part, not contributing much to speculative-based expansions of credit.

In particular, Tooke was critical of the bullionists for not appreciating the fact that in the years 1808 to 1814, when depreciations of the paper currency were at their highest, the values of exportable commodities measured in gold were in general relatively lower in Britain than in the European markets, notwithstanding the price inflation in Britain over that period.[48] This factually contradicted the argument of Ricardo and other bullionists that the relative cheapness of gold to other exportable commodities was proof that the depreciation of the paper currency was ultimately a consequence of an excess quantity of money under restriction.[49] Instead, Tooke contended that exportable products were relatively cheaper than gold and that the adverse balance of payments causing the depreciation could not be corrected by the flow of relatively cheap British exports to Europe because of the blockade.[50] He argued that it was largely because of Napoleon's continental blockade that gold was actually dearer and not cheaper than other exportable commodities.

In conclusion, Tooke believed the alteration in Britain's system of currency to effectively a fiat-based one during the restriction period 1797–1821 contributed to general price movements through the effect of variations in the foreign exchange rate on the cost of imported commodities. This mainly consisted of depreciations in pound sterling contributing towards higher price inflation. During the restriction period, Tooke (1838, II: 346) ascertained that price inflation persisted from 1797 to 1814, after which a deflationary phase occurred. In his empirical analysis, Tooke established that during the period in which the average rate was high by historical standards, there was considerable instability in the price level, with periods of high rates of inflation followed by periods of deflation (for a picture based on Tooke's statistics, see Figure A3.1, p. 235). As shown earlier in this chapter, Tooke contended that the main cause of the price inflation was real forces, what he called natural and political forces, that were connected with the French Wars of 1793–1801 and 1803–1815, that adversely affected conditions of supply and, thereby, persistently raised the costs of production of a broad range of commodities. It was also real forces connected to the French Wars acting on Britain's external position which, as shown above, Tooke believed was the main cause for the extensive depreciations of the pound sterling exchange rate. The essential point was that these extensive currency depreciations could occur under restriction whereas under a (gold/silver) convertible system of currency, Bank of England policy would not have been able to accommodate the depreciation:

> the restriction admitted of a greater depression of the exchanges, than could have occurred in a convertible state of the paper. And as the depression of the exchanges constituted an element of increased cost of all imported commodities, and thus, directly and indirectly, affected the prices of a considerable proportion of native productions, the restriction may be considered to have been the condition without which so much of the rise of prices as was attributable to increased cost by adverse exchanges could not have occurred. Besides that, it is the general tendency of a fall of the exchange to raise prices of exportable commodities.
>
> (Tooke 1838, I: 168)

Nevertheless, Tooke argued that it was possible the currency depreciations could have been averted had the Bank of England been prepared to sacrifice internal monetary stability by countering the influence of the real disturbances on the balance of payments and the exchange rate with a highly restrictive monetary policy. It is evident Tooke (1838, II: 163–8) believed that in the extraordinary circumstances created by the French Wars, the Bank of England was correct in not being guided by the foreign exchange rate and, if unwittingly, conducted monetary policy in a sound manner during the restriction period. In all, Tooke believed restriction contributed, in the sense detailed above, to only part of the high inflation phase from 1793 to 1814. With regard to the effective resumption of cash payments by the Bank of England in 1821, as previously indicated, Tooke (1838, I: 170–3) believed it made a smaller one-off contribution to price deflation equal to the magnitude by which the market price of gold was lowered to the restored pre-1797 mint standard. After Britain officially establishes the gold standard in 1821, there is no longer much scope in monetary policy for any trade-off between the stability of internal monetary conditions and a depreciated exchange rate since the market price of gold cannot diverge substantially from its mint standard.

5.6 On the effect of the mid-nineteenth-century gold discoveries

Post-1821, when Britain's monetary values were fixed to the gold standard, the money prices of commodities were determined by their exchange (or relative) value to gold; that is, by the gold price of commodities. Therefore, the price level depended heavily on factors that determined the value of gold. This was well understood by classical economists and, as indicated in the previous section of this chapter, by Tooke. But despite Tooke recognising the importance of the value of gold in explaining price movements under a convertible system of currency, little of his writings are devoted to its analysis until volumes V and VI of *History* (1857). It appears the reason behind this omission was that Tooke found no a priori evidence for believing anything other than the value of gold remained relatively invariable from 1821 to the mid-nineteenth century. However, in 1848 Tooke believed the prospect of a progressive rise in the production of Russian gold mines was likely to alter its future value:

> There is, however, one other consideration which must not be lost sight of in any view to future prices; and that is the value of gold. I believe that the circumstances operating upon the supply of gold, relatively to the demand for it in the markets of the world, have been for many years past such as to preserve it *at a nearly constant value. At least there have been no indications, taking the ordinary tests, of any material variation*. But there are in prospect causes which may produce a considerable alteration. The most important of these is the extraordinary production of gold in Russia.
>
> (1848a, IV: 40; emphasis added; also see 1844: 12n.1)

Tooke argued that if the 'quantity of gold relatively to its uses should increase so as sensibly to affect its value', the lowering in its value will result in 'an increased price of corn, and of labour, and of commodities generally' (1848a, IV: 41). If the 'production of silver should be comparatively stationary', Tooke argued it will also result in 'an increased price of silver, and our par of exchange reduced with foreign countries whose standard is silver' (1848a, IV: 41). An 'extraordinary' increase in gold production did in fact occur over the following decade as a result of gold discoveries in California and the East Australian colonies rather than any large growth in the output of Russian mines. The economic effects of the substantial increase in the world supply of gold which stemmed from these discoveries were the subject of detailed study by Tooke and Newmarch in Part VII of volume six of *History* (1857).

In this study Tooke and Newmarch (1857, VI: 145–54) estimated that, as a result of the discoveries in the New World, increased production had added £174 millions to the value of the stock of gold over the period 1848 to 1856. This represented an approximate increase of 27 per cent in the world's stock of gold. Tooke and Newmarch (1857, VI: 154–8) estimated that nearly all this additional gold was coined and put into monetary circulation. Indeed, Tooke and Newmarch ascertained that the demand for gold as money well exceeded its production over the relevant period, the deficit being largely satisfied by the conversion of existing plate into coin and the drawing out of gold from existing hoards.[51] This great increase in the stock of metallic money was, according to Tooke and Newmarch (1857, V: 341–7; VI: 158–78), accompanied by a substantial trend rise in the general money prices of commodities and money wages. However, Tooke and Newmarch (1857, VI: 194–7, 225) rejected the orthodox doctrine that the increase in the quantity of metallic money was the major cause of this persistent inflation in money prices. While they acknowledged that the increase in the supply of gold tended to reduce its exchange value, this was more than offset by an increased demand for it stemming from an expansion in international trade and production:

> the increase of Trade, Enterprise, and Production have, during the last Eight or Nine years, counteracted almost entirely the apparent *à priori* tendency of the New Supplies to depreciate Gold as compared with Silver and other Commodities, – in other words, to raise the Prices – as stated in Gold – of all Commodities.
>
> (Tooke and Newmarch 1857, VI: 197)

Tooke and Newmarch (1857, VI: 193–218) argued that the gold discoveries raised the price level through a process by which increased supplies of gold stimulated an expansion in international income and expenditure. This involved the diffusion of gold from regions of production to the international economy as payment for imported goods or as remittances for foreign capital investment. Non-producing countries absorbed the additional supply of gold according to their relative export performance and balance of payments positions. Relying on the views of Senior (1830) and J.S. Mill (1848 [1909]: 619–28), Tooke and Newmarch (1857, VI: 205–10) argued that the distribution of the precious metals among countries in the international economy ultimately depended on the relative productivity of their industries. Hence, a greater proportion of the additional supply of bullion was absorbed by the United Kingdom because of the superior skill and efficiency of its industry and the superior quality of its exports which caused them to be in high demand abroad.[52] Tooke and Newmarch (1857, VI: 210–12) maintained that in the first instance, the greater part of increased gold went to England, whose exports were in the greatest demand in California and the Australian colonies, from which it was 'conveyed to other parts of the world' through international payments on its imports. Importantly, this process was seen by Tooke and Newmarch to generate rising incomes and expenditures in the commercial world by which gold was absorbed by demand into the monetary circulation of countries.

In Tooke and Newmarch's explanation of the economic impact of the mid-nineteenth-century gold discoveries, there were two main ways in which the increased supply of gold was seen to have stimulated higher levels of expenditure and production in the world. First, an exogenous increase in the export demand of the gold-producing regions provided a stimulus to industry in Britain as well as North-East America and Western Europe. In this connection Tooke and Newmarch (1857, VI: 219–21) ascertained that the 'opening out of new fields of enterprise' in these regions, in particular, for investment in railways and the telegraph, was an important source of stimulus for additional expenditure. It also opened up new markets for trade, especially in the American West. Second, they argued that the increased supply of gold bullion facilitated an expansion in international trade and capital investment which was the driving force of rising 'real wealth'. An important aspect of this argument was that, together with freer trade, large-scale British investment in railways and other communications infrastructure in Europe, North America and India provided new sources of raw materials and export markets for an expansion in international trade over the period 1848–1856. Essentially Tooke and Newmarch (1857, VI: 220–3) were of the view that this economic development was facilitated by the availability of larger gold reserves to 'national' banks, enabling a greater volume of international transactions to be expedited than would have otherwise been possible given the constraint of maintaining a minimum reserve to ensure convertibility of its paper currency. In relation to Bank of England policy, Tooke and Newmarch (1857, V: 561–98; VI: 200–4) contended that higher reserves accommodated by the increased supply of gold afforded lower rates of interest (the discount rate) than would have otherwise occurred (see Chapter 7, n.34). By way of summarising the argument, they appealed to Adam Smith's well-known analogy, likening the monetary function of the stock of gold in the international economy to the function of a highway: 'A Highway facilitates and encourages traffic; and the broader, smoother, and longer it is, the greater its efficacy as an instrument or machine conducive to production' (Tooke and Newmarch 1857, VI: 216).[53]

In these ways Tooke and Newmarch believed that the mid-nineteenth-century gold discoveries contributed to higher levels of income and expenditure in Britain, through which it tended to raise money prices in general. Hence, according to Tooke and Newmarch (1857, VI: 224–5), it was by manner of its causal role in 'the gradual growth of a larger demand' that the gold discoveries contributed to the higher level of prices.

A feature of the Tooke and Newmarch's explanation is that the rise in the level of money prices was attributed to factors that acted directly on commodities other than gold: raising their prices (and wages) *relative* to the gold standard. What is interesting about this explanation, which Jevons (1863: 15–16) noticed, is that Tooke and Newmarch rejected the possibility that the gold discoveries led to a reduction in the cost of production of gold:

> Now there is good reason to believe that this supposition of a diminished Cost of Gold since 1850, is almost wholly erroneous. It might be shown very clearly, that combining together the extent, and cost, of the agency which has been employed to raise the 174 Millions of New Gold from the soil; the large army of Labourers and persons dependent upon them; the expenses of conveying those Labourers to the distant regions of the Gold Diggings; the expense of Tools; the cost of Living; and the value of the commodities with which the Gold has been purchased of the Diggers; – and placing this combined Total of outlay against the quantity of Gold produced, it would appear that the operation, as a question of investment to be tested by mere figures of profit and loss, has been strikingly unsuccessful. It would appear, in other words, that the amount of Labour and Capital which has been expended in producing Gold; might have been expended to greater advantage in producing commodities; – *provided* that such commodities could have found as ready and brisk a market as has been found by the Gold.
>
> (1857, VI: 226)

Tooke and Newmarch therefore ascertained that the new gold fields of California and Eastern Australia were no more productive per unit of inputs than pre-existing deposits so that the 'large addition [to the world's stock of gold] took place without affecting in any way that can be discovered the relative value of Gold' (1857, VI: 232).[54] However, this view is not very plausible since it is inconceivable that there would have been sustained investment in these regions without the realistic prospect of earning higher rates of return offered by more productive gold mines. Indeed, a priori evidence for the relatively higher fertility of the newly discovered gold mining regions is provided by their meteoric production which, as Tooke and Newmarch (1857, VI: 145–54) calculated, added more than 25 per cent to the world stock of gold in the short period between 1848 and 1856. Subsequent studies by Jevons (1863, 1869), Giffen (1886) and Soetbeer (1888: 159–63) as well as the 'Final Report' of the Gold and Silver Commission (1888: 9–11, 69) supported the argument that the gold discoveries directly induced a reduction in the value of gold (measured against silver). These studies tended to employ a marginalist approach, explaining the decline in the value of gold by virtue of an increased supply of gold in relation to its demand.

From the standpoint of the classical approach, it is difficult to conceive how the additional output of gold was absorbed into monetary circulation in absence of a prior causal reduction in its cost of production which directly raised the general price level. In all plausibility, it would involve a process in which the discovery of the more fertile gold mines of Eastern Australia and California at the pre-existing worldwide demand for gold would, at least initially, bring about a significant reduction in the cost of production at the new least-productive mine that supplants the old but now unprofitable one. The reduction in the value of the gold would, as the monetary standard, lead directly to an increase in the general level of money prices worldwide which, in turn, would tend to cause an increase in the demand for money and, thereby, the worldwide demand for gold for monetary circulation. If, over time, the demand for gold should increase to a level at which the least productive mine profitably employed is the old one, then the pre-existing cost of production of gold will be restored. Indeed, this appears to be what Tooke and Newmarch believed occurred.

As previously discussed in Section 3.5, Tooke and Newmarch appear to have adopted the position that because gold was 'universally marketable', its demand would increase to absorb the higher output of a gold industry with an enlarged productive capacity. However, this reasoning lacks plausibility in the classical approach to value in absence of the foregoing causal process by which the cost of production of gold declines as a result of the discovery of more fertile mines. Indeed, the analysis of Senior (1840: 52–5) showed that the discovery of new mines could only plausibly induce an increased demand for gold as money if it brought about a reduction in the cost of production of gold. While the economic forces which Tooke and Newmarch (1857, VI: 204–13, 218–23) identified as raising levels of income are likely to have contributed towards increasing the monetary demand for gold, the most important single factor was surely a permanent lowering in the value of the gold standard (relative to other commodities) which, thereby, causes a trend rise in the general price level. By contrast, Tooke and Newmarch (1857, V: 341–7) largely explained the rise in the price level in the decade after the gold discoveries by reference to factors which increased the cost of production of commodities other than gold in relation to gold.

Overall, then, the explanation of the effect of the gold discoveries on the price level in Tooke and Newmarch (1857, VI: 213–29) is not altogether convincing. It is also not altogether consistent with Tooke's banking school position. Perhaps this analytical shortcoming reflected the influence of the principal author of the explanation, Newmarch, who had a tendency to emphasise the causal role of demand in the movement of prices. But it also suggests Tooke himself did not fully grasp the classical approach to explaining the long-run value of money in an economy such as Britain with a gold standard. As already discussed in Section 3.5, following Ricardo (1823: 85–7, 193), this approach was most clearly elaborated by Senior (1840) and read but apparently not fully understood by Tooke.

5.7 Tooke's explanation of secular price movements, 1792–1856

In Tooke's large-scale study of prices over the period 1792 to 1856, three main phases of movement in the price level are identified. These phases are graphically represented in Figure A2.1 (p. 233). The first phase is an upward trend in the price level which Tooke (1838, II: 346) dated from 1792 to 1814. Tooke attributed this upward trend in 'general prices' to natural and political factors that tended to restrict the supply of commodities brought to market and raise their normal costs of supply.

The natural factor consisted of a long-run deterioration in climatic conditions that adversely affected the productivity of British agriculture. Tooke (1838, II: 346–7) maintained that the 'frequent recurrence of seasons of an unfavourable character' of which 'some were of a desolating character' caused a reduction in the level of agricultural (corn) output and considerably raised the average price of corn. Because these unfavourable seasonal conditions extended 'over the greater part of Europe' (1838, II: 347), the average price of corn imported by Britain at times of domestic shortfalls was also similarly high. Political factors connected with the French Wars of 1793–1815 were also central to Tooke's explanation of the causes for this phase of persistent price inflation. First, wartime obstructions and prohibitions raised the price of imports. Early in the wars, naval obstructions mainly affected food imports from across the Atlantic; while, in particular, Tooke emphasised the 'destruction of a great source of supply of transatlantic produce by the revolution in St. Domingo, which rendered sugar and coffee, and most other West India produce, scarce and dear' (1838, II: 347). According to Tooke (1838, II: 347) a more substantial obstruction to British trade, 'especially during the latter years of the war', was the operation of Napoleon's continental blockade, effective from 1806 to 1812, which systematically raised the price of north European imports 'of articles of which, whether as raw materials of our manufactures, or naval stores, or food, we stood in urgent need' during the course of the wars. Second, Tooke maintained that a major cause contributing to a sustained increase in the cost of imports was the very high wartime freight and insurance charges that he attributed to the 'commercial hostility' characteristic of the French Wars. Third, Tooke held that the price of imports was raised by the wartime depreciation in the sterling exchange 'which in the last five years of the war averaged 20 per cent, thus adding so much to the cost of all imported productions' (1838, II: 347). He believed the depreciation in the currency was essentially attributable to a combination of political factors connected with the French Wars: namely, the strong international demand for gold (specie); the extraordinary foreign payments by the British government to subsidise European allies and to finance its military operations abroad; an ongoing trade deficit on the balance of payments caused by increased imports of corn and naval stores as well as the impediment to British exports of Napoleon's Continental blockade.[55]

Fourth, Tooke argued that a 'higher rate of interest constituting an increased cost of production' (1838, II: 347) significantly contributed to a higher long-run price level. Tooke attributed the higher average rate of interest to the British government's policy of debt-financing its massive war expenditures: to 'the absorption by the war loans of a considerable proportion of the savings of individuals' (1838, II: 347). He therefore also regarded the higher interest rate to be the result of political factors arising out of the French Wars. It is notable that wages growth was not seen by Tooke to be a major inflationary factor. He ascertained that the increase in money wages was less than the general increase in the money price of 'provisions' such that the real wage of (most) workers significantly declined over the relevant period. Moreover, in Tooke's picture, the upward trend in the price level was accompanied by a fundamental shift in the distribution of income from the wages of workers and, to a much lesser extent, from the profits of capitalists (in civilian industry), to the rent of landowners and net profits of (corn) farmers.

The second phase consisted of a downward trend in the general price level, which Tooke (1838, II: 348) dated from 1814 to 1837. This secular decline in price inflation is attributed by Tooke to a reversal in natural and political factors affecting supply conditions and facilitating a long-run lowering in the cost of production of commodities in general. A major reversal identified by Tooke was the long-run improvement in climatic conditions, raising the productivity of domestic agriculture and, in particular, lowering the secular price of corn. After the desolate season of 1816 and 'the great scarcity of 1816–17, which extended over Europe', Tooke ascertained:

> A succession of more favourable seasons, there having been in the last twenty years, namely, from 1818 to the present time, only five seasons in which the produce of wheat was decidedly deficient; and in none of them was the inclemency of the season, or the scarcity resulting there from, at all comparable to some of those which occurred during the war; nor was there any one of them that extended over Europe.
>
> (1838, II: 347)

In this phase Tooke did not believe the Corn Laws successfully operated to artificially raise the average price of corn (see Section 4.4). A second major reversal was the reduction in the cost of imports that followed the cessation of war. According to Tooke (1838, II: 347) this was the effect of the 'removal of obstacles from the several sources of supply' and of the 'great reduction of the charges of importation, by low freights and insurances incidental to a state of peace'. Tooke also recognised that a change in the geo-political environment after the French Wars in favour of Britain provided 'a great extension of some' and 'the discovery of new' sources of foreign supply for commodities.[56] Another factor contributing to lower British import prices identified by Tooke was the 'rise of the foreign exchanges, in consequence of the cessation of the great foreign war expenditure, and the consequent reduction of the cost of all imported commodities' (1838, II: 347). Clearly, Tooke believed this factor operated quickly after the war and prior to 1821 when effective restoration of the gold standard ruled out any persistent depreciation of sterling exchange below par.

A third major reversal identified by Tooke stemmed from the reduced demands placed on the London financial market by the cessation of extraordinary government war expenditures financed by massive public debt accumulation. Tooke believed these altered institutional circumstances in the financial market led to a 'reduction of the general rate of interest, and a more extensive application of individual accumulations [of savings] to reproduction at a diminished cost' (1838, II: 347). Lastly, Tooke listed technical progress as an important factor in lowering prices with '[I]mprovements in machinery, in chemistry, and in the arts and sciences generally, all tending to reduce the cost of production of numerous articles, or to provide cheaper substitutes' (1838, II: 348–9). This is also associated with his view that 'improved, and cheaper, and more rapid internal communications' (1838, II: 348) tended to lower the regional transport cost of bringing goods to market. Tooke ascertained that in response to the long-run decline in the price level, money wages fell. However, given that the prices of corn and other provisions were held to have fallen by more than money wages, Tooke believed the real wage of workers rose over the period. In Tooke's overview, this was associated with a re-distribution of income from landowners and farmers back towards industrial capitalists and workers.

The third phase consisted of a moderate upward trend in the general price level from 1838 to 1856. Though this phase was not explicitly delineated by Tooke, it is nevertheless consistent with the findings of his study. As already outlined in Section 4.1, Tooke ascertained a long-run deterioration in climatic conditions which contributed to a decline in the productivity of agriculture over the period. Tooke believed that this led to a persistent dependency on imported corn by Britain which, together with the disaster of the European potato famine in the 1840s, caused a trend rise in the price of corn from 1838 until after the repeal of the Corn Laws in 1846. Although Tooke established that seasonal conditions were no better after 1848 to 1856, he believed free trade in imported corn facilitated a levelling in its price. Natural factors were therefore seen by Tooke to systematically raise the average prices of 'the most necessary articles of food' throughout the 1840s. By contrast, Tooke (1848, IV: 43–80; 1857, V: 341–7) ascertained that the general prices of other commodities remained flat in this decade before trending upwards in 1850s. A major factor identified by Tooke in his analysis was technical progress, which he believed tended to lower prices during the period. In particular, Tooke and Newmarch (1857, V: 373–5) contended the rapid development of the railway network and telegraph in Britain operated to lower the costs of bringing commodities to market:

the more rapid and perfect the means of conveying to the manufacturer the desires of the consumer, the less will be the quantity of stock he will find it necessary to have beforehand. And it is obvious, that by means of railways and telegraphs, the expenses and risks of all trades concerned in the production and sale of manufactured articles, have been greatly diminished; and the diminution of these risks and expenses must have the effect, so far as they go, of a fall in the cost of production.

(1857, V: 375)

Tooke and Newmarch (1857, V: 193–4; VI: 534–6) also believed that 'inventions and improvements' in machinery, especially in steam-powered engines, significantly increased productivity and reduced the costs of production in both manufacturing and agricultural industry.[57] Furthermore, Tooke and Newmarch (1857, V: 191–5) contended that land reclamation, the greater utilisation of fertile land and the adoption of improved methods of farming all operated to lower the cost of agricultural production.

The main counteracting factor identified by Tooke for the upward movement in the price level in the 1850s was the large increase in gold production that resulted from the discoveries in California and the East Australian colonies. As was shown in the previous section of this chapter, Tooke argued that, together with freer international trade and the opening up of new (colonial) markets, it facilitated strong economic activity in Britain, associated with persistent demand pressures on the supply of commodities. Tooke and Newmarch (1857, VI: 171–88, 204–13, 233) also contended that it lay behind strong growth in money wages for both skilled and unskilled workers. A political event that Tooke believed significantly contributed to higher prices was the short-lived Crimean War of 1854–1856. Hence, according to Tooke's analysis, the moderate upward trend in the price level in this phase was largely attributed to a long-run average deterioration in climatic conditions reducing productivity in agriculture and the impact of gold discoveries on economic activity, which more than counteracted the effect of technical progress.

Overall, then, Tooke argued that the secular movement in the general level of money prices in Britain over the period 1792 to 1856 was due to real factors that systematically determined the conditions of production and the normal costs of bringing commodities to market. These mainly consisted of natural and political factors so understood. Another important factor was technical progress mainly in connection with improvements in machinery and in the development of transport and communications infrastructure. Not directly related to conditions of production, Tooke also argued that politico-institutional factors which determined the long-term rate of interest on capital in the financial market were also important. By contrast, Tooke did not believe money wage behaviour was a prominent explanatory factor.

6   The monetary thought of the pre-banking school Tooke, 1819–1838

Tooke's pre-banking school monetary thought has been much neglected in the literature. Understandably, the focus has been on Tooke's more original banking school theory and, connectedly, with his prominent role in the all-important currency–banking school policy debates of the 1840s. Only studies by Gregory (1928) and Arnon (1991) wholly devoted to Tooke's work and its development deal in any depth with his pre-banking school monetary thought.[1] This inattention has tended to obscure the development of Tooke's monetary thought in the 1820s and 1830s which help explain why he was eventually to challenge the central propositions of the classical economists' quantity theory of money and to propose an alternative banking school theory to explain the behaviour of the monetary system. In particular, what has gone unnoticed is the dissenting nature of Tooke's pre-banking school views on orthodox monetary theory which led him on the road to his banking school position. So while Tooke's pre-banking school monetary thought remains within the bounds of orthodoxy there developed within it the seeds for his eventual rejection of it. To use Gregory's (1928: 76) expression, the orthodoxy of Tooke's pre-banking school monetary thought can be described as 'eclectic' in the sense of being capable of reconciling different possibilities in the causal relationship between money and prices according to circumstances established by reference to the empirical evidence.

Tooke's position certainly did not accord with strict versions of the classical economists' quantity theory of money, which was most clearly articulated by Ricardo (1811a) and which, in particular, supposed a stable proportional relationship between the overall structure of paper credit and Bank of England notes and coin (or specie reserves). As Gregory commented: '[H]e *never* was a strict Bullionist, and, in fact, from his earliest writings, deprecated the extremes to which he thought that this point of view had been pushed' (1928: 16). Only in the pamphlet *Considerations on the State of Currency* (1826) did Gregory (1928: 76) consider that Tooke showed an 'attitude' that 'is largely Ricardian'. Closer to the mark, Arnon (1991: 3, 58–9) considered Tooke to be a 'modified bullionist', by which he meant that the pre-banking school Tooke subscribed to the quantity theory of money in the long-run but not in the short run:

He thought the quantity theory to be basically true, i.e. if other things do not change, prices are determined by the quantity of the medium in circulation. However, other things do change. Hence, in practice, in many cases, the quantity theory, while continuing to represent a fundamental long-run tendency, does not provide a good explanation for short-run phenomena.

This view places Tooke's pre-banking school monetary thought close to the orthodox position articulated by Henry Thornton (1802). It should be kept in mind that the version of the quantity theory of money adopted by most English bullionists in the early part of the nineteenth century was closer to that proposed by Thornton than that proposed by Ricardo. As is shown in this chapter, from the beginning Tooke was considerably influenced by Thornton, something which he appears to later acknowledge: '[T]he treatise by the latter [Henry Thornton] entitled, "An Inquiry into the Nature and Effects of the Paper Credit of Great Britain", is in every way a remarkable work' (1848a, IV: 85).[2] But while Thornton's position can be usefully regarded as the starting point of Tooke's pre-banking school monetary thought, it is certainly not the ending point. By 1838 Tooke believed the quantity theory had little explanatory power and had abandoned it in all but principle.

This chapter is concerned with elucidating the formation of Tooke's pre-banking school monetary thought over the period 1819 to 1838. It begins in Section 6.1 with an examination of Tooke's strong support for the resumption of cash payments by the Bank of England and restoration of the gold standard in 1821. In particular, it is shown that, while Tooke in 1819 supported Ricardo in the return to the gold standard, he differed with him on the practical issues of the manner by which the policy was effected and its subsequent economic impact, which reflected a deeper theoretical difference on the relationship between money and prices. Section 6.2 then examines in detail Tooke's analysis of money, credit and prices in the context of the orthodox monetary theory of the time. This detailed examination will proceed by reference to three important theoretical propositions of the classical quantity theory: first, external adjustment in terms of the price–specie–flow mechanism; second, the autonomous control of the Bank of England (the central banking authority) over the whole quantity of money and credit in circulation; and, third, the causal relationship between the quantity of money (and credit) in circulation and prices and economic activity. A substantial issue on which Tooke dissented with orthodox theory was the nature of the relationship between the rate of interest and the rate of profit. In Section 6.3, this dissenting position of Tooke's is examined together with his theory of the determination of the rate of interest and of its role in the conduct of monetary policy. Lastly, Section 6.4 considers Tooke's pre-banking school views on institutional reform of the English banking system and then examines, in some detail, his position on the appropriate conduct of monetary policy by the Bank of England in order to secure financial and economic stability.

6.1 On the resumption of cash payments and the gold standard

The earliest of Tooke's publicly expressed views on monetary questions are found in his evidence before the Commons and Lords parliamentary committees on the expediency of the Bank of England resuming cash payments in 1819. In this evidence Tooke (1819a: 127, 132; 1819b: (Q 83–8) 179–80) gave strong support to resumption and, thereby, to the restoration of the gold standard. Indeed, as noted by Hilton (1977: 43n.51), Tooke was in fact the only witness besides Ricardo who believed an immediate return to convertibility by the Bank of England could be immediately put into train. It is perhaps for this reason that Fetter (1968: 104) claimed: 'Tooke had taken a view close to that of Ricardo – not only supporting the re-establishment of the gold standard but accepting a basically monetary explanation of price changes.' However, as Arnon (1990: 44) pointed out, it is important to distinguish between Tooke's support for the gold standard and the content of his early views on monetary behaviour. Indeed, from the very beginning Tooke disagreed with Ricardo on the practical manner of return to convertibility by the Bank of England, implemented in 1821, and its subsequent effect on price inflation and economic activity. This disagreement belies a major difference in Tooke's theoretical approach from that of Ricardo.

The parliamentary committees on the resumption of cash payments were established in 1819 by the Liverpool Government with the purpose of overcoming opposition to resumption and to pressure the Bank of England to do so as soon as practicable.[3] Reflecting the pre-determination of the government to return to the metallic standard, both committees dismissed opposing arguments and came down in favour of compelling the Bank to resume cash payments by a fixed date. After the interim reports of these committees, the central issue was how and when the Bank of England would be required to resume cash payments (Hilton 1977: 43–5). It was in this very context that Ricardo's Ingot Plan became prominent in evidence given before the committees and subsequently formed the basis of 'Peel's Bill' for the resumption of cash payments (Sraffa 1952: 350–64). Ricardo had originally set out his Ingot Plan in the 1816 pamphlet, *Proposals for an Economical and Secure Currency*. The plan entailed a system of currency which, on the resumption of full convertibility of paper money, enabled making the Bank of England notes payable in bullion (bars) rather than coin. Its purpose was to economise on the use of scarce gold and silver specie as coin in internal monetary circulation consistent with securing gold as a stable standard of monetary values in the British economy. The plan therefore envisaged that internal circulation would be overwhelmingly carried on by paper money (rather than coin) whose value would be rigidly fixed to the official mint price of bullion.

The feature of the Ingot Plan which most interested the resumption committees was the graduated scale of reduction of the market price of bullion towards its mint price at which the Bank of England would redeem its notes over time. This graduated scale presented a practical mechanism by which the Bank of England could be coerced to actually prepare for resumption by a gradual contraction of its banknotes in circulation. It also provided a way of easing the expected deflationary effects of the preparations for resumption. Hence, Peel's 1819 Act adopted this graduated scale for resumption. It stipulated that the Bank was to convert notes into bullion on demand at a specified price (close to the market price) from 1 February 1820 and, then at successively lower bullion prices, until resumption of payments in cash (coin) at the mint price was secured by 1 May 1823. But, having speedily accumulated specie, the Bank of England sought and was given permission by the government to abandon the Ingot Plan altogether and pay in cash from 1 May 1821. This action greatly annoyed Ricardo who had hoped that his Ingot Plan would have been permanently adopted. He accused the Bank directors of mismanaging resumption by capriciously contracting its notes which, associated with its large purchases of specie, forced up the value of gold and thereby imposed harsh deflationary pressures on the economy (Ricardo 1819–1821: 359–60; 1821–1823: 15, 122–3, 140–1). What particularly piqued Ricardo was that the Bank's actions left him, as the main public advocate of resumption, open to criticism from those who opposed it. The role of Tooke in this episode is revealing of his early differences with Ricardo.

In evidence to the Lords committee on resumption, Tooke was asked to comment on Ricardo's Ingot Plan. In reply, he read out a written answer stating that he thought the plan 'admirable for its Ingenuity and Simplicity' and had 'no Doubt of its Convenience and Cheapness' (1819b: (Q 89) 180–1). Tooke believed it was 'particularly well calculated to serve as an intermediate Measure, for limiting and regulating the Paper circulation till Arrangements can be made for establishing the whole Currency on a permanent Footing' (1819b: (Q 89) 181). However, Tooke added, 'if proposed in itself as a permanent System, I cannot but consider it as objectionable' (1819b: (Q 89) 181). The reason Tooke gave for this opinion 'above all' was the 'extended inducement to Forgery' provided by a monetary circulation consisting entirely of paper currency. He also argued that being 'so frail a Material' and 'resting so exclusively on Credit and Confidence', paper currency was 'exposed to the danger of frequent Derangement, and in some cases total Destruction' (1819b: (Q 89) 181).

A more substantial reason for Tooke's objection to the Ingot Plan is found in the following statement: '[I]ndependent of these Objections to an exclusive Paper Currency, it strikes me that many Contingencies and Exigencies might arise, wherein an abundant Stock of the precious metals might be of essential Advantage' (1819b: (Q 89) 181). Although Tooke did not elaborate this point in his written answer, as shown in Section 6.2.1, it sprang from reservations about the practical operation of the price–specie–flow mechanism which he disclosed in later writings. In short, Tooke objected to Ricardo's Ingot Plan as a 'permanent system' on the grounds of its impracticality. The point is that he only supported the plan as an 'intermediate measure' to facilitate the resumption of cash payments by the Bank of England. In reply to the question of 'what Steps would be most expedient' for effecting resumption, Tooke answered:

I have heard no Measure better adapted, than the one which has been suggested, of obliging the Bank by an Act of the Legislature to sell Gold
Bullion at certain stated Prices progressively downwards, till it shall have
reached the Mint Price; because I conceive, that there would be very great
Danger of any Measure short of this failing of its Effect, as no Words
merely conveying the Promise of a resumption of payments in Specie can
satisfy the public that it will actually take place at the Period fixed; such
Promises having, previous to the renewal of the restriction in 1816, been
given in Words as strong as Language can convey.

(1819b: (Q 83) 179–80)

Tooke's position was agreeable to the Liverpool Government which only wanted
to use Ricardo's plan as a means to compel an unenthusiastic Bank of England
to actually abide by Parliament's decision to resume cash payments. Tooke
hoped that resumption would actually be achieved in a shorter period than envisaged by the plan's timetable in order to relieve 'the Suspense and more or less
Uncertainty in undertaking all commercial Operations, which may be influenced
in their results by the State of the Currency while they are in Progress' (1819b:
(Q 84) 180). As Hilton (1977: 87–91) has shown, like Tooke, government ministers standing behind Peel's Act of 1819 'had no particular affection for the Ingot
Plan' as a permanent system and 'gladly agreed to jettison the use of ingots now
that the Bank was prepared to resume at once'.[4]

Unlike Ricardo and most other witnesses who appeared before the resumption
committees of 1819, Tooke did not fear that an immediate resumption of payments in cash by the Bank of England would have a serious deflationary effect on
the economy. Instead, Tooke believed the depressed state of trade and prices provided favourable circumstances for an easy return to the gold standard. When
asked by the Lords committee, 'Would it in your Judgment be practicable and
safe for the Bank of England to resume Cash Payments on the 5th of July next?',
Tooke replied in the affirmative: 'I see no Reason to apprehend any Difficulty in
restoring the Exchanges, and reducing the Price of Gold by the 5th of July, so as
to make the Fact of the actual Resumption a matter of minor Importance' (1819b:
(Q 2) 168). Tooke (1819a: 127; 1819b: (Q 3–4) 168) believed that little, if any,
contraction of the amount of Bank of England notes in circulation would be
necessary in 1819 to restore the foreign exchanges to par and reduce the price of
bullion to the mint standard. He was of the opinion that the 'depression of trade'
and 'stagnation of markets' would continue to bring down domestic prices, as
particularly induced by a 'glut of corn' and decline in the price of corn, and
improve the balance of payments position (Tooke 1819a: 132). In this situation,
Tooke (1819a: 127) argued that 'diminished confidence' would tend to raise the
'value of money' as traders and bankers attempted to shore up their liquidity positions. This would operate like a reduction in the amount of banknotes in circulation, thereby also contributing to an improvement in the foreign exchanges. Thus,
in 1819 Tooke believed economic and financial circumstances favoured an early
resumption of cash payments by the Bank of England.

The depression in prices, especially in agricultural prices, in the period 1819 to 1822 saw a strong reaction against resumption, especially by the agricultural sector. Much of the public criticism was directed against Ricardo (1819a: 385, 392; 1819b: 417–18), who steadfastly maintained that, at most, the return to the metallic standard would induce a 5 per cent depreciation in domestic prices as measured by the premium of the market (paper) price of gold over its mint value. As previously discussed in Section 2.1, Tooke defended Ricardo on this question before the Agricultural Committee of 1821. According to Tooke (1821b: 295–6) the return to the gold standard involved about a 10 per cent reduction in prices, calculable by a 4 per cent decline in the market price of gold to its mint price and a 6 per cent appreciation of gold in relation to silver (and, therefore, other commodities). However, Tooke believed that as gold was actually restored to its mint price the foreign exchanges improved to par on their own accord:

> perhaps the Committee will give me leave to observe, that I am not clear that if Parliament had not interfered in 1819, the state of things, as far as the currency concerned, would not by this time have been nearly the same as it now is.
>
> (1821b: 295)

Hence, Tooke argued that under Peel's 1819 Act, preparations for resumption by the Bank of England that caused the value of gold to rise relative to silver contributed no more than a 6 per cent depression in domestic prices on the assessment that silver did not depreciate in value. He strenuously argued to the committee that the depression (of well over 30 per cent) in the price of agricultural commodities (i.e. corn) was due to abundant harvests and excess supplies on the domestic market.

In later writings devoted to this question, Tooke vindicated his 1819 position, denying that preparations of resumption by the Bank of England exerted any significant deflationary effect on domestic prices. Appealing to the historical evidence, Tooke (1823, i: 166–7; 1826: 53n.; 1829a: 6–26; 1838, II: 96–107) denied the Bank of England contracted its issues in order to comply with Peel's Act. Instead, Tooke (1829a: 8–11; 1838, II: 107–9) maintained that as a result of a favourable balance of payments position, the foreign exchanges actually rose above par, making it unnecessary for the Bank to adopt a deflationary stance in preparation of resumption of cash payments at the official mint price of gold.[5] On this basis Tooke categorically refuted longstanding charges of mismanagement made against Bank directors by Ricardo and others (also see Rist 1940: 193–4):

> Mr. Ricardo does not appear to me to have sufficiently appreciated this state of things, when he charged the Bank directors with mismanagement, in having prematurely and unnecessarily enhanced the value of the currency by their large purchases of gold after the passing of Mr. Peel's bill. His mode of expression conveys the idea that the directors made an effort to buy gold; that they created a demand for it by a designed reduction in their issue for that

specific purpose. Now, the truth is, that they were perfectly passive, and moved only in the ordinary routine of their business: they bought gold simply as it was brought to them at or below the Mint price; and it was a matter of indifference, as concerned the amount of the currency, whether the gold was taken by the importers to the Mint, and thence brought directly into circulation as coin, or were taken in the shape of bullion to the Bank in return for its notes.

(1829a: 22n.; 1838, II: 108n.)

Indeed, in contrast to Ricardo, Tooke (1821b: 295) approved of the early resumption of payments in cash by the Bank of England because it brought to an end the 'capricious fluctuation of the currency' which arose from being on so 'indefinite footing'. Hence, though Tooke and Ricardo were allies in the return to the gold standard, they did differ on the practical questions of the manner by which it was implemented and its subsequent impact on trade and prices. Whereas Ricardo tended to believe that the ongoing depression in trade and prices made resumption more difficult to achieve because of its deflationary effect, Tooke believed the economic situation actually made resumption easier to achieve without having to impose any deflationary policy on an already depressed economy.[6]

It was shown in Section 5.5 that Tooke ascertained that the imposition of the restriction of cash payments had only a minor inflationary impact on the British economy. He also argued that the return to a convertible system of currency had only a minor deflationary effect on prices. Tooke (1829a: 27–38; 1829b: 46–53; 1838, II: 94–116) continued to defend Peel's Act of 1819 from criticism for nearly twenty years after its enactment. His strong support for the gold standard was based on the contention that it would impart stability onto prices and enhance the confidence of traders entering into commercial transactions. In the first place, and unlike a regime under restriction, a convertible system of currency eliminated the possibility of the Bank of England (or the government) from accommodating an amount of paper money in circulation which induced persistent depreciation in its value through the depreciation of the foreign exchanges. For Tooke, the gold standard eliminated any significant depreciation in the foreign exchanges which, by raising import prices, had an inflationary impact. Moreover, by limiting the fluctuation of the exchanges around par, it ensured stability in the value of the paper currency.

Second and more importantly, Tooke (1829a: 20–21n.) believed the gold standard provided a stable unit of account for money. This viewpoint was fully elaborated by Tooke in the following passages:

> in stating and proving that a standard meant a certain quantity of gold … an important distinction [exists] between two functions of money: the one, that of serving as an instrument of exchange; the other, that of being the subject of contracts for future payment. It is in the latter capacity that the fixity of a standard is most essential.

(1848a, IV: 145)

As a mere instrument or medium of exchange, at the same time and in the same place, invariableness of value, though desirable, is not of so much importance; the immediate purpose of money in this capacity being to serve as a point, or rather scale, of comparison more convenient than actual barter between any two commodities or sets of commodities. It is in the latter capacity, that is to say, as the subject of engagements or obligations for future payment, that in every view of justice and policy, the specific thing promised, in quantity and quality, should be paid at the expiration of the term.

(1848a, IV: 146)

Both the seller and the buyer of the goods, and the lender and borrower on mortgage, are willing to take their chance of what the value of gold may be at the expiration of the term. It is true that gold may vary in value; but there is no other commodity, silver perhaps excepted, so little liable to vary. And there is, accordingly, no other commodity than gold, or silver, which it would suit both parties to look for eventual payment.

(1848a, IV: 146–7)

In this role the gold standard was considered by Tooke to lessen the uncertainty of traders about the future value of (or payment on) contractual obligations, thereby enhancing commercial activities. In support of this argument, Tooke (1848a, IV: 148–50) quoted frequently from Samuel Bailey's *Money and its Vicissitudes in Value* (1837: 100–5) and cited approvingly Ricardo's pamphlet, *The High Price of Bullion* (1811a). In fact Tooke's viewpoint was commonly held by classical economists (bullionists). It was based on the supposition that compared to any other commodity, the intrinsic value of gold was highly stable over time. The justification for this supposition came from the Ricardian theory of the determination of the value of gold (or silver) as a scarce resource. The conditions for the stability in the value of gold based on this theory detailed in Section 3.5 do not appear to have been known to Tooke until the 1840s, after he read Senior (1840). So, while from the beginning Tooke assumes the value of gold to be stable, only in his banking school writings is there evidence that he understood the conditions underpinning its long-run stability.

6.2 Money, credit and prices

In consideration of Tooke's pre-banking school position on the relationship between money, credit and prices, it will be instructive to do so in terms of the basic propositions of the classical economists' quantity theory of money. This will enable the consideration of Tooke's position in relation to the monetary orthodoxy of nineteenth-century classical economics.[7] What follows in this section will proceed by reference to three important theoretical propositions of the quantity theory: external adjustment in terms of the 'price–specie–flow' mechanism; the autonomous control of the Bank of England (the central banking authority) over the whole quantity of money and credit in circulation; and the causal relationship between the quantity of money (and credit) in circulation and prices and economic activity. For the most part, our investigation of Tooke's pre-banking school monetary thought concerns his position on monetary behaviour under a gold convertible system of currency that operated in the British economy after 1821.

6.2.1 External adjustment

In general, Tooke subscribed to the price–specie–flow doctrine as a *long-run* mechanism of external adjustment. However, he had major reservations about its *short-run* efficacy. When he appeared as a witness to the Lords Committee on Resumption in 1819, Tooke was questioned on the external adjustment process by which the foreign exchanges are restored to par. In the hypothetically proposed case of an autonomous 'reduction of Banknotes' which induced a decline in the prices of domestically produced commodities, Tooke (1819b: (Q 13–14) 170) was clear that an improved trade balance depended on the response of foreign and domestic demand to the relative price change. Tooke acknowledged that this response was conditional on '[T]he Wants, of effectual Demand of Foreign Countries, as well as at Home', but maintained them to be 'very much influenced by the Price' since 'a Quantity of Commodities, which is much beyond the Vent at one Price, may be within it at another' (1819b: (Q 15) 170). On the conditions necessary for an improvement in export revenue, Tooke stated: 'in almost all Cases of increased Exportation in consequence of reduced Prices, the Total Amount in Value at the low Prices exceeds what it would have been in the Case of a smaller Quantity at higher Prices' (1819b: (Q 16) 170).

On the import side, Tooke appears to have believed that a reduction in the relative price of domestic products would more easily lower the domestic demand for foreign products, perhaps because there was greater scope for substitution in industrial England than in foreign countries.

While Tooke certainly believed that a favourable change in relative prices would improve the trade balance, in contrast to Ricardo's position, for example, he did not regard the adjustment process as automatic but rather as a tendency whose effective operation was subject to wider circumstances. This is clear from the answer he gave to a question about whether 'Foreign Countries will be able and willing to purchase a larger Amount of Value' following a reduction of prices:

> I should say, that in general that would be the Effect, or that in general such is the Tendency of reduced prices, taking a greater or shorter Length of Time to produce the full Effect, according to Circumstances, too numerous to detail; such as Distance, the bulk or quality of the articles, &c.
>
> (1819b: (Q 17) 170)

These wider circumstances, variously elaborated upon in later writings by Tooke, governed the period of time over which adjustment in the balance of trade occurred. The kind of circumstances (in peacetime) mentioned by Tooke (1826: 90–1, 113–14) included prohibitions and other legislative restrictions on trade, the state of credit conditions in foreign markets, the distance of transit of commodities between foreign and domestic markets, and supply conditions (principally of re-exports) affecting the ability to satisfy effectual demand abroad. Since these circumstances were 'incidental to all extensive commercial relations' (Tooke 1826: 90, 114) contended that the adjustment in trade flows 'requires an interval of some length' before it induced bullion flows.[8]

Prominent in Tooke's thinking on the process of adjustment of the balance of payments was the role of capital flows, consisting of foreign loans, international debt payments and discretionary payments in bullion unrelated to transactions in trade (including foreign exchange speculation and government military expenditure abroad). Tooke believed the level of the rate of interest, relative to other countries, played a key role in regulating the direction of commercially related international capital movements. Thus, in explaining to the Lords Committee on Resumption how the 1819 monetary contraction could restore the exchanges to par, Tooke argued that:

> there is a Tendency to an Increase of the Rate of Interest of Money, which may have the Effect of bringing back some Part of the British Capital which had been forced out by the previous artificial Reduction of the Rate of Interest at Home.
>
> (1819b: (Q 13) 170; also see (Q 32) 172)

And then, more than a decade later, he stated to the Committee on the Renewal of the Bank Charter in 1832:

> Q 3948 If the mode by which the Bank endeavours to rectify the Exchanges is contracting its issue, how does that contraction of the issue of the Bank act upon the Exchanges? – Tooke: It operates in two modes, namely, by its tendency, *ceteris paribus*, to reduce prices and to raise the rate of interest; it therefore tends ultimately, though perhaps not immediately, to increase the export and to diminish the import of commodities and to check the transmission of capital.
>
> (1832: 286)

It is evident that in Tooke's analysis the rate of interest is the key mechanism in the short-run adjustment of the balance of payments and the foreign exchanges to par. For him, a deficit on the balance of payments leading to a net outflow of bullion and depreciation of the foreign exchanges below par tended to raise the (relative) rate of interest and arrest net capital outflows; and vice versa. Thus, when a deterioration in the foreign exchanges occurred, Tooke (1826: 93–6; 1838, II: 287, 296) believed the accompanying rundown in bullion reserves caused the Bank of England to adopt a tougher monetary stance and accordingly raise its discount rate on commercial bills (or equivalently shorten the term of the discount). The resulting rise in market rates of interest tended to correct the foreign exchanges by attracting bullion from overseas investors in domestic securities. On the other hand, under circumstances when the foreign exchanges rise above par, Tooke (1838, I: 194) believed that an accompanying inflow of bullion would tend to reduce market rates of interest on securities, often in relation to an unchanged discount rate charged by the Bank of England. Tooke (1826: 46–55; 1838, II: 148–9, 191) also noticed instances when the Bank of England autonomously brought down the structure of interest rates on securities relative to 'prospective' returns overseas, thereby inducing capital outflows and placing pressures on the exchanges. In this way Tooke believed by exerting influence on the short-term market rate of interest, the Bank of England could, via its direct effect on capital flows, effectively correct the balance of payments in the short run and ensure stability of the foreign exchanges around par. This was distinguishable from the indirect effect of the rate of interest on the foreign exchanges, which was conceived by Tooke to operate in the long run according to the influence of changes in monetary policy on (relative) prices and trade flows.

Tooke maintained that periodically Britain's balance of payments and its foreign exchanges were seriously disrupted by natural and political events which, in particular, included large importations of grain as a result of climatically induced reductions in the domestic production of corn and the sudden collapse of export markets as a result of war or social revolution (1838, I: 217, 241, 246–52, 272–3, 295–6, 303–6, 353–5; II: 8–10, 154–6). In addition, Tooke (1826: 90n.; 1829a: 70–2; 1838, II: 139–40) showed an awareness of irregular cycles in the position of the balance of payments according to the timing of export receipts and import payments, sometimes referring to the delay in 'returns' on export sales and, especially, to the adverse effect of the Corn Laws, by its tendency to increase the lumpiness of import volumes at high duties. With regard to external adjustment, Tooke believed the price–specie–flow mechanism worked only slowly over the long run according to the aforementioned indirect effect of monetary policy on (relative) prices. The point is that he regarded it as a fundamental long-run tendency rather than as an automatic self-correcting mechanism. Tooke believed that, in the short run, external adjustment operated through the direct effect on capital flows of policy-induced variations in the level of the interest rate relative to overseas (as further clarified in Section 6.2.3).

6.2.2 Policy control over the quantity of money

The pre-banking school Tooke believed the power of the Bank of England, as the central banking authority, to autonomously control the *whole* quantity of money, and credit in circulation (i.e. 'circulating medium') was heavily constrained in the short run. This view stemmed from Tooke's position on the causal relationship between the circulating medium and price fluctuations. From the beginning he believed the Bank of England could autonomously control its own banknotes in circulation, but subscribed to Thornton's (1802: 75–80, 90–102, 212–24) position that their velocity of circulation was subject to variation. To the Commons Committee on Resumption, Tooke (1819a: 132) contended that this velocity usually varied with 'what is called confidence' when '[G]oods change hands freely upon notes, or other means of credit, and therefore the currency has fewer functions to perform, and is less detained in the hands of the different classes who have to part with it'. These short-run variations in velocity were considered to be associated with alternations in economic activity (in the 'rapidity or stagnation in the circulation of commodities') and fluctuations in the prices of commodities. According to Tooke (1819a: 127, 132), for a given amount of Bank of England notes and coin, 'the value of currency depends very much upon the rapidity of its circulation', rising (or declining) with a low (or high) 'state of confidence' and 'slowness' (or 'rapidity') in its velocity of circulation.

Although Tooke did not dissent from the premise that the Bank of England, through the management of its banknotes, can influence the whole quantity of money (and credit) in circulation, he contended in particular that the amount of country banknotes could vary independently of Bank of England notes and coin. This is evident in his answer to the following question:

> Have you observed, within your own experience, in the city of London, what is called abundance, and sometimes a scarcity, without any corresponding increase or diminution, at the same periods, in the amount of the bank of England paper? – Tooke: ... in the case of bank issues, there may be, from distinct causes, an increase or diminution of country bank notes, without a corresponding change in the amount of bank of England paper ...
>
> (1819a: 131)

Among those 'distinct causes' affecting the quantity of country banknotes, Tooke emphasised the supply conditions of corn because it had a considerable influence on the 'general prices of other commodities, as well as of corn' (1819a: 132).

In his not always clearly stated argument about the inter-relationship between the conditions of production, the movement in prices, the role of confidence and speculative activity in commodity markets, Tooke (1819a: 127–32) came very close to contending that variations in the structure of credit depended on prices. This position was developed more firmly on empirical grounds in *High and Low Prices*, with Tooke (1824, i: 93, 106–19) finding 'little coincidence' between variations in the quantity of Bank of England notes and in 'private paper', ascertaining that 'the most striking instances of a great rise of general prices occurred without any increase of Bank notes' and 'the most memorable instances of a sudden fall took place contemporaneously with large additions to the Bank circulation'. In the *Considerations*, Tooke argued that a major difficulty for the Bank in regulating the whole 'paper circulation' arose 'out of the nature of the country bank circulation' which seemed 'to be dependent on circumstances not immediately under the control of the Bank of England' (1826: 86n.). Those circumstances were the afore-mentioned state of market conditions and prices of agricultural commodities. It was this reasoning that lay behind Tooke's opinion to the Commons Committee on the Renewal of the Bank Charter in 1832 that 'I conceive that the Bank of England has a very imperfect power of controlling the country circulation' (1832: (Q 3906) 282).

As well as the paper money circulation in the country, Tooke (1824, i: 63–8) argued that monetary circulation affected by cheques (i.e. deposit transfers) and bills of exchange in the City of London also varied in the short run independently of Bank of England notes and coin. On the basis of the dependence of country banks on their correspondent London banks for readily convertible funds, Tooke maintained that variations in country notes were usually associated with changes in the amount of 'book credits' of London deposit banks and the circulation of bills of exchange in the City: 'In fact, a speculative advance of prices generally originates in London, and then it affords the means and inducement to an extension of country bank paper' (1829a: 31n.). In rebutting the position of the Bullion Committee of 1810 that in the short run the quantity of Bank of England notes was a limitation on the extension of country banknotes in circulation, Tooke argued that:[9]

> The error ... is in the assumption that the whole amount of London circulation is commensurate or identical *at any given time* with the Bank of England paper circulating in the metropolis, and accordingly the conclusion that a demand upon the country bankers for bills on London is equivalent to a demand for Bank of England notes and requires an increase of these to support extended issue of the country bankers, is incorrect, as referring to any limited period.
>
> (1829a: 31–2n.)

In his *Letter to Lord Grenville*, Tooke (1829a: 117–27) supported his position by reference to a paper by James Pennington which was published as Appendix I of this work. Pennington's paper expounded the process by which London deposit banks expanded and contracted their book-credits on the basis of a given amount of Bank of England notes and coin necessary to meet 'occasional demands' made on them.[10] This 1829 paper, together with some clarifications made by Pennington in a follow-up letter published as Appendix C of Tooke's *History* (1838, II: 369–78),[11] is particularly significant because, based on fractional reserve banking, it set out a credit-creation process in which loans advanced by banks generated re-deposits. In the analysis of Pennington, the process depended on, and was limited by, first, the cash reserve requirements of the banks, second, the proportion of currency which is habitually held as banknotes and coin rather than as book-deposits and, lastly, whether the circumstances of trade are conducive to the extension of loans by deposit banks overall. The analysis lent considerable support to Tooke's (1832: (Q 3819–20)

270, (Q 3836) 272; 1838, I: 172, 203; II: 123–4, 334) general argument that in the short run the whole quantity of paper money and credit varied in proportion to its 'basis', consisting of Bank of England notes and coin, according to the state of market activity: increasing with a 'spirit of speculation' and high confidence and declining with 'stagnation and despondency' in commodity and share markets.

6.2.3 Relationship between the price level and money

By *History* (1838, I, II) the pre-banking school Tooke had taken the firm position that the variation in the whole circulating medium was predominantly the *consequence* of short-run fluctuations in the price level. Moreover, he contended that in sympathy with price fluctuations, the velocity of circulation of the 'basis' of the currency was often accompanied by an inverse change in the quantity of Bank of England notes in circulation. This position was largely outlined in the following passage:

> it may be remarked of this portion of the circulating medium [country banknotes], that, supposing it to bear for local purposes a certain due proportion to the basis of the currency, the deviations from this, its due level, have been, not only during, but before and since the restriction, very considerable, expanding under circumstances, and in a state of opinion, favouring a rise of prices, and collapsing under the opposite circumstances; and these expansions and contractions have, in the majority of instances, not been preceded by any corresponding variations of the Bank issues, although eventually they have come under the limitation and control of the Bank regulation.
>
> The same, and perhaps in a still greater degree, may be said of those other component parts of the circulating medium, bills of exchange, and book credits.... The expansion and contraction of these and country bank notes, are, as will be abundantly exemplified, the *consequences, and not the causes,* of a rise and fall of prices.
>
> (1838, I: 148–9; emphasis added)

Nevertheless, as indicated in this quotation, Tooke believed the Bank of England, through the regulation of its issues, could influence, albeit imperfectly, the whole circulating medium, limiting its variations in the short run and bringing it under control in the long run.

In his pre-banking school writings and parliamentary evidence, but especially his discussion of the regulation of banknote issues in Section III of the *Considerations* (1826), Tooke identified four main ways in which the Bank of England influenced the wider 'paper circulation'. First, by directly altering the rate at which it discounted commercial bills of exchange brought to its door in relation to the market rate of interest. Thus, according to Tooke (1826: 73–83), by lowering (or raising) the bank rate in relation to the market rate on short-term bills of exchange, the Bank was able to induce an enlarged (or reduced) application for discount facilities upon which its banknotes could be expanded (or contracted). Second, by altering the volume of commercial bills of exchange it discounted (i.e. loans) at a given bank rate. It is evident though that Tooke (1826: 77–80; 1829a: 54–7; 1832: (Q 4080–3) 299–300) believed the effectiveness of this rationing method depended on the state of the money market; with a policy of extending or reducing its accommodation more effective when there were pressures in the money market and a relatively high market rate of interest was inducing a greater demand for discount facilities at the Bank than when market conditions were slack and the market rate low. Third, by the sale or purchase of securities, in particular government exchequer bills issued on the open market, the Bank of England could alter its notes in circulation as well as exert an influence on the market rate of interest (Tooke 1826: 73–4; 1832: (Q 5454) 441–2, (Q 5478) 444). Fourth, through advances to and repayments from government, the Bank could influence the amount of its notes in circulation (Tooke 1826: 79–81; 1829a: 61–71; 1832: (Q 4084) 300). However, Tooke believed that this method was not really at the discretion of the Bank of England, but rather at that of the British government according to whether it was cheaper to borrow funds in the open market or at the Bank.[12]

From his various discourses on the subject, it is evident that Tooke believed the Bank of England regulated its banknotes mainly through the second and third channels. Indeed, given the non-discretionary nature of government funding arrangements and the institutionalised policy of the Bank of England to charge a fixed discount rate under the constraints of the usury law, these were the two most effective channels available for regulating its banknotes in circulation. According to Tooke the latter policy position especially hampered the ability of the Bank to regulate its issues:

> One of the great difficulties which the directors have experienced in the regulation of their issues, has arisen from the uniformity of the bank rate of discount, while market-rate of interest has been subject to frequent and sometimes great variations. The consequence of this has been, that when the market-rate has been above the rate charged by the bank, the applications for discount have been so numerous and urgent, that the issues through that medium have tended to an excess; while, on the other hand, when the market-rate has fallen below the bank-rate, the channel for keeping up the circulation of paper through the medium of discount, seems almost wholly to have failed.
>
> (1826: 77–8)

That Tooke focused on this difficulty is an indication of his interest in the transmission process by which the Bank of England could effectively conduct policy (see Section 6.4). More so than most of his contemporaries, Tooke did associate the regulation of the Bank of England notes in circulation with alterations in the rate of interest.[13]

In spite of the constraints mentioned above, Tooke believed the Bank of England had the power to control the whole circulating medium in the long run by affecting the reserves of the commercial banks, in particular the country banks and, by the late-1830s, the provincially established joint-stock banks. However, as will be clarified below (pp. 140–43), Tooke believed this power was largely asymmetric: the Bank could restrain the commercial banks and force them to reduce their paper circulation, but it could not cause them to expand it and, thereby, increase the whole circulating medium independently of economic activity and prices. Thus, Tooke conceded that in circumstances when trade and manufacturing were 'flourishing' and 'confidence was entire', the commercial banks could, in the short run, counteract or even undermine a restrictive policy stance of the Bank of England. But he argued that this would:

> not proceed far, nor last long, under a resolute reduction of its securities by the Bank of England. The reserves of the country banks must be in gold or Bank of England notes: these they would have an increasing difficulty to possess themselves of, the resource of re-discounting in London being greatly curtailed, so that the means of making advances, as well by discounts and by book credits, as by issue of notes, would be abridged, and the whole of the country circulation would thus be more or less restrained ...
>
> (1838, II: 287–8)

Tooke (1838, II: 302) indicated that this process entailed the eventual adoption by provincial banks of the higher rate of interest 'established in London'.

In Tooke's view it was also possible for the Bank of England to exert an influence on credit conditions and the whole circulating medium in the short run, chiefly through the effect of its operations on the market rate of interest on short-term bills. This was based on the notion that the level of interest had an influence on speculative activity in both the share and commodity markets. According to Tooke (1826: 36–47, 55–8, 83–4; 1838, I: 194; II: 148–9, 191, 344–5) a low rate of interest facilitated credit-financed buying of shares and commodities by traders intent on making windfall profits from expected price hikes; while a high rate discouraged this speculative activity. But significantly, Tooke (1832: (Q 3845–6) 274–5) believed that an accommodating monetary policy and low interest rate was not the 'moving power' but rather acted to encourage the heightening of speculative activity. He also came to believe that a low rate was a greater inducement to share speculation than to speculation in commodities. In reference to a speculative upturn in commodity and share markets in 1835–1836, Tooke wrote:

> although, as regards the markets for goods, there is not a trace of any *direct* influence of the amount of the currency, or of the rate of interest, on the rise of prices of produce in 1835–6, the case, as relates to the share markets, is different; both the inducement to adventure, and the means of investment in joint-stock companies, are alike promoted, by a low, and above all, by a falling rate of interest.
>
> (1838, II: 326)

Tooke (1838, II: 177–81, 287, 298, 302) believed that if well-managed, monetary policy was capable of suppressing speculatively driven expansions in paper credit. Its effectiveness largely rested on how quickly the Bank of England was able to identify speculative activity and, by reducing its issues and raising the discount rate on bills, dampen confidence in the markets before a 'spirit of speculation' gained momentum. For Tooke (1826: 42–54, 87–90; 1832: (Q 3849) 275–6), this policy action may often involve the Bank having to adopt a restrictive stance in absence of any signs of depreciation in the foreign exchanges or rundown in its bullion reserves. He strongly believed the most effective mechanism for immediately influencing monetary conditions was by direct alterations of the bank rate in relation to the market rate of interest. Hence, the aforementioned limitations to varying the bank rate was seen by Tooke (1826: 77–8; 1829a: 58–61) to be a significant handicap on the capacity of the Bank of England to exert a restraining influence on short-run inflationary expansions of the whole circulating medium.

It was shown in the previous chapter that Tooke believed the primary causes of price variations were natural and political factors affecting the supply conditions of commodities. From these causes short-run price fluctuations were considered by Tooke to be accommodated by changes in the whole circulating medium, usually associated with sympathetic variations in the velocity of Bank of England notes and coin. Hence, for the most part, causality was held by Tooke to run from prices to the whole circulating medium, while its basis, the quantity of banknotes and coin in circulation, separately depended on the policy stance of the Bank of England. Yet, despite this position, the pre-banking school Tooke adhered 'in principle' to the quantity theory of money. To the Bank Charter Committee of 1832, Tooke stated: '[A]s a general proposition I am quite prepared to admit, and I have never denied, that all other things being the same, an increase of the circulating medium would tend to produce a rise of prices, and vice versa' (1832: (Q 4019) 294; also see 1832: (Q 5439) 440). A reconciliation between these two apparently conflicting positions lies with Tooke's view on the permissive role of credit in price fluctuations and the policy response of the Bank of England. This is best explained in terms of Tooke's conception of the anatomy of price fluctuations.

Tooke (1824, i: 63–6) argued that the *original* cause of short-run price fluctuations was natural and political factors which induced an imbalance between the demand for and supply of a major commodity (i.e. corn) or group of commodities. The resulting fluctuation in the price level will often be associated with, and aggravated by, speculative activity in the markets. According to Tooke, the circumstances that gave rise to a 'spirit of speculation' and 'overtrading' are those of excess demand in the markets for major commodities, either as a result of an actual or anticipated deficiency in supply or as a result of an anticipated higher demand from the 'opening up of new and extensive markets'. The speculatively driven upward movement in the price level is accommodated by an expansion in paper credit. For Tooke the extent to which speculative activity is 'excited' and permitted to raise prices depended heavily on the supply of credit provided by the banking system.

While Tooke believed the enlargement in the circulating medium was always the consequence of the speculative ascent of prices, the banking system could nevertheless have an influence on the latter through the effect of its banknote issues on credit conditions.[14] It is evident Tooke (1838, I: 148–9; II: 312–14, 332) believed that subject to the institutional structure of the banking system, only the Bank of England possessed the power to autonomously influence banknote circulation and monetary conditions. Hence, according to Tooke, if the Bank adopted an expansionary policy that extended credit facilities and provided a further stimulus to speculation, it will contribute to a higher range of prices. This position was crystallised by Tooke in the following way:

> Now my firm belief is, that there is hardly a single instance in which the Bank of England issues can be adduced as the origin of the rise of prices. As I have said before, when the increase takes place coincident with a disposition to speculate from other causes, then it very naturally contributes to extend the range of speculation.
>
> (1832: (Q 3845) 274; also see (Q 5448–9) 441)

Tooke added, moreover, 'it is a subject on which I think more delusion prevails than any other I am acquainted with' (1832: (Q 3845) 274). Tooke argued a speculatively driven increase in prices would inevitably lead to 'overtrading', and from a lack of 'consumption' demand, eventually to an excess supply in commodity markets which would cause a collapse of prices. Tooke (1824, i: 66–8) maintained that the greater the speculative upturn, the more violent would be the 'recoil' in commodity markets and decline in prices which followed, and the deeper the 'stagnation and despondency' in financial markets. Hence, according to Tooke (1838, II: 177–88, 191–2, 286–97, 344), to the extent that Bank of England policy contributed to a speculative boom, it will also have contributed to the subsequent commercial discredit and contraction of the circulating medium.

The pre-banking school Tooke believed monetary policy to be an auxiliary cause of short-run price fluctuations. The Bank of England's influence though was considered by Tooke to be largely asymmetric. It was capable of accommodating an expansion in credit which aggravated a speculative upturn in prices and, by the adoption of a restrictive policy stance when confidence in the markets was beginning to wane, to also bring on the inevitable turnaround and decline in prices. But Tooke was of the view that, except when it was a reaction to a speculative boom, the Bank was less capable of extending a decline in prices as a result of an excess supply in commodity markets caused by natural and political factors (e.g. an abundant domestic harvest of corn). In his empirical studies covering the period from 1792 to 1837, Tooke (1826: 2–35; 1838, II: 46–55, 172–89, 280 et seq.) ascertained that the Bank of England contributed significantly to price variations in 1817, 1824–1825 and 1835, by accommodating a speculatively driven expansion in the circulating medium. It is notable Tooke fully appreciated that on the latter two occasions, the speculative booms which led to financial crisis in 1825–1826 and 1835–1836, applied especially to shares and foreign investments rather than to commodities. Therefore, for the greater part, Tooke believed that in practice the Bank of England exerted little influence on price fluctuations:

> In the research I have had occasion to make into the fluctuations of prices, with a comparison of precise dates of the occurrence of enlarged issue, and likewise of the occurrence of advanced prices, as likewise of a contraction of paper and a fall of prices, I have been struck with great surprise at finding that in point of fact the sequence did not answer the previous expectation; that the most signal instances of a rise in prices, and the most signal instances of a fall of prices, have been totally unconnected in their origin with the Bank of England issues; that is, the rise of prices has *preceded* any large issue of Bank of England paper, and a fall of prices has *preceded* contraction, and in some instances it proceeded consistently with a very enlarged issue of paper.
>
> (1832: (Q 3976) 289; emphasis added)

In his writings, especially in *History* (1838, I, II), Tooke continuously presented evidence to repudiate the position of the 'partisans of the currency doctrine' that the main cause of price fluctuations were variations in the quantity of Bank of England notes in circulation.[15]

The pre-banking school Tooke did not abandon the 'general principle' that changes in the quantity of circulating medium causally influenced the price level. However, Tooke acknowledged it only as a long-run tendency that did not work in practice. Before the Bank Charter Committee of 1832 Tooke stated: 'I have always acknowledged the general principle, that, other things being same, variations in the amount of the circulating medium have a tendency to influence prices' (1832: (Q 5439) 440); and then, to the question, 'But your notion of that tendency arises from general principle, rather than from any observation of facts?', replied, 'Certainly' (1832: (Q 5440) 440). The only circumstance in which Tooke believed the Bank of England exerted a lasting influence on the price level occurred during the restriction period when, as already considered in Section 5.5, a passive monetary policy allowed the depreciation of an inconvertible paper to persist, so raising the cost of imports. Even in this instance, Tooke was of the view that the original causes of this depreciation were natural and political factors. In a convertible system of currency, Tooke believed that through the regulation of its issues, the Bank could not have such a persistent influence on the price level incompatible with the market price of gold being around its mint standard.[16] Tooke (1832, Q 4013–14: 293) believed the Bank of England's obligation to maintain convertibility of its banknotes placed a limit on its capacity to causally influence the price level. This relates to Tooke's view about the Bank's role in the external adjustment process.

To begin with, according to Tooke, the indicator (or test) for ascertaining an excess or deficiency in the circulating medium was the depreciated or appreciated state of the foreign exchanges, irrespective of its original causes, largely attributable to natural and political factors. In particular, when the foreign exchanges fell below par and there was a serious rundown in the country's bullion reserves, Tooke (1832: (Q 3880–1) 279) contended that external adjustment involved the Bank of England adopting a restrictive policy which, by constricting the facility for credit provision, tended to reduce domestic prices. However, Tooke believed the price–specie–flow mechanism worked so slowly that in practice external adjustment largely relied on the more immediate effect of a higher rate of interest attracting capital flows from abroad. Moreover, it is evident from Tooke's (1826: 56–60; 1838, II: 160–71, 283 et seq.) analysis that he believed a decline in general prices, especially if in reaction to a speculative rise, would often quickly undermine confidence and lead to the widespread withdrawal of credit, which acted to raise the market rate of interest on bills. Hence, the Bank's role in facilitating external adjustment was dependent on the state of credit conditions in relation to the (irregular) cyclical movement of commodity (and share) prices. The important point is that Tooke did not regard external adjustment as being an automatic self-correcting process but, instead, one often requiring skilful management by the Bank of England to prevent a drain of bullion that endangered the convertibility of the currency.

6.2.4   The evolution of Tooke's pre-banking school monetary thought

A consideration of the evolution of Tooke's pre-banking school monetary thought shows that he progressively attached less relevance to the explanatory power of the classical economists' quantity theory of money so that, by 1838, he had all but abandoned it except in principle. Basically, he subscribed to it only as a general proposition which had little practical relevance to explaining the movement in the general level of money prices. From the beginning Tooke rejected Ricardo's rigid version of the quantity theory with its supposition of a stable proportional relationship between the overall structure of paper credit and Bank of England notes and coin (and specie reserves). In contrast, Tooke maintained this proportion normally varied in the short run in correspondence with price fluctuations. The emphasis that Tooke placed on the permissive role of credit, in particular the link he made between it and commercial confidence, in his evidence to the resumption committees of 1819, attests to the early influence of Henry Thornton and, before him, Adam Smith. Like Thornton, Tooke believed there was considerable elasticity in the English monetary system with paper credit able to accommodate variations in the price level largely independent of Bank of England policy. However, Tooke was much more sanguine than Thornton about the causal influence of monetary policy on the level of prices and the power of the Bank of England to nullify it by stringency, even in an inconvertible system of paper currency.

On the basis of his empirical study, *High and Low Prices* (1823, 1824), Tooke ascertained that monetary policy was largely an auxiliary cause and *not* an *originating* cause of price movements in England during the period of restriction and afterwards to 1822. In the *Considerations* (1826) and subsequently in the *Letter* (1829a) and *Second Letter to Lord Grenville* (1829b) he criticised the

quantity theory for its lack of practical application in explaining monetary behaviour and providing a reliable basis for policy-making. As shown in Section
6.2.1, Tooke rejected the automatic nature of the price–specie–flow mechanism
of external adjustment claimed by Ricardo and some other classical quantity theorists. He argued that given the periodic occurrence of exogenous disturbances
by real economic forces, financial stability demanded an *active* policy on the part
of the Bank of England under a post-1821 convertible system of currency.

It was shown in Section 6.2.3 that by 1832 Tooke had taken the position that
the quantity theory was a general principle with little practical relevance. By
History (1838, I, II), Tooke had adopted the radical position that causality tended
to run in reverse from prices to the whole circulating medium and that, in particular, country banknotes in circulation were mainly the consequence of variations in the (relative) price of agricultural commodities. In this way Tooke
steadily dismissed the influence of quantitative changes in monetary circulation
to explaining the movement in the general price level. Nevertheless, Tooke
maintained the Bank of England possessed the power to autonomously regulate
its own banknotes in circulation and, thereby, was able to exert a limiting influence on credit conditions and speculative activity in commodity and share
markets. In the short run, he believed the Bank's influence exerted through the
rate of interest was heavily constrained, with the effect of its policy stance
dependent on concrete circumstances. In the long run, he believed the Bank,
through a restrictive monetary policy, had the power to limit an inflationary
expansion in credit. In this connection it was his position that as a auxiliary
cause of price movements, the ill-judged adoption of an accommodating policy
stance by the Bank of England could well exacerbate speculatively driven price
rises.

6.3 On interest and profits

A major theoretical issue on which the pre-banking school Tooke dissented from
commonly received opinion was the relationship between the determination of the
money rate of interest and the rate of profit on productively employed capital. In the
Considerations Tooke began his analysis of the rate of interest by observing that '[T]
he commonly-received opinion, and that generally adopted by political economists
is, that the rate of interest is governed by the rate of profit' (1826: 6). This 'commonly received opinion' in the early nineteenth century can be attributed chiefly to
Adam Smith (1776 [1976]: 69–70, 105–6) and Ricardo (1821: 296–7), who maintained that the money rate of interest was ultimately governed by the rate of profit so
that, in the long run, changes in the normal rate of profit, an unobservable magnitude,
could be inferred from observing changes in the average rate of interest.

Adam Smith and Ricardo both conceived that the normal profit rate consisted of two parts: the money rate of interest as the pure remuneration on loan
capital and a remuneration to compensate for the 'risk and trouble' normally
associated with employing capital productively. Of these two parts into which
profit resolves, they treated interest on money as the residual one, determined

by the deduction of the remuneration for risk and trouble from the normal profit rate. Based on the supposition that the remuneration for risk and trouble was a stable magnitude in relation to the normal profit rate, Smith and Ricardo believed that long-run changes in the profit rate translated into sympathetic changes in the money rate of interest.[17] Hence, the commonly held position among classical economists of the early nineteenth century was that the rate of interest was 'ultimately' and 'permanently' determined by those real forces that determined the normal rate of profit. In Adam Smith the real forces imprecisely consisted of an array of socio-institutional and technical factors that determined conditions of competition and economic development; while, in Ricardo, they consisted in a precise manner of the real wage in conjunction with the technique of production. This orthodoxy was challenged by Tooke in the 1820s when he argued that the money rate of interest was heavily influenced by institutional factors in the financial market independent of production conditions determining the rate of profit. By the late-1830s, Tooke had adopted the novel position that the institutionally determined rate of interest actually governed the rate of profit. With special reference to the role of monetary factors, this section is concerned with Tooke's explanation of the determination of the money rate of interest and his dissenting position on its causal relationship with the profit rate.

The first indications that Tooke had serious doubts about the commonly received view among classical economists of the causal relationship between the rate of profit and interest rate occur in questions on the subject he promoted at Political Economy Club meetings in 1825. At the meeting of 2 May 1825, Tooke sponsored the following three questions:

Is the rate of Interest a correct index of the rate of Profit?

Is the rate of Profit, as indicated by the rate of Interest any criterion of the rate of accumulation of national capital?

When it is said that the rate of Profit depends upon wages, is the term Wages confined to necessaries of the most common labourers, or does it include the higher remuneration for the various gradations of skilled labour?

(Higgs 1921: 25)

Two more questions for discussion were promoted by him at the meeting of 6 June 1825:

Into what component parts may return to Capital be divided?

Has not the term 'rate of Profit', as applied to particular portions of Capital, a very different meaning from '*Profit*' when applied generally in a national point of view?

(Higgs 1921: 25)

These questions formed the basis of Tooke's argument against the 'commonly received opinion' on the causal relationship between the two rates in Section I of the *Considerations* (1826).

The foil for Tooke's argument was an article by J.R. McCulloch (1824a) which set out a Ricardian explanation of the profit rate, positing that it was a mark of a country's 'power of accumulation' whose magnitude could be empirically verified by the 'customary rate of interest' over which it regulated.[18] To begin with, Tooke (1826: 11–12) conformed to the conventional conception of classical economists that the rate of profit consisted of the rate of interest on 'monied capital' and a remuneration for the 'risk', 'trouble' and 'professional skill' for the productive employment of capital. This conception is outlined in the following passages:

> I should define the rate of interest to be that proportional sum which the lender is content to receive, and the borrower to pay, annually, or for any longer or shorter period, for the use of a certain amount of monied capital, without any consideration for trouble in the collection of the income, or for risk as to the punctual repayment of the interest or principal at the stipulated periods ...
>
> In this view, the *rate of interest is the measure of the net profit on capital*. All returns beyond this, on the employment of capital, are resolvable into compensations under distinct heads, for risk, trouble, or skill, or for advantages of situation or connexion ...
>
> (Tooke 1826: 11–12; also 1838, II: 355)

In the 1820s Tooke appears to have taken the position that the rate of profit was determined by real forces of production, which included the 'degree of productiveness', without specifying a precise theory of how they did so. The third question promoted by Tooke at the Political Economy Club meeting of 2 May 1823 (quoted above) indicates that he clearly understood the Ricardian explanation of the rate of profit, although, as already shown in Section 3.2.3, he rejected it. Nevertheless, having taken the position that the profit rate was generally determined by (technical) conditions of production, Tooke challenged the orthodox notion that the rate of interest was explained by, and consistently moved in sympathy with, the rate of profit: 'My only purpose, at present, is to inquire in what respect the rate of interest is an index of the rate of profit, and how far the former depends upon the latter' (1826: 6).

With regard to the form of the relationship between the two rates, Tooke (1826: 7) readily acknowledged that in the long run the 'average' rate of interest must 'bear some proportion' to the rate of profit because it 'indicates the degree of expectation of profit' on funds borrowed for productive purposes which must on average be realised (see also Arnon 1991: 82). The long run is an 'indefinite number of years', sufficient to balance out an array of possible natural and political disturbances which are a 'source of miscalculation' in the capital market (Tooke 1826: 7). Thus, for Tooke, the long-run average rate of interest is that rate established by the regularity of those forces he identified as persistent and not accidental ones. However, while the two rates tend to move in sympathy in the long run, Tooke argued the proportion that the rate of interest bears to the rate of profit changes according to fundamental alterations in the politico-institutional and conventional forces operating in the financial market in relation to the conditions of reproduction of profitably employed capital. In the short run, consisting of a period from as short as three years to up to ten years, Tooke (1826: 7–8, 11) held that a proportionality rule was not applicable, with the possibility of the two rates actually moving in opposite directions under some circumstances.

In substantiation of this argument, Tooke (1826: 9–12) claimed that 'commonly received opinion' on the relationship between the two rates is based on 'unsound premises' about the workings of the financial market (see also Panico 1988: 23). In the first place, not all funds are borrowed 'with a view to reproduction, or in other words, for profitable employment' (Tooke 1826: 10). In this context, funds borrowed for unproductive purposes, especially by the government, are seen by Tooke as highly significant in the determination of the level of the money rate independent of the profit rate. The second 'source of error' consisted in overlooking disparities between the supply of monied capital (i.e. loan funds) by lenders looking for a secure investment and the demand for it by borrowers able to offer 'good security' (Tooke 1826: 10). As shown below (pp. 148–51), these disparities are closely linked by Tooke with the risk-return preference of portfolio investors in relation to the risk-return profile of available financial assets. Nevertheless, according to Tooke (1826: 10–11), if the supply of monied capital were to increase in a 'greater ratio' than its demand, the rate of interest on the 'best securities' would tend to decline in relation to the profit rate. Hence, in pointing out the analytical omissions of the orthodox position, Tooke denied that the rate of interest could be simply explained by reference to the rate of profit.[19]

There is little doubt Tooke (1926: 8–9) came to this position from an observation that average rates of interest were higher during periods of war than during the intervening periods of peace. In particular, he was heavily influenced by the upward trend movement in the rate of interest during the course of the French Wars and afterwards when there was a massive accumulation of national debt (also see Kurz and Salvadori 1995: 490). Given the constraints placed on the British economy by war, it was difficult to attribute this rise to an improvement in the conditions of production which would have raised the level of the rate of profit.[20] Instead, Tooke attributed the increase in the rate of interest to government policy for financing war debt. Since government war debt amounted to funds borrowed for unproductive purposes, this view accords with his above-mentioned reasoning for the independence of systematic variations in the rate of interest in relation to the rate of profit. Tooke's thinking was also influenced by the sharp decline in the money rate from 1822 until late-1825, which he largely attributed to an excess supply of monied capital attenuated by the adoption of an accommodating monetary policy by the Bank of England (1826: 24–64). An important element of Tooke's explanation of the severe financial crisis in late-1825 was that the reduction in the interest rate on safe government securities caused investors to seek higher returns on more risky assets. For Tooke this latter motive of investors was the major cause of the unsustainable boom in the share market in 1824 and 1825 which led to financial collapse. Tooke reasoned the increased supply of monied capital tended to affect the risk-return preference of asset holders in such a way as to cause the rate of interest to fall in relation to the rate of profit. Hence, the development of Tooke's position sprang from an empirically based view that much of the variation in the rate of interest during the course of the French Wars, and until 1825, was attributable to politico-institutional factors in the financial market, independent of the rate of profit earned on productively employed capital.

According to Tooke (1826: 11–24; also 1838, II: 355–62) the average rate of interest was determined in the long run by the conditions of supply and demand for monied capital in the financial market. In Tooke's conception 'supply' and 'demand' refer to the supply and demand of a level or amount of loan funds absent of any functional relationship to the rate of interest. On this point it should be kept in mind that an analysis in which the supply and demand for loan capital are functions of the rate of interest is a modern conception which can only be logically developed from the marginal theory of capital and distribution (see Section 1.2). As anticipated by our comment, by 'monied capital', which was also referred to as 'disposable' or 'floating' capital, Tooke meant loans advanced on the 'security of bills, that is, on discount, on mortgage, or any other kind of security' (1826: 11n.) by 'owners of capital' who are 'unwilling or unable to employ their money actively themselves' (1826: 12) to either borrowers who actively invested the funds with a prospect of commercial return or who expended them unproductively. Tooke argued that only capital that came onto the financial market in the form of loans, when it then constituted monied capital, could influence the money rate of interest.[21]

The approach taken by Tooke in explaining the rate of interest consisted of identifying classes of lenders and borrowers in terms of their broad institutional role in, and, influence on, the behaviour of the financial market (Panico 1988: 24–5). To begin with, Tooke (1826: 13–18; 1838, II: 356–8) divided lenders into three generic classes according to the degree of risk of repayment and trouble of collecting the interest income which they were willing to accept. The first consisted of lenders who were willing to advance funds only on the 'best securities' not attended with either risk or trouble (e.g. government stock). Among these lenders were banks of all kinds and any other lenders who were 'precluded by legal or other disability' from investing in risky securities. The second class of lenders were those who had a preference for investing their monied capital in 'mortgages', 'ground-rents' and 'loans on goods and other securities' of 'little or any risk' but 'involving the necessity of superintendence, and more or less of trouble and exertion in collecting the annual interest' (1826: 15). The third class of lenders consisted of those prepared to 'run an extra degree of risk' in order to earn a return higher than the 'common' interest on safe securities, but 'without bestowing personal labour, or possessing any technical knowledge or skill, to qualify them for the active management of such investment' (1826: 16–17). Among this class are investors in 'sleeping partnerships', 'joint-stock companies', 'foreign loans', 'mining schemes' and other ventures of the most 'hazardous nature'.[22]

With respect to borrowers, Tooke (1826: 19–20; 1838, II: 359) divided them into two basic groups. The first group were 'productive' borrowers who employed capital 'beyond their own funds' with the prospect of earning a rate of profit that would 'remunerate them for their trouble, and skill, and risk' (1826: 19). This group of investors also included businessmen who urgently required funds to meet engagements already entered into beyond the capacity of their existing capital.[23] The second consisted of 'unproductive' borrowers who used funds to finance unproductive expenditures beyond their income. It is evident that by unproductive expenditure, Tooke was referring to that which is not applied to reproduction and, thereby, has no prospect of earning a commercial return. The major class of borrower of this type was the national government which can 'mortgage the revenues of the state' (1826: 20). Others included 'agents of foreign governments who raise loans in this country' and wealth-holders with 'personal security to offer' (1826: 19–20).

On the basis of this generic classification of lenders and borrowers, Tooke proposed an explanation of variations in the average rate of interest by logical stages of analysis:

> to consider, in the first place, the effect of an alteration in each class of the circumstances under consideration separately, the others remaining the same, and then to trace the influence of any variation in each class on all the others.
>
> (1826: 20)

Unfortunately, Tooke did not develop this analysis much beyond the first step. Nevertheless, from related discussion, it is evident Tooke believed the average rate of interest was generally affected by a change in the risk-return preference of possessors of monied capital and by a fundamental change in the proportion of monied capital going to unproductive compared to productive borrowers. Thus, Tooke (1826: 16) held the 'prevalence' of 'habits of prudence' by wealth-holders, such that the greater proportion of them occupied positions in the first two classes of lenders above, would tend to ensure a low 'average' rate of interest. He also maintained that the average rate would be higher as a greater proportion of monied capital was used to finance unproductive expenditures. In particular, Tooke (1826: 15) believed a 'state of war' would raise the 'average' rate of interest in order to attract wealth-holders other than those of the first class to absorb the resulting increase in government war debt. On the other hand, in peacetime, a reduction in government debt, achieved by a 'sinking fund' or a re-conversion operation, would lower the average rate of interest (1826: 14).[24] Thus, Tooke believed the main cause of long-run changes in the rate of interest came from alterations in government debt which were directly associated with war finance requirements, so that the average rate would rise in wartime and decline in peacetime. Overall, Tooke's approach was to explain the long-run average rate of interest in concrete terms by reference to a complex of politico-institutional factors and conventional attitudes of wealth-holders (and bankers) towards the risk-return profile of securities which underpinned the supply of and demand for monied capital in the financial market.

An important aspect of Tooke's position was that monetary factors can only exert an influence on the rate of interest in the short run. At the end of a long footnote in the *Considerations*, Tooke wrote:

> When the amount of the currency has become settled, for any length of time, at a particular level, it is immaterial, as related to the rate of interest, whether the level of the currency be at one half or at double of its former value: *the rate of interest will then be governed entirely by the supply of, and demand for, capital, as resulting from circumstances independent of the currency*. But it cannot be too constantly borne in mind, that every alteration in the amount of currency produces a *temporary* effect upon the rate of interest.
>
> (1826: 23n.; 1838, II: 361n.; emphasis added)

Tooke argued that in the 'progress' of an increase (or reduction) in the amount of banknotes, beyond (or below) that consistent with a 'settled state of the currency', there would result a 'fictitious' or 'nominal' increase (or decrease) in monied capital, by which he meant an amount of monied capital which did not correspond to real capital in the form of commodities and labour when prices and wages were stable (also see Tooke 1832: (Q 3971–3) 288–9; Panico 1988: 28).[25]

In a clear statement of the transmission process by which Tooke believed the Bank of England could autonomously alter the currency in circulation, he explained the manner by which monetary factors temporarily influenced the rate of interest:

> during the progress of an increase of the currency there is a fictitious increase of *monied capital*, and this I have called *nominal*, which comes in competition with the pre-existing monied capital; and it is while in the state of increase that it both reduces the rate of interest, and diminishes the value of money. It cannot enter into circulation otherwise than by reducing the rate of interest, other things remaining the same; as it must inevitably, at the same it is issued, increase the number of lenders, or diminish the number of borrowers.
>
> ... as almost every increase of paper, excepting what is paid by the bank for bullion, is issued in the way of loan, either to government, or to individuals, it is likely to affect the rate of interest in the first instance, before it

comes into contact with commodities … and the converse holds with regard
to a diminution of the currency while in progress.

(1826: 23n.; 1838, II: 361n.)

However, Tooke (1826: 23–6; also 1838, II: 361–2) believed such 'nominal
capital' was usually the result of an increased demand for credit facilities by
agents engaged in speculative activity and that it could be supplied in the short
run by the financial system independent of Bank of England policy. Therefore,
Tooke was of the view that speculation in commodity and share markets
involved a nominal amount of capital in the form of credit coming onto the
money market and, according to the degree of monetary accommodation by the
Bank of England, was accompanied by an artificial lowering in the rate of interest below its long-run average. According to Tooke (1826: 26–30; 1838, II:
362–4), the inevitable 'recoil of speculation' and downturn in the markets would
be associated with a reduction in the supply of monied capital which, as lenders
attempted to shore up their financial position by calling up loans, led to an evap-
oration in nominal capital. Together with an increased demand for funds by a
larger proportion of borrowers with engagements well beyond their means, the
resulting shortage of liquidity caused a temporary rise in the rate of interest
above its long-run average. Thus, consistent with Tooke's position discussed in
Section 6.2.3, the alternation from a spirit of speculation in markets to one of
stagnation and despondency is associated with short-run variations in the rate of
interest below and above the long-run average rate, respectively.

In Tooke's picture, then, while the rate of interest is conceived to be determined by politico-institutional and conventional factors operating in the financial
market independent of the rate of profit, monetary policy can exert only a temporary influence on its determination. This dissenting position of Tooke's in the
Considerations (1826) had an important influence on the development of views
about the relationship between the rate of interest and rate of profit over the next
couple of decades. Its significance was recognised by Gilbart (1834: 166) who,
while agreeing with 'the opinion of most of our political economists' that in a
competitive financial market 'the rate of interest is regulated by the rate of
profit', emphasised '[T]his sentiment has, however, been attacked'.[26] The other
two leading members of the banking school, Fullarton (1845: 168–70) and
Wilson (1847: 20–2), also adopted Tooke's position. Moreover, as elaborated in
Sections 8.1 and 8.2, J.S. Mill (1844 [1874]) and Marx (1894) were both
strongly influenced by Tooke's arguments and adopted similarly dissenting positions on the interest–profit relationship.

By the late 1830s, Tooke adopted the novel position that not only was the rate
of interest independently determined in the financial market, but that it governed
the rate of profit on capital employed in production.[27] This causal relationship
stemmed from Tooke's view that the rate of interest entered into the cost of production of commodities and that its level was thereby a significant influence on
the general price level over the long run (see Sections 5.4 and 5.7). In this connection it is highly significant that in reproducing in Appendix A of *History*

(1838, II: 355–64) an extract from Section II of the *Considerations* (1826) containing his analysis of the rate of interest, Tooke largely excluded the reasoning he gave for systematic variations in the rate of interest *in relation to* the rate of profit discussed above (p. 148). This provides fairly clear evidence of a shift in Tooke's position to one in which the rate of interest, 'the measure of the net profit on capital', governs the rate of profit on the basis that in the long run the remuneration for risk and trouble does not usually move in the opposite direction to the average rate of interest on monied capital of the best security. As previously discussed in Section 3.2.3, in this interpretation Tooke proposed the normal rate of profit was ultimately determined by forces operating in the financial system that determined the average rate of interest. Nevertheless, consistent with this interpretation, there remains in Tooke's analysis the possibility that conditions of production affecting the opportunities of profitably employing capital can exert an indirect influence, chiefly by affecting the demand for monied capital by productive borrowers and the supply of monied capital generated by the accumulation process. In other words, conditions of production can affect the rate of profit but only indirectly through its contributing influence on overall financial conditions in the loan market determining the average rate of interest. This interpretation appears consistent with Tooke's later position developed more openly in conjunction with his banking school principles (see Section 7.3).

6.4 On monetary policy and the English banking system

From his analysis of money and prices, the pre-banking school Tooke formulated firm views about the appropriate conduct of monetary policy by the Bank of England and institutional reform of the English banking system. Tooke's views on these banking policy issues are mainly to be found in the *Considerations* (1826) and in evidence given to the Commons Committee for the Renewal of the Charter of the Bank of England in 1832. Views on monetary policy are also to be sporadically found in *Letter to Lord Grenville* (1829a) and *History* (1838, I; II) in the form of retrospective criticisms of Bank of England policy as connected with actual instances of commercial instability and financial crisis. As will be shown in what follows, in connection to monetary policy, the issue that concerned Tooke most was the level of bullion reserves which the Bank of England ought to routinely hold in the conduct of its policy. However, before examining Tooke's position on monetary policy, consideration is briefly given to his position on reform of the English banking system.

Tooke clearly believed the English banking system in the early nineteenth century was defective in many respects and contributed to financial instability which could, under certain circumstances, periodically threaten the convertibility of the currency. In the aftermath of the severe financial crisis of 1825, when Parliament considered government-sponsored legislative changes to the regulation of the banking system (see Section 2.2), Tooke (1826) campaigned in favour of certain reforms, which he further developed in his evidence to the Bank Charter

Committee of 1832. First, Tooke advocated the withdrawal from monetary circulation of small notes of less than £5, which country banks had been accustomed to issue, to be replaced by coin. Tooke's (1826: 126–8, 138–9) main argument against their circulation was that it exposed the 'lower classes', who were obliged to accept them in receipt of wages and other small payments, to unfair losses when the banks issuing them failed (also see Smith 1996a: 138). Second, and more importantly, Tooke (1826: 125–6) advocated the admission of joint-stock banking with limited liability for its owners, which the Liverpool Government subsequently enacted in 1826 on the basis that they operate outside a radius of sixty-five miles from London and the Bank of England be permitted to open branches outside this radius in any part of the country. Having come to the conclusion that England's unit banking system was inherently unstable, Tooke (1826: 125–6) argued that joint-stock banking would enhance the stability of provincial banking in England.[28] Indeed, Tooke (1832: (Q 3911) 282, (Q 3945–7) 286) argued that only joint-stock banks should be given the power to issue banknotes. He also advocated the prudential regulation of joint-stock banks, prescribing a minimum holding of portfolio capital in relation to their banknote circulation and to calls that could be made on 'subscribed' (or authorised) capital to shore up their position (1826: 141–3).[29]

Third, Tooke strongly advocated for greater public accountability of note-issuing banks and, in particular, of the Bank of England, in the form of regular published accounts of their financial position.[30] Given its central role in the monetary system, Tooke complained that the 'veil of secrecy and mystery' (1826: 33) surrounding the actions of the Bank of England generated needless uncertainty among agents in the financial market and impeded a time-consistent monetary policy in the face of the regular change in its management (i.e. Governor and Deputy-Governor). Essentially, Tooke (1826: 124–5) argued that to ensure the Bank conducted policy in the public interest its activities needed to be 'exposed to public scrutiny and discussion' and 'subjected to the constant control and correction of public opinion'.[31] Public accountability by the Bank of England was seen by Tooke (1832: (Q 5415) 437) to be important because it provided an essential check on the discretionary management of its policy. This reform was in fact partially implemented in 1833 when the Bank of England was required under the renewed charter to render a weekly confidential statement of accounts to the Chancellor with publication of a monthly summary. However, Tooke (1838, II: 279–80) remained dissatisfied with the amount of detail and precision of the monthly information published.

Fourth, Tooke supported the move towards monopoly control over the issue of banknotes by the Bank of England. In this connection, Tooke (1832: (Q 3866–8) 278) opposed the establishment in the City of rival banks of issue to the Bank of England, chiefly on the grounds that competition between them would increase the tendency of over-issue of notes. In support of this view, Tooke (1832: (Q 3908) 282) argued that in the 'present system of banking' competition between country banks of issue was a major source of derangement of the currency. According to Tooke (1832: (Q 5460–3) 442–3) the problem with banking competition is that it occasionally induces 'undue and imprudent enterprize' with the 'safety' of banks who acted prudently unwittingly endangered by those banks who acted imprudently. But while Tooke (1832: (Q 5467–8) 443) was prepared to support measures that extended the Bank of England's power to centrally control the whole paper circulation, he was not prepared in 1832 to advocate its 'unlimited monopoly', as given by exclusive power to issue banknotes. Fifth, and last, it is evident Tooke (1826: 62n.; 1832: (Q 3862) 277) favoured the repeal of the usury law that imposed a 5 per cent ceiling on interest rates charged on all loans.

With these institutional reforms Tooke was promoting a banking system in which a network of large capitalised joint-stock banks operated in regional England, while the Bank of England, through a permanent extension of its notes into the country's circulation, had a greater centralised control over the whole circulating medium.[32] He was also promoting greater public scrutiny of the banks and, in particular, of the Bank of England, on the belief that public opinion, formed from a 'real knowledge of all the facts' (1832: (Q 3878) 279) would contribute towards monetary policy being conducted better in the 'interests of the community' (1826: 124).

Turning to Tooke's views on the conduct of monetary policy, he believed the central policy objective of the Bank of England was to safeguard the value of paper currency in terms of the official metallic standard. Under the convertible system of currency instituted in England after 1821, this entailed suppressing unstable price fluctuations in commodity and share markets which could otherwise lead to an extensive depreciation of the foreign exchanges and to a drain of bullion which threatened the ability of the Bank to make cash payments on demand at the mint gold price. Repudiating the idea that the Bank should aim to accommodate the government or enhance commercial trade, Tooke stated his position clearly in the following answer to the Bank Charter Committee of 1832:

> it is the business of a Bank that administers a paper currency in exchange for gold, or in lieu of gold, to have no other end than that of preserving its paper strictly, correctly and invariably upon a level with the value of gold, and any assistance to trade, or any assistance to Government, involving an increase of issue not called for by the wants of circulation, is a departure from the legitimate objects of the institution.
>
> (1832: (Q 3830) 271)

In order to safeguard convertibility Tooke argued that basically the Bank needed to do two things in the conduct of its policy. First, it needed to maintain a large precautionary reserve of bullion in order to meet the periodic external outflow of specie which occurred when the balance of payments was in deficit. Second, the Bank needed to prevent or minimise an extraordinary internal demand for cash (i.e. liquidity demand) which would otherwise cause a rundown in its reserves to levels that endangered convertibility. These two basic sides of Tooke's policy position stem from his views on the behaviour of the English monetary system.

Tooke's strong advocacy for the Bank of England to hold, as a matter of policy, a large reserve of bullion was based on the view that balance of payments adjustment via the price–specie–flow mechanism worked too slowly to prevent the possibility of a serious external drain on reserves. This point was made in the *Considerations* (1826) by Tooke in reasoning he gave for rejecting the permanent institution of Ricardo's Ingot Plan on the grounds of its impracticality (see Section 6.1). The focus of Tooke's criticism was the adequacy of bullion holdings by the Bank of England envisaged by Ricardo (1816) and fellow advocate, McCulloch (1824b), under the plan. Tooke (1826: 101–6) argued that the small bullion reserve implied by the plan would not be sufficient to meet the periodic external outflow of specie associated with variations in the balance of payments. This was because, as discussed in Section 6.2.1, Tooke believed the process of adjustment through international trade would operate slowly and unreliably in reversing the outflow of specie. Therefore, in the 'common course of trade' an external deficit would place considerable pressure on the Bank to promptly tighten policy and raise interest rates in order to prevent its reserves from falling to unsustainable low levels.[33] Moreover, Tooke (1826: 103–6) believed a large precautionary reserve was necessary to guard against natural and political events occasionally causing an 'extraordinary' external drain. The most prevalent example of this phenomenon was an unproductive domestic harvest, leading to high corn prices, its sudden large importation and, thereby, 'extra-outpayments' on the external account.[34] Others variously mentioned by Tooke (1826: 104) included large-scale government remittances abroad, speculatively driven investment in foreign securities and unforeseen delays or losses in the receipt of foreign income from exports.[35] In these circumstances Tooke (1826: 104–10) argued a large gold reserve by the Bank of England was necessary to give it time to adjust policy and for the process of external adjustment to work before panic in the London money market was ignited by concerns about the inadequate level of reserves to meet prospective demand.

The main concern of Tooke was that financial market panic would otherwise lead to an internal drain which would force the Bank to suspend cash payments. In this connection Tooke linked the reserve holdings of the Bank of England to confidence in the financial market: 'The only rational foundation for confidence, on the part of the public, in a bank, is a knowledge, that the reserve is ordinarily of sufficient magnitude to serve as security against *casualties* and *emergencies*' (1826: 10; emphasis added). On what ought to be considered a safe level of reserves, Tooke stated the opinion:

> I do not consider that a Bank issuing paper money payable on demand, situated as the Bank of England is, and having to supply upon emergencies the demands of Country Banks, that is, of all other Banks of circulation in the country, can be considered perfectly safe, with a treasure much less than half of the amount of its notes in circulation …
>
> (1832: (Q 3874) 278)[36]

Tooke clearly recognised upholding public confidence in the Bank's capacity to handle contingencies was important in staving off internal demands for cash which could threaten its reserve position. However, Tooke objected to a prescribed policy rule on reserve holdings of the Bank of England, believing this ought to be left to the practical discretion of management, subject to the scrutiny of public opinion:

> I do not think that it would be expedient for Government to interfere in determining the proportion of bullion that should be kept in reserve by the bank against its liabilities; it would be sufficient, I should think, if by a regular publication of the state of its affairs it were under the constant check of public opinion. There might be circumstances in which the treasure might be reduced below the usual proportion, and upon extraordinary emergencies considerably lower; but at the same time there might be, upon a full view of the state of affairs, a most clear conviction in the public mind that the circumstances were of so temporary a nature that a reflux of the bullion would take place inevitably and speedily, and that consequently there was no ground for alarm.
>
> (1832: (Q 5415) 437)

According to Tooke the main threat to currency conversion came from an extraordinary internal drain caused by financial crisis, which he saw as the inevitable consequence of a speculative boom. To prevent this happening, Tooke argued that the Bank of England needed to adopt a far-sighted policy. This involved identifying the early stages of speculative activity in commodity and share markets, and taking action to suppress it by restraining the expansion of credit facilities. At any sign of speculative activity, Tooke advocated the adoption of a non-accommodating stance by the Bank of England, chiefly by raising the level of its discount rate above the short-term market rate of interest. By this course of action, which in modern parlance is referred to as 'leaning against the wind', Tooke believed speculatively induced rises in the price of commodities and share prices could be moderated, thereby also moderating the demands for liquidity on the Bank when the downturn in the markets brought 'stagnation and despondency'.

Most of Tooke's criticism of Bank of England policy was for accommodating credit-based speculation. Thus, for example, Tooke was particularly critical of the Bank's role in the financial crises of 1825 and 1836–1837. In the first case, Tooke (1826: 31–64; 1838, II: 140–92) believed an easy policy stance by the Bank in 1824 and 1825 facilitated an expansion in credit and, thereby, encouraged an unsustainable boom in the share market, which had all the hallmarks of the speculative mania of the famous 1720 South Sea Bubble: 'The Bank had not kindled the fire, but, instead of attempting to stop the progress of the flames, it supplied the fuel for maintaining and extending the conflagration' (1838, II: 178–9). The collapse of this boom in late-1825 led to a severe financial crisis with bank closures, widespread bankruptcy and an internal drain of bullion reserves which forced the

Bank of England to nearly suspend cash payments on demand (for an account of this crisis and its aftermath, see Fetter 1965: 111–26; Hilton 1977: 202–31; Smith 1996a: xvi–xxvii). Tooke contended that by accommodating the boom the Bank had substantively contributed to the aftermath, endangering convertibility. Similarly, in the second historical case, Tooke (1838, II: 286–95) was highly critical of the Bank for not tightening policy and raising the interest rate in 1835 and 1836 to restrain speculation, especially that in foreign securities and other overseas ventures. Again, Tooke (1838, II: 296–301) contended this inaction contributed to the subsequent financial crisis and the accompanying 'commercial discredit', which placed considerable pressures on its reserves. These criticisms of the Bank illustrate Tooke's view that monetary policy ought to be directed towards suppressing speculative activity seen to be the main cause of instability in prices and of the financial system. Importantly, consistent with his position on the limited powers of the Bank of England, previously discussed in Section 6.2.2, Tooke did not consider it possible for Bank policy to counteract the rise (or the fall) in the (gold) price level fundamentally caused by natural and political factors. Instead, monetary policy could only counteract an *extension* of the rise in the price level *propelled* by credit-financed speculation.

Tooke was clearly of the view that the conduct of monetary policy towards ensuring the stability of the value of the currency was no easy task, with the Bank of England always having to cope with unforeseen events which altered circumstances in the financial market. Given the influence of extraneous factors on monetary conditions, Tooke (1826: 87–8) acknowledged that the best 'criterion' by which the Bank can determine whether their notes in circulation are excessive or not was the 'state of the exchanges'. Nevertheless, Tooke claimed a major difficulty for the short-term management of the currency was that the foreign exchanges were not able to 'indicate quickly enough and with sufficient precision' (1826: 88) the 'strength of the tide' of gold inflows or outflows which 'sets in' and the 'precise level at which its force is likely to be spent' (1826: 96). Hence, Tooke (1826: 88–9) believed an excess in the circulation and a depreciation in the value of the paper currency in terms of gold may exist for 'several months' before the exchanges signal its occurrence and there is a 'decided' external drain of bullion reserves. This was another reason Tooke (1826: 99–100) gave in support of his argument that the Bank of England needed to hold a higher safe reserve of bullion to give it more breathing space in adjusting its policy stance. Moreover, as the following statement indicates, Tooke believed the Bank of England could better avoid difficulties if it took a far-sighted approach in the formulation of its policy stance, by going beyond just the state of the exchanges and also looking towards the state of trade as an additional guide:

> I am not aware that the Bank should be considered as necessarily bound in the regulation of its issues to look to anything but the amount of its treasure and the Exchanges. Its treasure might be at par, yet the Exchanges might be affording an indication that a drain would soon commence; that is a case, in my opinion, in which the Bank is bound by considerations other than that of

the state of its treasure. The Directors might, indeed, as mercantile men, take into consideration the state of trade as an additional guide in their issues, but they are perhaps not in strictness bound to do so.

(1832: (Q 3850) 276)

Tooke particularly had in mind the signs of a spirit of speculation and the gathering clouds in commodity and share markets which may not yet be indicated by a weakening in the exchanges or any discernible efflux of bullion.

In view of the above-mentioned difficulties, Tooke argued the Bank of England needed to be able to quickly adapt its policy stance to deal with changing circumstances and unforeseen events. He believed the most effective way the Bank could alter its policy stance and exert an immediate influence on monetary conditions was through its commercial discounting of short-dated bills:

> it is not only the most beneficial in extending the means of commercial enterprise, but that it is the most manageable, because, the bills having only a short time to run, afford to the Directors the means of constant control over the amount of their issues; whereas, in the case of advances to Government they possess no control.

(Tooke 1829a: 52–3)

Unlike the case of government advances, the Bank had considerable discretion to readily alter its portfolio of short-dated securities in the commercial bill market. Nevertheless, through this avenue, Tooke believed the expediency of monetary policy depended heavily on the level of the Bank's discount rate in relation to the short-term market rate on bills. As discussed in Section 6.2.3, Tooke (1826: 77–9, 86; 1829a: 52–61) was highly critical of the Bank of England's management for adopting the policy rule of fixing its bank rate and rationing its commercial discounts on the basis of the bona fides of bills brought to it. In combination with the sale and purchase of securities on the open market, Tooke advocated for the Bank to conduct policy through the active adjustment of its bank rate on commercial bills discounted at its door.[37] Importantly, according to Tooke, this was the best way for the Bank of England to exert a regular influence over monetary conditions and thereby quickly counter any commercial activity which posed a threat to the stability of the currency.

Overall, then, the pre-banking school Tooke advocated discretionary management of monetary policy on the part of the Bank of England. Tooke believed the Bank required scope for discretion in the conduct of its operations, chiefly attained by holding a high average reserve of bullion, to cope with the extraordinary demands for liquidity that would occasionally be made on it. These extraordinary demands were usually the result of political and natural events which disrupted markets and often induced speculative activity. Tooke also believed in the need for active management of policy by the

Bank to counter speculative activity which could otherwise have an unstable effect on the financial system and endanger convertibility of the paper currency. He considered the price–specie–flow mechanism worked too slowly to be of any practical use in the short-term management of the currency. Instead, while the foreign exchanges provided the main guide to policy in a gold convertible system, Tooke proposed a more far-sighted approach in which, as an indicator of the state of credit conditions, activity in commodity and share markets be taken into consideration. For Tooke, monetary policy worked most effectively through flexible use of the bank rate as the main way of influencing credit conditions. Hence, notwithstanding Tooke's apparent scepticism of the Bank of England's role as lender-of-last-resort, his emphasis on the role of discount policy and his appreciation of the difficulties faced by it in managing monetary conditions would strike a familiar chord with the modern central banker.

7 The monetary thought of the banking school Tooke, 1840–1857

Tooke's prominence is owed most to his role in the currency–banking school debates of the 1840s. It was in the course of these famous monetary debates that Tooke re-assessed his position and developed novel principles in monetary thought more compatible with his explanation of prices. These principles formed the basis of the banking school theory. On the basis of his newly developed monetary analysis, Tooke then criticised the position of the currency school. This transformation in Tooke's monetary thought from his pre-banking to banking school theory first became evident in volume III of *A History of Prices* (1840a: 247–79) when consideration was given to the currency schools' proposals for institutional change of the Bank of England.[1] In this published work and in evidence to the Commons Select Committee on Banks of Issue in 1840, Tooke outlined the propositions that formed the basis of his banking school position. This position was given its most coherent exposition in Tooke's masterly pamphlet, *An Inquiry into the Currency Principle* (1844). No less important was Part III of volume IV of *A History of Prices* (1848a) in which Tooke made use of contributions by Fullarton (1845), J.S. Mill (1844) and Wilson (1847) to further develop and refine various aspects of his banking school theory. After 1848 the main focus of Tooke's writings and parliamentary evidence was directed towards exposing the adverse consequences of the practical operation of the Bank Charter Act of 1844, which he continued to strenuously oppose from the standpoint of his banking school theory. Tooke further elaborated his views on the appropriate institutional setting and conduct of monetary policy in evidence to the 1848 Commons and Lords Committees on the Causes of Commercial Distress in 1847–1848, and then in the pamphlet *On the Bank Charter Act of 1844* (1856). In the latter work and in volumes V and VI of *History* (1857), Tooke clarified some aspects of his thinking without making any substantial advance upon his banking school theory. There is no doubt Tooke considered his banking school theory to be a constructive alternative to the quantity theory approach of the classical economists.

The major catalyst for Tooke's re-assessment of orthodox monetary thought was the emergence of the currency school and its plan for compelling the Bank of England to regulate its notes *pari pasu* with changes in its bullion reserves. This plan originated with Torrens (1837) and was largely developed by Norman

(1838) and the leader of the currency school, Overstone (1837, 1840a, 1844).[2] The currency school's position was that stability of the price level and the foreign exchanges depended on the Bank of England's autonomous control over the quantity of banknotes in circulation. They proposed a strict interpretation of the classical economists' quantity theory based on two fundamental propositions. First, that by controlling the quantity of its banknotes in circulation, the Bank of England was able to govern the superstructure of credit in the economy. This implied that the velocity of circulation of banknotes and coin was fixed in the short run (Overstone 1840b: (Q 2663–6) 343, (Q 2733–5) 373–5). Second, the currency school supposed that the price–specie–flow mechanism worked effectively in the short run (Overstone 1840b: (Q 2755–6) 382–3). From this standpoint, the currency school argued that if the Bank of England regulated its banknotes strictly in accordance with changes in its bullion holdings, short-run fluctuations in prices and economic activity would be moderated.

In order to compel the Bank of England to operate in this way, the currency school proposed that its public function of issuing notes in exchange for coin (or bullion) be institutionally separate from its private business of banking, consisting of receiving deposits, buying and selling securities in the open market and discounting bills brought to its door. The hearings of the Commons Select Committee on Banks of Issue in 1840 opened the way for Peel's government to. implement the currency school's 'plan of separate issue' in the Bank Charter Act of 1844 (see Clapham 1944: 171–82; Horsefield 1944: 180–5; Fetter 1965: 172–97). The main feature of the Act was that the Bank of England be divided into an 'Issuing Department' and a 'Banking Department'. The issuing department was enabled to issue £14 million of banknotes against government securities, beyond which additional notes could only be issued in exchange for coin. This meant the banking department could only extend its issue of notes on bills discounted by exchanging its bullion for notes at the issuing department. The Act also contained provisions to extend the Bank of England's monopoly control over banknotes issued in England and Wales, which was subsequently extended to Scotland and Ireland under companion legislation passed in 1845. From the beginning Tooke (1840a, III: 248–53) was strongly opposed to the currency school's plan, which was contrary to his pre-banking school position. However, Tooke's criticism of the currency school and their plan was formulated on the basis of his newly developed banking school views about the operation of the English monetary system.

The object of this chapter is the illumination of the monetary thought of the banking school Tooke. Section 7.1 considers Tooke's conception of the distinctive functions of money and credit in the operation of the English monetary system as embodied in his 'dual-circulation' framework. This framework is shown in Section 7.2 to be crucial to Tooke's conception of endogenous money which lies at the heart of his banking school theory. It is also shown in Section 7.2 that Tooke considered the conception of endogenous money to be relevant not only to a monetary system in which the paper currency is fully convertible into gold at the official mint price, but that it is also relevant to a monetary system based on an inconvertible paper currency. Perhaps the most important though neglected aspect of Tooke's banking school theory is his position on the relationship between the rate of interest, monetary spending and the price level. Section 7.3 carefully considers this vital aspect of Tooke's banking school theory. In Section 7.4 Tooke's position on banking policy, including the appropriate monetary policy of the Bank of England, is considered. It is shown that Tooke's banking school position on banking policy is largely consistent with his pre-banking school position. Section 7.5 then considers Tooke's arguments against the Bank Charter Act of 1844, which constituted an important element of the currency–banking school debates. By way of an analytical reconstruction, Section 7.6 provides an overall picture of Tooke's banking school position, showing that within the theoretical framework of classical economics it represents a coherent alternative to the quantity theory of money approach.

7.1 The 'dual-circulation' framework: money and its functions

A major issue in the hearings of the 1840 British Parliamentary Committee on Banks of Issue concerned the definition of money. This issue arose because as the object of control under policy proposals which were subsequently embodied in the 1844 Bank Act, the currency school defined money narrowly as banknotes and coin circulating 'outside the walls of banks'. The definition was essentially based on the reasoning that banknotes and coin were 'the common medium of exchange of the adjustment of all transactions, equally at all times, between all persons, and all places' (Overstone 1840b: (Q 2663) 344; also (Q 2663–70) 343–7). The 1840 committee closely questioned Overstone on this definition which, notably, excluded bank deposits and bills of exchange.[3] The latter were instead regarded to be credit instruments. The banking school Tooke was highly critical of the currency school's narrow definition of money for its relevance in explaining the behaviour of the British monetary economy. This criticism was firmly based on his newly developed conception of the operation of the monetary system and the institutionally based functions of money within it.

According to Tooke, money consisted of all mediums of exchange used to expedite transactions. It was therefore defined widely by Tooke to consist of not only coin and banknotes, but also cheques (i.e. bank deposit transfers), bills of exchange, exchequer bills and any other forms of credit used to make payments in the economy. Tooke believed that different kinds of money were significant because of the different functions they fulfilled in the operation of the monetary economy. In evidence to the 1840 Committee on Banks of Issue, Tooke classified money into three basic categories according to 'considerations of economy, convenience and security'. The first category was what Tooke called 'currency', consisting of 'coin of the realm', Bank of England notes, country banknotes and 'cheques upon bankers' in the hands of the public. Tooke was actually uncertain as to whether drawn cheques ought to be included because, unlike the other currencies, they 'require the signature of the party passing the draft, and that they do not pass from hand to hand' (Tooke 1840b: (Q 3278) 297). He conceded to the committee though that they should be included on the grounds of 'their perfect similarity to bank notes, in many of the purposes for which they are employed' (Tooke 1840b: (Q 3278) 297). The second category was what Tooke (1840b: (Q 3284) 298) termed 'circulation', consisting only of Bank of England notes and country banknotes 'payable on demand'. It was therefore a sub-group of the first category. The third category was what Tooke called 'circulating medium', consisting of 'all instruments of interchange by which the productions and revenues of the country are distributed' (1840b: (Q 3285) 298). As well as 'currency', it therefore included bills of exchange, trade credit and other forms of money in active circulation.

Significantly, Tooke did not regard bullion, coin and banknotes 'inside the walls of banks' as currency because they were inactive. Similarly, while bank deposits 'unemployed and inert' were considered by Tooke to be money, it was not currency. Only cheques drawn on demand deposits which, thereby, affected money transfers were considered by Tooke to be currency. Tooke (1840b: (Q 3290) 298; (Q 3810) 365) acknowledged to the 1840 committee that these definitions involved fine distinctions between monetary instruments according to their different degrees of 'convenience'. However, Tooke argued that it was really a question of 'nominal classification' and that deriving precise definitions of these categories was of 'very little practical importance' (1840b: (Q 3291) 298). For Tooke, the significance of different monies lay in their functional role in the operation of the English monetary system. Tooke's conception of the operation of this monetary system was largely embodied in his dual-circulation framework expounded in the *Inquiry* (1844).

As already outlined in Section 3.2, Tooke's dual-circulation framework derived from Adam Smith's conception that the 'circulation of every country may be considered as divided into two different branches; the circulation of the dealers with one another, and the circulation between the dealers and the consumers' (Smith 1776 [1976]: 322; quoted in Tooke 1844: 33). The conception was based on Smith's distinction between value added in the intermediate processes of production and distribution and the 'gross product' of final output.[4] Thus, consistent with his analysis of distribution and prices, Smith wrote that:

> [T]he value of the goods circulated between the different dealers with one another never can exceed the value of those circulated between the dealers and the consumers [because] whatever is bought by the dealers ... [is] ... ultimately destined to be sold to the consumers.
>
> (1776 [1976]: 322; quoted in Tooke 1844: 34, 71)[5]

In Tooke's framework, the functions of money are defined by their institutionally based role in these two different branches of monetary circulation. The monetary circulation between dealers and consumers was seen by Tooke (1844: 33–4) as facilitating 'the distribution and expenditure of incomes' through a large number of small-size transactions. These transactions mainly consisted of the 'payments of wages, which constitute the principal means of income' (1844: 33–4), the 'payment of rent, dividends, salaries' (1840a, III: 276) and the final expenditures by consumers. Tooke argued that these transactions were predominantly facilitated by banknotes and coin, which were the main constituents of what he defined as currency.

The monetary circulation between 'dealers' and 'dealers' is conceived by Tooke as facilitating 'the distribution and employment of capital' (1844: 33) in the intermediate stages of production and distribution of products. Tooke (1840a, III: 275; 1844: 35–6; 1848a, IV: 229) maintained that transactions between dealers and dealers required only a small amount of banknotes and coin. This was because these transactions were mainly carried on by bank loans and other forms of credit with the settlement of debts usually effected by way of bills of exchange and cheques. The 'wholesale markets for provisions' was an exception because Tooke (1844: 35) maintained that rural trade between farmers, cattle dealers and millers was mainly conducted with country banknotes. In this branch of monetary circulation, Tooke (1844: 13–16) also included international transactions on the grounds that they constituted 'transfers of capital' which were ultimately settled by the transmission of bullion between different 'national' banks.

In Tooke's conceptual framework, the duality in monetary circulation is mirrored by a dichotomy in the functions of the banking system between 'administering' the circulation of the currency and effecting the 'concentration' and 'distribution' of capital. The first-mentioned function of banks, referred to by Tooke as 'business over the counter', entails the receipt of 'deposits of the incomes of their customers, and to pay out the amount, as it is wanted for expenditure' (1844: 36). It essentially consists of country banks accepting deposits and paying out banknotes or coin on demand by depositors (1844: 38). With respect to London deposit (and non-issuing) banks, Tooke believes its functions consist of facilitating, by way of cheque, the payments of 'upper' and 'middle' class persons, 'who are in the habit of employing bankers' (1844: 24), only on consumer expenditures. However, given the vast majority of the population did not use bankers for expediting consumer expenditures, Tooke considered the circulation of the currency largely occurred 'outside the walls of the banks'. Hence, Tooke regarded the role of the banks in this branch of monetary circulation as minor. The second and main function of banks, referred to by Tooke as 'business behind the counter', entails the collection of 'capital from those who have not immediate employment for it, and to distribute or transfer it to those who have' (1844: 36). For Tooke, this consisted of banks collecting unemployed capital (i.e. 'disposable capital') and facilitating its productive employment through intermediation, either directly by way of loan advances or indirectly by way of discounting bills of exchange at their door. As indicated above (p. 165), Tooke believed bank credit was predominantly used by dealers to facilitate transactions associated with the production and wholesale distribution of commodities. Tooke (1844: 24–5) considered this role of the banking system to be crucial because most of these transactions, involving 'capital transfers', were settled by 'drafts on bankers' or acceptances of bills of exchange. In this connection, Tooke (1848a, IV: 183–4) believed most banknotes were issued by way of advances by the Bank of England and note-issuing country banks. In addition, Tooke (1844: 12–16) believed that, as the central holder of bullion reserves, the Bank of England effectively facilitated international transactions by the provision of bullion to settle any outstanding debt of English merchants and investors.

The main purpose of Tooke's dual-circulation framework was to show that, contrary to the position of the currency school, most monetary expenditure in the economy was transacted by the use of cheques and bills of exchange without the intervention of banknotes. Indeed, according to Tooke, banknotes and coin were mainly used to transact exiguous expenditures by tradesmen and consumers who were not in the habit of using bankers and for making income payments, especially for wages and for rent. For these reasons, Tooke (1844: 20–31) criticised the currency school for excluding cheques and bills of exchange from its definition of money as the target of policy control. The other purpose of the dual-circulation framework was to show the considerable elasticity of credit in the English monetary system, consistent with Tooke's (1819a: 127–32; 1824, I: 63–8; 1829a: 31–2; 1832: (Q 3819–20) 270; 1838, II: 148–9) long-held position that the 'circulating medium' varied with prices in the short run in relation to the 'currency' (i.e. banknotes and coin). Tooke (1844: 36) argued that whereas the amount of banknotes and coin remained relatively constant, the amount of 'circulating medium' among dealers and dealers varied considerably. This amounted to a criticism of the currency school's assumption of a constant velocity of circulation of banknotes and coin (see, in particular, Overstone 1840b: (Q 2663–6) 343, (Q 2733–5) 373–5). Tooke's conception of an elastic relationship between the internal monetary circulation and external specie flows affecting the stock of gold reserves was related to this viewpoint. In short, Tooke (1844: 101–2) argued that, in relation to a more stable quantity of banknotes in internal circulation, the stock of bullion reserves at the Bank of England varied considerably in response to changes in the balance of payments.

7.2 A conception of endogenous money

The central principle of Tooke's banking school theory was that the *whole* quantity of money in circulation was endogenously determined by the demand for money. Consistent with Tooke's real explanation of prices, this principle meant that, in reverse to the quantity theory of money, causality ran unambiguously from the general level of prices to the quantity of money. The principle is clearly stated in the following passage:

> prices of commodities do not depend upon the quantity indicated by the amount of bank notes, nor upon the amount of the whole circulating medium; but that, on the contrary, the amount of circulating medium is the consequence of prices.
>
>   (Tooke 1844: 123; see also 1840a, III: 200; 1840b: (Q 3299) 299)

This principle meant that the banking system, in particular the Bank of England, did not have the power to alter the whole quantity of money in circulation without recourse to those circumstances independently determining economic activity and the general level of money prices. In a repudiation of the currency school position, it also meant that, as a whole, note-issuing banks did not have the power to influence autonomously the quantity of banknotes in circulation. Tooke believed his conception of endogenous money was *most* relevant to a monetary system in which banknotes were strictly convertible on demand into gold at its official mint price as was the case in Britain post-1821. Nevertheless, as shown below (pp. 170–71), Tooke believed his conception was also relevant to explaining the behaviour of a fiat monetary system in which banks (or a central authority) issued inconvertible banknotes.

Tooke's conception of endogenous money was developed in conjunction with the dual-circulation framework discussed in the previous section. There were two aspects to his argument. The first consisted of what he called the 'mode of issue', which concerned the transmission process by which money went into circulation outside the walls of banks. The second aspect consisted of the 'law of reflux' which concerned the manner by which monies, principally banknotes, returned to the banking system from their circulation outside it. This law of reflux was in fact developed by Tooke in association with Fullarton (1845).[6]

Tooke (1844: 49–52; 1848a, IV: 183–5) argued that it was through loans advanced and bills of exchange discounted by banks that the demand for money was principally met. He maintained that under England's convertible system of currency, the 'borrower' or 'discounter' 'has the option of receiving [bank]notes or gold, or a book credit' (Tooke 1848a, IV: 184) according to the purpose for which the funds are required.[7] Since by far the greater proportion of money demanded was to expedite transactions between dealers and dealers associated with the inter-mediate processes of production and distribution of products, Tooke (1844: 35) considered most funds borrowed were received in the form of a 'book credit' (as actuated by cheque) and therefore remained within the 'walls of banks'. Only a small proportion of money demanded was held to be taken in the form of banknotes and coin in order to expedite transactions between consumers and dealers largely associated with the retail trade and the payment of incomes. Hence, Tooke (1848a, IV: 184; also see 1840b: (Q 3723–5) 352; 1844: 62–3) contended 'the amount of loans and discounts by the Bank of England, or other banks of issue' was 'no measure of the amount of their notes in circulation'. In this respect, Tooke (1848a, IV: 195) disputed the orthodox view that note-issuing banks could autonomously increase the quantity of banknotes in circulation by an extension of loans and discounted bills. According to Tooke's law of reflux, any unwanted banknotes would simply be returned to the issuing banks as deposits.

Importantly, Tooke (1844: 70–1; 1848a, IV: 186) considered the law of reflux to apply strictly to a system of convertible currency in which holders of banknotes are 'entitled to demand gold' from the central banking authority (i.e. Bank of England). The essentials of Tooke's reasoning are embodied in his principle of limitation, which proposed that effectual demand was ultimately limited by the 'quantity of money constituting the revenues, *valued in gold*, of the different orders of the state under the head of rents, profits, salaries, and wages, destined for current expenditure' (1844: 71; emphasis added). In accordance with the dual-circulation framework, Tooke argued that total consumption expenditure, being effectual demand for final commodities sold by dealers to consumers, depended on social income, the largest part of which consisted of wages.[8] It is apparent Tooke (1844: 71–2) conceived the monetary value of social income (or 'revenues' of the community), especially wage and salary income, remained relatively constant in the short run because it was tied closely to the value of gold which, as shown in Section 3.5, he considered to be highly stable even in the long run. For this reason Tooke believed consumption expenditure also remained relatively constant, varying little in the short run. Tooke maintained that, in a convertible system of currency, social income, and therefore effectual demand, changed only slowly with a permanent change in the conditions of production (including gold) and the normal prices of commodities. Hence, the demand for banknotes and coin also remained relatively constant, with issues of banknotes in excess of what were wanted at any given time quickly returning to the banking system, without any intermediate effect on consumption expenditure and, thereby, (gold) prices. Thus, Tooke (1848a, IV: 190–4) argued that with the monetary value of deposit 'obligations' (i.e. debts) tied to gold, note-issuing banks were compelled in a convertible system of currency to make advances 'for such short periods, and on securities so solid and convertible, as to insure the return of the money advanced in time to meet the utmost of their engagements' (1848a, IV: 193).[9] By contrast, Tooke believed the demand for credit by producers and dealers to finance capital expenditures varied considerably in the short run with economic activity and the fluctuation of market prices. Therefore, Tooke (1848a, IV: 184–5) argued short-run variations in the amount of loans and discount facilities provided by the English banking system had little effect on the amount of banknotes in circulation unless it was coincidently associated with a change in income and effectual demand. The point is that for Tooke the law of reflux meant it was not possible for the banking system to increase autonomously the issue of convertible banknotes by conferring upon consumers additional purchasing power and, thereby, directly generating a 'fresh demand' in the economy.

In Tooke's principle of limitation, the gold value of social income does not only limit the quantity of banknotes in circulation in the short run, but also ultimately limits the whole circulating medium in the long run. On the basis of his dual-circulation framework, Tooke conceived that the whole circulating medium, including amount of loans advanced and discount facilities provided by banks, was determined by the demand for credit by manufacturers and dealers connected with activity in the intermediate processes of production and distribution of commodities. It is evident Tooke (1844: 72) conceived that in the long run when the supply of commodities had adjusted to effectual demand at which normal (gold) prices (i.e. 'cost of production') are established, the whole circulating medium so determined corresponded with an amount of banknotes and coin normally required to facilitate transactions between consumers and dealers. However, in the short run, Tooke argued the whole circulating medium varied in relation to the amount of banknotes and coin in response to changes in intermediate trade between dealers and dealers and when market prices deviated from cost of production. Thus, Tooke held that a rise in prices, caused usually by an exogenous reduction in the supply of the relevant commodities, would be accommodated by an endogenous expansion in credit, involving a rise in the velocity of circulation of banknotes and coin. When this rise was heightened by speculative buying, Tooke conceived this involved stock building principally by dealers, based on an expectation of making profits from selling at higher wholesale prices in the future. Tooke made it clear the accompanying increase in credit was the effect of higher market prices when he wrote in relation to the role of bills of exchange: 'so far from being a cause, [they] are the effect of price' whereby '[*T*]*he prospect of advantage supplies the motive, and the credit of the buyer constitutes the power of purchase*' (1844: 73). What ultimately limited this rise in prices was effectual demand (1844: 74–5). While speculative activity among dealers may raise 'wholesale' prices, ultimately they must conform to 'retail' prices according to the final expenditure of 'consumers at home and abroad'. The 'eventual fall' in prices inevitably involved some dealers making losses as retail prices could not realise the 'return for capital expended in production'. Conversely, in Tooke's picture the downturn in prices is accompanied by a decline in the velocity of circulation of banknotes and coin and tight liquidity conditions. This downturn will be limited by the cost of production of commodities since in the long run it will not be sufficiently profitable for producers to supply at prices below it.

Tooke therefore conceived that in a system of convertible currency, a short-run downturn in prices was limited by cost of production and a short-run upturn in prices was limited by the purchasing power of consumers. A significant aspect of Tooke's conception is that, whereas changes to supply conditions are seen to be the main cause of price fluctuations, and that speculative activity by 'dealers' can exacerbate them, effectual demand by 'consumers' for the final product exerts a stabilising influence on prices. Through its determination of real aggregate consumption expenditure, the gold value of social income, especially wage income, constituted a *limitation* on short-run upward movements in the general level of prices (Tooke 1844: 71–2; for a similar interpretation, see Rist 1940: 214–18). This is precisely what Tooke meant when he wrote:

> It is the quantity of money constituting the revenues of the different orders of the state, under the head of rents, salaries, and wages, destined for current expenditure, according to the wants and habits of the several classes, that alone forms the limiting principle of the *aggregate of money prices*, – the only prices that can properly come under the designation of *general prices*. As the cost of production is the limiting principle of supply, so the aggregate of money incomes devoted to expenditure for consumption is the limiting principle of demand for commodities.
>
> (1840, III: 276)

This principle of limitation gave effect to the notion that market prices fluctuated around normal money prices fixed to a gold standard (see also Tooke's (1848a, IV: 195) quotation of a passage from Wilson (1847: 83–4)).

Tooke argued that only in a system of inconvertible currency in which the principle of limitation did not operate was it possible for the authority issuing paper money to influence autonomously the quantity of money in circulation. However, according to Tooke, the degree to which the issuing authority was able to influence autonomously the quantity of inconvertible money in circulation and, thereby, affect money prices, depended on its mode of issue. To begin with, Tooke (1848a, IV: 186) argued the 'power of issue is unlimited' in a system in which 'compulsory' paper monies, such as the French *assignats* of the early 1790s, are issued by the government (or another issuing authority). While Tooke acknowledged that a 'small proportion, may, indeed, be returnable in payment of taxes', he contended that 'the Government may immediately re-issue the amount so returned, and then keep up or extend the quantity, according to its own pur-poses' (1848a, IV: 186). Tooke (1844: 70–1) considered the unlimited power of issue was specifically connected with the issue of compulsory paper money for the purpose of financing government expenditure, through which the issuing authority was able directly to affect money income, monetary expenditure and money prices. He emphasised that this mode of issue involved paper money being forced directly into circulation by way of government expenditure: con-sisting of the government issue of paper money usually in payment for 'personal expenditure of the Sovereign', 'public works and buildings', 'salaries of civil servants' and the 'maintenance of military and naval establishments' (1844: 71). According to Tooke (1848a, IV: 186), the expansion of paper money in this way would raise money prices (the price level) by directly creating an additional demand for commodities for given conditions of supply in the economic system. However, Tooke contended that by a different mode of issue such an autono-mous expansion in inconvertible money may not necessarily raise money prices. Thus, following up a proposition of J.S. Mill (1844: 589n.), Tooke (1848a, IV: 197–8) argued that if the expansion in government issued paper money was used to purchase 'national debt', then, because it would not directly induce a short-run increase in demand, the effect on the price of commodities would be minor. Instead, he held that this monetary operation would raise the price of public securities and, thereby, lower the rate of interest, stimulate net capital outflow and, thereby, a net outflow of specie which may indirectly raise prices (of imports) according to the depreciation in the foreign exchanges.

Tooke (1844: 19–20; 1848a, IV: 173–83, 198) pointed out that the issue of inconvertible paper money for the purposes of directly financing government expenditures was unusual in England. He showed that this direct mode of issue was mainly employed to finance high wartime expenditures by national govern-ments on the Continent (e.g. Napoleonic France and Russia) which possessed a monopoly control over the issue of paper money (Tooke 1848a, IV: 209–18). The usual mode of issue which operated in England during the restriction period 1797–1821 consisted of banks issuing inconvertible banknotes for commercial purposes to the private sector by way of loan or by discounting bills of exchange brought to them. This indirect mode of issue in a system of inconvertible currency was in fact only explicitly considered by Tooke in the context of Ricardo's (1811b: 216–17) famous hypothesis of a gold mine discovered on the premises of the Bank of England introduced 'for the purpose of proving that the [banknote] issues of the Bank of England would add to the amount of the currency in the same manner and degree as the issue of so much gold so discovered' (1848a, IV: 199–200). Tooke argued that providing the Bank of England issued any additional gold coin by way of discounting short-dated bills of a bona fide commercial character, it would be unlikely to have a significant effect on the demand for commodities and, therefore, on prices. When issued in this way, Tooke contended gold coin is subject to reflux, which acted as a 'counteracting force' to any autonomous expansion by the Bank. As its corollary, Tooke (1848a, IV: 199–200) argued that, during the restriction period, inconvertible banknotes issued by the Bank of England were similarly subject to reflux because under its strict rules they were issued by way of discounting bills of exchange of only a bona fide commercial character with a maturity 'not exceeding sixty-one days'. Tooke indicated that by discounting at a rate 'decidedly' below the market rate of interest, it was possible for the Bank of England to 'slowly' overcome the reflux and permanently increase the amount of inconvertible banknotes (or gold coin) in circulation. However, this required for an increase in the public's demand for currency generated by higher monetary expenditure and income in the economy. But Tooke (1848a, IV: 200–2) considered that in the normal course of commercial banking there was no reason why the issue of inconvertible banknotes by way of loan should necessarily be the *originating* cause of higher effectual demand.

The above shows Tooke considered his conception of endogenous money applied as much to an inconvertible as to a convertible system of currency. Two important points of clarification need to be made in this respect. First, for Tooke, whatever the kind of monetary system, the law of reflux was based on the notion that the quantity of money is demand-determined according to the prior causal determination of prices and trade. According to Tooke, the *force* of the reflux of banknotes was greater the less the demand for commodities (or demand for currency) was affected in the course of their issue. In a convertible system of currency, reflux operated forcefully because, irrespective of the mode of issue, it was not possible to permanently expand the amount of banknotes in circulation by raising effectual demand and, thereby, raising the demand for currency. The reason for this was the operation of the principle of limitation previously explained. However, in an inconvertible system of currency, the principle of limitation did not operate since money income and prices were not tied to the long-run value of gold. Nevertheless, Tooke believed that in this kind of monetary system reflux was ineffective only when the mode of issue consisted of inconvertible paper money being directly forced into circulation by way of increased government expenditure.

Second, as indicated above, Tooke believed that in an inconvertible system of currency the issue of banknotes on short-dated bills of exchange of a bona fide character limited their potential expansion by limiting the demand for currency. In this regard, Tooke adhered to the 'real bills' doctrine in so far as he believed that providing banknotes issued by way of bank loans facilitated only non-speculative transactions, their issuance could not contribute to higher money prices and, thereby, to a higher permanent demand for money. He believed that in any kind of monetary system, the capacity of the banking system, through its lending, to facilitate speculative activity which raised money prices depended much on the effect of the level of interest on the inducement to purchase commodities. But in the case of an inconvertible system of currency, because Tooke's principle of limitation did not operate, any credit-financed speculative upturn could lead to permanently higher money prices and, thereby, higher income, which required a larger quantity of banknotes in circulation. In relation to price fluctuations, Tooke clearly believed they were prone to be more violent and of a longer duration in an inconvertible system of currency than a convertible one in which the principle of limitation operated forcefully.

7.3   Interest, spending and the price level

Unlike most of his contemporaries, Tooke fully recognised that the power of the banks, more particularly the Bank of England, to alter the whole quantity of circulating medium depended on the indirect effect of variations in the rate of interest (relative to the rate of profit) on the inducement to spend in the economy. In classical economics, Thornton (1811: 335–9) and Ricardo (1811a: 91–2; 1821: 363–4) had ultimately relied on this causal relationship during the bullionist controversies to substantiate their proposition that by lending at a rate below the market rate of interest, the Bank of England was able to issue an excess amount of inconvertible banknotes which would be absorbed by a higher induced demand for money in the process of causing price inflation. This transmission mechanism of monetary policy, incompletely articulated, was not greatly improved upon by classical economists after Ricardo. Nevertheless, by the 1840s the orthodox position was that expansions in the whole quantity of money involved a lowering in the rate of interest that facilitated increased bank borrowing for the purposes of commodity speculation which, thereby, raised prices; while a contraction in the whole quantity of money, vice versa (see, for example, Gilbart 1834: 163–73; 1841: 6–7; Bosanquet 1842: 65–8). Thus, in 1840 Tooke wrote:

> The commonly received opinion is, that a low, and especially a declining, rate of interest operates necessarily as a stimulus to speculation, not only in government stocks and in shares both at home and abroad, that is in both British and foreign public and private securities, but also in the markets for produce.
>
> (1840a, III: 151)

Consistent with his pre-banking school position (see Section 6.2.3), the banking school Tooke (1840a, III: 151–2) believed the rate of interest was a 'primary consideration' in the inducement to invest in shares and other financial securities. According to Tooke (1840a, III: 165; 1844: 86), a decline in the market rate of interest on short-term bills tended to induce speculative investment in longer-dated securities, thereby raising the prices of government stocks and shares. It is evident Tooke believed this speculation was essentially based on arbitrage when, in reference to the example above, he wrote:

> on such occasions, the anticipation of the prices to which they ought to attain, may be an exaggerated one, but the foundation for the rise would substantially exist in a tendency to an adjustment of the relative value of different securities for investment.
>
> (1840a, III: 165)

Upon this reasoning, a rise in the market rate of interest would induce a reduction in the prices of all securities 'quite independently of any forced contraction of the circulation by the Bank [of England]' (1840a, III: 165). Tooke also considered the rate of interest to exert an important influence on the inducement to invest in large investment projects financed by share capital which held out 'the prospect of increased income to the subscribers' (1840a, III: 165). On the one hand, a fall in the interest rate would 'favour' such projects, while, on the other hand, a rise in the interest rate is 'necessarily attended with a fall in the value of projects in actual operation, and with discouragement to the formation of new ones' (1840a, III: 166). In addition, Tooke contended that a low rate of interest 'favours' though 'does not originate, building and land speculations, the facility of borrowing being essential to the extension of such speculations' (1840a, III: 165). In regard to speculation in long investments in general, Tooke conceived the inducement to invest depended not only on the level of the rate of interest, but also on the expected rate of return of the project as determined independently by trade conditions as well as relevant political factors (more on this below, pp. 174–5). However, Tooke (1840a, III: 152, 166) was of the view that this relationship between the rate of interest and the price of securities had 'no analogy in the market for commodities' and that 'with reference to the influence of the rate of interest, and the operations of the Bank on speculations in produce' he maintained that 'I am more especially disposed to question the prevailing opinion'.

An important element of Tooke's banking school position was the rejection of any robust inverse *functional* relationship between the rate of interest and the inducement to spend. In particular, Tooke denied that the facility to borrow at a low rate of interest on its own provided a sufficient inducement to an increased expenditure on commodities:

> upon general grounds, there is so little reason to suppose that the mere facility of raising money at a low interest forms a sufficient motive for persons having marketable securities, or being in good credit, to borrow for the purpose of purchasing commodities with a view to resale ...
>
> (1840a, III: 155)

In volume III of *History*, Tooke (1840a: 159–65) supported this argument by reference to historical evidence showing that the 'facility of credit' was not an important factor in the most 'memorable' speculations in commodities. In the *Inquiry* (1844: 79–80), Tooke fully developed this negative argument by reference to what he called the 'money market theory' articulated by Gilbart (1841).[10]

Distinct from the 'currency theory' which 'connects prices with bank notes', the 'money market theory' was defined by Tooke (1844: 85) to connect prices with the rate of interest. According to Tooke (1844: 77–9), Gilbart claimed that the facility of obtaining credit was the 'moving cause' of speculation in commodities because it would increase the 'power of purchase' of merchants in the economy.[11] Tooke denied the ability to borrow at a low rate of interest was the moving cause of speculation in commodities because it would increase the power of purchase, arguing that the 'error is in supposing the *disposition* or *will* to be co-extensive with the power' (1844: 79; also see 1840a, III: 152–5, 159–65). Tooke (1844: 82–3) contended the necessary motive for additional speculative buying of commodities by merchants (or dealers) was the prospect of profit from their resale, which depended on the future advancement of their prices as ultimately determined by their supply conditions. Hence, in answer to the proposition 'that a facility of borrowing at a low rate of interest not only confers the power of purchasing, but affords the inducement – applies the *stimulus* to speculation in commodities', Tooke wrote:

> borrowers are not *stimulated* to purchase commodities speculatively, merely because they can borrow on low terms; they are but too happy if they can borrow at all. But to suppose that persons entitled to credit are likely to be induced – *stimulated* is the favourite term – by the mere circumstance of a low rate of interest to enter into speculations in commodities ... argues a want of knowledge of the motives which lead to such speculations. These are seldom if ever entered into with borrowed capital, except with a view to so great an advance of price, and to be realised within so moderate a space of time, as to render the rate of interest or discount a matter of trifling consideration.
>
> (1844: 81–2)

> It is not the mere facility of borrowing, or the difference between being able to discount at 3 or 6 per cent., that supplies the *motive* for purchasing, or even for selling. Few persons of the description here mentioned ever speculate but upon the confident expectation of an advance of price of at least 10 per cent.
>
> (1840a, III: 153)

While Tooke believed a low rate of interest could play a facilitating role, it could not therefore be the moving cause of commodity speculation (Rist 1940: 222–3; Panico 1988: 42–3). Upon the same reasoning, Tooke (1844: 81–2) believed that though a higher rate of interest may have a restraining influence, an unsustainable speculation in commodities could only be effectively limited by banks being careful to provide credit on 'reasonable security of repayment'. Therefore, Tooke's proposition that the banks, in particular the Bank of England, did not have the power to autonomously expand or contract the whole quantity of money in circulation is premised on a rejection of any systematic causal influence of the rate of interest on spending (Pivetti 1991: 77–8). It was from this standpoint that Tooke concluded 'the prices of commodities are little, if at all, affected by temporary alterations in the rate of interest' (1840a, III: 166).

With regard to permanent alterations in the rate of interest, Tooke proposed that these did have a systematic influence on prices 'directly opposite to those which are commonly supposed' (1840a, III: 166). The banking school Tooke conceived that the permanent rate of interest constituted a cost of production of commodities, which thereby entered into the determination of their normal (gold) prices. As the following passage well illustrates, Tooke argued that a persistent reduction in the rate of interest constituted a reduction in the cost of capital in production which, through competition, would tend to cause a *lasting* decline in the general price level:

> A general reduction in the rate of interest is equivalent to or rather constitutes a diminution of the cost of production. This is more especially and very obviously a necessary effect where much fixed capital is employed, as in the case of manufactures, but it likewise operates in all cases where an outlay of capital is required, according to the length of time ordinarily occupied in bringing the commodities, whether raw produce or finished goods, to market; the diminished cost of production hence arising would, *by the competition of the producers*, inevitably cause a fall of prices of all the articles into the cost of which the interest of money entered as an ingredient.
>
> (1844: 81; emphasis added)

On the basis of the same reasoning, Tooke (1844: 123–4) argued that a permanent rise in the rate of interest would, through competition, tend to bring about a lasting increase in the general price level (also Tooke 1840a, III: 166–7; 1857, V: 583–4).

Evidently, Tooke developed this conception of money interest as a cost of production from statistical evidence of a strong correlation between long-run movements in the rate of interest and the general price level. Indeed, Tooke had this conception in mind as early as 1823 when, in *High and Low Prices*, explaining the general decline in prices in the period 1818–1822, he wrote 'a reduction in the rate of interest again tending to diminish the cost of production, and thus being a fresh element of cheapness' (1823, i: 165). However, this argument was subsequently expurgated from the text of the second edition of this work (1824, i: 117–19). The argument was then fully adopted in Tooke's explanation of the long-run secular movement in the general price level in England over the period 1792–1837 provided in volumes I and II of *History of Prices* (1838, II: 346–9), in which the long-run movement in the average rate of interest was identified as a major contributing factor (see Section 5.7).

This conception of money interest as a normal cost of production is also the basis of Tooke's position expounded in Section 3.2.3 that, compatible with his adding-up approach to prices and distribution, the money rate of interest systematically governs the normal rate of profit, the latter determined by the sum of the average money rate of interest and the remuneration for risk and trouble on the employment of capital in production. The banking school Tooke adhered to the explanation of the determination of the money rate of interest developed in his pre-banking school phase.[12] As elucidated in Section 6.3, in this explanation Tooke conceived that in the long run the average rate of interest was determined by politico-institutional and conventional factors in the financial market which, in conjunction with normal conditions of production and the process of capital accumulation, systematically governed the supply of and demand for loan capital. The only significant difference is that the banking school Tooke believed greater consideration needed to be given to Britain's international financial relations, especially with the United States of America, in explaining the rate of interest in London:

> I have only here to add, that the circumstances which have, since that explanation was given, developed themselves in our foreign commercial relations, not only with the United States of America, but with the rest of the world, are calculated to give additional force to the causes there enumerated in disturbing the rate of interest.
>
> (1840a, III: 143)

Most significantly, the banking school Tooke continued to maintain his pre-banking school position that, through the conduct of its monetary policy, the Bank of England had the capacity to exert an influence on rate of interest in the short run but not in the long run: 'it is quite impossible for the Bank or any other institution to exercise any *permanent control* over the rate [of interest] paid for the use of [capital], a rate of course determined by the law of supply and demand' (1856: 72; also see 1840b: (Q 3802) 364; 1857, V: 556).

It was chiefly through its 'considerable temporary' influence over the market rate of interest that Tooke (1840b: (Q 3728) 352, (Q 3761) 357; 1844: 124; 1848c: (Q 3132) 351) considered the Bank of England was best able to affect credit conditions and, thereby, the state of commercial trade in the economy. Tooke (1840b: (Q 3723–32) 352–3; 1844: 102–3) continued to believe the most effective way for the Bank to influence the market rate of interest was through the 'forcible' purchase and sale of securities in the open market. However, with the Bank having adopted the practice from the mid-1840s onwards of frequently adjusting its discount rate on bills brought to its door, the banking school Tooke (1840b: (Q 3801) 364) gave more prominence to the influence of its discount policy on the market rate of interest.

Tooke (1848b: (Q 5344–5) 416) believed that in the short run the bank rate set by the Bank of England had an important bearing on the 'general rate of interest'. Indeed, as is discussed in the next section of this chapter, the banking school Tooke was of the view that, through its discount policy and open market operations, the Bank of England was capable of stabilising the rate of interest around its long-run average level. He considered the main cause of short-run variations in the rate of interest was a change in the position of the balance of payments which, via external flows of bullion, altered the level of specie reserves held by the Bank of England (Tooke 1840a, III: 187–8). In particular, because of London's central role in the provision of bullion reserves for the international capital market, Tooke (1840a III: 143–4, 241–3) believed monetary pressures in foreign financial markets (i.e. North America) were a major source of disturbance to the rate of interest. Nonetheless, Tooke argued that by 'forcible action' on its securities the Bank of England was able to counteract these external influences on the rate of interest. Tooke (1840b: (Q 3769) 359; 1844: 102–3; 1848b: (Q 5448–9) 429) especially maintained that, by forcibly raising the rate of interest in relation to foreign rates, the Bank of England possessed an 'infallible' means of inducing the net capital inflow necessary to shore up its bullion reserves and to quickly correct the foreign exchanges.

While the banking school Tooke believed that in the short run the Bank of England, as the central banking authority, had considerable power to influence the rate of interest, it had limited power to influence the price level. The reason for this is that Tooke denied any systematic inverse relationship between prior causal alterations in the rate of interest and monetary expenditure in the economy. However, this did not mean Tooke ruled out the possibility of the Bank's monetary policy influencing the price of commodities in the short run. As indicated above (pp. 172–3), Tooke certainly believed policy-induced changes in the rate of interest had a systematic effect on share prices and, connectedly, credit conditions in the financial market. Tooke acknowledged that by altering the willingness of banks to provide credit to merchants and the degree of confidence of commodity dealers to provide trade credit to each other, Bank of England policy could also influence commodity prices in the short run. Consistent with his pre-banking school position, Tooke (1844: 103) believed the influence of Bank policy on prices largely depended on the wider economic conditions determining the state of commodity trade. It is evident though he considered the influence of Bank policy on prices to be largely asymmetric, with a high interest rate policy more likely to be effective in depressing commodity trade and prices than a low interest rate policy stimulating trade and raising prices. Thus, as indicated above (pp. 174–5), Tooke (1840a, III: 268; 1840b: (Q 3088) 346; 1848a, IV: 294–5; 1857, V: 585–90) argued that when political and natural factors gave rise to speculative activity in commodity markets, an accommodating policy by the Bank of England, which kept the rate of interest low, would extend the range of increase in the prices of affected commodities than would have otherwise occurred. But Tooke (1840a, III: 268) held that in absence of circumstances favourable to speculation, it was 'not within reasonable probability' that an expansionary policy by the Bank could on its own raise the level of prices.[13]

In contrast, when commodity markets were stagnant and there was no prospect of a future advance in prices, Tooke believed a stringent Bank policy which significantly raised the rate of interest could induce a large number of credit-reliant dealers to sell stocks and thereby lower prices. This viewpoint was best articulated in the following passage:

> as the rate of interest acts, and is in its turn acted, upon by the state of credit, an influence on prices *may*, in *certain states of the market*, be exercised by the rate of interest through the medium of Credit; for, inasmuch as a higher than ordinary rate of interest supposes a contraction of credit, such goods as are held by means of a large proportion of borrowed capital may be forced for sale by a difficulty in obtaining Banking accommodation, the measure of which difficulty is in the rate of discount, and perhaps in the insufficiency of the security. In this view, and in this view *only*, a rate of interest higher than ordinary may be said to have an influence in depressing Prices.
>
> (Tooke 1857, V: 584; emphasis added; also see 1840a, III: 166–8; 1840b:
> (Q 3624–5) 341–2; 1844: 103)

Tooke (1840a, III: 266–8; 1848b: (Q 5451–2) 430; 1848c: (Q 3094–6) 347) readily conceded that by the adoption of an extremely stringent policy, involving the forcible sale of its securities such as to violently raise the rate of interest, the Bank of England was capable of inducing 'commercial discredit' that would inevitably depress commodity prices. However, Tooke argued, for the Bank to exercise this power by means of a 'violent operation' would involve it acting 'wholly inconsistent with its professed rules and its ordinary practice' (1840a, III: 267). He also argued that the 'power of producing such a depressing effect' (1840a, III: 267) could only be temporary since a high interest rate induces an influx of bullion (i.e. capital inflow) which would endogenously relieve the 'pressure' on London's financial market. Overall, it was Tooke's position that except in the implausible case when a violent operation is implemented, the Bank of England had limited power to purposely influence the level of money prices because there is no predictable connection between the rate of interest, spending and economic activity.[14]

In Tooke's picture, then, the Bank of England's power to influence economic activity and the price level was confined to the short run. In the first place, Tooke contended that this power was exercised through its influence over the short-term rate of interest and, thereby, the foreign exchanges and credit conditions in the economy. On the basis of his conception of endogenous money explained in the previous section of this chapter, Tooke maintained that in a convertible system of currency it was not possible for the Bank to exercise this power through direct control over its banknotes in circulation. Therefore, according to Tooke, the capacity of the Bank of England to stabilise the price level depended heavily on the effect of changes in the rate of interest on the inducement to purchase commodities. Second, as just shown, Tooke denied there was any systematic inverse causal influence of changes in the rate of interest on the demand for commodities and, thereby, on the price level. Instead, Tooke believed that, except in the case of an aggressively adopted restrictive stance, the effect of the

Bank's monetary policy on the price level was not predictable, being dependent on how it affected credit conditions and, thereby, the demand for commodities by merchants in the context of *wider economic circumstances*. Hence, the effect of the Bank's policy on the economy at any given time could only be explained by reference to the *concrete* situation. Third, in the long run, when Tooke conceived permanent changes in the rate of interest did have a systematic though uni-directional effect on the general price level, he denied the Bank of England had any significant direct influence over its average level. Only indirectly, by shaping conventional opinion in the financial market about the risk-return profile of securities and by facilitating government borrowing operations, is there scope in Tooke's theory for the Bank to significantly influence the demand and supply conditions of disposable capital which determine the long-run average rate of interest.

Lastly, Tooke's position on the determination of the rate of interest and its relationship to the price level is entirely consistent with his view about external adjustment and the capacity of the Bank of England to exert a strong influence over the foreign exchanges in the short run. An implication of Tooke's position is that a permanent rise (decline) in the rate of interest which acts to raise (lower) the cost of production of commodities will tend to reduce (increase) a country's international competitiveness. This is in fact compatible with his longstanding view that in response to alterations in the relative price of tradable commodities, the process of adjustment in the volume of imports and exports occurred over the long run (see Section 6.2.1). In contrast, Tooke believed changes in the net flow of capital (and, thereby, bullion) between countries in response to alterations in their relative rates of interest could occur in the *short run*. As Tooke was careful to emphasise in the following footnote, the ability of the Bank of England to correct the foreign exchanges by effecting a rise (fall) in the rate of interest and inducing net capital inflow (outflow) was confined to the short run:

> It is urged that if a low rate of interest is a cause of cheapness, by parity of reasoning, a high rate of interest must be cause of dearness: it should seem, therefore, to follow, that the Bank in raising the rate of interest with a view to redress the exchanges would raise the prices of commodities, thus exhibiting the anomaly of advanced prices co-existent with an effort on the part of the Bank to restore an influx of bullion. The answer to this objection is, that in the argument leading to the conclusion that a low rate of interest is a cause of cheapness, I have expressly assumed that the reduced rate should be of such duration or permanence as to enter into the cost of production, and the converse holds of a rise in the rate of interest. Now, the operation of the Bank in raising the rate in order to counteract a drain, *cannot be considered of such permanence as to affect the cost of production.* And the greater the rise in the rate of interest from a forcible operation of the Bank on its securities, the less must be the probability of its duration.
>
> (1844: 123–4n.; emphasis added)[15]

Thus, in Tooke's (1848c: (Q 3106–7) 348) conception, monetary policy could influence trade flows in the short run by altering the foreign exchanges and by affecting the facility of credit to London's international trading houses, but could not do so in the long run.

In accordance with the above reasoning, the banking school Tooke conceived that in the short run causality ran unsystematically from the rate of interest to spending and money prices and, then, systematically to the whole quantity of money in circulation. Given his rejection of the notion that changes in the rate of interest was the moving cause for expenditure on commodities, Tooke believed the Bank of England had limited power to influence the whole circulating medium. Instead, well-established during his pre-banking school phase, Tooke held that short-run variations in the whole circulating medium mainly depended on political and natural factors which caused price fluctuations. On the basis of his dual-circulation framework (see Section 7.1), the banking school Tooke conceived that these variations in the whole circulating medium were predominantly due to expansions and contractions in the amount of credit money in that branch of monetary circulation that expedited transactions between dealers and dealers, corresponding to an increase and reduction in the velocity of circulation of banknotes mainly used to expedite transactions between dealers and consumers. In this connection Tooke contended the amount of banknotes in circulation remained relatively stable in the short run, changing more in response to prior causal changes in economic activity than in money prices:

> a further Investigation into the Rationale of the Connexion between Prices and the Circulation has perfectly satisfied me that Bank Notes are simply the Effect of Transactions. They may or may not be the Effect of Prices; but I should say generally that they vary more according to the Nature and Amount of pecuniary Transactions connected with the State of Trade than according to Prices.
>
> (Tooke 1848c: (Q 3129) 351)

Only by a violent contraction in its securities which induces a high rate of interest, causing a depression in economic activity and prices that leads to a considerable reduction in the amount of credit money and, thereby, in the whole circulating medium, did Tooke (1848c: (Q 3094) 347) believe the Bank of England could effectively reduce the amount of its own banknotes in circulation. Except in circumstances when there was a rapid drain of bullion reserves below a safe level, Tooke considered that the effective implementation of such a stringent policy by the Bank was improbable. In this overall sense, Tooke denied the Bank of England could alter *at will* the quantity of its banknotes in circulation.

7.4 Banking policy

The banking school Tooke's views on banking policy were largely articulated in the context of the currency–banking school debates in which he was the main opposer to the currency school's plan for the separation of the banking and note-issuing functions of the Bank of England as instituted by the Bank Charter Act of 1844. Tooke's strenuous opposition to the 1844 Bank Act is best understood in terms of his own position on the appropriate institutional framework for the English banking system and for the conduct of monetary policy by the Bank of England. For the most part, this position was consistent with that which he had developed in his pre-banking school phase. Nevertheless, on various points the banking school Tooke refined his views on banking policy and, in particular, showed a greater appreciation of the role of the Bank of England as a central bank acting in the public interest.

The main issue in banking policy that concerned Tooke was the level of bullion reserves which the Bank of England ought to routinely hold in the conduct of its policy. As was shown in Section 6.4, the pre-banking school Tooke believed that after the restoration of the gold standard in 1821 the major problem with the management of the currency in England was the inadequate precautionary reserve of bullion which the Bank of England routinely held to meet the contingency of an 'extraordinary' demand for cash. The banking school Tooke (1848b: (Q 5353–9) 417–18; 1848c: (Q 3044–5) 341) also continued to believe this was the major problem with Bank of England policy throughout the late-1830s and in the 1840s. Thus, in reference to the Bank's role in the 1836–1837 and 1839 financial pressures, Tooke argued its 'fundamental error' was in 'attempting to regulate the large united amount of circulation and deposits upon too small an average reserve' (1840a, III: 185).[16] Tooke therefore argued in 1840 that '*the* [Bank's] *directors should undertake to hold in reserve a much higher average amount of bullion than they have hitherto considered it necessary or consistent with the interests of their proprietors to maintain*' (1840a, III: 185).

To calculate the average amount of bullion that ought to be held by the Bank of England, Tooke adopted the precept from the 'Palmer Rule' that a 'safe' level of bullion reserves would constitute approximately one-third of its liabilities. Applying this precept to the 'eventful experience of the last fourteen years, viz., since 1824', Tooke (1838, II: 330–1) proposed that '*not less than ten millions can ever be considered as a safe position of* [the Bank's] *treasure, seeing the sudden calls to which it is liable*'. As indicated by Tooke (1840a, III: 188–9; 1840b: (Q 376–6) 358–9) in subsequent writings and committee evidence, this safe level of £10 million was based on it being an average (equivalent to a medium) of a 'latitude for variation' in bullion reserves between £5 million and £15 million (Fetter 1965: 189; Morgan 1965: 141). Following 'the experience [in 1847] of a drain so much larger than I could reasonably have had in contemplation' (1848b: (Q 5359) 418), Tooke revised upwards this safe level in 1848 to £12 million on the basis of an allowable variation in reserves of between £6 million and £18 million. This allowable variation in reserves was based on what Tooke (1840a, III: 187–9) identified from historical experience to be the medium variation in the Bank of England's stock of bullion associated with cyclical movements in foreign trade flows in response to changes in the foreign exchanges. It consisted of the notion that when the stock of bullion was high, the resulting appreciation in the foreign exchanges would tend to induce a trade deficit (and capital outflows) and, thereby, a rundown in reserves; and when the stock of bullion was low, vice versa.

The important thing for Tooke was that in the event of an extraordinary external outflow of bullion, the Bank of England should conduct policy so as to ensure its reserves did not decline below the lower limit and require it to implement a violent action which would induce a state of commercial discredit (Laidler 1975: 212–13). To this end, Tooke proposed 'guidelines' for the conduct of monetary policy consistent with the above-mentioned cyclical variation in the Bank's reserves of bullion. First, Tooke (1840a, III: 187–8; 1848b: (Q 5361) 419) argued that when the trade balance was favourable and there was an external inflow of bullion, the Bank of England should allow its reserves to accumulate up to the maximum limit (of £15 million or £18 million) by holding its discount rate above the market rate of interest. In this way the Bank was able to achieve the average level of reserves specified above over the course of Britain's cycle of trade flows.[17] According to Tooke (1840a, III: 185–7), the reason why the Bank of England had failed to hold a sufficient average level of reserves was its tendency not to allow the level of reserves to much exceed safe levels (of £10 million or £12 million) when an external inflow of bullion was occurring. Tooke attributed this tendency to the Bank's practice of lowering its discount rate and making open market purchases in order to increase its stock of interest-bearing securities in preference to non-income earning bullion:

> Hitherto, at least since 1830, whenever, by the tide of the metals inwards, the amount of bullion has reached ten millions or upwards, the Bank has taken active measures to convert a part of so unproductive stock into securities; and consequently the intervals during which the amount was at a high rate were very short.
>
> (1840a, III: 186–7)

Second, Tooke proposed that when the trade balance became unfavourable and an external drain set in, from a position of holding the maximum limit of bullion reserves, the Bank should be passive in allowing them to decline down to the safe level. Tooke (1840a, III: 188) argued that 'in the majority of cases' this export of bullion (of £5 million to £6 million) would by itself induce a favourable turn in the foreign exchanges and a turnaround in the trade balance.[18] Only if bullion reserves continued to decline below the safe level 'so as to give reason to apprehend the existence of more extensive and deeper seated causes of demand for the metals' should the Bank take 'active measures in raising its rate of discount or selling its public securities' to counteract the drain (1840a, III: 188). In the event of such an extraordinary drain, Tooke (1848b: (Q 5363–9) 419–20) contended that unless reserves declined dangerously below the lower limit (of £5 million to £6 million), moderate counteractive measures would only have to be applied by the Bank of England 'without producing alarm and disturbance of the money market' (1840a, III: 188). Based on historical experience, Tooke (1848b: (Q 5370) 420) ascertained that any extraordinary drain could be met by the export of £10 million to £12 million of bullion, at which point, being the lower limit, the tide would begin to turn. As discussed above, Tooke argued that with a favourable turn in the cycle of foreign trade (and foreign exchanges), the Bank should adopt a firm policy to ensure the steady accumulation of its reserves up to the maximum limit.

The purpose of Tooke's policy guidelines was to ensure the Bank of England maintained an adequate precautionary reserve of bullion which would afford it greater scope to deal with any extraordinary drain without resorting to violent restrictive measures that would induce unwanted pressure in the money market. In particular, Tooke (1840a, III: 189–90) claimed that, by conducting monetary policy with a large average reserve, the Bank could secure greater stability (or 'uniformity') in the market rate of interest and credit conditions favourable to commercial activity. He contended, perhaps somewhat ambitiously, that under his policy approach, '[T]he utmost alteration of the rate of discount to which the Bank might have occasion to resort would probably not exceed 1 per cent.; and the occasions for an alteration even to that extent would probably be rare' (1840a, III: 189). It was Tooke's view that, prior to the 1844 Bank Act, Bank of England policy had contributed to instability in the rate of interest and credit conditions 'inconvenient' to commercial activity by operating with a small average reserve. As already suggested, Tooke believed the Bank tended to conduct policy on an unsafe average reserve because it was more profitable to hold interest-bearing securities than bullion, especially when there was an external inflow of bullion and the price of public securities was rising. On this point Tooke wrote:

> The main objection or difficulty in the way of maintaining so large an average amount of treasure as ten millions, is in its unproductiveness, and its consequent drawback from the profits of the Bank; but against this must be set the greater security of its position; and, after all, the amount is not larger than any prudent banker would deem it right to hold against liabilities so large and so fluctuating as those of the Bank of England.
>
> (1844: 117)

In this connection Tooke (1840a, III: 92–4, 194–5) identified a conflict between the public duty of the Bank of England and the private interest of its proprietors.[19]

Tooke believed the private interest of Bank of England proprietors was conveniently joined by that of 'merchants and traders' who regarded 'accommodation' by the banking system as a 'claim of right' (1840a, III: 94, 104). It is evident that Tooke believed this mutual understanding was ostensibly justified by the 'vague doctrine' that the Bank had a 'duty' to support commercial credit and, thereby, accommodate the trade of the country. Tooke (1840a, III: 102–14) was highly critical of this doctrine as justification for Bank of England policy which he considered far from being in the public interest. Nonetheless, Tooke (1840a, III: 194–5; 1848b: (Q 5354) 417–18) acknowledged that to get the Bank to conduct policy with a higher average reserve of bullion, it would be necessary for the government to compensate the proprietors for reduced profits under arrangements for the renewal of its charter in 1844. Tooke (1840a, III: 195–7) also acknowledged the adoption of his policy guidelines would reduce the competitiveness of the Bank of England, which may lead to the gradual replacement of its banknotes in provincial regions by country banknotes. To prevent this from occurring, Tooke suggested that, as part of compensation for holding a higher precautionary reserve, the Bank could be offered the 'exclusive' right to issue paper money in the whole country (Morgan 1965: 141).

The banking school Tooke (1848b: (Q 5393) 423 (Q 5423) 427–8; 1848c: (Q 3053–8) 342–3) was a strong advocate of allowing the Bank of England considerable discretion to conduct monetary policy for the same reasons he did so in his pre-banking school days (see Section 6.4). Therefore, Tooke (1840b: (Q 3715) 351; 1848b: (Q 5379–80) 420–1) rejected the proposition that his policy prescription discussed above should be the basis of any 'regulation' in which the Bank of England was compelled to follow 'rules' such as holding a fixed proportion of bullion to its liabilities or holding no less than a certain average level of bullion reserves. Instead, Tooke advocated renewal of the Bank's charter ought to be based on an 'understanding' that management would conduct monetary policy with a higher average reserve of bullion (in relation to its liabilities). Tooke (1848b: (Q 5392) 423) believed that, while his guidelines provided the basis for sound monetary policy, it nevertheless depended on the ability of the Bank's management to make prudent judgements according to the different circumstances prevailing at any given time. He clearly believed that in banking discretion was inescapable, with bankers especially called upon to make prudential judgements in the provision of credit. For Tooke (1840a, III: 262; 1844: 81) prudent banking basically involved the advancement of credit on 'reasonable security of repayment' and with a sufficient reserve to cover contingencies. But Tooke (1840a, III: 195–6; 1844: 87–8) maintained there was no possible regulation that could prevent banks from occasionally engaging in imprudent lending practice which contributed to commercial distress.

Tooke (1848b: (Q 5424) 428) was a strong supporter of the institutional independence of the Bank of England, in particular rejecting the idea that its 'Governor' be appointed by the government.[20] Instead, Tooke advocated reforms to the system of administration of the Bank of England which would increase the discretionary powers of its governors and improve the professional competence of its management overall. In the first place, Tooke recommended a change in the system of electing Bank directors and governors in order to increase their term of office. He believed the existing system of annually electing eight new directors to a Court of twenty-six from which the Governor and Deputy-Governor were then elected produced a high turnover of personnel that deprived the Bank of 'competent and experienced' management (1848b: (Q 5425–6) 428; 1857, V: 617–21). To overcome this problem, Tooke and Newmarch (1857, V: 623–5) proposed the tenure of both governors and directors be extended from one to three years, with all governors and twenty of the remaining twenty-four directors eligible for triennial re-election. This reduced the likely turnover of directors of the Bank of England to four every three years.[21] Tooke and Newmarch (1857, V: 623–5) also proposed that three governors instead of two should be elected, consisting of a 'Governor', 'Sub-Governor' and 'Deputy-Governor'. He believed a third governor, primarily responsible for the regulation of the securities of the Bank, would enhance the united authority of the governors with the Court of Directors in setting policy (see below, pp. 185–6).[22] However, Tooke and Newmarch (1857, V: 631–2) acknowledged that this proposal for electing governors was likely to be opposed on the grounds that an increased amount of time would have to be devoted to the Bank's management by office-bearers at the neglect of their own commercial affairs. To meet this objection, Tooke proposed an alternative system, whereby the positions of governors be made full-time, attracting high salaries and elected by the Court of Directors from an open field of candidates (i.e. including persons who were not directors of the Bank).[23]

Second, Tooke advocated a change in the administrative procedure by which policy decisions of the Bank of England were made. At the time the administrative procedure of the Bank of England involved the governors, after conferring with a Committee of Treasury, to refer policy measures of importance to the Court of Directors for decision at weekly meetings. In particular, this included the fixing of the Bank's 'minimum' bank rate to be charged on bills discounted. While admitting he had no precise knowledge of how these meetings were conducted, Tooke nevertheless considered it to be a cumbersome method of decision-making:

> I consider that a Board, consisting of twenty-four Directors and two Governors, is too numerous for deliberation and discussion on questions of importance, involving points of difficult solution, and affecting the interests and convenience of the Public; and at the same time, requiring prompt decision.
>
> (1857, V: 620–1)

In particular, Tooke objected to important policy measures being ultimately 'decided by a simple and bare majority' (1857, V: 627) of Bank directors largely on the grounds that it would lead to a lack of consistency in policy-making. He agreed with the argument by the parliamentarian George Carr Glyn, given in evidence to the 1848 Lords Committee on Commercial Distress, that 'there may be a majority one week which may be a minority the next, and the principle of the system may be upset by an adverse vote, though it may be prudent and right' (1848: (Q 1782) 210; quoted in Tooke and Newmarch 1857, V: 608–9, 612). To remedy this problem, Tooke (1857, V: 627–31) proposed rules of procedure that would invest greater discretionary powers with the governors over the Court of Directors in making policy decisions. These rules consisted of requiring a two-thirds majority of all Bank directors to overrule any recommendations of the governors; that all policy questions and, in particular, alterations in the Bank's discount rate, should be discussed at Court meetings only at the instigation of the governors or Committee of Treasury; and, as mentioned above, three governors should be elected to formulate a united position on policy recommendations to the Committee of Treasury and the Court of Directors.[24] In advocating these institutional changes Tooke was promoting the establishment of a body of professional managers to determine Bank of England policy in the public interest, more akin to the operation of a modern central bank.

With regard to the Bank of England's public accountability, the banking school Tooke was much less pre-occupied with this issue than the pre-banking school Tooke. Nonetheless, by the late 1840s, Tooke expressed dissatisfaction with the weekly publication of the Bank's accounts, largely on the grounds that they failed to provide a useful 'guide by which to judge the general propriety of the conduct of the Bank in its management' (1848b: (Q 5410–15) 426–7; 1848c: (Q 3144–5) 353) and possessed the disadvantage of giving rise to 'alarm' and 'panic' when reserves were shown to be small. To remedy these deficiencies, Tooke (1848b: (Q 5416) 427) recommended quarterly publication of the Bank of England's accounts.

A banking policy issue the banking school Tooke did consider was free banking, which he defined as 'an unlimited competition in banks, whether of issue or of deposit' (1848b: (Q 5384) 422). The issue of free banking arose from its proposal by Parnell (1827; 1833) and Gilbart (1834, 1841), leading lights of what has been called the free banking school (for an account of this school, see White 1984: 51–80; Schwartz 1989). It has been claimed by Arnon (1991: 130–1, 166–8) that from the *Inquiry* (1844) onwards, Tooke adopted a free trade position on the issue of banknotes. However, this claim is not supported by the evidence. To the 1848 Commons Committee on the Causes of Commercial Distress, Tooke stated quite definitely: 'I do not admit the doctrine of what is called free trade in banking' (1848b: (Q 5384) 422). In defence of the privileges of the Bank of England, Tooke (1840a, III: 172–4) had earlier expressed considerable hostility to the free banking school. Indeed, though a strong supporter of free trade in general, Tooke made an exception to banking on the grounds that '*the issue of paper substitutes for coin is no branch of productive industry*' (1840a, III: 207). He argued unfettered freedom by banks to issue promissory notes of any denomination would lead to more serious 'derangement's of the currency' and more frequent instances of fraud, agreeing with the observation of an American writer that '*free trade in banking is synonymous with free trade in swindling*' (1840a, III: 206). For this reason Tooke believed banking '*is a matter for regulation by the state, with a view to general convenience, and comes within the province of police*' (1840a, III: 207; also see 1848b: (Q 5384–5) 422).

Tooke's opposition to free banking is consistent with his longstanding position that banks should be regulated to prevent them from issuing small notes under £5, adhere to prudential requirements and meet certain standards of public accountability (refer to Section 6.4). It is also consistent with the alteration in Tooke's position from that taken in his pre-banking school phase on the desirability of the Bank of England extending its control over the issue of banknotes from the City of London to the whole country. Informed by his newly developed conception of endogenous money, the banking school Tooke no longer believed that 'unlimited competition' between note-issuing banks was any more likely to produce commercial revulsion than that between non-issuing (i.e. deposit only) banks:

> The danger of unlimited competition of banks does not apply more to banks of issue, always supposing the notes to be perfect, than to non-issuing banks. The mischief of commercial revulsions from overtrading, whenever trace-able to the banks, has been from over advances of capital, on insufficient or inconvertible securities, or both. Banks, whether of issue or not, may, in competition for business, make advances to persons undeserving of credit, and may discount large amounts of doubtful bills, thus adding to the circu-lating medium, without adding directly to the amount of the circulation, that is, of notes.
>
> (1844: 157–8)

Tooke (1844: 155–6) was 'prepared to maintain' that a 'sufficient security' against an unlimited competition of note-issuing banks ever producing an 'exces-sive' issue of banknotes was provided by their 'convertibility into gold'. Hence, Tooke (1844: 151–3) no longer supported an increase in the Bank's power over the issue of banknotes in order to facilitate its autonomous control over the quan-tity in circulation.[25] Instead, the banking school Tooke (1840a, III: 194–7) was in favour of the Bank of England maintaining a dominance over the issue of ban-knotes in the United Kingdom in order to preserve its competitive position and, thereby, continue to act as the central banking authority with the capacity to exert a strong influence over monetary conditions in the public interest. It was from this standpoint that Tooke (1840a, III: 206–7) opposed the free banking school's campaign to remove the Bank of England's monopoly over the issue of banknotes in the 'City' of London (or 'metropolis').

The banking school Tooke well appreciated the central banking role of the Bank of England, both as banker to the government and lender-of-last-resort to the financial system. This is shown in the following extracts from Tooke's evid-ence to the 1848 Committee on Commercial Distress:

> Q 5386 Do you consider that the existence of the Bank of England is an advantage to the public? – Tooke: Unquestionably; its existence upon its present scale arises from the circumstance of its being the Government Bank; but taking it all in all; I should say that it is an institution which, if it did not exist, and you were constructing a [financial] system *de novo*, it would be desirable to have.
>
> (1848b: 422)

> Q 5387 What advantages do you consider to flow from the existence of the Bank of England? – Tooke: ... that upon a general failure of credit there is

this vast establishment, with its enormous capital and its unquestioned credit, which can come in and fill the vacuum created by such a general derangement of credit as might otherwise occasion a total suspension of business.

(1848b: 422)[26]

In this central banking role, Tooke (1848b: (Q 5388) 422) believed the Bank of England underpinned the elasticity of credit in Britain's gold-based monetary system essential to the well-being of its trade and commerce.

The banking school Tooke showed a much better appreciation of the Bank of England's lender-of-last-resort role than the pre-banking school Tooke. Nevertheless, he continued to emphasise the need for the Bank to adopt an active monetary policy to prevent financial pressures from occurring. This involved the Bank taking a firm stance to discourage moral hazard in the banking system as a whole and to prevent expansions in credit that accommodated unsustainable speculative booms in shares and commodities. Given the possibility of unforeseen contingencies, Tooke believed the Bank's management needed discretion in the conduct of its policy. As previously shown in this section, Tooke advocated for Bank of England policy to be conducted on the basis of a large precautionary reserve to give policy-makers a safe margin for error and adequate time to implement measures to counteract any extraordinary and sudden demand for bullion (i.e. liquidity). By adopting this policy, Tooke (1857, V: 535–6) believed the Bank of England would be in a sounder position to fulfil its lender-of-last-resort role in the event of commercial discredit and, thereby, better equipped to deal with any financial crisis with the potential to endanger convertibility of the currency. Moreover, by conducting policy in this manner, Tooke (1844: 103–5) believed the Bank of England would be able to secure greater stability in the rate of interest and credit conditions, which he considered to be a goal of banking policy second only to the preservation of the convertibility of the paper currency.

7.5 Tooke's opposition to the Bank Charter Act of 1844

Throughout the 1840s and until the mid-1850s, Tooke was a relentless critic of the institutional separation of the Bank of England's note-issuing and banking functions advocated by the currency school and given legislative form in the Bank Charter Act of 1844. There were three major parts to Tooke's criticism of the 1844 Bank Act. First, on the basis of his banking school monetary analysis expounded above in this chapter, Tooke attacked the premises upon which the 1844 Bank Act was based. Second, from the standpoint of banking policy, Tooke criticised the 1844 Bank Act ex ante for the probable consequences of its practical operation for the stability of the financial system. Third, after its inception, Tooke attacked the 1844 Bank Act ex post, by reference to its role in the actual behaviour of England's financial market and economy over the period 1844–1856. These three parts of Tooke's criticism of the 1844 Bank Act are considered in what follows.

In the introduction to this chapter it was shown the 1844 Bank Act was based on the currency principle which, according to Tooke, consisted of the principle that 'bank notes in circulation should be made to conform to the gold, into which they are convertible, not only in value, but in amount' so that they 'vary exactly in amount as the coin would have done if the Currency had been purely metallic' (1844: 2). Upon this principle the currency school proposed the 'test of good or bad management' by the Bank of England was 'the degree of correspondence between variations in the amount of bullion, and variations in the amount of bank notes in circulation' (1844: 2). The currency principle constituted a strict version of the classical economists' quantity theory of money in which the velocity of circulation of banknotes was conceived, if anything, to move in sympathy with prior causal variations in the quantity of banknotes in the short run. The currency school therefore supposed that the whole circulating medium varied strictly in correspondence with the quantity of banknotes in circulation. It was shown in Section 7.3 that Tooke disputed the fundamental proposition underpinning the currency school's theory that the Bank of England had the power to control at will the quantity of its own banknotes and, thereby, the whole quantity of circulating medium in Britain's convertible system of currency.

In the first place, Tooke (1840b: (Q 3723–8) 352, (Q 3732) 353; 1844: 102–3) argued the Bank of England could only influence monetary conditions by the purchase and sale of securities (i.e. by altering its outstanding advances) through which it could influence the rate of interest and credit conditions in the economy. He strenuously maintained that, contrary to the view of the currency school, causality tended to run from credit conditions and, according to the effect on prices and trade, to the demand for banknotes in the economy, and not vice versa:

> Q 3623 Do you not suppose that an increase in the amount of bank notes in circulation will afford facilities for the enlargement of the circulating medium, and of credit generally, so as to facilitate an increase of prices? – Tooke: Not at all. I conceive that it is enlargement of credit under the influence of opinion respecting prices, that, by entailing an increase in transactions, may, according to the nature of the transactions rather than the amount of them, call out an additional amount of bank notes.
>
> (Tooke 1840b: 340–1)

An apparent 'confusion' of members of the 1840 Committee over currency matters was:

> traceable to the deep-seated impression ... that the amount of bank notes in the hands of the public was the main point for consideration, as having a direct and an important influence on prices, and on credit and on trade, instead of being as it is, – a mere effect or indication of the circumstances which call out and maintain that amount.
>
> (Tooke 1844: 103)

Moreover, Tooke contended that 'unless there is a demand for gold, the great bulk of the transactions of the Bank of England' are 'accompanied with as little effect upon the amount of bank notes in the hands of the public as are the transactions of the country banks of issue' (1844: 58; also see 1840b: (Q 3725) 352). Only in the special case when inconvertible paper money was issued through the agency of increased deficit-financed government expenditure did Tooke concede that it was possible for a note-issuing authority to directly influence prices and credit (see Section 7.3).

From this standpoint Tooke (1844: 19–20, 70–1) accused the currency school of confounding the power of the English banking system to regulate the quantity of convertible banknotes in circulation with that of a government authority issuing compulsory and inconvertible paper currency. In this connection, Tooke (1848a, IV: 178–83) challenged the currency school to explain precisely *how* the Bank of England could regulate the quantity of *convertible* banknotes in circulation at its own discretion. Tooke charged the followers of the currency principle with the error of assuming rather than providing such an explanation:

> The same wedded attachment to the doctrine of the Currency principle which looks to bank notes, and to bank notes only, as the primum mobile in our monetary system, may account for the little research which the [1840] Committee made into the causes and effects of variations in the rate of interest, and for the strange misconception which pervaded the questions relating to that point, of those members who took a leading part in the examinations. They seem from the first to last to have looked upon variations in the rate of interest as of importance only, inasmuch as those variations might be supposed to affect the amount of the circulation.
>
> (1844: 103–4)

The currency school failed to comprehend the significance of this charge, let alone attempt to answer it. It was not until 1858 that Torrens (1858: 314–19), the chief defender of the currency school position, referred to the role of the rate of interest in effecting the demand for credit accommodated by bank loans. Nowhere does Torrens tackle the crucial question dealt with by Tooke of the causal effect of the rate of interest on the inducement to purchase commodities (see, for example, Torrens 1844: 43–55; 1848: 83 et seq.; Clay 1844: 29–42; while Overstone did not reply to any of Tooke's criticisms of his position).

Second, Tooke argued that, contrary to the currency school position, the whole circulating medium usually varied in the short run with price fluctuations independently of the quantity of banknotes in circulation. Tooke had long maintained the English monetary system possessed considerable elasticity with short-run price movements largely accommodated by variations in credit, consisting of bank advances, discounted bills of exchange and various forms of trade credit, associated with the distribution and employment of capital. By contrast, he maintained the quantity of banknotes in circulation remained relatively stable in the short run, referring to evidence of 'the apparent steadiness of the amount of the notes in circulation, during certain periods, compared with deposits and the securities or the bullion' of the Bank of England, concluding that the 'comparative uniformity indicates a very great degree of regularity in the demand for banknotes' (1840b: (Q 3739) 354). In this connection Tooke (1844: 102, 107–8; 1848a, IV: 185) believed increases (decreases) in the bullion reserves of the Bank of England, which came from external influxes (drains), usually involved expansions (contractions) in its deposits with little change in the demand for its banknotes (also see Tooke's 1848a, IV: 291 quotation of J.S. Mill 1844: 596). Tooke argued that the exchange of bullion for Bank of England notes was only significant in times of commercial discredit and its aftermath. However, in absence of a serious depression in trade, Tooke considered an internal drain of bullion did not so much imply a contraction in the amount of Bank of England notes as a contraction in credit monies (and country banknotes).[27] This was because an acute demand for liquidity would involve a substitution from credit monies to Bank of England notes and coin which, presumably, reversed when confidence had been restored to the London financial market. Hence, according to Tooke, even if an effective system of regulation could be instituted to enable the Bank of England to directly control the quantity of its (convertible) banknotes in circulation, it would not have the power to control the whole circulating medium, nor to stabilise the price level, in the short run.

In all, Tooke challenged the central premises of the 1844 Bank Act by, first, denying the Bank of England had the power to regulate at will its own banknotes in circulation and, second, by showing that the velocity of circulation of their banknotes varied considerably in the short run in response to the demand for credit. In this way he showed that controlling the quantity of banknotes in circulation was not an appropriate *target* of banking policy.[28] Moreover, Tooke (1844: 121; 1848c: (Q 3104–5) 348, (Q 3126–7) 350) repudiated the currency school's argument that variations in the quantity of convertible banknotes in circulation in relation *to* the quantity of bullion at the Bank of England implied a change in the *value* of the currency. Instead, Tooke argued that irrespective of the lack of correspondence between the quantity of banknotes and bullion or, indeed, of the state of the foreign exchanges, the value of the currency ultimately depended on its convertibility into gold (cash) on demand by the Bank of England at its official mint price. Hence, in answer to the question, 'If the paper circulation is to be preserved constantly conformable in value to gold, must it not conform in quantity constantly also to gold?', Tooke stated to the 1840 Committee on Banks of Issue: 'Not at all; as long as the paper is strictly convertible into gold, it cannot be said that the value of the currency is impaired; there may be a very considerable occasional demand for the export of the precious metals, without any ground of inference that the originating cause of it has been any excess of the circulation of this country' (1840b: (Q 3744) 355; also see Tooke 1848c: (Q 3119) 350).

The second part to Tooke's criticism of the 1844 Bank Act was that it would contribute to greater monetary instability and increase the danger of inconvertibility rather than provide a safeguard against it. Well before the Act's inception Tooke (1840a, III: 179–84, 251–3) argued that under the currency school's 'plan of separate issue' fluctuations in the rate of interest, state of credit and prices *'would be more frequent, more abrupt, and sometimes of greater extent'* (1840a, III: 253). This argument is based on the standpoint of Tooke's own banking policy position explained in the previous section of this chapter. First, Tooke (1844: 157–9) contended that under the currency school's plan the Bank of England would be no better able to prevent an expansion in credit which financed speculatively driven upturns in commodity and security prices than it was under the pre-existing system (Laidler 1975: 219–20). In the absence of a strong demand for cash, which induced a rundown in bullion reserves, Tooke contended the plan placed no greater imposition on the Bank of England to adopt a firm policy stance than would be the case under the existing arrangements. Given Tooke (1840a, III: 181–3, 251) believed credit-financed speculative booms usually occurred at times when an external inflow of specie secured a relatively high level of bullion reserves, he failed to see how the provisions of the 1844 Bank Act could compel the Bank of England to adopt a policy which prevented any undue extension of credit.

Second, Tooke argued the 1844 Bank Act would handicap the Bank of England's ability to deal with a drain on its bullion reserves and intensify the resulting pressure on Britain's financial market. This was because, according to Tooke (1840a, III: 178–9), the separation of the Bank of England into a banking (or 'deposit') department and an issuing (or 'circulating') department to be instituted under the 1844 Bank Act would effectively reduce the amount of bullion available to conduct monetary policy. Tooke (1844: 105–10) illustrated his argument by reference to a scenario originally advanced by Torrens (1840: 11–13). This scenario assumed the Bank of England started with the balance sheet in Table 7.1.

It was then supposed that, as a result of an external efflux of bullion, there was a £3,000,000 withdrawal of deposits from the banking department. To meet this demand for gold, the banking department would be required to exchange an equal amount of its banknotes for bullion at the issuing department. Tooke argued that faced with this situation the Bank of England would have to quickly 'sell securities, or allow the existing ones to run off, and they must inexorably shut their doors to all applications for advances or discounts' (1844: 108; also

Table 7.1

Issuing department	
Banknotes in circulation	£18,000,000
Securities	£9,000,000
Bullion reserves	£9,000,000
Banking department	
Deposits	£9,000,000
Securities	£6,000,000
Reserve in banknotes	£3,000,000

see Tooke 1840b: (Q 3843) 368). The situation would be characterised by 'extreme' pressure on the reserves of London banks in general, causing them 'to the utmost extent practicable' to 'call in their loans, and resolutely refuse further accommodation' (1844: 108). Tooke contended that to be 'effectual in restoring its reserves in sufficient time to meet the exigency' (1844: 109), the Bank would have to implement a violent restrictive monetary policy that pushed up the rate of interest to high levels and deny the facility of short-term credit to commercial trade. But in the event the efflux was 'strong' and 'urgent', Tooke (1844: 109) argued that there was a real possibility the 'forced sale of securities might prove insufficient in point of time to arrest the demand' and lead to the 'absurd' situation where the banking department would have to stop payment for lack of cash, while the issuing department 'would still have £6,000,000 of bullion'. In fact Tooke prophetically claimed that to meet such an 'emergency' the government would have to suspend the provisions of the 1844 Bank Act 'to authorise a temporary transfer of coin from the issuing to the banking department' (1844: 109).

Tooke's main point was that in the face of only a moderate drain, at the very least the Bank of England would be compelled under the Act to adopt a violent restrictive policy attended with much 'inconvenience to the public' than would be necessary under the existing system of the union of its note-issuing and banking functions. By 'inconvenience' Tooke meant very high rates of interest and a 'deranged' state of credit which adversely affected economic activity. In support of this point Tooke (1844: 110) referred to evidence showing that in 1828–1829 and 1831–1832, £3,000,000 or £4,000,000 of the Bank's bullion was exported under the existing system without any significant pressure on the financial market. Tooke (1844: 110–14) also contended that the external drain of over £4,000,000 in bullion which led up to the monetary pressure of 1839 would have been more intense under the proposed measures of the 1844 Bank Act. In particular, he used this example to argue that, under the Act, the Bank of England would be required to 'take forcible measures for self preservation upon the first manifestation' of a drain which 'could not fail to be attended with very important and highly inconvenient effects' (1844: 113–14; also see Tooke 1840a, III: 183–4). Moreover, Tooke argued that, by effectively locking up bullion reserves in the proposed issuing department, the Act would, in particular, weaken the Bank of England's ability to cope with an extraordinary drain and, therefore, significantly weaken the Bank of England's capacity to preserve the convertibility of pound sterling (for a similar opinion, see Fullarton 1845: 199–200, 246–9).

The third part of Tooke's criticism of the 1844 Bank Charter Act was that from its commencement it *actually* contributed to greater monetary instability in the period 1844–1856. Although with the inception of the 1844 Bank Act, Tooke and his banking school followers lost the critical battle over banking policy, the currency–banking school debates were revived by the financial crisis of 1847. This was because the crisis forced the British government to temporarily suspend the 1844 Bank Act to permit the transfer of bullion from the issuing department to the banking department in order that the Bank of England could continue to make payments in cash on demand and secure the convertibility of the currency. The role of the Act in the 1847 crisis was the central issue in the inquiries of the Commons and Lords Committees on the Causes of Commercial Distress in 1847–1848. Tooke took the opportunity to renew his criticism of the currency school and the 1844 Bank Act in volume IV of *History* (1848a: especially 293 et seq.) as well as in evidence given to both these committees. However, while the 1844 Bank Act came under criticism by the majority of witnesses before the above committees for exacerbating the crisis and, in its 'Report', the Lords committee weakly recommended a relaxation of its restrictive clauses, Parliament baulked at any amendments (Fetter 1965: 211–16). Nevertheless, though public controversy over the 1844 Act died down, Tooke (1856; 1857, V: 485–639) continued to criticise its practical operation.

Tooke argued the 1844 Bank Act played an instrumental role in the financial crisis of 1847, the worst in Britain since 1825 (on its severity and aftermath, see Tooke 1848c: (Q 5457–61) 430; and, in comparison to the 1825 crisis, Tooke 1848a, IV: 329–48). There were two aspects to Tooke's argument. First, Tooke contended the 1844 Bank Act created the environment in Britain's financial market that promoted the spectacular railway investment boom of the middle 1840s which inevitably led to the crisis. Second, as he had predicted, Tooke argued the Act handicapped the Bank of England's capacity to deal with a serious external drain in 1847.

According to Tooke, a low discount rate policy adopted by the Bank of England 'immediately' on the institution of 1844 Bank Act, 'tended to facilitate and promote the railway speculations which were then in progress' as well as 'the spirit of adventure which was then abroad for other undertakings involving the outlay of borrowed capital' (1848a, IV: 294–5). It was Tooke's (1848a, IV: 333–4; 1848c: (Q 3083–91) 346–7; 1857, V: 557–8) contention that this policy by the Bank during the mid-1840s contributed to the crisis by accommodating an extension of credit which prolonged and heightened the unsustainable speculative boom (King 1936: 134–8). The adoption of a low interest rate policy by the Bank of England was held by Tooke (1848a, IV: 294–5; 1857, V: 59) to be the result of the 1844 Bank Act in the sense that it gave the Bank a free hand to compete more aggressively for banking business against private bankers and money dealers when bullion reserves were at a relatively high level (Fullarton 1845: 196–9, 250). In adopting this policy stance, Tooke (1848a, IV: 62–3, 294–6; 1848c: (Q 3050–1) 342) argued the Bank of England was acting entirely in accord with the 'spirit' of the 1844 Act which, according to its propounders, intended that in the issuing department the currency would be regulated by a self-adjusting process, thereby leaving the banking department free to compete as if it were a private bank.[29] In support of his argument, Tooke quoted from the parliamentary speech of Prime Minister Peel (6 May 1844) advocating the legislation for the Bank Charter Act of 1844:

> The *principle of competition*, though unsafe, in our opinion, when applied to issue, *ought, we think, to govern the business of banking*. After the issue of

paper currency has once taken place, it is then important that the public should be enabled to *obtain the use of that* issue on as favourable terms as possible.

(1848, IV: 294)

Hence, Tooke clearly saw that underlying the 1844 Bank Act was the wrong-headed notion that with the Bank of England's note-issuing function regulated in accord with the currency principle, its public duty was met, thereby leaving it free to pursue its own private interest by competitive banking operations.[30]

Tooke argued the 1844 Bank Act aggravated the 1847 crisis by limiting the Bank of England's ability to extend accommodation and relieve the demand for liquidity before panic in the financial market had set in. In the face of an external drain, the Bank of England was compelled in mid-April of 1847 to raise its discount rate and severely restrict accommodation to the financial system despite there being in excess of £6 million bullion in the issuing department. Tooke maintained: '[T]he effect of this severe contraction of accommodation was to paralyse nearly all transactions of credit throughout the country' (Tooke 1848a, IV: 305). At the same time, Tooke (1848a, IV: 304–6; 1848c: (Q 2998–3003) 336) contended the alarm at the low and declining reserves in the banking department brought on an internal drain, which severely hampered the Bank of England's ability to stem the tide of bullion flowing from its coffers.[31] When, following a series of commercial failures, the internal drain resumed in October 1847, Tooke (1848a, IV: 315–20; 1848b: (Q 5333–8) 415–16, (Q 5346) 417) argued that under the auspices of the 1844 Bank Act, the Bank of England had no other recourse but to restrict again its accommodation by a violent increase in its discount rate which only exacerbated the panic in the London financial market and aggravated the liquidity crisis.[32] When reserves in the banking department had fallen to unsafe levels in late-October 1847:

It was then quite upon the cards that a few days of the prevailing alarm, which was causing a general hoarding of bank notes and coin, might exhaust it altogether; thus realising the predictions of those who, with myself, had pointed out, as a not improbable effect of the [1844 Bank Act], *if strictly enforced*, as it was intended to be, that the ridiculous, although lamentable catastrophe, might be witnessed, of the banking department being compelled to stop payment, while there was more than six millions of bullion in the issue department.

(Tooke 1848, IV: 317–18)

Without the government's permission in late-October 1847 to suspend the 1844 Act in order to allow the transfer of bullion from the issuing to the banking department, Tooke (1848c: (Q 3026) 338–9) considered the Bank of England was in 'imminent danger' of having to stop payments in cash.

By contrast, Tooke argued, had the Bank of England conducted its operations on the basis of the total bullion reserve otherwise available under a union of its banking and note-issuing functions as existed prior to the 1844 Bank Act, the 1847 crisis would have been considerably moderated. With a larger accessible reserve, Tooke (1848a, IV: 347–8) claimed the Bank would have been in a position in early-October 1847 to extend accommodation and relieve the internal demand for liquidity. Indeed, Tooke contended that under a union of its departments, it is likely the Bank of England would have overcome the financial crisis without bullion reserves declining below £7 million to £8 million and without 'the slightest Apprehension on the Part of the Public of the Power of the Bank in its entire State to meet all its Engagements without the least Inconvenience' (1848c: (Q 3039) 340). Tooke (1848a, IV: 380–400) opined that it could have done so with much less instability in the rate of interest and, thereby, unnecessary harm inflicted on commercial trade.[33]

An ongoing criticism by Tooke (1857, V: 586–9) was that the 1844 Bank Act induced systemic instability in the rate of interest, which had an adverse effect on commercial activity in the British economy. Tooke (1857, V: 562–7) supported his criticism by reference to statistical evidence showing the frequency and extent of alterations by the Bank of England of its minimum rate of discount on short-term bills accepted at its door over the period from the Act's inception in September 1844 to the end of 1856. This evidence was presented by Tooke (1857, V: 570–6) to show clearly that alterations in the Bank's rate of discount over this period depended on the state of its cash reserves in the banking department and were made largely independent of the amount of bullion in the issuing department and the amount of Bank of England notes in active circulation. A picture of Tooke's statistical evidence is provided by Figure A4.1 (p. 235). By reference to this evidence, Tooke highlighted that '[D]uring the Three Years from September, 1844, to October, 1847, the rate of discount was altered *Fourteen* times' and '[D]uring the Nine Years from October, 1847, to the end of December, 1856, there have been *Thirty-Six* alterations' (1857, V: 567). He further pointed out that these alterations were particularly more frequent at times of monetary pressure in 1847, 1853, 1855 and 1856.[34] With respect to the 1847 crisis, Tooke (1848a, IV: 330, 400; 1857, V: 565–6) showed the Bank of England altered its minimum rate of discount on no less than thirteen occasions during 1847, ranging from 3½ per cent up to 8 per cent at the height of the pressure, before declining to 5 per cent by end-year.[35] Thus, to the 1848 Lords Committee on the Causes of Commercial Distress, Tooke declared: 'I never knew any Year in which there was so great and so violent an Alteration in the Rates of Discount as during the Year 1847' (1848c: (Q 3006) 336). Tooke argued the main cause for the Bank of England's frequent and often violent alterations in its discount rate was the separation of its departments under the 1844 Bank Act which deprived the banking department of bullion reserves adequate to comfortably deal with ordinary (external) drains which, predominantly, involved the withdrawal of deposit funds. By comparison, Tooke argued that under a union of banking and issuing functions as existed prior to the 1844 Bank Act, had the Bank of England conducted policy astutely in accordance with his guidelines for holding a large precautionary reserve of bullion, the discount rate would have remained steady so exerting a stabilising influence on market rates of interest and credit conditions over the period 1844–1856 (Tooke 1857, V: 573).

7.6 The formation of Tooke's banking school theory

The formation of Tooke's banking school position stemmed from a longstanding dissatisfaction with the classical economists' quantity theory of money. As explained in Section 6.2.4, Tooke progressively attached less relevance to the explanatory power of the quantity theory in his pre-banking school phase so that by 1838 he had all but abandoned it in principle. But it was only with the development of what he believed was an alternative theory of monetary behaviour that the banking school Tooke was able to finally abandon the quantity theory in principle. Notwithstanding Tooke articulated most of his banking school theory in the context of criticising the premises underlying the currency principle, he clearly meant it to be a constructive alternative to more substantive versions of the quantity theory of money than that proposed by the currency school.[36] In volume IV of *History* (1848a: 84–402), after he had established his banking school position, Tooke wrote a review of the progress of monetary debate in England from 1797 to 1847 in which he was critical of Ricardo and the bullionists in general. This critique of the classical economists' quantity theory by Tooke (1848a, VI: 84–142) was informed by his newly formulated banking school theory. Before consideration is given to the transformation in Tooke's monetary thought from his pre-banking school to banking school position, it is pertinent to clarify the latter by bringing together all the theoretical elements detailed previously in this chapter.

Tooke's banking school theory essentially consists of three related principles. The first and central principle was that in a convertible system of currency the quantity of money in circulation, consisting of all forms of means of payment, is endogenously determined by the aggregate monetary value of all transactions in the economy. Its corollary was that causation ran from the price level to the quantity of money in circulation. The main implication of this proposition is that the Bank of England, as the central banking authority, did not have the discretionary power to autonomously regulate the quantity of money in conflict with the requirements of trade. Any attempt by the Bank of England (or the banking sector as a whole) to autonomously expand its convertible banknotes in circulation which was not justified by public demand would be returned to the banking system; while, alternatively, effective measures to withdraw banknotes and coin from active circulation in relation to public demand would result in their substitution by other less convenient monetary instruments (i.e. credit). Hence, Tooke proposed that the velocity of circulation of banknotes and coin would vary considerably in the short run in response to changes in the demand for money according to the institutional structure of the financial system and the conduct of monetary policy in response to economic circumstances. Only in an inconvertible system of currency did a central authority responsible for issuing paper money have the power to autonomously influence the quantity of money. However, looking at history, Tooke believed the only plausible way that this power could be systematically exercised was by the government issuing compulsory money to finance its expenditures and, thereby, force it directly into circulation. But, when, in the ordinary course of commercial banking, inconvertible banknotes were issued by way of short-term loans and discounts, as occurred in England during the restriction period 1797–1821, the central issuing authority (i.e. Bank of England) had limited power to autonomously regulate the quantity of money. Therefore, with qualification, Tooke proposed that the quantity of money in circulation was normally demand-determined in a fiat-based monetary system as well as in a gold-based one. Importantly, Tooke's conception of endogenous money was entirely compatible with his long-held explanation of prices considered in Chapters 4 and 5, which attributed price movements in England to natural and political factors affecting the supply conditions of commodities.

The second banking school principle of Tooke's was the negative one that the rate of interest has no systematic inverse causal influence on the inducement to spend in the economy. This meant that, while the Bank of England could exert a temporary influence on the rate of interest, it could *not* thereby exert a systematic and predictable influence on expenditure and the public's demand for money. Instead, Tooke argued that through its effect on the rate of interest, the Bank could influence credit conditions and, according to the state of markets, economic activity. In regard to credit conditions, Bank of England policy was conceived to have a systematic effect on portfolio investment, with a lower (higher) discount rate tending to promote higher (lower) prices of shares and government securities. Bank policy was therefore conceived to have a reliable influence on share market activity. Through adjustments in its discount rate, the Bank could also reliably influence short-term capital flows and, thereby, the reserves of bullion which underwrote liquidity (and 'confidence') in Britain's gold-based money market. Nevertheless, by affecting credit conditions, the Bank of England's influence on monetary expenditure was unsystematic, depending on the concrete situation. Thus, under circumstances favourable to speculation, a low rate of interest could play a role in facilitating additional borrowing and increase the purchase of commodities (by dealers), but it could not be the moving cause of higher monetary expenditure. Alternatively, a high rate could have a restraining influence on speculative buying pressure in commodity markets. Based on empirical evidence, Tooke proposed that, if anything, a restrictive policy, especially a violent one, involving the Bank of England raising its discount rate, was more effective in reducing expenditure by dealers on commodities, mainly in credit-laden markets, than a low interest rate policy was in stimulating higher spending.

The third principle was that the long-run average rate of interest entered into the normal cost of producing commodities so that permanent changes in this rate exerted a positive causal influence on the long-run price level. Consistent with this notion, the banking school Tooke implicitly proposed this average rate governed the normal rate of profit. As previously shown in Sections 6.3 and 7.3, Tooke had long argued this average rate of interest was determined in the financial market by politico-institutional and conventional factors, largely independent of Bank of England policy. Hence, in the long run, the monetary authorities were conceived by Tooke to have limited power to indirectly influence the rate of interest and, thereby, the price level.

On the basis of these principles and in accordance with his dual-circulation framework, Tooke's banking school theory can be represented in terms of the income form of the monetary equation. The following two monetary equations are employed for this purpose:

$$M_n^* V_n^* = P_n Y_n \qquad\qquad (7.6.1)$$

$$M_n V_n = P_n Y_n \qquad\qquad (7.6.2)$$

where P_n is the normal general price level; Y_n is the normal level of aggregate real income (or gross output); M_n^* is the normal quantity of the total money in circulation (i.e. including all forms of credit in what Tooke called 'circulating medium') and V_n^* is its normal income velocity of circulation; M_n is the normal quantity of Bank of England notes and coin in circulation; and V_n is its normal income velocity of circulation. With respect to the relationship between these two equations: $M_n^* > M_n$ and $V_n^* < V_n$.

These two equations are conceived to correspond to a long-period position of the economy in which monetary equilibrium is established. In this position the normal outputs of all commodities are conceived to have adjusted to their effectual demands and, for a given technique of production, normal (relative) prices of commodities are determined on the basis of a uniform net rate of profit on capital (see Section 1.2). The normal general price level, P_n, is calculated according to the composition of commodities making up the value of gross output, whereby, in a convertible system of currency, the normal money prices of commodities are expressed in terms of gold at its official mint value. It is also conceived that, for a given level of income (and wealth), V_n and V_n^* are determined by the institutional structure of the monetary system in relation to the conventions and habits of agents in expediting payments. In this equilibrium, M_n and M_n^* will correspond with a certain reserve of (gold) bullion at which the foreign exchanges are at par and the money (or paper) price of gold is at its mint value.

In the long run, Tooke argued that changes in the general price level, P_n, are determined by natural and political factors permanently affecting the normal costs of producing and bringing to market a major group of commodities in relation to gold (see Section 5.7). Given the normal level of output, Y_n, changes in the price level are conceived to endogenously determine monetary circulation, consisting either of $M_n^* V_n^*$ or $M_n V_n$ on the left-hand side of equations (7.6.1) and (7.6.2), respectively. The conception that, for a given technique of production and given the institutional structure of the financial system, causality runs from nominal income to monetary circulation, is entirely compatible with classical economics. As shown by Green (1992: 12–17), the classical economists, including Ricardo, conceived that a permanent change (rise) in the general price of commodities in relation to gold (or silver) would result in an endogenous change (increase) in monetary circulation associated with a sympathetic change (rise) in the production of gold (or silver). The distinctive feature of Tooke's banking school theory was that compatible with this conception, for a given level of normal real income (and aggregate output), long-run causality ran from the average rate of interest to the normal price level to an endogenously determined quantity of money in circulation.

It was in relation to short-run monetary disequilibria, when economic variables deviated from their normal values, that the monetary thought of the banking school Tooke differed so markedly from the classical quantity theorists. Indeed, Tooke's differences with the currency school centred on the short-run position of the economy (Laidler 1975: 218–19; Green 1992: 15–17, 207–9). In relation to equations (7.6.1) and (7.6.2), this short-run disequilibrium position can be expressed as truisms by the following equations:

$$M^{*}V_{m}^{*} \equiv P_{m}Y_{m} \tag{7.6.3}$$

$$MV_{m} \equiv P_{m}Y_{m} \tag{7.6.4}$$

where P_{m} is the short run general price level calculated on the basis of the *market* prices of commodities at which their demands and supplies are not equal and a non-uniform net rate of profit on capital rules; Y_{m} is the short-run level of aggregate real income (and gross output) different from its normal level; M^{*} is the actual quantity of circulating medium associated with V_{m}^{*}, its short-run income-velocity of circulation; M is the actual quantity of Bank of England notes and coin, and V_{m} its short-run income-velocity of circulation. In contrast to the classical quantity theorists, Tooke proposed that, in a convertible system of currency, *short-run causality* went from fluctuations in nominal income, $P_{m}.Y_{m}$, according to changes in prices and economic activity, to the quantity of circulating medium (M^{*}) associated with variations in its velocity of circulation (V_{m}^{*}). This will be associated with relatively larger variations in the velocity of circulation of Bank of England notes and coin (i.e. $\Delta V_{m} > \Delta V_{m}^{*}$), the extent of which will depend on the policy of the Bank of England in relation to the circumstances behind the particular change in nominal income.[37] Within his dual-circulation framework, Tooke believed these short-run changes in nominal income (around normal levels) were predominantly due to fluctuations in the price level as connected with variations in the number of commodity transactions (or trading activity) between dealers and dealers accommodated by sympathetic variations in the amount of credit.[38]

Tooke's conception of endogenous money is entirely consistent with his explanation of short-run price fluctuations. It was shown in Chapters 4 and 5 that from the beginning the pre-banking school Tooke attributed price fluctuations mainly to real factors affecting supply in relation to the demand for (a major group of)

commodities. In the anatomy of price fluctuations Tooke believed the main catalyst was a supply shock that caused a shortage in the market for a major commodity (or group of commodities) so that $P_m > P_n$. The banking school Tooke argued
such an upturn in the price level (and nominal income) was accommodated by an
increase in the facility of credit available to dealers so that in relation to the equations above: $M^* > M_n^*$, given $V_m^* \approx V_n^*$, and $V_m > V_n$. When this upturn is extended
by speculative buying by dealers then, as a result of increased confidence in the
provision of credit (especially of bills of exchange), income-velocity of the circulating medium will tend to rise so that $M^* > M_n^*$ will be accompanied by $V_m^* > V_n^*$.
This will particularly occur when commodity speculation is accompanied by a
speculative boom in the share market.[39] Should the Bank of England adopt a low
interest rate policy which helps accommodate speculative activity, the income-
velocity of Bank of England notes and coin will tend to be greater. According to
Tooke's principle of limitation, a rising price level will eventually be brought to
an end by an insufficient effectual demand as limited by a relatively stable level
of social income (in gold). By contrast, a downturn in the price level (so that
$P_m < P_n$) is the result of an excess supply in markets for a major group of commodities. In Tooke's analysis, this excess supply is usually caused by either an
exogenous increase in supply (e.g. an abundant harvest) in relation to demand or
in reaction to a collapse of a speculatively based upturn in commodity prices
demand falls in relation to supply. This will induce a contraction of credit so that
$M^* < M_n^*$, and with market confidence low, $V_m^* < V_n^*$. Furthermore, as a result of
widespread efforts to shore up liquid positions, the demand for Bank of England
notes and coin will tend to increase so that $M > M_n$, associated with $V_m < V_n$. Tooke
(1848a, IV: 125–6) believed such an intense demand for liquidity will on its own
tend to raise the market rate of interest. Tooke also believed this will occur in a
situation where the Bank of England adopts a violent restrictive monetary policy
which effectively depresses economic activity as well as the price level.[40] On the
basis of Tooke's principle of limitation, notwithstanding losses incurred by commodity traders in the adjustment process, the downturn in prices (and therefore
the price level) will be ultimately limited to the 'cost of production' (in gold) at
which producers can profitably supply the market.

Of particular interest is the implication of Tooke's banking school position
for the external adjustment process. It was shown in Section 6.2.1 that the pre-
banking school Tooke believed the price–specie–flow mechanism was not automatic and worked only slowly in establishing external adjustment in the long
run. However, this mechanism is completely repudiated by his banking school
principles. In particular, as shown in Sections 7.1–7.3 of this chapter, Tooke
rejected that (a) there was any systematic relationship (even in a purely metallic
system) between external specie flows and the internal quantity of money in circulation, and that (b) a change in the quantity of money would (via the rate of
interest) systematically cause a change in domestic expenditure and the price
level. Nevertheless, Tooke considered variations in relative prices in international commodity markets would affect trade flows and contribute to external
adjustment in the long run. From his monetary analysis it is apparent Tooke

believed the trade adjustment process relied on three kinds of price mechanisms. In the first place, Tooke believed that when exports were high, there was a tendency for supply on the domestic market to decline in relation to demand, imparting upward pressure on prices; and when exports were low, vice versa. Second, when export income was high (low), the resulting increase (decrease) in the nation's income and prices would tend to raise (lower) import expenditures.[41] Third, Tooke believed changes in the foreign exchanges within the gold points under a gold-convertible monetary system contributed to trade adjustment. Accordingly, when a trade surplus (deficit) resulted in a balance of payments surplus (deficit), an appreciation (depreciation) in the foreign exchanges would, by reducing (improving) price competitiveness, tend to reverse the flow of trade. It needs to be emphasised though that Tooke considered this adjustment process to be a tendency subject to natural and political factors which often disturbed international market conditions. In the short run, Tooke had long held the position that, besides the cushion provided by variations in bullion reserves at the Bank of England, external adjustment relied heavily on the effect of variations in the rate of interest (relative to overseas rates) on net capital flows. He argued that to ensure monetary stability, this adjustment process needed to be managed by the Bank of England through discretionary policy, involving the alteration of its discount rate. As shown in the previous section, Tooke argued this task was made more difficult by the operation of the 1844 Bank Act.

The transformation from Tooke's pre-banking school position to his banking school position expounded in this chapter fundamentally consisted of developing monetary principles more compatible with his real explanation of prices formulated from exhaustive empirical analyses. With an increasing uneasiness, the pre-banking school Tooke reconciled this explanation of prices with the quantity theory approach to money. It was largely because of his inductive approach to the study of economics that Tooke was slow to reject the quantity theory in the face of accumulated evidence of its weak explanatory power. Indeed, in the context of defending Tooke against claims of inconsistency for this transformation by members of the currency school, Fullarton made reference to this very point:[42]

> In the first place, [Tooke's views] have never, till very lately, been brought before the public in a condensed or popular shape, but have had to be searched out among the dry details of statistical work, in which few general readers have the courage to look for them. Secondly, Mr. Tooke himself has been exceedingly slow in following out his original conclusions on the subject of price to all their consequences. The germ of his present opinions may be traced in the facts, which he collected and laid before the public in the first edition of his great work [i.e. *High and Low Prices*] but at the time of that publication, in 1823, Mr. Tooke's mind appears to have been still strongly imbued with the prevailing notions, that prices are liable to rise and fall with the increase or diminution of the amount of Bank notes in circulation, that banks have it in their power to increase at pleasure the quantity of paper money, and that the efflux and influx of gold are to be regulated by regulating

the issues of the banks. He adhered to these doctrines even after he had refuted them by his discoveries, and seems to have parted with them at last only by degrees and with reluctance, under the pressure of his growing convictions. The progress of those convictions may be traced through their successive stages in his various publications, and in the evidence delivered by him before diverse Parliamentary Committees ...

(1845: 18–19)[43]

The catalyst for the transformation of Tooke's monetary thought was the controversies of the late-1830s which saw the emergence of the currency school and its advocacy of banking policies which had the intent of giving practical effect to the currency principle. Thus, when asked by the 1848 Lords Committee on the Causes of Commercial Distress in 1847–1848 to explain 'the Nature of the Phenomena which have come within your Observation and have led to an Alteration of your Opinions', Tooke replied:

As well as I can now remember it was the Controversy which took place consequent upon the monetary Derangement in 1836–37, which led me to suspect the Existence of the Error which, as I now believe, lies at the Bottom of the Theory which ascribes to the Bank of England and other issuing Banks a direct Power over the Amount of the Circulation, and thence an Influence on Prices, being the Theory upon which the Act of 1844 has been founded. It is an Error in which I participated.... I did not sufficiently perceive that Bank Notes issued on Loan for short Periods, and strictly convertible, are simply the Effect of Transactions and not Causes of them. But in the renewed Researches which I was led into on that Occasion, *I found that the Facts were totally irreconcilable with the Theory in question* [i.e. the Quantity Theory], and a further Investigation into the Rationale of the Connexion between Prices and the Circulation has perfectly satisfied me that Bank Notes are simply the Effect of Transactions.

(1848c: (Q 3129) 351; emphasis added)

It was at the end of the 1830s when Tooke was preparing volume III of *History of Prices* for publication in 1840 that he began to formulate his banking school principles first articulated in that work.[44] However, the process of transformation is likely to have begun earlier when Tooke was preparing volumes I and II of *History* (1838), entailing a re-assessment and re-writing of his historical analysis of prices from 1792 to 1822 contained in *High and Low Prices* (1824) and, on the basis of fresh research work, extending the analysis to 1837. In this connection a major factor in the timing of Tooke's transformation was his retirement from Russian trading business in 1836 which afforded him much more free time for reflection in writing on political economy. Although Tooke subsequently became Governor of the Royal Exchange Assurance Corporation in 1840, a position he held until 1852, this role was not a full-time one and continued to afford him significant time for carrying on his work in political economy.[45]

In the light of Tooke's growing dissatisfaction with the classicals' quantity theory of money during his pre-banking school phase, the transformation to his banking school position is much less radical than has been supposed in the literature (see Gregory 1928: 79–88; Arnon 1991: 120). In the first place, the banking school Tooke's conception of endogenous money is anticipated in his long-held belief in the permissive role of credit in Britain's monetary system. In particular, as indicated by Gregory (1928: 81), this is reflected in his pre-banking school view that the quantity of country banknotes in circulation depended on the level of agricultural prices (see, for example, Tooke 1819a: 130–2; 1824, i: 63–8; 1826: 37–41, 86n.; 1832: (Q 3836) 272, (Q 3906) 282; 1838, I: 148) and compare with Tooke (1844: 38–43). It is also reflected in Tooke's pre-banking school view that monetary circulation effected by bank deposit transfers in the City of London systematically varied in the short run independently of Bank of England policy, often in connection with variations in the country banknote circulation, and often associated with speculative activity in both commodity and financial assets (see Section 6.2.2). Moreover, by 1838 the pre-banking school Tooke argued short-run variations in the general price level were accommodated by changes in the whole quantity of circulating medium largely independent of the quantity of Bank of England notes in circulation (see Section 6.2.3).

In the second place, from the *Considerations* (1826) onwards, the pre-banking school Tooke showed a strong interest in the process by which Bank of England policy could influence credit conditions and economic activity.[46] He emphasised that Bank policy chiefly operated through the rate of interest and, connectedly, was concerned with ascertaining how changes in its level actually affected activity in the share market and commodity market. An important aspect of Tooke's banking school theory is the key role of the interest rate in the power of Bank of England policy to autonomously influence economic activity. Indeed, at the heart of Tooke's banking school criticisms of the currency school was its lack of a transmission process to plausibly support the premise that the Bank of England (or banking system) could autonomously determine the quantity of money in circulation.

In retrospect, then, the evolution of Tooke's monetary thought to his banking school position was a long and torturous one, which, in the heat of the currency–banking school debates, culminated in the development of an alternative monetary theory to the classical economists' quantity theory of money.[47] From this standpoint, it is highly significant that, despite this development in his monetary thought, the banking school Tooke's position on banking policy remained largely the same as the one he held during his pre-banking school phase. While, from 1848 onwards, the banking school Tooke adopted a more enlightened view on the institutional role of the Bank of England as a central bank, the main development in his position consisted of refining already well-established views about the best way for the Bank of England to conduct monetary policy (with a higher precautionary bullion reserve) in a discretionary way in order to secure financial stability and, thereby, promote commercial activity. In essence, Tooke's new banking school principles supplied more substance to his longstanding position on banking policy against that of the currency school.

8 Tooke's legacy

Among nineteenth-century classical economists, only Ricardo and Thornton rival Tooke for influence on the development of monetary economics. The large-scale empirical analysis of Tooke and Newmarch's six-volume *History of Prices* (1838–1857) has been an invaluable source for monetary economists as well as historians.[1] As Ricardo had hoped in 1822 (see Chapter 2, n.18), Tooke showed himself in this work to be the predominant analyst of market prices in classical economics. Indeed, Tooke's empirical-based analysis of short-run price fluctuations by reference to temporary and specific factors affecting the interaction between demand and supply represents an important legacy in demonstrating the approach to explaining market prices in the classical tradition. In conjunction with Tooke's considerable writings on monetary behaviour and policy, this empirical analysis has exerted an important influence on figures instrumental in the development of monetary thought. Of Tooke's contribution it is his novel banking school ideas that have undoubtedly left the most enduring legacy. However, at the time of their promulgation in the 1840s and 1850s these ideas were controversial and received a mixed reception. The currency school, which acknowledged a debt to Tooke's pre-banking school contributions, were highly critical of his banking school position.[2] The strongest critic was Torrens (1840, 1844, 1848, 1858), chief defender of the currency school, who relentlessly sought to expose Tooke's banking school views as 'grand Tookean Fallacies'.[3] Other currency school members who lined up to criticise Tooke in the currency–banking school debates included Clay (1844), Johnson (1856) and Arbuthnot (1857). Tooke dealt with most criticisms, especially those of Torrens, in volume IV of *History* (1848a: x, 171–209). The criticism was matched by support from a number of contemporary writers inspired by Tooke's banking school ideas. Chief among these was John Fullarton, who made it clear his renowned publication, *On the Regulation of Currencies* (1845), was written with the aim of contributing towards the 'completeness' and 'consistency' of Tooke's banking school theory (1845: 19–20). Based on Tooke's ideas, Fullarton (1845), in particular, further developed the law of reflux and significantly advanced the analysis of hoarding behaviour. Another adherent to Tooke's banking school views was James Wilson, inaugural editor of the *Economist*, and author of *Capital, Currency and Banking* (1847), a collection of articles on banking policy issues published in the years 1845–1847. Fullarton and Wilson became leading members of the banking school, closely subscribing to Tooke's position and strongly defending it against Torrens and other currency school critics.

In addition to Fullarton and Wilson, Tooke obtained support from Newmarch, who assisted him with his work in the 1840s before becoming co-author of volumes V and VI of *History (*1857). Besides this partnership with Tooke, Newmarch (1857) advanced the banking school position in evidence to the Commons Select Committee on the Bank Acts in 1857. Tooke's contributions were also well received by the prominent banker and writer J.W. Gilbart. A peripheral member of the banking school, Gilbart (1841; 1849, I: 113–51) did not subscribe to a lot of Tooke's constructive theory, but he did earnestly support his criticisms of the currency principle and the 1844 Bank Act. Although Tooke lost the battle in his opposition to the 1844 Bank Charter Act, chiefly through the agency of Bagehot (1873), his banking school ideas did exert an influence on the development of British central banking policy in the last quarter of the nineteenth century (Smith 2003: 54–6). In monetary policy debates in Continental Europe, Tooke's ideas gained considerable popularity, largely as a consequence of their dissemination by Adolph Wagner (1857), an influential German writer on money (Wicksell 1898: 38–50; Rist 1940: 181–2; Schumpeter 1954: 709, 726, 851). In the United States, Tooke's banking school ideas also exerted considerable influence through Laughlin (1886; 1903), a major authority in late-nineteenth-century debates over bimetallism, instrumental in the foundation of the Federal Reserve Bank in 1913 and a trenchant critic of the quantity theory (Girton and Roper 1978; Skaggs 1995). However, the influence of Tooke's banking school ideas waned on both sides of the Atlantic in the early twentieth century as the quantity theory of money became dominant in correspondence with the seminal development of marginalist economics. This submergence is much reflected in the commentary on Tooke surveyed in Section 1.1 of this book.

This chapter is concerned with the lasting influence of Tooke's banking school theory on the development of monetary economics. This influence has been exerted in two different theoretical traditions. First, Tooke's banking school ideas have had a *constructive* influence on the development of monetary thought in the classical tradition. In the nineteenth century, this line of influence ran through fellow members of the banking school, from Fullarton and James Wilson, to J.S. Mill and to Marx. The rehabilitation of classical economics as well as the emergence of Keynesian economics in the twentieth century has revived this line of influence. Second, Tooke's banking school criticisms of the classicals' quantity theory exerted an important influence on the reconstruction of the quantity approach to money in the marginalist tradition. In this tradition, Wicksell and Marshall stand out as the two most important progenitors of twentieth-century monetary thought. Tooke's contributions significantly assisted Wicksell and, to a lesser extent, Marshall, in developing their seminal monetary theories within the framework of the newly founded marginal analysis.[4] In consideration of these lines of influence, the chapter begins in Section 8.1 with an examination of Tooke's influence on J.S. Mill and, then, in Section 8.2, his influence on Marx. Section 8.3 considers Tooke's influence on Wicksell and Marshall in the marginalist tradition. In Section 8.4, the constructive value of Tooke's banking school ideas are considered in the light of the rehabilitation and constructive development of classical economics since Sraffa (1960). Finally, Section 8.5 identifies Tooke's main legacy to economic science.

8.1 The influence on J.S. Mill

The most eminent contemporary to support Tooke's opposition to the Bank Charter Act of 1844 was J.S. Mill. In a famous review article published in the *Westminster Review* (1844), Mill lent considerable support to Tooke's banking school position against criticism by Torrens (1844). In this article, Mill (1844: 579–80) showed himself to be an admirer of Tooke, praising him 'as an authority of the highest order'. Indeed, from his earliest writings, Mill's position on monetary questions was much influenced by Tooke. This influence on J.S. Mill's monetary writings is first apparent in the article, 'Paper Currency – Commercial Distress', published in the *Parliamentary Review, Session of 1826* (1826), in which Mill endeavoured to explain the causes of the financial crisis of 1825–1826. Mill's notion of 'over-trading', which was at the centre of his explanation, was evidently influenced by Tooke's authoritative account of the crisis in his *Considerations* (1826).[5] A more important early influence on Mill was Tooke's (1826: 5–31) theory of the rate of interest in its relationship with the profit rate. Indeed, Mill basically adopted Tooke's approach in his essay 'On Profits and Interest', written in 1829–1830 though not published until 1844 in *Essays on Some Unsettled Questions of Political Economy*. Much of the explanation provided in this essay was subsequently incorporated into Mill's *Principles of Political Economy* (1848 [1909]: 405–21, 637–50).

Unlike Tooke, J.S. Mill of the *Essays* (1844 [1874]: 90–106) adopted Ricardo's theory of the rate of profit, essentially arguing that the normal profit rate depended on real forces determining the real wage rate.[6] As is well-known, Mill subsequently changed his position on the determination of the normal profit rate in the *Principles* (1848 [1909]), when he effectively discarded the core of Ricardo's theory of distribution and value (Dobb 1973: 126–31; De Vivo 1984; Bharadwaj 1989).[7] Nevertheless, Mill continued to believe the normal rate of profit was determined by real forces, though not consistent with Ricardo's theory. In accordance with the common position of classical economists, in 1829–1830, Mill conceived that the normal rate of profit resolved itself into two parts: the rate of interest and a compensation for the risk and trouble of productively employing capital, which he called the 'wages of superintendence'.[8] Adopting Tooke's position, Mill treated the compensation for risk and trouble as the residual part and the interest rate as the autonomous part of the profit rate: 'it would be decidedly more correct, that the wages of superintendence are regulated by the rate of interest, or are equal to profits *minus* interest' (1844 [1874]: 108). In Mill's conception, the general rate of profit, determined by real forces, is a maximum limit to the average rate of interest, with the interest rate determined by forces operating in the financial system independent of the profit rate. Inspired by Tooke's (1826) dissenting position, Mill developed a conception that allowed him to argue:

> although the rate of profit is one of the elements which combine to determine the rate of interest, the latter is also acted upon by causes peculiar to itself, and may either rise or fall, both temporarily and permanently, while the general rate of profit remains unchanged.
>
> (Mill 1844 [1874]: 114)

In explaining the rate of interest, Mill closely followed Tooke's approach of classifying different generic groups of lenders and borrowers that determine the supply of and demand for loan capital, and then, to consider how these groups behave in relation to the determination of the rate of interest (see Section 6.3). Just like Tooke, Mill divided borrowers into 'productive' borrowers, who employ capital productively with the prospect of earning profits, and 'unproductive' borrowers, who use funds to finance unproductive expenditures beyond their income. It is evident that, by unproductive expenditure, Mill (1844 [1874]: 111), following Tooke, meant expenditure that was not applied to reproduction and, therefore, had no prospect of generating a commercial return. The major borrower of this kind was the national government. With respect to classifying lenders, whereas Tooke identified different groups of lenders in terms of the trouble and risk they were willing to accept, Mill (1844 [1874]: 109–10) classified lenders according to their institutional role in the financial market. The notion of liquidity preference present in Tooke's analysis in terms of the risk-return profile of financial securities demanded in relation to those supplied is therefore not present in Mill's analysis.

The first distinct group of lenders in Mill's analysis consist of those who act as intermediaries in the financial market, being 'bankers, bill brokers, and others, who are money-lenders by profession' (1844 [1874]: 109) and who earn profits from their activities. Mill regarded the capital of banks as contributing to the supply of loan capital to the market. The second distinct group of lenders, referred to as the 'monied class' by Mill (1844 [1874]: 109), consisted of non-professional wealth-holders such as 'widows and orphans', 'public bodies', 'charitable institutions' and 'a great number of persons unused to business, and who have a distaste for it, or whose preoccupations prevent their engaging in it'. Mill (1844 [1874]: 109) argued that this group were 'habitually, and almost necessarily, lenders' by reason of their reliance on interest-earning income just as the 'productive class' are 'habitually borrowers' because they desire to extend their business beyond their own capital.

On the basis of this classification Mill, similar to Tooke, explained the average rate of interest by reference to politico-institutional factors determining the demand and supply conditions in the market for loan capital. Hence, Mill (1844 [1874]: 112–17; 1848 [1909]: 638–41) contended that with a growing proportion of national wealth going to the monied capital class, the amount of disposable capital on the loan market would progressively grow over time and have the tendency of lowering the average rate of interest. Mill believed this institutional development would be facilitated by strong growth in deposit banking. Mill also contended that a major cause for a permanent change in the rate of interest in relation to the rate of profit was changes in 'unproductive' borrowing by the government to finance war-related expenditures. In this connection Mill (1844 [1874]: 112–14) agreed with Tooke's (1826: 7–8, 11) thesis that the substantial increase in British government debt to finance the long-running French Wars permanently raised the rate of interest in relation to the rate of profit. This approach to explain the interest rate was employed as well by Mill in the *Principles* (1848 [1909]: 637–50). Thus, Mill (1848 [1909]: 643) referred to the large 'absorption' of disposable capital in the construction of railways, which occurred during the railway boom of the mid-1840s, as a cause of a higher average rate of interest. In addition, Mill (1848 [1909]: 642, 646–7) maintained, as Tooke and Newmarch (1857, V: 597) did, that the substantial increase in the supply of gold that followed the gold discoveries of the late-1840s increased the supply of loan capital and, thereby, tended to lower the rate of interest.

Although heavily influenced by Tooke, Mill's analysis of the financial market did possess some distinctive features. He indicated that, independent of the level of interest, the demand for funds by productive borrowers was limited by the amount of their own capital which could be secured for collateral and by the uncertainty felt about realising returns on the employment of borrowed capital.[9] In addition, Mill indicated that changes in the rate of interest can affect savings when, in connection with the temptation of a higher rate to investors, he wrote: '[T]he same temptation will also induce some persons to invest, in the purchase of new stock, what would otherwise have expended unproductively in increasing their establishments, or productively, in improving their estates' (1844 [1874]: 113). A major difference between the analysis of Mill and that of Tooke concerned the role of banks. Whereas Tooke regarded banks as largely passive middlemen between lenders and borrowers, Mill (1844 [1874]: 114–17) argued that the institutional development of deposit banking would tend to lower the average rate of interest over time by the more efficient mobilisation of idle funds and, progressively, to increase the supply of disposable capital. As is discussed in the next section, Marx took up this theme, though from a different standpoint. However, with regard to the role of the Bank of England, Mill (1848 [1909]: 647–9) shared Tooke's view that monetary policy could exert a temporary but not a permanent influence over the rate of interest.

As already indicated, Tooke's banking school ideas exerted a significant influence on the development of J.S. Mill's monetary thought. In support of Tooke's position in the currency–banking school debates, Mill (1844: 592) largely agreed with the argument that the quantity of banknotes in circulation, especially country banknotes, was the consequence rather than the cause of variations in prices. Mill (1844: 591–3) also adopted Tooke's argument that normally an increase in the general price level was the result of speculative activity accommodated by credit and independent of the quantity of banknotes in circulation.[10] Based on his interpretation of Tooke's dual-circulation framework, Mill (1844: 588–9; also see 1848 [1909]: 532–6, 652–6) argued that an increase in the quantity of money could only raise the price level if there was an increase in the 'purchasing power of the community' enabled by an increase in the 'aggregate money incomes of the community'. In a convertible system of currency, Mill (1844: 590–2) contended that it was only at 'speculative times' when confidence was running high that a 'new' purchasing power over commodities could be created by an increased facility of credit. Moreover, Mill (1844: 594–6) acutely appreciated that Tooke's denial of the banking system's power to influence prices was based on a refutation of the common opinion that a lowering of the rate of interest conferred an increased power of purchasing which provided the stimulus to commodity speculation. However, Mill did not indicate agreement with Tooke's argument on this point. Instead, by reference to Tooke's argument on the importance of the transmission process, Mill (1844: 596–8) claimed the 'mode of issuing and recalling' banknotes had a considerable influence on the loan market, arguing that, in this respect, the 1844 Bank Act would tend to be destabilising.

It is in Book III of Mill's *Principles* (1848 [1909]), in which there are numerous and all favourable citations and quotations from Tooke's works, that the influence of the latter's banking school ideas is most evident.[11] In the *Principles* it is true Mill softened his opposition to the Bank Charter Act of 1844 and advanced a version of the quantity theory of money. Nevertheless, the influence of the banking school is evident in the careful manner in which Mill re-stated the classical quantity theory and the heavy qualifications he placed on its application.[12]

J.S. Mill believed the quantity theory was most applicable to a purely metallic system of currency or one with an inconvertible paper currency (1848 [1909]: 495–6, 542–55). For him, it had only limited application to Britain's highly developed monetary system in which credit played a key role in financing business transactions. Developing Tooke's view, Mill (1848 [1909]: 523–41) argued that credit was the major facilitator of 'purchasing power', responsible for accommodating most variations in the price level. However, while Mill accepted much of Tooke's argument denying the power of the Bank of England and other banks to arbitrarily increase the quantity of banknotes in circulation, he did not fully subscribe to Tooke's conception of endogenous money (Wicksell 1898: 85–7). Mill (1848 [1909]: 653–4) maintained that when markets were in a 'quiescent state' in which 'producers and dealers do not need more than the usual accommodation from bankers and other money lenders' the 'law of reflux' would ensure that banknotes in circulation did not increase beyond the public's demand. But when markets were in a 'speculative state' in which the expectation of a profitable rise in prices caused producers and dealers to unduly expand their operations by means of 'a more than ordinary use of their credit', Mill (1848 [1909]: 654–6) indicated that the law of reflux would fail to prevent banks from autonomously increasing their issue of banknotes and extending the speculation. Mill's exposition of the anatomy of a speculative-based rise in prices, in which the market eventually collapses and leads to 'commercial revulsion', conforms closely to Tooke's long-established explanation. Overall, then, despite the eclecticism of Mill's monetary theory, it is evident he was much influenced by Tooke's banking school theory.

8.2 The influence on Marx

Tooke's banking school ideas exerted a considerable influence on Marx's monetary analysis and, connectedly, the position he developed on the relationship between the interest rate and profit rate. Marx's most elaborate writings on money and interest are to be found in volume III of *Capital*, posthumously published in 1894 and consisting of unfinished notes written in the 1860s and orderly arranged by its editor, Engels.[13] In Part V of this volume there are numerous, mostly favourable, references to Tooke (and Fullarton).[14] It also includes the whole of chapter XXVII devoted by Marx (1894: 442–60) to critically appraising the views of the banking school on the distinction between currency and capital. As was Marx's method, the formulation of his monetary analysis proceeded from a critical study of the contributions of those from whom he derived the most revelation. The esteem in which Marx held Tooke was well expressed in a letter to Engels, written in 1858 a few days after Tooke's death, when he referred to him as 'the last English economist of any value' (1983: 284).

In contrast to Mill, Marx incorporated much of Tooke's banking school theory into his own monetary analysis without qualification. Thus, Marx (1859: 169–87; 1894: 454–7, 546–51) fully accepted Tooke's main argument that the quantity of money in circulation was endogenously determined by prices together with the volume of output. Furthermore, Marx (1894: 443–60, 528–30) essentially constructed his analysis of money and banking on the basis of Tooke's dual-circulation framework, distinguishing between monetary circulation that facilitated the 'expenditure of revenue' from that which facilitated the 'transfer of capital' (for a reconstruction of this analysis, see Panico 1988: 61–70). Following Tooke, Marx (1894: 443–6) maintained that the circulation of money promoting the 'expenditure of revenue' involved transactions between 'consumers and retail merchants'; while that promoting the 'transfer of capital' involved transactions between 'dealers and producers'. Whereas the amount of money that facilitated the 'transfer of expenditure' circulated 'outside the banks' walls', the amount of money that facilitated the 'transfer of capital' circulated 'inside the banks' walls'. However, in adopting this approach, Marx (1894: 442–6) was critical of Tooke and the banking school for confounding capital in the form of credit (and currency) with real capital employed in production. Specifically, Marx was critical of Tooke for his tendency to regard only those transactions facilitated outside the banks walls as involving the circulation of money in the form of coin and banknotes while treating those transactions that are facilitated inside the bank's walls through deposit transfers (and bills of exchange) as requiring only a money reserve to enable the circulation of capital.[15]

Marx believed Tooke overlooked the relationship between the two spheres of circulation, in which the same money, though circulating in different forms, can perform both the function of consumption expenditure and the purchase of intermediate products by merchant traders.[16] Marx therefore believed that Tooke's distinction between 'currency' and 'capital' was wrongheaded:

> a certain quantity of money *circulates* in the transactions between dealers as well as in the transactions between consumers and dealers. It is, therefore, equally *currency* in *both* functions.... To reduce the difference between circulation as circulation of revenue and circulation of capital into a difference between currency and capital is, therefore, altogether wrong.
>
> (1894: 443–4)

For this reason Marx disagreed with Tooke's position that, while matters of currency could exert a temporary influence on the rate of interest, in the long run, the average rate was 'governed entirely by the supply of, and demand for, [disposable] capital as resulting from circumstances independent of the currency' (Tooke 1826: 23n.; 1838, II: 361n.). In this particular respect, Marx more firmly established a position in which the average rate of interest is determined by monetary forces in the financial market independent of conditions of production. This position is closely connected to Marx's (1894: 420–1, 514–19) criticism of the currency school for confounding capital in the form of credit (and currency) with real capital employed in production. Marx (1894: 485–501) contended that the main factors that influenced the demand for loan capital and its expansion were connected with the nature and organisation of the financial system independent of the amount of real capital employed in production (Panico 1988: 74–7). In all, despite the differences mentioned, Tooke's dual-circulation framework was an important foundation upon which Marx developed his own analysis of the operation of the financial system.

The dissenting positions of Tooke and J.S. Mill on the interest–profit relationship in the 1820s heavily influenced Marx in developing a conception of the rate of interest as an autonomous variable in the sense of being determined by forces independent of the rate of profit. Within Marx's surplus approach to value and distribution, the normal rate of profit is, following Ricardo, determined by the real wage for a given technique of production. The normal rate of profit so determined by real forces was conceived by Marx (1894: 358–60, 370–9) to be divided into two component parts: the average rate of interest going to the lender (or 'money-capitalist') and the profit of enterprise going to the productive borrower (or 'industrial-capitalist'). Of these two component parts, Marx (1894: 358–60, 370–9) treated the average rate of interest as the autonomous part, which could permanently establish levels up to the 'maximum limit' set by the normal rate of profit and, therefore, he regarded the profit of enterprise as the residual part (Pivetti 1991: 66–9). On the basis of this constraint, Marx developed the arguments of Tooke and Mill to explain the average rate of interest by reference to a complex set of economic, institutional and conventional factors which governed the operation of the financial system, including the monetary authorities (Panico 1988: 70–4). A distinctive feature of Marx's explanation of money interest was that industrial capitalists, insofar as they are borrowers of capital, and money capitalists are seen to be antagonists, each with an interest in obtaining a larger portion of profits at the expense of the other. Marx therefore conceived of the above-mentioned factors explaining the level of the average rate of interest and, thereby, determining the division of profit between 'interest' and 'profit of enterprise', as reflecting the balance of power existing between these two kinds of capitalists.

According to Marx, the average rate of interest 'cannot be determined by any law' and, hence, 'there is no such thing as a natural rate of interest in the sense in which economists speak of a natural rate of profit and a natural rate of wages' (1894: 362, 364–5). Instead, Marx (1894: 362–5) believed the average rate of interest was the average of rates of interest on long-term loans over the business cycle, rates which are determined at any point in time by the supply of and demand for loan capital and independent of competitive forces operating in the production system. In this regard, Marx believed the rate of interest was conventional in character: 'there is no other method of determining [the interest rate] than by the opinion of borrowers and lenders in general; for right or wrong, in this respect, are only what common consent makes so' (1894: 362–3). Among those monetary factors that Marx (1894: 364n.68, 358, 367–8) believed entered into the conventional determination of the rate of interest was the discount policy of the Bank of England and, acknowledging 'the greater or lesser approximate equalization of the rate of interest in the world market', he contended that there was a 'direct influence exerted by the world market on establishing the rate of interest, irrespective of the economic conditions of the country'. In particular, Marx referred to the influence of longstanding conventional factors rooted in 'customs' and 'juristic tradition' (1894: 364) in the determination of the average rate of interest.

It was in explaining why the average rate of interest varied independently of the general rate of profit that Marx enlisted arguments by Tooke and J.S. Mill. Hence, Marx (1894: 361–2) referred approvingly to the argument that 'many borrow without any view to productive employment' and that the expanding 'class of rentiers' in England would increase the growth of loan capital supplied to the financial market. More particularly, Marx agreed with Mill that the rate of interest would systematically fall in relation to the rate of profit with

> the development of the credit system and the attendant ever-growing control of industrialists and merchants over the money savings of all classes of society that is effected through the bankers, and the progressive concentration of these savings in amounts which can serve as money-capital.
>
> (1894: 362)

Within his elaborate monetary analysis, Marx (1894: 420–4) argued that this institutional development of the banking system, especially that associated with the proliferation of large-scale deposit banking, would bring about a progressive concentration of the financial system's cash reserves, enabling banks to expand the amount of loans in proportion to 'reserve funds'. Marx (1894: 558) contended that, against this development, the purpose of the regulatory provisions of the Bank Charter Act of 1844 'was to make money dear' and, thereby, to improve the profitability of English bankers. Along the same lines as Tooke (1848a, IV: 347–8; 1848b: (Q 5386–8) 422; 1857, V: 535–6), Marx argued that the decentralisation of British bullion reserves, which occurred as a result of the 1844 Bank Act, caused 'continual large fluctuations' in the rate of interest, with the effect of sustaining a higher average rate of interest.[17] He clearly believed the 1844 Bank Act was an institutional change that reflected a shift in the balance of power from industrial capitalists to money capitalists, especially to bankers (Marx 1894: 560–4). Overall, Marx's monetary analysis was built on the foundation of banking school theory that was principally developed by Tooke. In particular, Marx's conception of the rate of interest as an autonomous variable in relation to the rate of profit clearly owes a great debt to Tooke, directly as well as via J.S. Mill.

8.3 The influence on monetary thought in the marginalist tradition

Tooke's influence on the development of monetary analysis in the marginal tradition has largely gone unnoticed in the literature. The two major pioneers of twentieth-century monetary theory, Alfred Marshall and Knut Wicksell, were highly appreciative of Tooke's illuminating criticisms of the classical economists' version of the quantity theory of money. In the preface to his *Interest and Prices*, Wicksell wrote that 'in the criticisms [of the quantity theory] by the school of Tooke there is much that is correct and instructive' (1898: xxiii). Furthermore, in volume II of *Lectures of Political Economy* (1906), Wicksell included among the most important writings on money and prices, Tooke's *Inquiry* (1844) and his *History of Prices* (1838–1857) as well as Fullarton's *On the Regulation of Currencies* (1845). There are numerous references to Tooke by Wicksell (1898: 36, 43–6, 82–92, 99–101, 112; 1906: 127, 161, 172–5, 182, 186–7, 194, 202) in these two works, both of an approving and critical nature. Given his practice of rarely citing sources, it is highly significant that Marshall referred to Tooke on two occasions in the *Official Papers* (1926: 4–6, 59), a posthumously published work of his evidence to several British parliamentary committees containing his most original and systematic dissertations on monetary questions. There are also three references to Tooke on historical questions in Marshall's last work, *Money, Credit and Commerce* (1923: 22, 54n., 306). As a gauge of Marshall's high opinion of Tooke, C.R. Fay relates how the great economics professor told him when he was a junior lecturer at Cambridge:

> [T]hat after long years of thought he had come to the conclusion that in the great currency controversy of Tooke versus Ricardo, Tooke was more right than Ricardo, in token whereof he lent me for the space of 6 years (i.e. to

the outbreak of World War I) his second copy of Tooke's 'History of Prices', then a rare six-volume work.

(1960: 35)

Both Marshall and Wicksell valued highly Tooke's historical study of English prices with its rich empirical analysis covering an extensive range of economic relationships, though predominantly relevant to the field of monetary economics. Just as valuable to them, though, as the quotations of Wicksell and Marshall above highlight, was Tooke's banking school based critique of the quantity theory of money in classical economics to the construction of their own seminal monetary analysis within the emerging and different theoretical framework of marginalist economics.

In the construction of his monetary analysis, Wicksell benefited from Tooke in two particular respects. First, Tooke's criticisms of the classicals' quantity theory focused Wicksell's mind on the need to provide a plausible transmission mechanism by which the banking system could autonomously regulate the quantity of money in circulation. This is evident in the discussion by Wicksell (1898: 81–101; 1906: 182–7) of Tooke's rejection of any systematic connection between the rate of interest, spending and the price level. Wicksell's transmission mechanism essentially relied on a demand function for loans, inverse elastic with respect to interest, as derived from a saving–investment analysis based on the new marginal theory of capital and distribution. As is well-known, Wicksell made a seminal contribution to the development of the marginalist theory of capital and distribution in *Value, Capital and Rent* (1893) and then in volume I of *Lectures on Political Economy* (1901) (Pivetti 1990; Uhr 1991: 87–114).

It was Wicksell's theory of capital and distribution that provided the theoretical foundations for his monetary theory. A crucial part of these foundations was the interest-elastic demand for savings function (derived from the demand function for capital as a stock) which, in the saving–investment analysis, provided a logical basis for supposing that the demand for loans (credit) is an inverse function of the rate of interest. In this theory, the 'natural' rate of interest (or normal rate of profit) is determined by real forces, consisting of the technical conditions of production and the social propensity to save that underpin the demand and supply functions of 'real capital' respectively. The observable ruling money rate of interest on loans is conceived to gravitate around the natural rate according to the short-run influence of monetary forces on the demand for and supply of loans. On the basis of the demand function for loans, Wicksell (1898: 102–56; 1906: 190–208) argued that the banking system could regulate the quantity of money (and volume of credit-funds) by altering the rate of interest on loans in relation to the natural rate of interest at which the demand for savings is equal to the supply of saving at full-employment output. Hence, in Wicksell's monetary analysis, the banking system can autonomously increase (contract) the quantity of money through increased (reduced) lending, by lowering (raising) the loan rate and making it profitable for firms to borrow more (less) funds for capital expenditure. With the resulting increase (reduction) in monetary expenditure, the demand for money would eventually rise (decline) to absorb its exogenous supply.

From the standpoint of his own monetary analysis, Wicksell (1898: 43–7; 1906: 182–8) was critical of Tooke's banking school position (Pivetti 1991: 81–6). But, importantly, Tooke's alternative views helped Wicksell to clarify the theoretical issues in constructing a plausible version of the quantity theory of money consistent with marginal economics (Uhr 1991: 88). In this sense, Wicksell gained as much from Tooke and the banking school as he did from the quantity theorists in the classical tradition. Indeed, on the basis of his transmission mechanism, Wicksell was able to contemplate the notion of endogenous money in what he called 'an elastic monetary system', in which

> the supply of money is more and more inclined to accommodate itself to the level of demand ... in our ideal state every payment, and consequently every loan, is accomplished by means of cheques or *giro* facilities. It is then no longer possible to refer to the supply of money as an independent magnitude, differing from the demand for money.... The 'supply of money' is thus furnished by the demand itself.
>
> (1898: 110)

For Wicksell (1898: 110), the main implication of an elastic monetary system was that the money rate of interest could deviate from the natural rate 'for a long time' with a considerable 'cumulative' effect on the price level.

Second, Tooke inspired Wicksell to develop an explanation of price variations consistent with *the observed facts* about the working of the monetary system. In this regard Wicksell accepted Tooke's empirically based observations on the actual movement of the volume of money, volume of credit, the interest rate and the price level in relation to each other, notwithstanding that they lay behind much of Tooke's objections to the classical economists' quantity theory. They basically consisted of the following observations:

1   That there was a strong correlation between actual movements in the general level of prices and the rate of interest (i.e. the 'Gibson Paradox').
2   An increase in the price level was usually accompanied by an expansion in credit and a rise in the velocity of circulation of currency; and a decline in the price level, vice versa (Wicksell 1906: 173–4, 184–5).
3   A rise and fall in the price level usually preceded an increase and decrease respectively in the quantity of paper currency in circulation (1906: 182–3).

Wicksell believed that a plausible explanation of money and prices needed to conform to these stylised facts.

In Wicksell's monetary analysis, price movements are explained by reference to deviations between the money rate of interest on long-term loans (ultimately regulated by the 'discount rate' of the monetary authorities) actually ruling and the natural rate of interest. Based on this notion, the explanation of cumulative price movements developed by Wicksell (1898: 164–77; 1906: 200–16) conformed closely to Tooke's 'facts'. What is particularly significant in this connection is that Wicksell well recognised that if price movements stemmed from monetary forces which acted on the money rate of interest and changed it in relation to the natural rate of interest on real capital, then his explanation would conform to stylised facts (2) and (3) but not (1). This is because as the observed level of the rate of interest declines or increases in relation to the unobservable natural rate, the price level will move in the opposite direction. In reference to the statistical relationship underlying (1), the Gibson Paradox, Wicksell wrote '[T]he correctness of this observation is beyond dispute; later statistics have frequently confirmed this fact' (1906: 182; also 1898: 88). Hence, in order that his explanation conformed to the Gibson Paradox, Wicksell (1906: 202–5) developed the ingenious 'trailing rate' doctrine (Ellis 1934: 300–8). On the basis of this doctrine, Wicksell (1898: 166–8; 1906: 205–7) argued that the main cause of price variations was *not* exogenous changes in the money supply but rather real factors affecting technical conditions of production and, thereby, the natural rate of interest, in conjunction with slowness in the operation of monetary forces, including monetary policy, which brings about adjustment in the money rate of interest. According to this explanation favoured by Wicksell the price level and the statistically observed interest rate move in sympathy with each other because as the natural rate exogenously increases (decreases) in relation to the money rate the latter will belatedly increase (decrease) with price inflation (disinflation) in the adjustment process.

Through this influence on Wicksell, Tooke made a significant contribution to traditional monetary analysis. Needless to say, the influence of Wicksell on modern monetary thought is enormous, exerted chiefly through the Swedish and Austrian schools and, from the late-1920s, through members of the Cambridge School (Laidler 1991: 146–9).

It was mainly through the writings of J.S. Mill that Tooke and the banking school exerted an influence on Marshall.[18] This line of influence is apparent in the emphasis that Marshall placed on the demand for money and the process by which exogenous changes in the supply of money could affect monetary expenditure and the price level. In this connection, Marshall's 'cash balance' version of the quantity theory focuses attention on the motives for holding money and the monetary transmission process. Nevertheless, like Wicksell, Marshall's transmission mechanism relied heavily on the demand for loan capital as an inverse function of the rate of interest. The precursor to Wicksell, it was in fact Marshall who first explained price movements by reference to deviations of the money rate of interest (as regulated by the 'discount rate' of the monetary authorities) from the 'real' rate corresponding to equilibrium between the demand for and supply of savings.[19] Marshall also explained variations in the price level broadly consistent with Tooke's stylised facts. While Marshall (1926: 49–52, 194, 274) believed monetary disturbances were the original cause of most price variations, interestingly, he argued that the phenomena of the Gibson Paradox was attributable to real factors which affected what he called the 'state of business confidence' and, thereby, the demand for liquidity. Furthermore, it is significant that Marshall's explanation of price variations is based heavily on a conception of trade cycles that he developed in *The Economics of Industry* (1879: 152–7) from Overstone as well as Bagehot (Bridel 1987: 48). It is evident from his writings that much of Overstone's description of the cyclical variation in business activity and prices was in turn derived from Tooke's empirical-based explanations of economic crises.[20] In general, the influence of Tooke and the Banking School on Marshall is manifested in what his biographer has described as Marshall's 'complex views' on the quantity theory of money which admitted that besides the quantity of money, the price level was affected by many real forces (see Groenewegen 1995: 349–50).

Marshall's influence on the formation of modern monetary thought is vast. His analysis pre-dated and, indeed, influenced Wicksell (1898: 76). Nevertheless, in published works, Wicksell's monetary analysis is more systematically worked out than Marshall's. This was because most of Marshall's substantive monetary thought is provided as part of oral evidence given to the Royal Commissions on the Depression of Trade and Industry (1886) and on the Value of Gold and Silver (1887–1888) published in *Official Papers* (1926: 1–195). Indeed, much of Marshall's lasting influence on twentieth-century monetary economics was exerted through the oral tradition of his teaching, by which he provided the foundations for the development of monetary thought by the Cambridge School, consisting of Robertson, Hawtrey and his outstanding pupils, Pigou, Lavington and Keynes (Bridel 1987). The far-reaching nature of Marshall's influence on the development of monetary analysis is manifest even in Keynes' revolutionary contributions in the 1930s.

8.4 Tooke and modern classical economics

A fresh light has been thrown on Tooke's political economy by the modern reconstruction of classical economics which, as discussed in Section 1.2, chiefly stemmed from a clarification of the classical theory of value and distribution by Sraffa (1951; 1960). In particular, this revival has clarified many theoretical issues in classical economics enabling a more precise assessment of Tooke's monetary thought. It was shown in Section 7.6 that from the standpoint of classical economics Tooke's banking school theory was as coherent as the quantity theory approach. Moreover, within the framework of modern classical economics, Tooke's banking school theory makes an important constructive contribution to explaining the distribution of income, the behaviour of the general price level and the operation of the monetary system.

The first element of Tooke's theory that makes a constructive contribution is his conception of endogenous money, essentially consisting of the argument that, given the institutional structure of the monetary system, the quantity of 'circulating medium' is determined by the demand for money of the non-bank public according to the level of nominal income of the economy. In this conception, Tooke proposed that, on the basis of a *given* level of output (or real income), short-run fluctuations in the price level would be accommodated by variations in the velocity of circulation of banknotes and coin. As was shown in Section 7.2, Tooke believed this conception was not only relevant to a gold-based monetary system but was also relevant to a fiduciary monetary system. It has been argued by Green (1992: 203, 207–8) that a major weakness in the position of Tooke was his adherence to Say's Law because it ruled out the possibility that adjustment to monetary disturbances involved changes in output as well as in prices and the velocity of circulation. However, Tooke maintained that such disturbances were usually the result of natural and political factors which, by influencing the conditions of production and distribution of commodities, acted on the general price level. Except in the special case of a government issuing compulsory money to finance its expenditures, Tooke disputed the fact that monetary disturbances could in the first place stem from monetary policy acting directly on the quantity of money. Moreover, as explained in Section 5.4, Tooke invoked Say's Law only as a long-run equilibrium condition. He fully grasped that in the short run there could be 'general gluts' from 'overproduction' or, alternatively, an excess in aggregate demand. From Tooke's standpoint, the response to these temporary states of disequilibrium between aggregate demand and aggregate supply was a change in output sympathetic with price fluctuations so that adjustment fell upon the velocity of circulation.

Nevertheless, it is true that by adhering to Say's Law Tooke neglected to account for the determination of output and income in his monetary analysis. Indeed, he adopted Say's Law essentially because he lacked a saving-investment analysis and theory of output. In the absence of such an analysis to explain the determination of equilibrium output, Tooke was unable to account adequately for the interaction between financial and expenditure flows consistent with his conception of endogenous money. However, Tooke's shortcoming should be seen in the context of the absence of any coherent saving–investment analysis and theory of output in classical economics (see Section 5.4). Hence, the precise theoretical shortcoming in question is present in the monetary analysis of all classical economists, even those such as Malthus who opposed Say's Law but did not possess a theory of output. It was not until the ascendancy of marginalist economics in the late nineteenth century and the subsequent development of a saving-investment analysis, chiefly by Marshall as developed by the Cambridge School and by Wicksell, in the Austrian tradition, that the quantity theory was re-formulated in terms of expenditure flows and the determination of output.

In view of the primacy Tooke gave to the demand for money in his conception of endogenous money and the importance he ascribed to the rate of interest in the Bank of England's capacity to temporarily influence monetary conditions, Tooke showed a much greater appreciation of the transmission mechanism by which monetary policy could be effected than his contemporaries. Tooke's main attack on the currency school consisted in exposing the absence of a plausible transmission mechanism in its quantity approach to money (see Section 7.5). The currency school simply took it for granted that the banks possessed the power to regulate exogenously the quantity of money in circulation. For this reason, aside from other members of the banking school and J.S. Mill, Tooke's classical contemporaries could not comprehend his notion that the quantity of money was contingent on and not the cause of changes in economic activity and prices. As remarked by Pivetti (1991: 77): 'Tooke has the great merit of managing to go to the heart of the matter; the question of the effects of changes in the rate of interest on the inducement to purchase commodities.' It was shown in Section 7.3 that Tooke denied any functional inverse causal influence of changes in the rate of interest on the demand for commodities, thereby disputing that monetary policy could in a predictable way influence economic activity in the short run. On this point, Tooke stood on firm theoretical ground. This is because the theoretical basis in monetary economics for a functional inverse relationship between short-run changes in the rate of interest and changes in monetary expenditure has been the interest-elastic demand for saving (or investment) function derived from the marginalist analysis of distribution and production, specifically from the marginal productivity premises underlying the demand function for capital (Garegnani 1983a: 24–8; 1990b: 58–61). By contrast, in classical economics, there is separability between the analysis of distribution and the determination of output which rules out any such functional relationship between the rate of return on capital and investment-related expenditure (see Section 1.2).[21]

Instead, in classical economics, there is scope to argue that changes in the rate of interest can exert a *short-run* influence on monetary expenditure but only in an unsystematic manner, consistent in fact with the approach taken by Tooke.[22] As was shown in Section 7.3, Tooke's analysis admitted the possibility of a causal relationship through the systematic influence of the rate of interest on the value of share capital which, thereby, could affect large-scale investment projects and, indirectly, by way of a wealth effect, could affect consumption expenditure. Moreover, it will be recalled Tooke believed the most common way changes in the rate of interest influenced spending in the short run was by its impact on the facility of credit to merchant traders. Tooke also believed that an increase in the money rate of interest was generally more effective in depressing monetary expenditure in the short run than a decrease in the money rate was in stimulating monetary expenditure. But, importantly, Tooke maintained that the effect of a temporary change in the rate of interest on spending was contingent on a wide set of factors and could only be ascertained by reference to the concrete situation under consideration.

With respect to the *long-run* influence of the rate of interest on monetary expenditure, in contrast to the position in marginalist economics, it is possible in modern classical economics to argue that a permanent change in the money rate of interest will exert a lasting influence on aggregate demand and, thereby, real income and output. This argument will be elaborated in the next section of this chapter. As is anticipated in our discussion below in this section, in large part, this argument originally derives from Tooke's conception of the long-run average rate of interest as a cost of production. Nevertheless, in Tooke's picture, monetary policy can only influence economic activity and prices in the short run through its temporary effect on the rate of interest and, thereby, through its unsystematic effect on spending, with the quantity of circulating medium endogenously determined by the resulting demand for money. Hence, while Tooke rejected any systematic influence of short-run changes of the rate of interest on spending, unlike the classical quantity theorists, he well-appreciated that it was through interest rates that monetary policy could influence financial conditions and the wider economy.[23]

Tooke's banking school theory of endogenous money in which the quantity of money in circulation is demand-determined in the short run as well as in the long run is entirely compatible with classical economics. However, as suggested above (p. 219), this theory can only be properly formulated in connection with a saving–investment analysis and theory of output which provides a congruent framework for developing an analysis of the interaction between expenditure and financial flows in relationship to the capital stock of a monetary economy. The Keynesian demand-led theory of output provides that congruent framework in modern classical theory. In this connection, the principle of effective demand is capable of explaining the level (and structure) of output compatible with the classical approach to the determination of (relative) prices and distribution.[24] This is because in the classical approach long period normal prices and distribution are determined for *given* quantities of gross outputs (Kurz and Savaldori 1998b). Therefore, as discussed in Section 1.2, in classical economics the aggregate level of output is open to determination by the principle of effective demand (Passinetti 1974: 44; Milgate 1982: 100–1; Garegnani 1983a: 61–3; 1990a: 122–4). On the basis of this principle, economic growth is conceived to be determined by the growth in effective demand (Serrano 1995). As is well-known, according to the Keynesian principle of effective demand equilibrium income, output and employment are determined by effective demand on the basis of a given propensity to spend and given levels of expenditure exogenous of income. An important feature of this theory of output is that providing there is unutilised productive capacity, saving can always be generated by increases in aggregate demand.[25] The non-existence of a factor–price mechanism characteristic of marginalist theory which acts to adjust aggregate demand to a level of output at full-employment means that in classical economics unutilised productive capacity can be conceived to be the norm. Indeed, the evidence of history is that labour unemployment is the norm, though its rate may vary.

This demand-led theory of output, with its postulate that via the multiplier the volume of saving endogenously adjusts to the level of investment, is also consistent with the conception that, subject to the institutional structure of the financial system, the overall quantity of money (and its composition) is endogenously determined by a demand-driven process. An important aspect of this latter demand-driven process in a developed monetary system is the role of credit-creation in which money, in the form of bank deposits, is created on the basis of fractional reserve holdings of liquid funds by banks. It was earlier shown in Section 6.2.2 that by the late 1820s Tooke was well aware of the credit-creation process in which bank deposits could be generated as a multiple of a bank's cash reserves. In Tooke's banking school theory, bank loans are clearly conceived to be exogenous as they represent the major way in which the demand for money is met with bank deposits created endogenously according to a reflux mechanism (see Section 7.2). But Tooke does not articulate this demand-driven process in terms of expenditure flows and income creation. In this connection the Keynesian theory of effective demand supposes that the financial system is capable of creating credit in order to finance any levels of net investment which happen to exceed planned saving for the period of time it takes for the operation of the expenditure-multiplier process to raise the level of income and generate the additional savings necessary to restore equilibrium.[26]

From this theoretical standpoint, the demand-driven credit-creation process can in simple terms be conceived to involve, for example, the advancement of loans by banks to meet an exogenous demand for funds to finance new investment, the expenditure of which endogenously generates additional bank deposits and, in turn, enables an expansion in bank loans, corresponding to the increased transactions demand for money associated with the expansion in income, output and, thereby, saving, generated in the expenditure-multiplier process. Deriving from a net expansion of bank credit and deposits, the banking system will require additional cash reserves the net demand (of existing supply) for which is conceived to be ultimately met in the short-term money market by the central bank at its set rate of interest on liquidity.[27] This simple example illustrates that the flows of expenditure and income in the Keynesian demand-led theory of output are congruent with the flows of credit funds and the volume of money in which the latter is conceived to be endogenously determined in a demand-driven process. Hence, Tooke's conception of endogenous money is capable of being developed to incorporate a credit-creation process on the basis of a demand-led theory of output compatible with modern classical economics.

The second element of Tooke's banking school theory which makes a constructive contribution is the conception that as a constituent part of the normal money cost of production of commodities, the average rate of interest exerts a positive causal influence on the general price level in the long run. As was explained in Section 7.3, this conception is underpinned by his argument that the long-run average rate of interest governs the normal rate of profit. However, there is a major shortcoming in Tooke's articulation of this concept in the adding-up theory of prices and distribution as the latter is analytically deficient because it fails to account for the interdependence between the real wage and rate of profit in the determination of normal prices for a given technique of production (see Section 3.3). As a result, Tooke was impervious to the full implications for distribution theory of his conception that the money rate of interest, as an independently determined variable governing the normal rate of profit, exerted a positive causal influence on prices. In classical theory, according to the surplus approach to prices and distribution developed by Ricardo and Marx, and reconstructed by Sraffa (1960), for a given technique of production, there is an inverse relationship between the rate of profit and the real wage. Hence, Tooke's conception implies imputing to the money rate of interest the main role in determining distribution through the determination of the rate of profit and, thereby, for a given technique, the real wage as a residual.

On the assumption that the real wage is not determined by, and normally stands above, the subsistence requirements of workers, Tooke's conception is entirely consistent with this classical theory of prices and distribution. Indeed, based on this assumption, Sraffa (1960) proposed that the rate of profit in an economic system producing a positive surplus product can be taken (necessarily lower than the technically maximum possible rate of surplus value) as the autonomous distributive variable so that real wage is determined residually along with normal prices. For Sraffa, this manner of determining distribution could find plausibility in the idea that the money rate of interest regulated the rate of profit:

> The rate of profits, as a ratio, has significance which is independent of any prices, and can be 'given' before prices are fixed. It is accordingly suscepti- ble of being determined from outside the system of production, in particular by the level of the money rate of interest.
>
> (1960: 33)

This proposition entailed a two-fold conception about the relationship between the rate of interest and rate of profit that Tooke had originally formulated. First, that the rate of interest is an autonomous variable in the sense that it is systemati- cally determined by forces 'outside the system of production' and can be explained without resort to the rate of profit on productively employed capital. Second, the money rate of interest, as the main component of the normal rate of profit, systematically regulates the normal rate of profit on capital employed in production. In this way, Tooke's conception has become the basis of the 'mone- tary explanation of distribution', which supposes that it is primarily through the determination of the long-term rate of interest in the financial market that socio- economic and politico-institutional factors determine the distribution of income between wages and profits in a capitalist society.

In the monetary explanation of distribution the normal rate of profit is con- ceived to be determined by two autonomous components: the long-term rate of interest, which is the 'opportunity cost' of employing capital in its financial form, plus a remuneration for the normal 'risk and trouble' of productively employing capital. It is envisaged that the normal remuneration for risk and trouble is determined by longstanding factors specific to particular lines of capital investment and independent of the money rate of interest, so that a per- sistent change in the money rate causes the normal rate of profit to (uniformly) change in the same direction (Pivetti 1991: 24–32). The long-run average rate of interest is therefore conceived to regulate the normal rate of profit and, thereby, exert a decisive influence on the distribution of income between wages and profits. As already mentioned, this explanation of distribution supposes that the real wage is not determined by the necessary subsistence of workers but, instead, is conceived to be normally determined at levels at which wages share in the surplus product along with profits. In this connection, it is interesting to note that Tooke believed the real wage was normally determined above necessary subsist- ence, essentially proposing, as shown in Section 3.2.2, that the lower limit to the real wage was determined by social welfare provision as a kind of social wage.[28] On the basis of a prior determined normal rate of profit and a given technique of production, the (surplus) real wage is conceived to be determined residually at a rate normally above the social wage along with normal (relative) prices. Accordingly, permanent changes in the money rate of interest, which cause uni-directional changes in the normal rate of profit, induce inverse changes in the real wage for a given technique of production.

This explanation of distribution is most relevant to a fiat-based monetary system characteristic of modern capitalism in which monetary values are not tied to any produced-commodity standard. In the fiat-based monetary system money prices can be normalised by an exogenous (homogeneous) money wage, which is seen to be determined independently by wage-bargaining.[29] The monetary explanation of distribution then consists of the argument that, as a component of normal money costs of production, for a given technique, a lasting increase (reduction) in the money rate of interest will cause enterprises in general to raise (lower) money prices and, therefore, the general price level, in relation to the *given* money wage in order to earn higher (lower) normal rates of profit on capital consistent with free competition. The resulting increase (reduction) in the price–wage ratio means that the real wage declines (increases), associated with a redistribution of income from wages (profits) to profits (wages). This change in distribution will involve a change in relative prices. Hence, according to this explanation, the money rate of interest exerts a lasting influence on the distribution of income, relative prices and the general price level (Pivetti 1991: 20–41). With regard to the latter, Tooke's argument that, as a part of the normal money cost of production, the long-run average rate of interest exerts a positive causal influence on the long-run price level entirely accords with this explanation of distribution and prices.

The monetary explanation of distribution is also relevant to a gold-based monetary system in which, like pre-1914 Britain, monetary values were tied to a gold standard, providing the real wage is not determined by necessary subsistence (Smith 1996b: 35–9). In this kind of economy, the monetary explanation of distribution relies on the historically plausible proposition that productive enterprises hold the balance of power over (organised) workers in the determination of the long-run normal (gold) money wage so that, for a given technique, the normal gold money wage and, hence, the real wage, adjusts to accommodate any lasting changes in rate of interest and, thereby, in the normal rate of profit.[30] Thus, Tooke's notion that the money rate governs the rate of profit can be the basis for a monetary explanation of distribution in a gold (or silver) based monetary economy such as nineteenth-century Britain as well as fiat-based monetary economies of modern twentieth- and twenty-first-century capitalism.

However, Tooke's argument of a long-run causal relationship going from the interest rate to the price level cannot be sustained in a gold-based monetary system as existed in Britain from 1821 to 1914, in which money prices are normalised by the official money value of converting currency into gold (Pivetti 1991: 79; Smith 1996b: 47). In such a commodity-based monetary system, for a given technique of production, a permanent increase (or reduction) in the rate of interest and, thereby, the normal profit rate, will *not* systematically raise (or lower) the general price level, which is approximately fixed to the gold standard. Instead, according to the classical theory of value and distribution, it will only induce a change in the relative prices of commodities.[31] It is perhaps significant therefore that Tooke's conception of the positive causal influence of the rate of interest on the price level originally sprang from empirical evidence of a strong correlation between long-term movements in the rate of interest and money prices over the period of restriction, 1797–1821, when Britain's monetary system was effectively fiat-based. But while Tooke's explanation of the Gibson Paradox is not theoretically feasible in gold (or silver) based monetary economies relevant to old capitalism, it is theoretically feasible in fiat-based monetary economies of modern capitalism.[32] Indeed, from the standpoint of modern classical economics, Tooke's fundamental view that long-run causality runs from the rate of interest to the general price level and then, endogenously, to the quantity of money, is highly applicable to contemporary capitalism (Smith 2001: 45–8).

The third element of Tooke's banking school theory which makes a constructive contribution within modern classical economics, which follows from the previous one, is that as an autonomous variable the rate of interest is determined causally prior to the normal profit rate by factors exerting their influence in the financial system. It was shown in Section 6.3 that Tooke explained the long-run average rate of interest by reference to politico-institutional and conventional factors which directly determined the demand for and supply of 'monied capital' in the financial market. It was also shown that while Tooke believed the Bank of England chiefly conducted monetary policy through the setting of its discount rate, curiously he insisted that its monetary policy could exert only a temporary influence on demand and supply conditions in the loan market and, thereby, on the rate of interest. However, this insistence by Tooke that monetary policy cannot exert a lasting influence on the rate of interest considerably weakens his argument that the latter is an autonomous variable which governs the normal rate of profit. If the rate of interest is autonomous on the grounds that it is directly determined by factors operating in the financial system, then the interest-rate policy of central banks must be considered one of the major factors.[33] Hence, in adopting Tooke's conception of the rate of interest as an autonomous variable, Marx included the discount policy of the Bank of England among the major factors determining its average level (see Section 8.2).

The most plausible way to give substance to Tooke's conception of an autonomously determined rate of interest is therefore to suppose, contrary to his own view, that the Bank of England had the power to exercise not only a temporary influence but also a lasting influence over the rate of interest (Caminati 1981: 101; Pivetti 1991: 86). As is shown in the next section of this chapter, the monetary explanation of distribution supposes that the general level of interest rates is determined by monetary forces, chief among them being the central bank's interest-rate policy, conducted through its direct control over short-term rates on liquid funds supplied to the financial system as well as other operations connected to debt management. This is entirely consistent with a theory of endogenous money as originally proposed by Tooke. Underlying this theory is the notion that the central bank, as the ultimate supplier of liquid reserves to the financial system and responsible for safeguarding its stability, is compelled to accommodate the system's demand for liquid funds but at a price of the central bank's choosing: the price being the short-term rate of interest on liquid funds (Dow and Saville 1988: 127–37; Goodhart 1989a: 208–11). It is this short-term rate of interest that constitutes the central bank's main monetary policy instrument. In this conception there is no inconsistency in the position held by Tooke that the central bank has little power to regulate the quantity of money, yet it has considerable power to influence the general level of interest rates.

Altogether, Tooke's banking school theory makes an important contribution to the development of monetary theory in modern classical economics. The conception of endogenous money, as articulated by reference to a demand-led theory of output, provides the basis for an alternative monetary theory to the traditional approach based on the quantity theory of money. An important aspect of this alternative monetary theory is Tooke's conception of the rate of interest as an autonomous variable that governs the normal rate of profit which, as shown above (pp. 222–4), can be logically sustained in the classical approach to the determination of distribution and prices. While Tooke did not subscribe to the notion that monetary policy exerted a persistent influence on the rate of interest, his conception of the latter as an autonomous variable is fundamental to sustaining this notion in the monetary explanation of distribution. In this explanation of distribution, the determination of the rate of interest by monetary forces is central to explaining the division of income between wages and profits in society. Hence, Tooke's conception of the interest–profit rate relationship provides the basis in classical analysis for being able to suppose that monetary forces can influence real variables in the long run, most directly by influencing the normal distribution of income. In addition, Tooke's related notion that the long-run rate of interest constitutes a normal cost of production of commodities makes an important contribution to better explaining price inflation in a fiat-based monetary economy. It informs that the inflationary process should not just be understood as a wage–price spiral in which expectations of future inflation fuels spiralling money wage and price increases but a process which includes the possible contribution made by persistently high and rising *nominal* long-term rates of interest also fuelled by inflationary expectations.[34] More generally, Tooke's explanation of price movements shows that the major *originating cause* of price inflation is natural and political factors that significantly restrict the supply of an essential commodity input not easily substitutable, such as oil today (equivalent to corn in early-nineteenth-century England) and/or a group of commodities constituting material inputs which, in relation to its existing long-run demand, induces a general increase in the cost of production of commodities in the economic system.[35]

8.5 Tooke's main legacy: overcoming money neutrality

There has been a renewed interest in Tooke's banking school theory in recent times by 'post-Keynesian' writers advocating the notion that the quantity of money is endogenously determined by demand against the traditional view that the quantity of money is exogenously controlled by the monetary authorities.[36] These writers have concentrated on Tooke's role in pioneering the notion of endogenous money (see Moore 1988: 5; Wray 1990: xiii, 102–10). No doubt a very important aspect of Tooke's legacy is as pioneer of the anti-quantity theory tradition in economic thought. But, while Tooke's conception of endogenous money represents an important contribution to the development of an alternative to the quantity theory approach, in our view a more important legacy to economics consists of his proposition that the rate of interest is an autonomous variable that can systematically govern the normal rate of profit because it opens up the possibility of supposing, in contrast to the tradition position, that monetary forces exert a *long-run* influence on real economic variables, in particular on income distribution and on aggregate output and employment.

Since the identification of profit as a category of income distinct from interest on money, by Turgot (1766: 68–71, 76–80, 87–8) and then, within a more coherent analytical framework, by Adam Smith (1776 [1976]: 65–81, 105–15), the traditional position in economic thought has been that in the long-run, causality runs from the profit rate to the rate of interest. This traditional position was well-articulated by Ricardo when he argued that, while 'subject to temporary variations from other causes' the rate of interest is 'ultimately and permanently governed by the rate of profit' (1821: 297). With the historical development of monetary theory, those 'other causes' have consisted of monetary forces, explained principally in terms of the supply of and demand for credit and the quantity of money as well as by reference to the role of a central banking authority. By contrast, the profit rate is conceived in economic theory to be determined by real forces in the system of production, so that however different the explanation, the traditional position supposes that the rate of interest is *ultimately* determined by those real forces which are specified to determine the profit rate. Thus, as is well-known, in Ricardo (1821: 110–27, 363–4) the real forces determining the normal rate of profit, and therefore, ultimately, the rate of interest, are the technique of production and real wage; while, in Wicksell (1898: 102–4, 122–34; 1906: 205–6), according to the marginalist approach, they are essentially the marginal productivity of real capital and the propensity to save of society that determines the relative scarcity of real capital.

Accepting it is chiefly through the rate of interest that monetary forces can transmit their influence on economic activity, the traditional position entails long-run money neutrality in which monetary forces can exert a temporary but not a permanent influence on real economic variables such as output and employment. Monetary forces, including monetary policy, are traditionally envisaged to exert an influence on real economic variables only when the rate of interest deviates from the rate of profit, after accounting for a magnitude to cover the additional risk normally associated with productive investment compared to investment in financial assets: with output and employment tending to decline temporarily when the money rate rises in relation to the normal profit rate and with excess aggregate demand and price inflation tending to occur when the money rate declines in relation to the normal profit rate.[37] Hence, monetary forces are traditionally envisaged to be a possible source of disequilibria as well as a means by which equilibrium is restored, chiefly through the gravitation of the money rate of interest to a level in sympathy with the normal rate of profit. It follows from this argument that to overcome long-run money neutrality, it is necessary to propose that opposite to the traditional position, causality runs from the rate of interest to the rate of profit logically consistent with the determination of normal prices and distribution.

In the history of economic thought there have been some notable dissenters to the traditional position. The best-known dissident is Keynes who by 1932 well-recognised the implication for monetary theory of the traditional position he inherited:

> the root of the objection which I find to the [Marshallian] theory under discussion, if it is propounded as a long-period theory, lies in the fact that, on the one hand, it cannot be held that the position towards which the economic system is tending … is entirely independent of the policy of the monetary authority; whilst, on the other hand, it cannot be maintained that there is unique policy which, in the long run, the monetary authority is bound to pursue.
>
> (Keynes 1971–1989, XXIX: 55 ['Lecture Notes', dated 14 November 1932])

From the *General Theory* (1936) onwards, Keynes proposed that the rate of interest was determined by 'purely' monetary forces, completely independent of those real forces in marginal theory that are envisaged to determine the normal profit rate (or equilibrium rate of interest).[38] Keynes went so far as to argue that of the two rates it was the profit rate on capital that would adjust to the rate of interest rather than the other way around: 'instead of the marginal efficiency of capital determining the rate of interest, it is truer … to say that it is the rate of interest which determines the marginal efficiency of capital' (1937b: 123). As shown earlier in this book (Sections 6.3, 8.1 and 8.2), over 100 years before Keynes, when classical economics dominated, Tooke dissented from the tradition position and was subsequently joined in that dissent by J.S. Mill and Marx. However, it was Tooke who from 1838 onward adopted the novel position that in the long run the average rate of interest systematically governed the normal rate of profit which, like Keynes' position post-1936, gives full force to the notion of an autonomous rate of interest. This notion is the basis of the monetary explanation of distribution in the classical theory of prices and distribution expounded in the previous section of this chapter.

In the monetary explanation of distribution, the long-run average level of interest rates is conceived to be determined by the longstanding interest-rate policy of the monetary authorities established on the basis of policy objectives and constraints of a social, economic and political nature, all of which can only be ascertained by consideration of the concrete historical situation. Among those factors that have been historically important in shaping interest-rate policy is the management of public debt, mainly in relation to minimising the debt-servicing burden on the government budget and meeting fiscal policy objectives, the constraint imposed by the external position of a country vis-à-vis the rest of the world and, connectedly, whether the main objective of policy-makers is price stability or achieving full-employment. Because of its implications for income distribution, interest-rate policy is also envisaged to be shaped more widely by the relative power of competing interest groups in society, in particular by organised labour on one side and productive enterprises on the other side in directly determining wage outcomes, as well as the banking and finance sector, which tends to represent the interest of portfolio wealth-holders. Moreover, the institutional form of the monetary system will play a crucial role in shaping interest-rate policy, not least because it defines the main objectives of monetary policy and the nature of the constraints on it. Indeed, institutional changes in the monetary system of economies have historically been accompanied by a change in conventional thinking about the role of monetary policy. As illustrated by Pivetti (1991: 10–19) and Smith (1996b: 39–43, 55–8), an appeal to history shows that a complex of these inter-related factors can explain longstanding monetary policy without any reference to the rate of profit (particularly, see Homer and Sylla 1996).

The important implication of the monetary explanation of distribution is that however interest-rate policy is explained on the basis of a complex set of social, economic and politico-institutional factors, by its determination of the long-run level of money interest, it exerts a lasting influence on the distribution of income, through which it can exert a lasting influence on real economic variables, in particular the level of aggregate output and employment, as well as the price level.

In modern classical economics, incorporating the Keynesian demand-led theory of output, monetary forces, most especially monetary policy, are conceived to exert a lasting influence on aggregate output and employment through their lasting influence on effective demand. On the basis of the monetary explanation of distribution, longstanding interest-rate policy, by influencing the determination of the normal distribution of income between wages and profits, can exert a systematic influence on consumption expenditure. Consistent with an under-consumption argument, on the highly plausible assumption that the propensity to consume of workers (or low-income earners) is lower than for capitalists (or high-income earners) in general, a lasting increase in the money rate of interest, which tends to redistribute income from wages to profits, would permanently reduce the overall level of real consumption. In the opposite case, a permanent lowering of the money rate of interest, by redistributing income in favour of workers (lower-income earners) would tend to increase consumption.[39] Permanent changes in the money rate of interest and, thereby, the normal rate of profit, can also be expected to exert a lasting influence on the inducement to invest, though the direction and force of this influence cannot be known with any certainty (Pivetti 1991: 45–6). Instead, the impact of a permanent change in the rate of interest on private capital expenditure will depend on a wide set of other existing factors such as technological development, the state of public infrastructure, commercial laws and trade regulations that affect entrepreneurial opportunity for profitable investment. Another avenue of influence is the impact of changes in the rate of interest on fiscal policy. Through its effect on debt-servicing costs, a lasting change in interest rates can affect the government's budgetary position and, thereby, its long-run fiscal stance. Thus, permanently lower interest rates that reduce the amount of government revenue that must be devoted to servicing public debt can accommodate either higher public expenditure and/or lower taxation which would contribute to stronger effective demand; while permanently higher interest rates will tend to have the opposite influence. However, this avenue of influence will depend critically on the objectives of fiscal policy-makers.

Overall, then, while a change in the rate of interest will exert a lasting influence on the level of output and employment through its effect on aggregate demand, the nature of that influence cannot be predicted with any certainty. It can only be ascertained by reference to the concrete historical situation under consideration. Nevertheless, by reference to the history of modern capitalism, it can be argued that, generally, a persistently low money rate of interest tends to support stronger aggregate demand, not only because it is likely to permanently increase private consumption expenditure (including spending on consumer durables) but, by reducing public debt-servicing costs, it better enables the government to adopt a more sustained expansionary fiscal policy, especially in the form of higher public capital expenditure.[40] Stronger private consumption and public expenditure is likely, in turn, to induce higher capacity-generating private investment as well as generally providing more profitable opportunities for investment in new products and technology.[41] But what is important here is that, from the standpoint of the monetary explanation of distribution in classical analysis, it is possible to argue, as indeed Keynes wanted to, that interest-rate policy can exert a lasting influence on the level and composition of output and employment.[42] This represents a dramatic departure from the long-run money neutrality of traditional economic theory.

Long-run money neutrality fundamentally stems from the traditional position in economic theory that the money rate of interest is ultimately determined by those real forces specified to determine the normal rate of profit (or natural rate of interest). It should be emphasised that this traditional position underlying money neutrality applies whether one supposes that the quantity of money is endogenously determined by demand (i.e. theories of endogenous money) or adopts the quantity theory approach to money (Pivetti 2001). Once it is acknowledged that monetary forces, including monetary policy, can exert its influence on a capitalist economy by acting on the money rate of interest, long-run money neutrality is seen to be the consequence of the traditional view that the money rate of interest must adjust to the normal rate of profit to restore long-run equilibrium. The implication for economic theory is clear: long-run money neutrality can only be overcome in a theory of value and distribution that can logically accommodate the conception that the long-run rate of interest systematically governs the normal rate of profit.

In the marginalist approach to value and distribution this conception cannot be accommodated because the normal prices of the factors of production are determined *simultaneously* by the technique of production, consumer preferences (especially with regard to saving-consumption decisions) and the given quantity of the factors of production available for use to society. Along with the normal real wage going to labour, the normal rate of profit on capital can only be determined in marginalist theory by the above-specified real forces which, thereby, must determine the money rate of interest in long-run equilibrium.[43] By contrast, in the surplus approach of classical economics, the distributive variables are determined *sequentially* in which either the real wage or the rate of profit is exogenously given and, on the basis of the prevailing technique of production, the other one is residually determined along with normal (relative) prices. As has been shown in our exposition of the monetary explanation of distribution, it is logically possible to sustain the conception in classical analysis that the money rate of interest governs the normal rate of profit, as originally suggested by Tooke. His main legacy to economics lies with this contribution towards opening up the possibility in the framework of modern classical analysis of supposing that monetary forces, in particular monetary policy, exert a lasting influence on the real economy, permanently affecting growth and distribution, as well as the price level.

Appendices

Appendix 1: Wheat price movements

A picture of movements in the price of wheat (as representative of corn) in the period 1782 to 1856 is shown in Figure A1.1. The wheat price index featured in the Figure is based on Tooke's series of annual average prices of wheat per Imperial Quarter presented in Appendix II (S) of *History* (1857, VI: 437–9). For 1856, the annual average price has been calculated from 'weekly average prices' up until end-August of the calendar year contained in a separate series in Tooke (1857, VI, Appendix V (A): 463–4). The index has been calculated by fixing the base 100 to the average annual price over the whole period, 1782–1856.

Appendix 2: General price movements

A picture of general price movements can be obtained by constructing indices from Tooke's data. These are depicted for the period 1782 to 1856 in Figure A2.1. Two weighted average general price indices have been constructed on the basis of price series for twenty-two commodities. The first index, consisting of

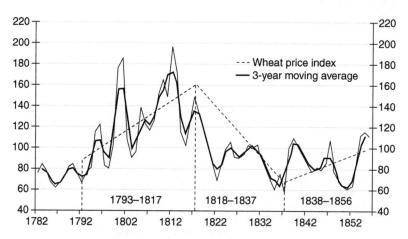

Figure A1.1 Wheat price movements, 1782–1856 (source: T. Tooke, *History of Prices* 1857, VI, 437–9, 463–4)).

all twenty-two commodities, may be regarded as representative of what today is called a 'production price index'. The second, consisting of thirteen commodities which are representative of 'provisions' entering into the real wage of workers, is a cost of living index. They have been constructed by calculating

Table A2.1 Weights of the price indices featured in Figures A2.1 and A3.1

Commodities	General price index	Cost of living index
1 Wheat	20.0	37.0
2 Coffee	1.0	2.5
3 Spirits	1.2	2.0
4 Sugar	4.8	8.0
5 Tea	2.2	4.0
6 Tobacco	0.3	2.0
7 Butter	6.0	4.0
8 Oils	2.0	3.0
9 Beef	10.5	10.0
10 Spices (pepper)	0.4	1.0
11 Wool	10.0	8.0
12 Tallow	1.8	3.5
13 Cotton	16.0	15.0
14 Silk	2.8	
15 Flax	3.5	
16 Hemp	2.5	
17 Saltpetre	0.5	
18 Timber	5.8	
19 Copper	1.5	
20 Iron	5.5	
21 Tin	1.2	
22 Tar	0.5	
	100.0	100.0

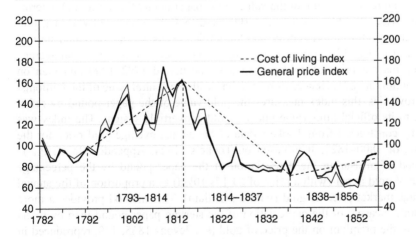

Figure A2.1 General price movements, 1782–1856 (source: T. Tooke, *History of Prices* (1838, I: 397–420; 840, III: 296–8; 1848, IV: 426–34; 1857, VI: 493–518)).

indices for each of the twenty-two commodities used with the base 100 fixed to the average annual price over the period 1782–1856. The composition of the commodities making up the two indices and the weights used in their calculation are set out in Table A2.1. The weights have been estimated by reference to British trade figures and limited production and consumption data for the period of the 1820s, 1830s and 1840s. But, given the lack of accurate historical information on patterns of consumption and output, an element of informed guesswork has gone into estimating these weights (compare with Hueckel 1973: 386–9). In this regard, it should be noted that there is a high degree of correlation between the movement of weighted average price indices so calculated and their corresponding unweighted average indices. The aim here is to obtain a statistical picture of general price movements from Tooke's data, consistent with his above-mentioned view that for such indices to be useful they need to weight the commodities included according to their 'comparable value' (see Section 5.1). Figure A2.1 shows that Tooke possessed a very good understanding of the long-run movement in the general level of money prices, derived from a comprehensive analysis of the prices of a range of commodities.

Appendix 3: The gold value of the paper pound, 1792–1821

A picture of the depreciation in the value of the paper pound against gold in relation to general price inflation in Britain over the period 1792–1821 is featured in Figure A3.1. The price index in this Figure has been constructed as a weighted average index from Tooke's price series for the weighted composition of twenty-two commodities prescribed in Table A2.1 of Appendix 2. It has been constructed by calculating indices for each of the twenty-two commodities used with the base 100 fixed to 1792. The annual inflation rate featured in the Figure is calculated on the basis of this price index. The gold value of the pound index in the Figure is a measure of the value of the paper pound (i.e. currency) in terms of the price of gold with the base 100 fixed to 1797 when gold was at it pre-restriction and resumption price and the foreign exchange rate of pound sterling was at par. It will be noticed in the Figure that calculated *as an* annual average price, this par price of gold prevailed in the period 1792–1800 and then on resumption in 1821. Hence, corresponding with the central issue of the bullionist controversies, this index measures the gold value of the paper pound by reference to its official mint value under a gold convertible system. The index was mainly constructed from Tooke's data of the annual average gold price for the period of 1800–1821. It is based on Tooke's (1824, Appendix No. 1, Pt. 1) method of measuring the depreciation of the paper pound by the percentage value of gold at par (with a price of £3 17s 10½d) as a proportion of the annual average market price of gold (with a premium). This method provides a more accurate measure of the depreciation of the sterling paper pound than by reference to the premium on the price of gold (see Jevons 1865: 139, reproduced in Arnon 1991: 17–18, with a diagram). The annual change in the gold value of pound featured in the Figure is calculated from our gold value of pound index.

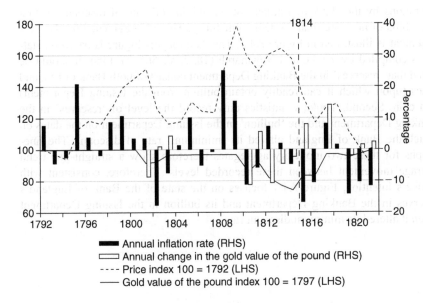

Figure A3.1 Movements in the gold value of the paper pound in relation to price inflation in Britain, 1792–1821 (source: T. Tooke, *High and Low Prices* (1824, Appendix to Part 1, No. 1, P. 1, 1838, II: 397–420)).

Appendix 4: The Bank of England's 'minimum' rate of discount, 1844–1856

As shown in Section 7.5, Tooke argued that in the period from September 1844 to end-1856 the 1844 Bank Act contributed to increased monetary instability and a greater fluctuation in market rates of interest as a result of more frequent

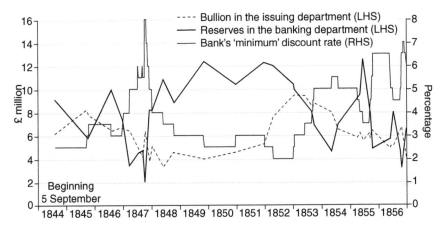

Figure A4.1 Alterations in the Bank of England's 'minimum' rate of discount after the inception of the 1844 Bank Charter Act, 1844–1856 (source: T. Tooke, *History of Prices* (1857, V: 565–7)).

alterations by the Bank of England of its 'minimum' rate of discount on first class bills of no more than 95 days to maturity. The main evidence for Tooke's argument is illustrated in Figure A4.1. The data for this Figure is based on statistics compiled by Tooke and Newmarch (1857, V: 565–7). First, it should be noted that 'reserves' in the Banking Department consist of both Bank of England notes (upon which it can readily obtain bullion from the Issuing Department) and coin. Second, Tooke's statistics only record the level of 'reserves' in the Banking Department and the 'bullion' in the Issuing Department on the dates on which the Bank of England altered its 'minimum' rate of discount. The line-graphs for these two monetary aggregates therefore show a straight-line trend average movement between these recorded levels. Therefore, consistent with Tooke's intention, Figure A4.1 focuses on the state of the Bank of England's reserves in the Banking Department and its bullion in the Issuing Department *when* it altered its minimum discount rate.

Notes

1 Introduction

1 A strong defender of the quantity theory, Mints (1945: 89–90, 94–5) was in fact puzzled by the views of those he called the 'real-bills writers', unable to discover any coherency in their position.

2 For the most part Viner (1937) was highly critical of the banking school, believing that their arguments against the possibility of an 'over-issue' of banknotes had been earlier discredited in the bullionist controversies.

3 The 1998 reference is an article by Pivetti titled, 'Thomas Tooke and the Influence of the Rate of Interest on Prices: Implications for Distribution Theory'. As the author explains in the opening footnote, much of this article draws heavily from Pivetti's *An Essay on Money and Distribution* (1991), and was originally published in a volume of commentaries to a German reprint of Tooke's *Inquiry into the Currency Principle* in 1997.

4 On the origins of the 'surplus approach' and its development up to Adam Smith, see Aspromourgos (1996). For an account of the surplus approach in Adam Smith, see O'Donnell (1990) and Aspromourgos (2009: especially 196–202). With respect to the development of the surplus approach in Ricardo, Marx and Sraffa, see Garegnani (1984; 1987). It should be noted that J.S. Mill has been excluded from this line of influence on the grounds that he did not contribute to the development of the surplus approach, notwithstanding that his economics sprang from the nineteenth-century classical framework.

5 The social wage is equivalent to what the classical economists called the subsistence wage. On the distinction between a social wage and surplus wage, see Smith (1996b: 35–9). As shown in Section 3.2.2, the notion of a wage standing normally above a minimum subsistence level is found in Tooke's writings. It is also implicit in the writings of J.S. Mill and Marx (Roncaglia 1978: 84–94).

6 The net rate of profit is the gross profit rate minus the remuneration for differential risk and trouble which normally characterises particular lines of capital investment. Hence, uniformity refers to competition establishing a system of differential normal rates of return on productively employed capital so that net normal rates of return are equal, which makes decision-makers allocating capital in pursuit of the highest returns indifferent between all possible lines of investment after accounting for systematic risk and trouble. As variously considered in Sections 6.3, 8.1, 8.2 and 8.4, in classical economics the net rate of profit is usually conceived of as the opportunity cost of capital approximated by the long-term money rate of interest and, by distinction, the gross profit rate is referred to as the normal (or natural) rate of profit (see also Pivetti 1991: 61–5).

7 The 'core' is similar to what Sraffa (1960: 33) referred to as 'system of production'.

8 The other major difference is that in classical economics demand is explained free of

methodological individualism and, indeed, of any functional relationship between quantity demanded and (relative) price, characteristic of marginalist economics. In classical economics consumer preferences are nevertheless conceived to figure in the explanation of effectual demands, which determine gross outputs. It is the content of these preferences which are important in explaining demand conditions, in which they are conceived to be shaped by social, cultural and economic factors, including the distribution of income among social classes, and by technical conditions of production. However, there is no logical basis in classical economics for supposing a functional inverse relationship between the relative price of a commodity and its quantity demanded from a rationalisation of consumer preferences according to the subjective notion of individual utility, which underlies the derivation of demand functions in marginalist economics. On this particular difference, see Garegnani (1990a: 127–32).

9 On the capital debates, see Harcourt (1972), Garegnani (1990b) and Kurz and Salvadori (1995: 427–67). Besides Sraffa (1960), key contributions to the debates included Garegnani (1966; 1970), Passinetti (1966; 1969), Samuelson (1966) and Robinson (1953–1954). In these debates, the critique primarily related to traditional long-period marginalist theory in which competitive equilibrium for the economic system is characterised by a uniform net rate of return on capital. It is claimed by some that this critique does not relate to the neo-Walrasian general equilibrium analysis in marginalist economics in which the endowment of capital as datum is specified in disaggregated form. The immunity of temporary and inter-temporal general equilibrium theory to this critique depends on supposing a disaggregated framework in which, implausibly, there exists no capital market to allocate capital (and other resources) across sectors of the economy in response to differential net rates of return. This supposition renders the theory an impressive mathematical artefact with little relevance to explaining economic phenomena.

10 On Sraffa's seminal contribution, see Garegnani (1998) and Roncaglia (1998). Garegnani (1983a; 1984; 1987; 1990a) and Pasinetti (1977; 1981) have also played an important role in the revival of classical economics. For the most thorough exposition of contemporary classical economics, see Kurz and Salvadori (1995).

11 Based on our definition of classical economics, who is a classical economist will remain problematic in the case of some writers on political economy. For example, Nassau Senior, who advanced some ideas such as profit is the reward for 'abstinence' which anticipated the marginalist approach, is still considered to be a classical economist on the grounds that his own theories were mainly developed in the classical analytical framework and he did make some contribution towards aspects of it (see Section 3.5). By contrast, there appear no such grounds for considering Richard Whately and Mountifort Longfield to be classical economists rather than mere precursers to the marginalist economists.

12 Classical economics did continue to be developed after the 1870s, largely on the basis of Marx's writings. Besides Dmitriev (1898–1904) and von Bortkiewicz (1906–1907 [1952]), works by von Charasoff, von Neumann and Leontief used concepts characteristic of classical economics and, in some important ways, contributed to its twentieth-century development (see Kurz and Salvadori 1995: 379–426; 1998c: 163–4).

2 Tooke's contributions

1 It also made provision for an annual Tooke Prize 'in connexion with the Statistical Society of London, to be awarded to the authors of Papers read before that Society, distinguished for eminent usefulness, or original research' (*Journal of the Royal Statistical Society*, 1858, vol. XXI, June: 200).

2 As an English chaplain, Reverend William Tooke was a regular attendant at the annual *diner de tolerance* given by the Russian Empress Catherine II to clergy of all

denominations. He also made contact with men of science on frequent visits to Poland and Germany, including a number of conversations with the 'profound and eccentric' philosopher, Emmanuel Kant, author of the *Critique of Pure Reason*, at Konigsberg (Nichols 1812–1815 [1967]: 376–7).

3 William Tooke also wrote the two-volume *History of Russia from the Foundation of the Monarchy by Rurik to the Accession of Catherine the Second* (1800). In addition, Reverend Tooke translated and enlarged on two large Russian historical works: *The Life of Catherine II, Empress of Russia*, 3 volumes (1798), written by the French author J. Castera; and *Russia, or a compleat Historical Account of all the Nations which compose the Empire*, four volumes (1780–1783), written by the German author Johann Gottlieb Georgi. As well as his contribution in bringing the most comprehensive works on Russian history to the English-speaking world, upon which he was perhaps the foremost authority, Reverend William Tooke also wrote prolifically on literature, being a regular contributor to the *Gentleman's Magazine* and the *Monthly Review*, and, among many other publications, was principal editor of the *New and General Biographical Dictionary*, published in fifteen volumes in 1798 (see Stephen and Lee 1885–1900, LVII: 976–7).

4 Tooke's younger brother, William Tooke (1777–1863), was a prominent lawyer and, following the passing of the electoral Reform Bill, was elected to the borough of Truro in 1832, which he served as a reformist Member of Parliament until 1837. He took a major role in the formation of the St. Katherines Dock Co., to which Thomas Tooke served as chairman (see below, pp. 14–15), and, as a member of its first council in 1823, played a prominent role in the foundation of London University (afterwards named University College) in Gower Street. Elected Fellow to the Royal Society in 1818, William Tooke was a literary contributor to journals, including the *Gentleman's Magazine*, editor of a number of publications and compiler of the two-volume historical work, *The Monarchy of France, its Rise, Progress, and Fall* (1855). He was also responsible for procuring the charter of the Royal Society of Literature, served as a treasurer to the Royal Literary Fund Society and was a leading member of the Society of Arts (see Stephen and Lee 1885–1900, LVII: 977–8). Thomas Tooke also had a younger sister, Elizabeth.

5 The rest of the Tooke family had returned from St Petersburg earlier in 1792 on the inheritance by Reverend William Tooke of a fortune from a maternal uncle.

6 In the prospectus for the company, it states that '[T]his important undertaking is supported by many leading merchants, shipowners and traders of the metropolis, who are deeply interested in promoting its commercial prosperity' (*The Times*, 2 July 1825).

7 A major figure in the establishment of the company was Captain John Macarthur, pioneer of the Australian wool industry. Originally the company was involved in pastoral activities in the Hunter region of the New South Wales colony before also becoming heavily involved in coal-mining. On the early history of the Australian Agricultural Company, see Gregson (1907).

8 See Tooke (1838, II: 275–6; 1840a, III: 278; 1848a, IV: 58, 63–4, 67, 72, 294–5, 299); while the dedicated account of the railway boom in Tooke and Newmarch (1857, V: 348–90) was written by Newmarch, though overseen by Tooke.

9 The Royal Exchange Assurance Corporation was established by Royal Charter in 1720 to pioneer and develop marine insurance. By 1840 it was one of the largest insurance companies in London, involved in fire and life insurance as well as marine insurance. After 250 years, the company was merged in 1970 with Guardian Assurance to become the Guardian Royal Exchange Group. The official historian of Royal Exchange Assurance (REA) refers to Tooke as a 'vigorous Governor' whose 'qualities of imagination and systematic thought which characterized his interest and writing in the field of economics and finance, must have proved relevant to his leadership of the REA at this crucial time in its history' (Supple 1970: 358).

10 Support for Tooke's election within the Society was very likely canvassed by his

father, Reverend William Tooke, a longstanding member, and his younger brother William Tooke, elected in 1818 (see Royal Society 1912: 363, 381–5). A contributory reason is suggested by Moore (1995: 104–5) that at a time when the scientific credibility of the Royal Society had been undermined by the breakaway and rise of other institutions chiefly in the natural sciences, it encouraged the induction of economists. Moore points out that, from around 1817, new Fellows elected included Malthus, Torrens and, on the fringes of economics, the publisher Macvey Napier and the politician Joseph Hume. Thus, Tooke's premature election may well have been the result of the desire by economists in the Royal Society to establish for political economy an identity in the scientific world.

11 According to Higgs (1921: xi–xiii, 1–5), the official historian of the Political Economy Club, a committee was formed in January 1820, at the instigation of Tooke, with the purpose of expounding the economic benefits of free trade and to exert influence on policy-makers to introduce legislation to this effect. The members of this committee who gave support to the Merchant's Petition drafted by Tooke were the founders of the Club. A preliminary meeting for the foundation of the Political Economy Club was eventually held on 18 April 1821, at the house of Swinton Holland, a partner in Baring and Co. Holland, Tooke, Torrens, Larpent, Norman, James Mill, Mallet, Mushet and Cowell were all present at this meeting at which it was decided the Club would meet regularly at the Freemasons' Tavern, London. James Mill was requested to draw up draft regulations for the Club to be considered at its first meeting held on 30 April 1821, attended also by Ricardo.

12 It appears that with the premature death of Ricardo in 1823 and the lack of interest of his disciple James Mill (who only attended three meetings after 1825 until his resignation in 1835), Tooke, as the 'founder of the society', played a dominating role in the promotion of debate from the mid-1820s onwards. Henderson's (1983) study shows that Tooke was the most active member in the whole history of the Club, having sponsored 36 questions discussed at meetings, more than any other member, and with one of the highest rates of attendance sustained over 37 years of membership. As indicated by J.L. Mallet's diary entries in Higgs (1921: xiii), Tooke was much respected by Club members, probably because of his organising skills as well as his practical approach to political economy combined with an ability to communicate ideas in an easily accessible manner. A pointer to Tooke's dominance in the Club in the mid-nineteenth century is given in a letter by Lord Overstone to G.W. Norman, dated 7 February 1853, warning that 'Tooke and some followers of his are getting an undue predominance in the Club' (O'Brien 1971: 564).

13 Politicians as well as prominent City businessmen attended meetings of the Club, either as members or invited guests of members. In 1834, Club members who became Cabinet Ministers were henceforth made honorary members as restricted to a supernumerary of forty, over the limit of thirty for ordinary membership (Higgs 1921: xvii–xviii).

14 Most of the evidence was attained at the work-site in manufacturing districts, consisting of interviews with factory owners, adult workers, employed children and their parents, foremen and medical practitioners, and carried out by nominated commissioners assisted by medical experts. According to the *Quarterly Review* of 1836, the amount of evidence collected was of a 'most repulsive magnitude' (vol. 57: 412). The commission in fact presented three reports: the 'First Report' and the major one (of 74 pages); a 'Second Report', which took account of delayed evidence by 'Medical Commissioners' (16 pages); and a 'Supplementary Report', which included evidence procured from a survey questionnaire (16 pages).

15 See 'First Report', P.P. 1833 (450), XX: 44–5. For an account of the Ten Hour Movement and its agitation against the Factory Commission, see Thomas (1948: 34–54).

16 The most important recommendation of the commission concerned the creation of a centralised inspectorate with factory inspectors given the powers of a magistrate to

police the regulations on hours and conditions of employment as well as education provided for children (Thomas 1948: 55–74; Inglis 1972: 365–6).

17 A possible contributing factor to his demise was the untimely death of his second son, Thomas Tooke junior, who was a Director of the Bank of England, at the end of 1857.

18 In a letter to Malthus dated 16 December 1822, Ricardo wrote:

> I saw Tooke for a few minutes, and was glad to hear from him that he had been writing, and was nearly ready for the press. I have a very good opinion of his judgement, and of the soundness of his view – he will, I think, from his practical knowledge, throw much light on the question of the influence of an over supply or an increased demand, without a corresponding supply, on price.
>
> (1821–1823: 250)

See also Ricardo to Mill letters of 17 September 1822 (1821–1823: 219), 10 October 1822 (1821–1823: 224) and 14 January 1823 (1821–1823: 266).

19 Part I is titled 'On the Effect of Alterations in the Currency'; Part II, 'On the Effect of War'; Part III, 'On the Effect of the Seasons'; and Part IV, 'A Table of the Prices of Various Commodities, from 1782 to 1822, with statements of Quantities; preceded by some General Remarks'. Pagination is separate for each Part.

20 Serving as a summary to the argument, Part IV was arranged into five sections and re-titled, 'On the Combined Effects of Alterations in the Currency, of War, and of the Seasons; with statements of Prices and Quantities'. Pagination is continuous for Parts I–IV and then renewed for the Supplementary section.

21 It is worth noting that the high praise for Tooke's *High and Low Prices* by Malthus and Torrens was no doubt connected with their campaign of showing the lack of empirical substance to the main propositions of Ricardian theory. As the chief opponents of 'Ricardianism' in the intense debates of the 1820s over the theory of value and distribution, they employed this line of attack against James Mill and McCulloch (see De Vivo 1984: 59–61, 71). Hence, Malthus, as quoted above, by 'our ablest writers' is clearly referring to the Ricardians; while in his praise of Tooke's work, Torrens (1829: xii–xiii) continues, '[I]t is practical rather than theoretical' and

> [I]t establishes its conclusions by an extensive induction from various and important facts; and, independently of its intrinsic merits, it derives an additional value from the circumstance, that its investigations are conducted in a manner which presents a striking and corrective contrast to the premature generalisations, and pure abstractions, of the Ricardo school.

22 In a letter to Lord Grenville, dated 24 November 1825, Tooke wrote:

> The gloom and apprehension which prevail in the City exceed anything that I have witnessed for many years; and according to all appearances the process of a wakening from the delusion into which the public had been lulled or rather I should say gulled in the last two years is likely to be attended by much more suffering than has yet been experienced.
>
> (Grenville Papers, British Library, Add. 69082)

Prime Minister Liverpool and President of the Board of Trade William Huskisson also anticipated collapse when, in March and April 1825, they each warned the public in Parliament that the government was not prepared to assist those who were ruined by speculative activity (House of Lords, 25 March 1825, *2 Hansard*, xii: 1195–6; House of Commons, 28 April 1825, *2 Hansard*, xiii: 288).

23 In reply to Tooke, Lord Grenville and Huskisson each wrote:

> I should be highly gratified ... by learning that the public is about to profit by a continuation of your valuable and useful labours. Few more important services can be rendered to the country than the establishing truths like these, not by a deduction

from remote, and questionable examples, of which we know not all the circumstances, but by reference made from time to time, to the transactions which are actually passing under our own eyes and which we are enabled to completely dissect and analyse. This could not be done but by a person uniting as you do, the most accurate knowledge of general principles with the most extensive practical experience.

(Grenville to Tooke, 23 November 1825, *Grenville Papers*, British Library, Add. 69082)

It is unnecessary for me to state how much I concur in the deduction which you have so clearly stated in the Summary of your intended publication. I am sure that by giving it to the public, about the time of the meeting of parliament you will do the country a great service, and what to me and others is not a matter of indifference, probably prevent, or at least check, a great deal of nonsense which, without some preliminary discussion to direct and guide the thoughts of those who do not think or enquire much for themselves, would probably find vent in the House of Commons.

(Huskisson to Tooke, 8 December 1825, *Huskisson Papers*, British Library, Add. 38747)

24 At meetings of the Political Economy Club, Tooke sponsored questions relating to variations in the price of bullion and the exchanges in relation to the value of the currency at the meeting of 5 April 1824; to the issue of Joint Stock Companies at the meeting of 10 January 1825; and on the relationship between the rate of interest and rate of profit on capital at the meetings of 2 May and 6 June 1825 (Higgs 1921: 21–5).

25 With respect to Tooke's access to the corridors of power in Whitehall, it is perhaps significant that in the late-1820s he lived at a Richmond Terrace address, four doors from Huskisson's residence and only a short walk from Downing Street.

26 Lord Grenville, William Wyndam (1759–1834), was a prominent Whig parliamentarian from the early 1780s until his retirement in 1823, occupying various Cabinet posts, including Prime Minister (1806–1807) and Foreign Secretary (1790–1801), and serving first in the House of Commons and then the Lords. Having established a group of followers in Parliament, the so-called 'Grenvilles', Grenville remained an influential figure in politics even after his retirement (Stephen and Lee 1885–1900, VIII: 576–81). In regard to his interest in political economy, Grenville was a supporter of resumption and a long-standing opponent to the Corn Laws as well as author of the tract, *Essay on the Supposed advantages of the Sinking Fund* (1828).

27 The debate was brought on in June by a bill to restrain the circulation of Scottish banknotes in England. It seems that some members of Parliament, unhappy with the elimination from circulation of small Bank of England notes (i.e. under £5) by April 1829, attempted to scuttle it. For an account of this debate, see Gordon (1979: 123–7) and Smart (1917: 452–4, 466–7).

28 In the first *Letter*, Tooke (1829a: 4–5) clearly outlines this object as the 'subject of another letter'.

29 In particular, Henry Parnell, advocate of free banking and author of *Observations on Paper Money, Banking, Overtrading* (1827), who argued for the maintenance of small notes on grounds of economy, and Joseph Hume, vociferous supporter of Ricardo, who now believed resumption was responsible for exerting deflationary pressures. Both had originally supported resumption in 1819.

30 Tooke (1838, II: 279–342) only made an incidental contribution to the monetary debates of the late-1830s in a discussion of the role of Bank of England policy in the financial pressures of 1837.

31 Including a comprehensive review of Lord Overstone's influential work, *Remarks on the Management of the Circulation, and on the Condition and Conduct of the Bank of England, and of the Country Issues, during 1839* (1840a), taking up nearly the whole of Chapter V.

32 To the 1840 committee, Overstone answered over 800 questions, covering over 100 pages of the minutes of evidence, while Tooke answered nearly 300 questions.

33 It consisted of three parts, with Part I providing an analysis of corn prices, Part II providing an analysis of prices of commodities other than corn and Part III providing an historical review of the 'currency question'. Newmarch provided important assistance with Part III and Danson assisted with Part I and 'the further essential service of conducting the whole of the work through the press' (Tooke 1848a, IV: viii–ix). Tooke acknowledged that, without the volunteered services of Danson, he would not have undertaken writing the volume.

34 The work contains a large number of extracts from the *Inquiry* (1844). Tooke defended this practice on the grounds that

> [I]f to avoid the appearance of quoting from a work of my own, I had stated afresh the same views, I am not sure that I should have expressed them better; and I could ill spare the time for such additional labour.
>
> (1848a, IV: ix–x)

35 It was incorporated as Part V of volume V of *History* (1857).

36 Given his advanced age, Tooke's explanation for the delay in preparing a much enlarged work compared to 'our original design' seems remarkable:

> To have hurried the Work to a speedy conclusion in 1855, would have laid us under the necessity of closing the narrative and the discussion in the very midst of the events which were gradually working out an answer to some of the most important and interesting questions.
>
> (Tooke 1857, V: x)

37 Much of the material in this Part was the basis of Newmarch's article, 'On the Recent History of the Credit Mobilier', published in the 1858 issue of the *Journal of the Royal Statistical Society*.

3 Tooke's approach to value and distribution

1 The long period method pre-dates Adam Smith but the form it took among earlier classical economists was more relevant to a pre-capitalist economic system. It was Smith who first developed the long period method with a conception of competition that made it relevant to a capitalist economic system, so providing the foundation for modern economic science. On this method and its origins, see Eatwell (1982), Aspromourgos (1996: 157–62) and Kurz and Salvadori (1995: 1–20).

2 On Adam Smith's conception of competition in the formation of natural price and in connection with distribution, see Aspromourgos (2009: 65–134).

3 However, it should be noted that, in correspondence with J.B. Say, Tooke indicated that due to monopoly elements the normal price was often above the cost of production established by competition (see n.6, below). See Tooke to J.B. Say letter, 12 March 1826, in Say (1848: 529) and Tooke to J.B. Say letter, 24 May 1828, in Say (1848: 537). It is apparent from this correspondence that Tooke believed any monopoly price established was 'in proportion' to the cost of production.

4 The view that Tooke propounded an 'income theory of prices', which was usually associated with the later monetary analyses of Wicksell (1898), Hawtrey (1913), Aftalion (1927) and Keynes (1930), is largely attributable to Gregory (1928: 20–2) and Marget (1938). In particular, Marget (1938) argued that, through its influence on Wicksell, the development of this theory had its beginnings with the 'Thirtienth Thesis' in Tooke's *Inquiry* (1844: 123). While Wicksell (1898: 45) maintained that the first sentence of Tooke's thesis 'does really provide a starting-point from which a theory of the value of money and of prices can be developed', he makes it perfectly clear that Tooke himself did not develop this 'suggestion' into a theory of prices.

Indeed, Wicksell believed correctly that Tooke explained price movements by reference 'to changes in the conditions of production of the commodities themselves' (1898: 45) rather than to changes in income and expenditure. The so-called 'Thirteenth Thesis' of Tooke (1844) instead concerns what is called his 'principle of limitation' on the fluctuation of the price level in a gold-convertible monetary system, elaborated in Section 7.2.

5 This correspondence was published in J.B. Say's *Oeuvres Diverses* (1848: 525–38). Extracts of this correspondence, which are quoted in this book, have been translated from French into English for the author by N. Fletcher, *Alliance Française de Sydney* and by Jean Jonnes.

6 In a letter to Say, dated 12 March 1826, Tooke wrote that 'too frequently Ricardo remains on the level of abstractions, drawing too many conclusions from a limited number of facts, and basing himself on hypothesis rather than on real life experience' (Say 1848: 529 [translated by N. Fletcher and J. Jonnes]). It was in fact a common criticism of Ricardo's theory in debates of the 1820s that it lacked factual basis (see Chapter 2, n.21). Moreover, this correspondence indicates that Tooke believed that the main *cause of value* was the 'limitation of the quantity supplied' of any product which must, as a pre-condition for its production, be '*able to be employed for use or enjoyment*' (Say 1848: 532 [Tooke to Say, 8 March 1828, as translated by N. Fletcher and J. Jonnes]). Tooke thought

> that this limitation is commonly and mainly caused by production costs, but it can be and in fact often is frequently influenced by other circumstances, such as, for example, a monopoly granted by the authorities or the possession of certain special advantages, such as the location of fertile land within reach of a large town, or a dock next to London Bridge, or the use of a water course in a populated canton

causing the 'value of the land product' to be 'out of proportion with labour and with every other advance devoted to the same production' (Say: 537 [Tooke to J. B. Say, 24 May 1828, as translated by N. Fletcher and J. Jonnes]).

7 The resolution of natural price into wages, profits and rent in Smith's adding-up theory of value and distribution is confined to a circulating capital model, whereby all products are consumed and reproduced in an annual production process. On this basis, by means of vertical integration, the value added of intermediate products, consisting of wages, rent and profits, are resolved into the final value of products consumed. For an account of Smith's analysis of value and distribution, see O'Donnell (1990: 32–8, 82–104).

8 Without always realising that this conception only strictly applied to a circulating capital model, most classical economists after Adam Smith adopted this conception. Most obvious in Ricardo's analysis of distribution, this conception was the basis for classical economists treating capital used in production as 'wages advanced' (Garegnani 1984: n.19, 300).

9 The significance of the labour theory of value to Ricardo was that it imposed the analytical constraint that an increase in either the wage rate or rate of profit *for a given technique* could not be supposed to be accommodated by an increase in natural price into which the distributive variables resolved. Instead, it could only be supposed to be accommodated by a reduction in the other distributive variable (see Garegnani 1984: 299–303). Hence, as Ricardo well knew, the labour theory of value is incompatible with Adam Smith's adding-up theory in which value is determined by reference to the aggregate of the prices of the inputs of labour, capital and land employed in production or, to put it another way, by reference to the costs of production.

10 The term 'adding-up' was first coined by Sraffa (1951: xxxiv–xxxvi) to distinguish in this way between Adam Smith's theory of value and distribution and that of Ricardo's theory. The adding-up theory is therefore fundamentally defined in terms of the

surplus approach of Ricardo in which (relative) prices are explained by reference to the determination of surplus value (rate of profit) as a residual share of social product (residual share as a proportion of capital employed). In this interpretation, consistent with our argument in Section 1.2, Ricardo overcomes deficiencies in Adam Smith's theory of value and distribution to develop a theory more compatible with the latter's notions of the social surplus and its determination (on the latter, see Aspromourgos 2009: 147–202). Most other interpretations of classical economics overlook the important analytical distinction identified here between Ricardo's theory of value and distribution and the theories of most of his contemporaries. A common interpretation is that, following Adam Smith, most classical economists, including Ricardo, held 'cost of production' theories of value, as distinguished from classical economists who (partially) held 'subjective' theories of value based on the concept of utility (see, for example, O'Brien 1975: 78–106; Sowell 1974: 97–110).

11 Tooke's critical comments in this passage on the inverse wage–profit relationship proposed in Ricardo's theory of distribution are in fact very similar to those made by Bailey (1825: 62–5) and Torrens (1829: x–xi).

12 Importantly, Adam Smith's conception is based on a circulating capital model, whereby there is no fixed capital and all commodities produced are consumed and reproduced in an annual production process (O'Donnell 1990: 35–9). Tooke appears to have understood this (see Chapter 7, ns.4 and 5).

13 Hence, with specific reference to Tooke in brackets, Marx (1894: 842) wrote:

> The fundamentally erroneous dogma to the effect that the value of commodities in the last analysis may be resolved into wages+profit+rent also expresses itself in the proposition that the consumer must ultimately pay for the total value of the total product; or also that the money circulation between producers and consumers must ultimately be equal to the money circulation between producers themselves (Tooke).

14 For a similar interpretation, see Rist (1940: 214–18).

15 The view that Tooke adopted an adding-up theory of prices is shared by Caminati (1981: 100), Panico (1988: 37) and Pivetti (1990: n.23, 44), but rejected by Arnon (1991: 71).

16 In this analysis, the rent going to landlords is clearly conceived by Tooke to be a component of, and therefore dependent on, the prior determination of profits going to farmers. Thus, in calculating the income of the 'agricultural interest', net of tithes and poor rates on the basis of estimates of gross revenue, Tooke concluded: 'there will remain a net profit of from twelve to fourteen millions per annum, or from twenty-four to twenty-eight millions in the two years, to be divided among the farmers and landlords, according to the terms of the leases' (1824, iii: 303). Also see Tooke (1838, I: 14–15, 186; II: 233–4n.).

17 While Ricardo (1821: 5) attributed priority for its invention to Malthus (1815) and West (1815), this appears unlikely as Ricardo (1815) articulated the theory in its most coherent form (see Kurz and Salvadori 1995: 306).

18 This meeting was held on 13 January, at which debate over the causes of rent was no doubt sparked by the following question:

> What improvements have been effected in the science of Political Economy since the publication of Mr. Ricardo's great work; and are any principles first advanced in that work now acknowledged to be correct?

This question was sponsored by Torrens and the account of discussion at the meeting is provided in J.L. Mallet's Diaries (Higgs 1921: 35, 220–4).

19 In this connection there is clear evidence that Tooke had adopted this conception of the interest rate as a cost of production as early as 1823 (see Section 7.3).

20 From the late-1820s onwards, the Ricardians, James Mill and McCulloch, adopted Ricardo's theory in forms that weakened the relevance of its core concept of the

determination of the rate of profit as an inverse function of the wage rate for a given technique. By contrast, non-Ricardian theories of the general profit rate were ad hoc, usually developed in terms of the demand for and supply of capital. This is also true of the explanations advanced by the less-influential Longfield (1834) and Bailey (1825); while, after rejecting Ricardo's theory, Torrens failed altogether to advance an alternative. On these matters, see Dobb (1973: 96–131), De Vivo (1984), Panico (1988: 30–1) and Bharadwaj (1989).

21 Tooke believed that in the short run a rise in money wages (in response to prior increases in prices) could indirectly heighten the price of provisions by increasing their demand when there was a general shortage of supply in the market. Hence, with the acute shortages of provisions in England in 1800 and 1801, Tooke argued that:

> The rise in the wages of labour, therefore, with the parish allowances, may be considered as having been, in the first instance, a consequence of the high prices of provisions, and subsequently a cause of the prices reaching a higher level than they could otherwise have attained.
>
> (1838, I: 227)

22 As this quotation makes clear, Tooke believed the King–Davenant Law was a useful empirically derived rule with no theoretical pretensions of explaining systematic market behaviour. The interpretation by Creedy (1986: 195n.4) and Endres (1987: 629–31) that Tooke used this law in the development of the 'elasticity concept' and was 'groping' towards '*ex ante* demand schedules' amounts to misreading a primitive marginalism into his analysis of market prices.

23 On this issue Tooke (1857, V: 78–80) quoted approvingly from this pamphlet.

24 These two cases of unanticipated gluts, on the one hand, and unanticipated shortages, on the other hand, are related by Tooke (1824, iv: 333) to the observed behaviour of commodity markets in England in 1816, 1817 and 1818.

25 This follows from Tooke's reasoning with regard to the opposite case:

> if the supply relatively to the estimated rate of consumption could be accurately ascertained, both as to the quantity actually in the market, and as to that which might eventually be forthcoming, there would quickly be an adjustment of the price in some regular proportion to the altered quantity, both actual and forthcoming. But it is not of many articles that the stock actually existing for sale can be ascertained, and there are still fewer of which the extent of contingent supply can be precisely defined.
>
> (1824, iv: 331)

26 For example, in considering whether the 'value of the precious metals' diminished such as to influence the 'state of prices' during the period of restriction from 1807 to 1819, Tooke (1823, i: 177–80) refers to the 'metallic price of corn'. In addition, see Tooke's (1823, i: 8–42) examination of the role played by the value of the precious metals, mainly gold, on the value of pound sterling and money prices during the restriction period of 1797–1821.

27 Tooke did qualify this view by stating that while 'gold is a commodity in such general demand' which 'can always buy all other commodities ... other commodities cannot always buy gold' (1844: 10). This suggests some limit on the demand for gold as its exchange value rises in relation to other commodities.

28 In the preamble to the 'Merchants Petition of 1820', reproduced in *History of Prices* (1857, VI: 331–5), Tooke wrote:

> In this country Dr. Adam Smith, whose great work, 'The Wealth of Nations', was published in 1776, is undoubtedly to be considered as the founder of the doctrine of Free Trade on systematic and scientific grounds, and as having placed the

practical application of that doctrine to commercial legislation in the clearest point of view.

(1857, VI: 331–2)

29 Malthus's proposition was advanced in the debates over the 1815 Corn Law which was intricately connected with the problem of post-war economic deflation and depression of industry. This is why the famous Malthus–Ricardo debates over value and distribution (i.e. the rate of profit) were connected to Say's Law and the role of demand in determining economic activity. As is widely known, Malthus (1820: 351–75, 463–522) supported the Corn Laws and the additional rental income it afforded the landlord class because he believed that their consumption of luxuries was necessary to maintain a higher aggregate effectual demand to prevent Britain's industry sinking into a post-war depression (also see Section 5.4).

30 In addition, he gave the following evidence:

> Supposing then, that from the superior advantages which we derive from our capital and machinery, and our better capacity of producing articles generally suited for the consumption of the world, that we are enabled to produce these manufactures at a rate so cheap, that the manufacturers of other countries cannot enter into a competition with us in the markets of the consumer; is it your opinion, or not that the high price of corn, and other food would be disadvantageous generally to the manufacturer? – Tooke: It would, of course, be disadvantageous to him; inasmuch as it would operate as a diminution of his profit; he must either pay a higher price, or have a worse quality.
>
> (Tooke 1821a: 235)

These questions were very probably asked by Ricardo himself, a member of the 1821 Agricultural Committee, in order to elicit answers from Tooke against agricultural protection.

31 After Adam Smith (1776 [1976]: 864–906), a well-known principle of public finance was that taxes and duties should not be imposed on 'necessaries' entering into the wage for the purpose of raising public revenue.

32 This view was put in evidence to the 1821 Agricultural Committee:

> If the British farmer is subject to taxes to which other classes are not subject, ought he not to have a protection against the foreign importer to that amount? – Tooke: I think that the British farmer may be entitled to a duty upon importation, to the amount precisely (if such a computation admits of being made) of such taxes as can be proved to fall directly and exclusively upon the land ...
>
> (Tooke 1821a: 231)

> You were understood to say on a former day, that all taxes affecting land immediately, ought to be taken into consideration in imposing a duty of any kind? – Tooke: Yes.
>
> (1821a: 291)

> You admit that the poor's rates is one of those taxes? – Tooke: It does appear that the poor's rates bear with greater weight upon landed than upon other property.
>
> (1821a: 291)

33 In a footnote to the quotation in the text above, Tooke wrote:

> Into the question of the amount of taxation, which falls *exclusively* on the production of corn, I will not now enter, further than to express, in general terms, my conviction that an accurate investigation of the items would bring the amount considerably under 10s. per quarter.
>
> (1829b: 88n.)

34 From the standpoint of Sraffa's (1960) interpretation of classical economics, the welfare gains of the classical economists' free trade argument could be represented by a rightward shift of the 'wage–profit' (or 'factor price') frontier that occurs with the adoption of superior techniques of production. The 'wage–profit' frontier in classical analysis shows an inverse monotonic relationship between the rate of profit and real wage for cost-minimising techniques of production in a multi-sectoral economic system with only single-product industries (see Kurz 1990). A rightward shift of this frontier would mean that for any given rate of profit (or real wage), the real wage (or rate of profit) will be unambiguously higher.

35 In the marginalist framework, those price mechanisms essentially rely on the adjustment in factor prices, most especially on the real wage and the rate of interest, according to the principle of factor substitution that underlies demand functions for labour and capital respectively. As argued in Section 1.2, no such functional relationships between factor prices and the quantities of factors employed can be logically established within the analytical framework of the classical economists. This point is illustrated by an appreciation that the classical economists proposed that the real wage is determined independently of the technique of production such that it can remain fixed in the face of changes in technique; or, to put it another way, increase equally as well as decrease irrespective of the factor-intensity of the technique adopted.

36 A major limitation on the classical economists' consideration of this demand constraint was the absence of a substantive theory of output (see Section 8.4). It may be commented that from the standpoint of the Keynesian theory of output, Tooke's belief that repeal of the Corn Laws would not lead to a demand problem in Britain is strengthened by reason of his position that it would tend to distribute income away from landlords in favour of wage earners that would, in all likelihood, increase society's expenditure 'multiplier'.

4 On Tooke's explanation of agricultural price movements

1 A basic commodity is a commodity which is employed as an input in the production of itself and of other commodities; a non-basic commodity is one which is not employed as an input to production (Sraffa 1960: 7–8).

2 This viewpoint appears to have exerted a considerable influence on the committee. See 'Report' of the Select Committee to whom Several Petitions Complaining of the Depressed State of the Agriculture of the United Kingdom were Referred, P.P. 1821 (668), IX: 1–27.

3 For example, in order to show that the average seasonal conditions in the period 1776–1793 were poor by the historical standards of the eighteenth century, Tooke (1838, I: 82) compared it unfavourably with the same period, 1730–1748, in the middle of the 'golden era' of English agriculture.

4 To quote Tooke:

> the fall and the low range of the price of corn, while money was undergoing, however slowly, a depreciation, prove how powerful must have been depressing circumstances operating upon the price of corn, to be sufficient, not only to prevent a rise corresponding with the diminished value of silver, but to cause a tendency in an opposite direction. The tendency to a decline of prices through so large a portion of last century occurred too, notwithstanding an increase, although slow, of the population, and a change which was in progress to the use of a higher diet.

(1838, I: 56)

5 This convenient quotation actually refers to the period 1792–1814 when Tooke is clearly referring to an upward trend in the general level of money prices rather than to only corn (agricultural) prices. It is evident from his table of wheat prices and

qualitative analysis in *History* (1838, II: 13–19, 23–7, 390) that the phase 1792–1817 must include 1816 as the 'twelfth' deficient season. Apart from 1816, Tooke finds the deficient seasons to be '1794 and 1795; 1799 and 1800; 1807 to 1812, inclusive' (1838, II: 346n.).

6 The five seasons that Tooke (1838, II: 226–40, 348n.) found 'decidedly deficient' were 1823, 1828, 1829, 1830 and 1831; while there was a series of abundant seasons in the years 1832–1835.

7 The deficient seasons were 1838, 1839, 1840, 1841, 1845, 1846, 1847, 1848, 1850, 1851, 1852, 1853 and 1855, with the harvests of 1846 and 1853 being particularly poor, and those of 1842, 1843 and 1854 being very abundant.

8 The comment by Tooke (1857, V: 175–7) that the cost of production serves 'so little as a regulator of the price' does not represent an inconsistency with this position because he is clearly referring to the market price (or 'current price') which in 'a practical and immediate point of view' is determined by supply in relation to demand for a *given* amount of land under cultivation. The cost of production as a centre of gravity for the prices of agricultural produce in Tooke's system is considered further in Section 4.3.

9 This is illustrated in the following passage:

> it was observed that the *relatively* high prices of barley and oats, and of other descriptions of grain and of pulse, had operated in causing a greatly increased consumption of wheat, as a substitute for these on the one hand, and on the other hand a considerable diminution of the breadth of land sown with wheat in the autumn and winter of 1835–36. The land so withdrawn from the cultivation of wheat was appropriated to the growth of barley and other corn and grain, which were comparatively high.
>
> (Tooke 1840a, III: 18–19)

With a reversal of the relative prices of this raw produce Tooke ascertained that by 1838–1839 there had been 'a restoration of the full proportion of wheat under cultivation, that had formerly been withdrawn, and possibly a further quantity of land appropriated to wheat, at the expense of other grain or pulse' (Tooke 1840a, III: 19). Tooke also made reference to the substitution of land use in the extraordinary case of the widespread failure of potato crops in the mid-1840s: 'In Ireland, and in those districts of England and Scotland in which the consequences of the potato failure of the two previous years [of 1845 and 1846] had been most severely felt, corn was extensively substituted for potatoes' (1848a, IV: 33).

10 This 'substitution' in consumption in response to an extensive change of relative prices is well illustrated by the following passage:

> The consumption of wheat in 1835 was not only on an increased scale for human food, in consequence of the more general employment, at full wages, of the population, and in consequence also of the *comparatively* high price of potatoes, and of oatmeal, and barley meal, and of animal food, but it was likewise greatly increased, by having served for cattle feeding and pig feeding, and for malting and distilling.
>
> (Tooke 1838, II: 238–9)

Also see Tooke (1838, II: 257; 1840a, III: 4, 19).

11 It is of interest that Tooke identified as a source of relief on corn prices in 1845–1846 the 'substitution' of vegetables for grain in human consumption and livestock feed, made possible by an 'open' winter season:

> little consideration is needed to show how great a saving of potatoes and corn is caused by an open, as contrasted with a severe, winter. In the former, cattle, sheep, and pigs, may be kept out and subsisted on green food and turnips so much longer

... in the winter of 1845–6, though potatoes were scarce and dear, turnips, and all other esculents, were abundant, and cheap. Indeed, it was with difficulty that the turnips could be fed off in the course of the spring; and it was said that, in several instances, farmers allowed their neighbours to send sheep to assist, gratuitously, in feeding off the surplus stocks. The abundance of turnips, and of beetroot, and cabbages, and turnip-tops, also added to the supply of human food, in aid, and to the great saving, of the consumption of bread.

(1848a, IV: 25)

12 In support of this contention Tooke quoted the following extract from Lowe (1823: 152):

The public, particularly the untravelled part of the public, are hardly aware of the similarity of temperature prevailing throughout what may be called the corn country of Europe, we mean Great Britain, Ireland, the north of France, the Netherlands, Denmark, and the north-west of Germany, and, in some measure, Poland, and the north-east of Germany. All this tract is situated between the 45th and 55th degrees of latitude, and subject, in a considerable degree, to the prevalence of similar winds. Neither the superabundance of rain which we experience in one summer, or its deficiency in another, are by any means confined to Great Britain and Ireland.

(1838, I: 53–4)

13 It is notable that with the progress of the nineteenth century, Tooke appears to have given more weight to the temporary influence of demand on corn prices on account of higher real wages giving greater scope for substitution in social consumption.

14 Under the 'contingent prohibition' of the 1815 Corn Law, imported corn was prohibited below an average (quarterly) price of 80 shillings (*s.*) per Imperial quarter and free above it; whilst under the 1822 protective regime imported corn was prohibited below an average price of 70*s.* and, above it, imported corn was subject to a limited sliding scale of duties. The 1828 Corn Law dispensed with any prohibition of corn and instead embodied a full sliding scale of duties for imported corn, with a maximum duty of 34 shillings (*s.*) 8 pence (*d.*) applied below an average weekly price of 53*s.*, sliding sharply down to 1*s.* as the price rose above 73*s.* In lessening this protection, the 1842 regime significantly reduced duties along the sliding scale. For an account of the English Corn Laws and the long-running debate over them, see Smith (2009: 345–50).

15 Criticizing the 'Report' of the Commons Agricultural Committee of 1833, Tooke noted that '[I]f the committee had simply stated that the corn law of 1828 had produced less fluctuation, and was less likely to produce it than the law of 1815, there would have been no ground for denying the assertion' (1840a, III: 25n.).

16 These incentives to speculation were somewhat mitigated by Peel's modifications in 1842 which made the graduation in the scale of duties to correspond more with the rate of upward movement in wheat prices from the 'pivot' price.

17 According to Tooke (1840a, III: 31), the Corn Laws also had a detrimental effect on the shipping industry. They did this by inducing sudden demands for the bulk shipment of imported corn at discrete intervals, causing sharp variations in freights which tended to impair the industry from adjusting its carrying capacity (through shipbuilding) to demand.

18 Significantly, it was in these periods that the 'landed interest', dissatisfied with the Corn Laws, clamoured for an increase in effective protection. Hence, parliamentary committees inquired into and reported on agricultural distress in the years 1820, 1821 and 1822, and then again in 1833, 1836 and 1837.

19 However, the analysis by Tooke and Newmarch (1857, V: 49–56, 180–5) of the importation of foreign corn over the period from 1821 to 1855, indicates that Tooke believed Britain, on the average of seasons, only became *heavily* dependent on imported grain from the mid-1840s onwards.

20 This view is made clear in the following passages:

> The failure of the present, and still more signal failure of the former corn laws, has arisen from the circumstance, that while possessing the power under certain conditions of artificially raising the price to a given height, there has been no provision in them for the application of a sustaining power. In order to be effectual in maintaining, as well as in merely occasionally raising the price, it is absolutely essential that there should be a bounty on exportation.
>
> (Tooke 1840a, III: 45)

> it has been suggested, that a bounty should be granted on exportation equal to the duty, which should never be remitted, on importation. And I am ready to allow, that if the policy or justice of granting any protection, as it is called, to the landed interest were admitted, this would be the only mode of making such protection effectual in keeping up a higher level of prices, and consequently higher rents.
>
> (1829b: 88)

21 The question to which Tooke here refers was as follows: 'In such case, if we could import grain from other countries, at less than two-thirds of the price of British corn, could British corn continue at its average value in the market?' (1821a: 288).

22 Tooke (1821a: 226) also estimated that the 'charges of conveying a quarter of wheat from Odessa to London' was 22*s*. 6*d*. bringing the imported price to 'upwards of 50*s*'. The shipment would involve a voyage of three to four months which, according to Tooke's argument, would make Black-Sea-grown wheat a very uncompetitive source of foreign supply under the operation of the Corn Laws.

23 To the 1821 Agricultural Committee, Tooke (1821a: 227–8) gave the following evidence in relation to the importation of Russian wheat under a free trade:

> What effect would be produced on the prices of wheat in those [Baltic] ports, provided the ports of England were always open for the reception of wheat? – Tooke: They would probably be higher than the present quotations at those ports.
>
> Can you inform the Committee what quantity of wheat might be obtained from those ports in case we were a regularly importing country? – Tooke: I do not imagine that any great increase of quantity could be obtained from those ports, except by a considerable advance of price upon those quotations.
>
> Can you form any estimates of what quantity could be obtained? – Tooke: The Russians have a saying, that price makes quantity, and in many respects they verify it; for if the price is inadequate, they keep back their own corn for several years, and bring it forward only to the shipping ports, when there has been demand during the autumn or winter preceding.

24 According to Fairlie's (1965: 574; 1969: 92, 106) price series, the difference between English and Prussian wheat prices averaged 32*s*. 8*d*. (i.e. 32 shillings 8 pence) in the period 1815–1827, 27*s*. 1*d*. in the period 1828–1841 and 15*s*. 1*d*. in the period 1842–1848. While Fairlie (1969: 92–3) provides only sporadic estimates of transport costs, these differences 'were more than ample to cover transport costs'.

25 It is worthwhile quoting Tooke on this historical experience:

> In a few instances the wages of agricultural labourers have been raised, but in a very trifling proportion to the rise of necessaries ... in the manufacturing districts there is not only no increase of money wages, but there is a falling off of employment, so that while the prices of provisions are in some instance doubled ... the earning of the work-people are reduced; they are thus suffering cruelly under the twofold evil of having their little income less, and of finding that reduced income going a much less way in the supply of their most urgent wants.
>
> (1840a, III: 52–3)

26 Besides the period of scarcity from 1838 to 1841, Tooke (1829b, 81–2; 1857, V: 76–7) observed that there had been food riots in 1794–1795, 1799–1801 and 1816–1817 when there were serious shortages of corn in England. In reference to these three latter instances of distress, Tooke wrote:

> it is well known that the peace of manufacturing districts was considerably disturbed; but if there had been reason to suppose, that any part of the rise in the prices of food had been produced by artificial means [i.e. Corn Laws], there can be no doubt that the tendency to popular commotion would have been greatly increased.
>
> (1829b: 82)

Tooke clearly understood the 'public feeling' that gave rise to the formation of the Anti-Corn Law League at the end of the 1830s, which campaigned relentlessly for the repeal of the Corn Laws. On the Anti-Corn Law League and its important role in the repeal of the English Corn Laws in 1846, see Barnes (1930: 239–82), Fay (1932: 88–108), Clark (1951) and Pickering and Tyrrell (2000: 165–90).

27 For a quantitative clarification of Tooke's position on the effects on distribution of the Corn Laws in comparison to that of Ricardo within a simple 'corn model', see the appendix in Smith (2009: 375–80).

5 An explanation of general price movements

1 This classification of commodity groups is used by Tooke in his analysis of general price fluctuations in Part II of *History* (1857, V: 228–347).

2 This is evident in the following viewpoint: 'the manufacturers, finding that the stocks of yarn and cotton goods had, in consequence of the great additional power which had been applied, by the erection of new mills in 1836, 1837, and 1838, outrun the consumption ...' (Tooke 1840a, III: 63).

3 In fact Tooke (1829b: 106) expressed dissatisfaction with the term 'overproduction' for conveying 'the idea of *too much*, or *more than ought* to be produced', with 'the meaning of evil' attached to it. He believed that while overproduction was only a temporary phenomenon, the permanent lowering in the prices of manufactures (given raw material costs) which stemmed from improved methods of production would be to the long-term benefit of consumers: 'the ultimate results are, extended means of enjoyment to the community, increased employment to the working classes, and the augmented sources of revenue to the state' (1829b: 107).

4 On the role of the extension of the market to facilitating greater specialisation (i.e. division of labour) and, thereby, productivity growth, in Adam Smith's theoretical system, see Aspromourgos (2009: 136–40).

5 As a result of the effective transfer of income afforded by railway expenditure, Tooke and Newmarch (1857, V: 369) argued that the 'working classes' were protected from the 'disastrous effects' of commercial distress, with the burden thrown largely onto the 'middle and wealthier classes'. In this regard, Tooke and Newmarch's analysis should not be interpreted as anticipating Keynesian ideas on expenditure–income determination. Other than the insight about the multiplier effect on indirect employment of capital expenditures, the analysis is essentially about the transfer of income and therefore expenditure between social groups. It is evident that in absence of the negative wealth effects flowing from the collapse in railway share prices, Tooke and Newmarch would have concluded a neutral impact on expenditure in the economy. Only through the effects on productivity derived from improved transport was railway expenditure seen by them to increase real income in society over the long run.

6 As evidence for this view, Gregory (1928: 14n.4) quoted Tooke (1826: 78n.), commenting that 'to form an opinion of the degree of variation' in its discount business

and cash and bullion holdings, the Bank of England furnished data to parliamentary committees in 1797, 1810 and 1819 'in as mysterious form as possible: *viz.* that of a scale'. Convinced of its correctness, Tooke (1826: 187) included this data showing the 'scale of cash and bullion' for the period 1782–1797 in Appendix D of the *Considerations.*

7 Among classical economists, the conception of a 'weighted' cost of living index naturally followed from considerations about the composition of commodities making up the real wage. This is apparent in a table presented by Tooke (1838, I: 228n.) which he extracted from an 'Appendix to the Report of a Committee of the House of Commons in the year 1800', providing an estimate of the 'expenses of house-keeping' for the years 1773, 1793, 1799 and 1800, as calculated on the basis of a given composition of commodities. It is also apparent in Tooke's (1838, I: 226–7n.) reproduction of the table of calculations by Young (1801: 285) to estimate the change in the real wage of a labourer.

8 This was illustrated by Tooke in the following manner:

> the article of Annatto, the whole annual importation of which is probably of a value not exceeding 20,000*l.*, is [in Porter's index] of equal influence in the result of the prices for the month or for the year as wheat, or cotton, or coffee, and sugar, articles which embrace as many millions as this does hundreds of pounds in value; and I rather think the first five articles in the list, would not embrace the value of a hundredth part of five other articles that might be selected, yet those of low value enter into the same line of comparison with those of the highest value; and I believe that I might undertake to select twenty-five out of the fifty articles which would not constitute the value of one tenth of the remaining twenty-five.
>
> (1840b: (Q 3615) 337; also see 1848a, IV: 464)

9 It is perhaps significant that despite the development in the statistical theory of weighted index numbers in the nineteenth century, notably by Laspeyres and Paasche, an empirically based weighted general price index was not accurately calculated until 1904 when the United States Bureau of Labour compiled a cost of living index on the basis of weights calculated from a survey of household expenditures carried out in 1901–1902. For a concise history of index numbers, see Diewart (1987).

10 This view was stated by Tooke in the following way:

> In the early part of the war, the extensive military operations were calculated to diminish the produce of the Netherlands, Germany, and Italy; and, at the same time, political convulsions attending the revolutionary period might affect the extent and quality of the cultivation of the land of France. In the subsequent periods of the war the course of military operations can hardly have failed to diminish the produce of Poland, Prussia, Saxony, and Russia, as likewise, of Spain, Portugal, and Italy.
>
> (1838, I: 115)

11 While the French had endeavoured to widen prohibitions in Europe against British trade during the early stages of the wars, it was not until Napoleon acquired hegemony over the Continent that an effective blockade could be imposed from 1806 onwards. It was imposed to counter Britain's maritime blockade against France, which, after the battle of Trafalgar in 1805, had virtual unchallenged control over the seas. The blockade had the twin aims of denying Britain its traditional supplies of grain and war materials (i.e. hemp, flax and timber) in northern Europe and, by depriving it of export markets, to weaken its financial position and ability to subsidise military operations on the Continent. On this economic warfare, see Heckscher (1922).

12 In particular, see the table in Tooke (1838, I: 309n.) showing that the charges for freight and insurance on imports from the Baltic were over ten-times more per average year over the period 1809–1812 than they were in 1837.

13 A cessation of hostilities in 1801 was officially ratified by the Peace of Amiens, signed in 1802. As Tooke (1838, I: 237) described it, this 'marked change for the better' in the 'state of politics' was connected to

> [T]he death of the emperor Paul of Russia, and the peace with Denmark, which followed the battle of Copenhagen, [that] had re-opened the navigation of the Baltic to British shipping, thus removing the obstruction which had been apprehended to supplies from thence.

14 The following passage shows Tooke was acutely aware that in these years of widespread scarcity in Western Europe, the competition for grain between France and Britain saw anti-commercial measures adopted with the twin aims of appropriating corn to meet domestic shortages and simultaneously denying supplies to the enemy:

> [The] Government had, early in 1795, and indeed, for some time before, taken the alarm at the indications of impending dearth, and adopted some extraordinary measures of precaution. All neutral ships bound with corn to France were seized and brought into this country, and their cargoes paid for, with an ample profit to the proprietors. This measure was adopted with a double view, of relief to ourselves and distress to the enemy, there being still a scarcity in France than in this country.
>
> (1838, I: 181)

15 For an account of these tax increases throughout the course of the French Wars, see Smart (1910: 3, 44, 53, 67, 100, 113, 166, 342–4, 360–1, 425). In the war years 1793 to 1815, tax revenue rose by over 300 per cent, compared with only 59 per cent over the previous comparable period (to 1770). Of this increase, customs revenue rose by over 300 per cent compared to 25 per cent, excise by nearly 250 per cent compared to 67 per cent, land tax by over 250 per cent compared to 64 per cent and revenue from the 'Property and Income Tax', instituted in 1799, grew rapidly to represent some 18 per cent of total government revenue by 1815 (calculated from Mitchell 1988: 576–7, 581).

16 As an indicator, revenue from poor rates rose some 60 per cent, from £5,348,000 to £8,647,000 between the years 1803 and 1813 (Mitchell 1988: 605).

17 In his main discussion of the effect of taxes on prices, Tooke wrote:

> It is not my intention, at present, to enter into a detailed statement of the grounds for this opinion, which would involve a discussion of the principles of taxation; a subject foreign to the purpose of this inquiry.
>
> (1838, I: 88; also see 1824, ii: 147)

18 This argument is based on the twin propositions that the increase in the money wages of labour would be passed backwards by farmers onto landlords through a reduction in rent and passed forward by manufacturers onto rich consumers through higher prices of manufacturing goods. Thus, Smith rejected the possibility that tax incidence could be shifted from wages onto profits (or interest).

19 Given Adam Smith's edict that '[E]very tax must finally be paid from some one or other of those three different sources of revenue' (1776 [1976]: 825), consisting of wages, profits and rent, his argument implied that ultimately taxes fall upon those 'superior ranks of people' whose income comes from rent (i.e. landlords).

20 This is evident in the following answers given by Tooke to the 1821 Agricultural Committee:

> However highly a country may be taxed, if the taxes be general and equal, will they have any effect in preventing us from competing with other countries? – Tooke: They cannot have that effect in my opinion. For instance, I cannot easily conceive, how an income tax of ten per cent, levied, if such a thing be practicable, with perfect equality, could affect prices; it would not affect the proportions of production and consumption; there would be no difference in the supply, nor do I

see how there could be any difference in the demand. I have confined myself, in this answer, to the effects of taxation on prices, as connected with foreign competition. The effects of taxation on the accumulation of capital, or national wealth, afford a distinct ground of consideration.

How then are taxes to be supported, unless it be by a general rise in the prices of articles produced? – Tooke: I do not think that a general rise in price, or high money prices, are essential to the revenue ...

(1821a: 292)

21 In the following evidence to the Agricultural Committee of 1821, Tooke acknowledged the constraints on free trade by the revenue-raising requirements of the government:

If a free trade existed, could any of the duties of customs or excise be levied in Great Britain? – Tooke: I all through mean, as far as is consistent with preserving an existing revenue.

A free trade could not exist under custom or excise duties? – Tooke: I mean a free trade as far as might be consistent with those.

Could you take off those duties before you pay off the national debt? – Tooke: I do not propose taking them off; I am alluding to those which are simply meant as protecting duties or regulations; such, for instance, as that under consideration relative to corn.

(1821a: 290)

22 On the shortcomings of Adam Smith's analysis of the incidence of tax on wage goods (or wages), see O'Donnell (1990: 105–6).
23 This argument was made by Tooke (1824, ii: 148; 1838, I: 89) on the understanding that the

controversy [over the effect of taxes on prices] has mainly turned upon the contrast between prices during the war and since the peace, till the close of 1822, the lowest point [of prices] having been reached before any remission of taxation.

The first time taxes and duties were reduced after the French Wars was in the British government's 1823 budget, followed by the 1824 'first free trade' budget, which instituted significant reductions in custom duties (see Smart 1917: 150–1, 192–222).
24 Total expenditure of the British government on 'Army, Navy and Ordnance' was approximately £850 million; while about £640 million was expended on subsidy payments (including loans) to foreign states. For these figures, see Sherwig (1969: 4, 365–9) and Mitchell (1988: 580, 587).
25 This burden was very heavy when it is considered that from the early-1820s to early-1850s, policy-makers gave priority to reducing taxes and duties, which tended to hold back growth in government revenue, over producing budget surpluses (and contributing towards a 'sinking fund') in order to reduce public debt.
26 The other significant contribution to this argument was provided in Section X, Chapter VII of Malthus (1820: 490–522) titled, 'Application of some of the preceding principles to the distresses of the labouring classes since 1815, with general observations'.
27 Tooke's 'adherence to the doctrine of M. Say' was noticed by Malthus (1823: 232).
28 Thus, Tooke (1823, ii: 10; 1824, ii: 151–2; 1838, I: 93) 'assumed that the quantity of money in circulation remains the same' noting that '[I]f a state of war includes the supposition of an increase in the quantity of money, then indeed the case would be different'. Tooke is here referring to inconvertible money which was in circulation during the French Wars.
29 Tooke continued with the following question:

If every market overflowed with commodities during the whole of that interval, and gave no encouragement for further production, was it probable, was it possible, according to any known law by which capital and reproduction are regulated, that all the products should have increased, and be in much greater quantity, as they proved to have been, at the end of that long interval than at its commencement?

(1824, ii: 204)

30 Thus, in reference to Say's Law, Blake wrote:

It appears to me that the error lies in supposing, first, that the whole capital of the country is fully occupied; and, secondly, that there is immediate employment for successive accumulations of capital as it accrues from saving. I believe there are at all times some portions of capital devoted to undertakings that yield very slow returns or slender profits, and some portions lying wholly dormant in the form of goods, for which there is not sufficient demand.

(1823: 54)

31 In this regard, Malthus (1820: 463–90) stressed the importance of 'unproductive' consumption of luxury commodities by the wealthier classes as an important element in generating greater demand and, therefore, employment in the economy.

32 The common misunderstanding that the classical economists' conception of Say's Law is the same as the conception in marginalist economics that 'supply creates its own demand' towards full-employment equilibrium, is owed to Keynes (1936: 18–21). Indeed, in *The General Theory* (1936), Keynes defined classical economics by reference to the adoption of Say's Law, when his main object of criticism was Pigou's *Theory of Unemployment* (1933), a work obviously based on marginalist, specifically Marshallian, principles.

33 Statistical evidence presented by Tooke (1824) consisted of population returns to Parliament, annual statistics on the number of marriages, on the number of animals slaughtered, on the value of imports less re-exports (including of cotton and wool), on the quantity of domestic products subject to excise and on sales of various domestically produced commodities.

34 Tooke wrote that 'the principal arguments in favour of this theory [of 'the stimulus of war-demand'] were brought forward in publications and speeches of some years back, when the transition from war to peace was comparatively recent' (1838, I: 111). However, in the second edition of his *Principles* published in 1836, Malthus did not alter his position on this question.

35 Other bullionists included Wheatley (1803; 1807), King (1803), Boyd (1801), Huskisson (1810), Horner (1803a; 1803b), Mushet (1811) and Malthus (1811). The position of the bullionists is well represented in the Bullion Report of 1810 which was principally drafted by Henry Thornton, with the assistance of William Huskisson and Francis Horner. On the formulation of the Bullion Report, see Cannan (1925: vii–xlvi) and Fetter (1954).

36 Thus, Ricardo contended that whether or not price inflation and a depreciation in the paper currency was caused by real factors, it was always the consequence of an accommodating monetary policy of the Bank of England. In this connection Ricardo argued that whatever the cause, price inflation could always be suppressed and the paper currency restored to its mint standard by the Bank of England judiciously restricting its quantity of banknotes and eliminating the excess supply of money in the economy. This position was well reflected by Ricardo's (1811a: 59–61) argument that 'an unfavourable balance of trade, never arises but from a redundant currency', upon which he criticised Thorton (1802: 151–3) for supposing that an unfavourable balance of trade may occasionally be the result of real factors such as a bad harvest or war blockades to export markets.

37 On these differences between the bullionists, in particular, see Fetter (1942: 364–73; 1965: 40–51) and Viner (1937: 138–48).

38 In addition, they included representatives of the Bank of England, whose contribution to the debates were made in the form of evidence given to parliamentary committees, in particular, in evidence given before the Bullion Committee of 1810 by Governor J. Whitmore, Deputy-Governor J. Pearse and Director J. Harman (Bullion Committee 1810: 79–82, 89–90, 94–8, 109–13, 119–22, 125–8, 142–4).

39 See the parliamentary evidence of the Bank of England's Deputy-Governor J. Pearse (Bullion Committee 1810: 95, 112) and Governor J. Whitmore (Bullion Committee 1810: 121).

40 See the evidence of J. Pearse (Bullion Committee 1810: 95) and Harman (Bullion Committee 1810: 143) and the criticisms in the Report (Cannan 1925: 45–51). It is evident Tooke was not impressed with their performance, remarking that they were 'under guidance of maxims and principles so unsound and of such apparently mischievous tendency, as those professed by the governors and some of the directors of the Bank of England in 1810' (1838, I: 158). Anti-bullionist statements of the 'real bills' doctrine are also to be found in Boase (1804: 4–7; 1811: 70–5) and Bosanquet (1810: 62–4).

41 The 'principle of limitation' is illustrated by Tooke (1819b: 181) in a paper presented as evidence to the Lords Committee on Resumption in 1819 from which extracts were subsequently quoted in *High and Low Prices* (1823, i: 9n.) and *History* (1838, I: 121–2n.). To illustrate his meaning, Tooke provides an example which goes as follows. Suppose a purely gold (or metallic) circulation consisting of twenty million sovereigns of the 'present weight and standard'. Then, suppose that by way of seigniorage, the intrinsic value of all the sovereign coins are uniformly reduced by 5 per cent. Providing the circulation was limited to the same twenty million sovereigns then, other things remaining the same, so that 'the relation of commodities to the numerical amount of coin was undisturbed', there would be no effect on money prices. Now, instead, suppose that the 5 per cent of gold abstracted from the coinage should be re-issued into circulation. The twenty-one million sovereigns now in circulation would 'exchange for no more than the former twenty million', such that the prices of all commodities including bullion would rise by 5 per cent. Similarly, in a mixed circulation in which paper currency is fully convertible into gold, if under these circumstances, paper circulation were to increase, there would also be a 5 per cent rise in prices. Thus, according to Tooke, when there was no limitation to the quantity of money in circulation, seigniorage would, in the same way as a debasement of the coinage (i.e. clipping), lead to a depreciation of money. An implication of this principle is that providing the intrinsic value of gold (or silver), as the monetary standard, remains constant, the purchasing power of a given amount of gold money in circulation would be limited. As is shown in Section 7.2, Tooke's conception of the principle of limitation changes considerably consistent with the development of his banking school theory of which it is an important element.

42 Tooke (1838, I: 123) likened the depreciation of coin to being 'rendered less valuable by being divested by law of some of the uses to which it might otherwise be applied', namely its use as a means of international payment (by 'exportation') and for 'consumption in domestic manufacture'.

43 Tooke (1838, I: 123) referred to an estimate of 1 per cent in Lord Liverpool's *A Treatise on the Coins of the Realm* (1805) and various estimates of three shillings and four shillings per ounce given in evidence to the Bullion Committee of 1810.

44 This is evident in the following answers supplied by Tooke to the committee:

> How do you ascertain that the value of gold has risen six per cent measured in silver since 1819? – Tooke: I am not clear that it amounts to proof that gold has risen, as the difference might equally arise from a fall in the value of silver.
>
> Do you believe that silver has risen in value, as compared with commodities, since 1819? – Tooke: I am not aware of any sufficient grounds for inferring that it has.

Is not [your] opinion, then grounded on the supposition and the belief, that silver has not varied in value? – Tooke: I assume that, having no sufficient ground for any different inference.

(1821a: 296)

45 On this development Tooke wrote:

notwithstanding the extended functions of money consequent on an increased population, and on an enlarged scale of pecuniary transactions, it is perfectly conceivable that a smaller numerical amount of coin and bank notes is now requisite to circulate commodities at the same prices than before that period.

(1838, I: 145)

46 This is stated by Tooke in the following answer:

You have stated, what in your opinion is the increase in the value of gold compared to silver since 1819; the Committee wish you to state, what in your opinion is the increase in the value of Bank notes, as compared with gold since that time? – Tooke: The Bank notes being exactly equal to gold at £3 17s. 10 1/2d. the increased value of the Bank note as compared with gold, is the difference between £4 1s. 6d. and £3 17s. 10 1/2d. or somewhat above four per cent.

(1821a: 296)

47 In support of his argument, Tooke quoted the following passage from Thornton (1802: 221n.):

In general it may perhaps be assumed, that an excessive issue of paper has not been the leading cause of a fall in the exchange, *if it afterwards turns out that the exchange is able to recover itself without any material reduction of the quantity of the paper*.

(1838, I: 157n.; emphasis added by Tooke)

Tooke (1838, I: 157n.) also quoted another passage from Thornton (1802: 225) cautioning the reader from automatically drawing the 'inference' that depreciation of the exchanges is due to an excess issue of 'paper'. In addition, Tooke (1848, IV: 136–42) presented evidence showing that during restriction there was 'uniform coincidence' between the recovery of the foreign exchanges and when there was no large foreign expenditures by the British government and/or large importations of grain adversely impacting on the balance of payments.

48 Tooke (1848a, IV: 100–13) was especially critical of the bullionists for not appreciating the fact that the depreciation of the paper currency in 1810 was associated with a rise in the value of gold and a decline in the money prices of commodities (see Figure A3.1, p. 235):

The assumption by the framers of the Bullion report and their partisans, of the relative state of prices of that period, so contrary to the actual facts of the case, is quite astounding; for, in reality, there had been a ruinous fall of prices in 1810, as compared with 1808 and 1809: and, so far from its being true, as affirmed by the Report, that 'the prices of all commodities have risen in price in common with them', – all commodities, provisions alone excepted (these being scarce from the effects of bad seasons combined with obstructions to importation), were actually falling, while gold was rising.

(Tooke 1848a, IV: 110)

49 As is well-known, Ricardo's (1811a: 52–9) argument was that under convertibility the export of gold would cause an internal monetary contraction that according to the price–specie–flow doctrine would cheapen British exportable commodities in relation to gold, increase the volume of exports, correct the balance of payments

and cause an appreciation of the exchange rate towards par. Also see Huskisson (1810: 48–54).

50 Tooke made this point mainly by quoting a long passage from a pamphlet he attributed to Hume (1834), of which the following is an extract:

> I remember well to have heard it frequently said of Buonaparte, at the time all this was going on, that he was constantly examining the English Price Current, in order to ascertain whether, and with what degree of success, his decrees were enforced by his own troops and obeyed by his allies. So long as he saw that gold was dear, and coffee was cheap, in England, he was satisfied that his continental system worked well. The English could see nothing in these documents but proof that the Bank was shamefully extending the issue of its notes.
> (Tooke 1848a, IV: 108–9; quoted from [Hume, J.D.] 1834: 29–31; also see Tooke 1848a, IV: 213–15)

51 Tooke and Newmarch (1857, VI: 154–5, 158) calculated that from 1849 to 1856 'total gold coinage' in England, France and the United States was £202 millions, adding about 30 per cent to the stock of gold in world monetary circulation.

52 Quoting Mill (1848 [1909]: 609), Tooke and Newmarch wrote:

> the United Kingdom has been in a pre-eminent degree the country whose Exportable Goods (native, or obtained elsewhere) have been 'most in demand abroad, – have contained the greatest value in the smallest bulk, – and have been (practically) the nearest to the Mining;' and therefore, that by far the largest proportion of the New Gold has been sent to this country.
> (1857, VI: 210)

53 However, with a distinctly 'mercantilist' tone, this analogy was taken a step further by Tooke and Newmarch than Adam Smith would have ever contemplated:

> if these illustrations have any force, it follows that, during some period, longer or shorter, an addition to the quantity of money is the same thing as an addition to the Fixed Capital of the country; and exerts on production an influence of the same kind as the provision of improved harbours, roads, or manufactories.
> (1857, VI: 216)

54 The possibility of a reduction in the cost of production of gold was considered to depend on the employment of improved methods of mining:

> We have now arrived, perhaps, at a point when the successful application of Machinery to the crushing of Quartz Rock may sooner or later effectually reduce the cost of producing Gold. It is quite possible that the Reduced Cost, and the increasing Quantity – for money produces its effects by means of volume as well as cost – may proceed more rapidly than the absorption of Gold in new countries, and by augmented dealings; – and so raise the range of General Prices.
> (Tooke and Newmarch 1857, VI: 227)

55 Another contributing factor in the deterioration in the trade balance alluded to by Tooke was the unfavourable terms of trade associated with the depreciation in the sterling exchange. Tooke noticed that this depreciation 'diminished the cost of all our exportable produce by so much to the foreign consumer' which brought about a 'depression of price of the latter description of productions, between 1808 and 1812' (1838, II: 347).

56 In particular, Tooke noticed the opening up of trade in South America after the independence of many states from Spanish colonial rule in the early-1820s.

57 In Appendix VIII of *History* (1857, VI), Tooke and Newmarch quoted an extract from a 1852 parliamentary (Mr Horner, chairman) report which was based on evidence of an 'eminent' engineer, providing a 'picture':

of Engines driven at higher speed; of Boilers augmented in Capacity; of Fuel saved; and of Invention constantly on the rack to discover new secrets of cheapening production; – contains an important warning against the hasty reception of views which involve the assumption in almost any form, that we have already exhausted the means of increasing the Gross Produce of our Manufactories.

(1857, VI: 533–4)

The extract particularly shows how technological advancements in steam-powered engines increased productivity in manufacturing, especially cotton production. As indicated elsewhere by Tooke and Newmarch (1857, V: 192–3n., 193), these advancements also increased productivity in agriculture as 'portable steam engines' (including 'Fowler's Steam Plough') was increasingly applied to farming around the mid-nineteenth century. Indeed, Tooke and Newmarch (1857, V: 193) presented statistics showing a significant increase in the number of portable steam engines of progressively higher horse-power sold to English farmers in the years 1852 to 1855.

6 The monetary thought of pre-banking school Tooke, 1819–1838

1 Rist (1940: 180–238) also discusses some aspects of Tooke's pre-banking school position, but the main focus is on Tooke's banking school monetary thought.

2 In order to elaborate on the 'great merits of Mr. Thornton's tract', Tooke (1848a, IV: 85–7) quotes long extracts from a review by Horner (1802: 173, 201) published in the *Edinburgh Review* praising the work.

3 The most influential campaigner for resumption within the Liverpool Government was William Huskisson and, outside of government, Ricardo. There were various sources of opposition to resumption. First, within the government, there was the Chancellor of the Exchequer, Vansittart, who was clearly concerned that the deflationary effect of resumption would undermine his system of re-financing public debt. It was partly to destroy Vansittart's system that Huskisson campaigned hard for resumption. Second, the Bank of England was concerned that, as a result of outstanding foreign loans and overseas investment flows, the unfavourable state of the exchanges would make it very difficult for them to prepare for resumption without inducing a severe deflation in the economy. The directors of the Bank were clearly worried about the adverse effect of deflation on the value of its very large holdings of government floating debt. Third, many bankers and merchants opposed resumption in the near future on the grounds that it would further aggravate the depression that was then being experienced in industry and agriculture. On the politics of the resumption of cash payments, see Hilton (1977: 31–77).

4 In contrast though to the claim by Hilton (1977: 91) that Tooke was 'outraged' by the Bank of England's early resumption of payments in cash (coin), the evidence in fact indicates he was quietly pleased with this outcome.

5 Tooke (1838, II: 107–8) attributed the improvement in the balance of payments and inflow of specie in 1819 and 1820 to the combined effect of (a) 'large sums due from abroad, for the unusually extensive exports of 1818'; (b) 'the shutting of our ports against importation of corn, and by the glut which prevailed here of other foreign products, in consequence of the large importations of 1818'; and (c) 'the improved state of finances which enabled and induced government to diminish the unfunded debt'. Interestingly, Tooke (1838, II: 109–10) offered 'contingencies which might have rendered Peel's bill operative in contracting the circulation': consisting of (a) a deficient domestic harvest which required a large importation of corn, (b) speculative activity in commodity markets and (c) large foreign loans and investment flows overseas, which all tend to induce an 'efflux' of specie.

6 Tooke indirectly referred to this difference in the following comment:

> It is curious to remark, that the state of things [i.e. depressed trade] which really rendered Peel's bill inoperative for the first few years after its enactment, should have been taken as the specific ground for the clamours against it, while, under opposite circumstances [i.e. an economic boom], when it would have been strictly coercive, there would not have been the slightest pretence for the complaints of those who have been most violently opposed to it.
>
> (1838, II: 110)

7 A similar approach has been taken by Arnon (1991: 46–54) in consideration of Tooke's earliest views, as principally contained in his evidence before the Resumption Committees of 1819.

8 In an illustration of the adjustment process, Tooke estimated that, after a reduction in the relative prices of tradable products, 'several months must elapse' before export orders are received from 'distant' foreign markets, while, additionally, in the 'common course of trade', a 'period of a year and a half, or two years, may elapse before the funds arising from such [resulting export] shipments can be made applicable to foreign payments' (1826: 106–7). This suggests that, depending on the logistics of foreign markets and the bulky nature of the commodities usually traded, the adjustment process, from the change in prices to the transmission of funds (i.e. credit/bullion) on traded products, may have taken from two to three years in duration.

9 The following passage from the Report of the 1810 Bullion Committee to which Tooke refers is very significant because it essentially underlies the argument of Ricardo and other classical quantity theorists for treating the velocity of Bank of England notes and coin as constant in the short run:

> If an excess of paper be issued in a country district, while the London circulation does not exceed its due proportion, there will be a local rise of prices in that country district, but prices in London will remain as before. Those who have the country paper in their hands, will prefer buying in London, where things are cheaper, and will therefore return that country paper being continually returned upon the issuers for Bank of England paper, the quantity of the latter necessarily and effectually limits the quantity of the former.
>
> (As quoted by Tooke 1829a: 31n.)

On this argument see Viner (1937: 154–65).

10 On the importance of the paper, Tooke wrote:

> I am indebted to my friend Mr. James Pennington for the means of making my conclusion on this point more complete. He has addressed a paper to me noticing an analogy, which has not, as far as I am aware, before been distinctly observed, between the book credits of the London bankers and the promissory notes of country banks. The point is so important, and bears so much upon the present subject, that I am induced, with Mr. Pennington's permission, to insert the paper containing his views upon it, and upon one or two topics connected with it, in the Appendix.
>
> (1829a: 32n.)

This paper was based heavily on an unpublished memorandum titled, 'Observations on the Private Banking Establishments of the Metropolis', prepared by Pennington for William Huskisson in 1826 (see Sayers 1963: xvii–xviii, xlv–li).

11 This letter was sent to Tooke to rebut the interpretation placed on the analysis of Pennington's 1829 paper by Torrens (1837). On this, see Tooke (1838, II: 337–8n.).

12 This is evident in the statement that

> when the market-rate is high, there must be an increased disposition on the part of government to apply to the bank for accommodation; as on the other hand, when it is low, to take the opportunity of paying off previous advances.

(Tooke 1826: 80)

For this reason, Tooke believed the debt-funding activities of the government tended to exacerbate pressures in the money market and the difficulties for the Bank in managing its issues. Also see Tooke (1829a: 52–3).

13 This concern was also expressed when, in a draft summary of the *Considerations* (1826) which Tooke sent to Lord Grenville with a letter dated 19 November 1825, he wrote:

> That the principal, if not the only medium, through which the Bank of England or indeed any Bank of circulation can extend its issue of paper money beyond what it may give out in the mere payments for purchases of bullion is that of loans to the state or to individuals and that it can only diminish its issues of notes, excepting such as may be cancelled against coin or bullion delivered from its coffers, by withdrawing or diminishing such loans; that consequently in extending or diminishing its issues beyond those limits it has a powerful influence on the rate of interest, as on the other hand its means of extending or contracting its circulation within limited intervals is very naturally affected by the rate of interest.

(*Grenville Papers*, British Library, Add. 69082, reprinted in Tooke 1996: 136–7)

14 This is illustrated in the following answers Tooke gave to the Bank Charter Committee of 1832:

> Q 5469 You have stated that the increased issues by the Banks would have an effect upon credit, rather than upon the prices of commodities; do you conceive that it would have any effect upon the prices of commodities? – Tooke: That must depend on the circumstances under which the enlarged issues were made; at the moment of an enlarged issue, if specially advanced to enable merchants to export or to import more or to work up more raw materials than they otherwise would have done, they would, *pro tanto*, add to the prices.
>
> Q 5470 Then the effect upon the prices is not produced by the addition to the circulating medium, but by the additional facility given to commercial transactions? – Tooke: Yes, at periods when, from the circumstances of trade, or of a particular commodity, there is a tendency from other causes to a rise in the price.

(1832: 443)

15 A 'partisan' who came in for much criticism by Tooke (1832: (Q 3840–6) 273–5, (Q 2994–5) 291, (Q 5439) 440; 1838, I: 10–11) was Robert Mushet, author of *An attempt to explain from facts the effect of the issues of the Bank of England* (1826).

16 This was linked to his view that under a convertible system of currency that 'there can be no great range in the actual quotations of the Exchanges' such that a bullion 'drain may be very considerable, while the indication of the Exchanges is not so' (1832: (Q 3884) 280).

17 Whereas Ricardo (1821: 90–1) conceived of the remuneration of risk and trouble as a magnitude proportional to the rate of interest so that both parts were stable *proportions* of the normal profit rate, Smith (1776 [1976]: 69–70) conceived of the magnitude of this remuneration as a percentage return on the capital employed in production so that a rise (fall) in the 'ordinary rate of profit' will be associated with a rise (decline) in the money rate as a proportion of the normal profit rate matched by a decline (rise) in the remuneration of risk and trouble as a proportion of the normal profit rate. On the respective conceptions of the relationship between interest and profit of Adam Smith and Ricardo, see Pivetti (1987: 63–8).

18 Central to the argument of McCulloch is the proposition that the '[T]he average rate of profit is the real barometer – the true and infallible criterion of national prosperity' (1824a: 8). Upon this basis and invoking the causal relation between the interest rate and profit rate that 'one is always directly as the other', he infers that where

> the rate of interest is low, as in Holland and England, it is an equally conclusive proof that the profits of stock are also low – that those are countries in which it is no longer possible to employ capital and labour with much advantage.
>
> (1824a: 9)

McCulloch's argument ultimately relied on the predominance of diminishing returns to agriculture which, in the absence of the free importation of cheaper necessaries, would lead to a higher proportion of output devoted to wages, and, thereby, a higher real wage, so driving down the rate of profit and slowing accumulation in relatively advanced countries.

19 Another 'source of error' identified by Tooke which is more specifically directed at McCulloch (1824a) seems to relate to deficiencies in the measurement of the rate of profit as a basis for empirical comparison with the money rate of interest:

> that while the returns to the whole national capital laid out with a view to repro-duction, are, and must be, estimated in kind (supposing that there were means of making such estimate), the rate of interest is always computed in money; con-sequently, profits estimated in money are not, necessarily, in the ratio of national profits estimated in commodities: the variation of the one is not, therefore, neces-sarily indicative of the variation of the other.
>
> (1826: 9–10)

This criticism by Tooke is significant in that it suggests he was fully aware of the so-called 'measurement problem' in Ricardo's theory of determining the rate of profit as a residual distributive variable. The 'measurement problem', which became the subject of debate among classical economists in the 1820s, concerns the problem with the labour theory of value in the general case of an economy which produces hetero-geneous products (see De Vivo 1984). Recognition of this theoretical problem by Tooke may in fact help explain his tendency of treating the profit rate as an exogenous distributive variable, as explained in Section 3.2.3.

20 On these grounds Tooke (1826: 9) claimed that the position of McCulloch (1824a; see n.18 above) led to the absurd proposition

> that the rate of profit, and the power of accumulation, must be greater in war than in peace; and the final conclusion would be, that perpetual war would be attended with perpetual prosperity: a conclusion so monstrous, that it must naturally lead to a suspicion, or rather to a conviction, that the premises are unsound.

21 It is worthwhile quoting Tooke fully on this to show the similarities with the concep-tion which was, in particular, later developed by Wicksell (1898: 102–21):

> A material consideration to be here borne in mind is, that it is only as long those capitals are floating, or disposable, that they operate on the rate of interest. When once they are invested, whether for a long time or a short time, they are out of the competition of *lendable* capitals, and ceased to affect, directly, the rate of interest. Thus, if I have invested my monied capital in the purchase of exchequer bills or in the discount of mercantile bills, however undoubted in point of security, and at however short a date, that sum is withdrawn from the amount of floating or dis-posable capital. I may, indeed, if I have a sudden occasion to require so much money for immediate use, re-sell or re-discount the bills, but then this sum must be withdrawn from the amount of floating or disposable capital in other quarters.
>
> (1826: 18)

22 Furthermore, Tooke considered 'the rate of interest at any given period may vary according to the length of the term and to the convertibility of the security' (1826: 14n.). He proposed that the interest rate would be higher on longer-dated securities and those with less marketability than those more easily convertible short-dated ones. On this basis, Tooke explained why the rate of interest on exchequer bills was lower than other government securities and why the rate on 'advances on mortgages of the best description' are usually higher than on 'mercantile bills of the most unexceptionable credit at short date' (1826: 14n.). Hence, to estimate 'the general rate of interest at any particular time', Tooke held that '[A]ll the circumstances which determine the greater or less eligibility of investment according to the greater or less *facility and certainty of conversion* are to be taken into account' (1826: 14n.; emphasis added).

23 On this distinction Tooke divided productive borrowers into two generic classes in order to show the change in the motive for borrowing which accompanied a speculative boom-and-then-bust scenario. This sub-classification was specifically adopted by Tooke to explain the role of the loan market in the speculative process leading up to the financial crisis of 1825 and its aftermath.

24 Interestingly, in a clear reference to the large-scale re-conversion of British government debt to a lower interest rate structure in 1822 and 1824, Tooke (1826: 21–2) argued that a reduction in the rate of interest on the 'best class of securities' (i.e. government securities) may well cause 'monied capitalists' to shift into more risky investments rather than 'submitting to a diminished income'. In accordance with Tooke's analysis, this involved a fundamental change in the attitude of wealth-holders towards risk, reflected by a shift from the first and second to the third class of lenders. This viewpoint in fact plays an important part in Tooke's explanation for the speculative boom in the London share market of 1824 and 1825 (see Smith 1996a: xvi–xix).

25 There is an inconsistency here between Tooke's analysis of the determination of the average rate of interest and his statement that equilibrium exists when '*capital* in the scientific use of the term as applied to the actual funds destined for reproduction, consisting of raw materials &c.' is 'identical' to '*monied capital*' (1826: 23n.; 1838, II: 361n.). As clearly shown above (pp. 150–51), Tooke believed a proportion of monied capital would always go to unproductive expenditures (i.e. military and naval supplies, civilian consumption of final goods etc.) which did not contribute to reproduction. In our view the interpretation given in the sentence is more consistent with Tooke's intended conception.

26 It is interesting to note that Gilbart recognised that in situations when the financial market was dominated by a government (or sovereign) borrowing funds for non-commercial expenditure, the orthodox view of interest and profit broke down:

> When a number of commercial men borrow money off one another, the *permanent* regulator of the rate of interest is the rate of profit; and the *immediate* regulator is the proportion between demand and supply. But when a new party comes into the market, who has no common interest with them, who does not borrow money to trade with, but to spend, the permanent regulator (the rate of profit) loses its influence, and the sole regulator is then the proportion between the demand and the supply ... in this artificial state of the money market, it appears reasonable to suppose that the rate of interest may have regulated the rate of profits, instead of the rate of profits regulating the rate of interest, which is the natural state.
>
> (1834: 168–9)

27 While Joplin (1823: 62–7) had earlier proposed 'profits of trade are regulated by the interest of money', he did not provide a convincing explanation for his position.

28 A strong case for joint-stock banking had been made earlier by Thomas Joplin in his influential pamphlet, *On the General Principles and Present Practice of Banking in Scotland and England* (1822).

29 With the renewal of the Bank of England's Charter in 1833, the British government introduced some regulations on joint-stock banks. These consisted of note-issuing joint-stock banks having to pay up one-half of their capital, the partners of deposit-only joint-stock banks subject to limited liability and all banks required to prepare a regular statement of its accounts for the confidential information of the government (see Thomas 1934: 173–5).

30 Tooke (1826: 125, 143, 195) advocated the publication of half-yearly accounts of banking transactions and profit and loss statements in the same detail as then provided by the Bank of France.

31 For Tooke's more considered views on this issue, see (1832: (Q 3872–8): 278–9, (Q 3897–9) 281, (Q 3918–19) 283, (Q 5416) 437).

32 In 1848, Tooke expressed satisfaction that

> [W]ith regard to the Country Banks, I consider that the Substitution of Joint Stock Banks for a large Proportion of the smaller private Banks has been the Cause of much greater Security of the Banking System than existed in 1825.
>
> (1848c: (Q 2986) 334)

33 Tooke (1826: 108) suggested a tough monetary stance might well impede trade adjustment by inducing 'a depression of credit, greater or less, in the places abroad with which we have any considerable intercourse', thereby arresting the foreign purchase of (cheaper) exports.

34 As discussed in Section 4.4, Tooke argued that after 1815 the English Corn Laws tended to increase the lumpiness of corn imports.

35 Among the causes of an external drain, Tooke (1826: 104) also listed monetary operations by foreign governments such as 'the conversion of the French rentes' or 'extensive re-coinages abroad', which cause a strong foreign demand for specie.

36 This position seems to accord with the 'Palmer Rule' which consisted of maintaining a bullion reserve approximately equal to one-third of the Bank of England's notes and deposits when the whole circulation was full and the exchanges were at the point of falling below par (i.e. depreciating). This rule formed the basis of the Bank's management of the currency under the Governorship of J. Horsely Palmer (1830–1833), who first revealed it in evidence to the Bank Charter Committee of 1832. On the origins of the Palmer Rule, see Horsefield (1940) and Fetter (1965: 132–3).

37 Tooke claimed that by adopting the 'rule of an invariable rate of discount' the Bank's 'control' over its note circulation was 'most unmanageable and irregular' since it tended 'to overflow, or run dry, according as the market rate of interest exceeded or fell short, in any marked degree, of the rate prescribed by the Bank' (1829a: 54–5). On the wrongheaded adoption of this policy rule by the directors of the Bank, Tooke wrote: '[T]hey might, indeed, in strictness be said to possess the power over the supply of paper through the medium of discounts, but they made a rule of not exercising it' (1829a: 55).

7 The monetary thought of the banking school Tooke, 1840–1857

1 This is chapter 5 of *History of Prices* (1840a, III) titled, 'Observations on a recent publication by Mr Samuel Jones Loyd, "On the Management of the Circulation, and on the condition and conduct of the Bank of England, and of the country issues, during the year 1839."'

2 Other significant contributors to the currency school include Samson Ricardo (1838) and Clay (1844). On the Currency School and its plan, see Fetter (1965: 165–72).

3 In particular, Overstone (1840b: (Q 3092–3132, 3147–8, 3151–9, 3176–92) 459–77) was aggressively cross-examined to the point of exasperation by Joseph Hume on why he did not regard bank deposits as money. On bills of exchange, see Overstone (1840b: (Q 3026–38) 446–8, (Q 3072–8) 449–53).

4 As noted in Chapter 3, n.12, Smith's conception is based on a circulating capital model. On this basis 'gross product' here is what Adam Smith called 'neat revenue', which he derived by deducting from 'annual produce' that part which is 'used for replacement and enhancement of *fixed* capital' so that it 'contains many materials and provisions which are needed for replacement – workers wages being the most obvious' (O'Donnell 1990: 38). Hence, according to O'Donnell (1990: 38), what Smith called '[T]he value … of what has been consumed and produced' (1776 [1976]: 675) or 'the consumable goods annually circulated within the society' (1776 [1976]: 340) was essentially a measure of social consumption. On this basis, by means of vertical integration, the cost of intermediate commodities will be imputed into the final value of commodities consumed.

5 That Tooke is likely to have understood that Smith's conception was limited to a 'circulating capital' model (as mentioned in Chapter 3, n.12) is indicated when, immediately after quoting this passage, he wrote:

> Assuredly, then, the prices at which commodities have gone into consumption, the result of them constituting the return for the *capital expended in the production*, may be considered with greater propriety than any other description as general prices.
>
> (1844: 71; emphasis added)

While according to Smith's adding-up approach to prices the value of the gross product *resolves itself* into income, it does not follow that in a circulating capital model the final expenditures by 'consumers' from 'dealers' will equal expenditures by dealers from dealers in the intermediate stages of production and distribution. This is because part of total consumption (out of gross income) will consist of expenditure on material inputs used in production by dealers from dealers. Nevertheless, this conceptual error in Tooke's dual-circulation framework does not significantly affect the conclusions of his monetary analysis. On this point, see also Mill (1844: 589) and Marx (1885, II: 479–81; 1894, III: 842; including quotation in Chapter 3, n.13).

6 While Tooke had essentially set out this law in the *Inquiry* (1844), he later acknowledged that a 'very clear and full statement' (1848a, IV: 185n.) of it had been provided by Fullarton (1845: 65–8). Indeed, so impressed was Tooke he quoted it at length in volume IV of *History* (1848a, IV: 178–81).

7 As pointed out by Tooke (1848a, IV: 184–5), in England gold coin could only be readily obtained from the Bank of England; while borrowers of country banks would often be accommodated by bills drawn on correspondent banks in the City of London (or Liverpool).

8 Consistent with the intention of Tooke's conception, social income is equivalent to the *net income* of society. However, as indicated in note 5 of this chapter, there is a lack of analytical consistency between this conception by Tooke (which he shared with most contemporaries) and his view of the determination of social income according to Adam Smith's method of resolution of value.

9 However, Tooke (1848a, IV: 193–7) conceded to Torrens (1844: 48–9) that a long-term loan on mortgage could, by keeping out banknotes for an extended period of time, facilitate increased expenditures which could contribute to a higher temporary rise in prices than would have otherwise occurred.

10 Tooke (1844: 79–80) also referred to and quoted from Bosanquet (1842: 73).

11 To make his point, Tooke quotes from two passages by Gilbart (1841: 7, 19). Essentially Gilbart argued that if, for example, the Bank of England were to purchase a million pounds sterling of exchequer bills on the open market, the resulting increase in bank deposits would increase the power of purchase of depositors who, 'to make the most advantageous investments, would have the effect of advancing the prices of commodities, and of stimulating a spirit of speculation' (1841: 19; also quoted by Tooke 1844: 78).

12 In reference to the extract from the *Considerations* (1826: 11–30) which was republished as 'Appendix A' of volume II of *History* (1838, II: 355–64), the banking school Tooke wrote: 'Of the causes which determine the rate of interest, I have given an explanation of some length in the former part of this work' (1840a, III: 143). Also see Tooke (1856: 72).

13 Tooke (1840a, III: 268) argued that even if such a policy was to be effectively employed, in a gold convertible system it could only be done so for a short period of time since there would be an external outflow of bullion and the foreign exchanges would decline, so exerting upward pressure on the rate of interest.

14 However, as is discussed in Section 7.4, Tooke believed Bank of England policy which contributed to interest-rate instability would have an adverse effect on commercial trade.

15 Despite this clarification by Tooke of the 'apparent inconsistency' (1844:123) in his position, Wicksell (1898: 99; 1906: 186–7) was not satisfied with his reasoning. With reference to Tooke's distinction between the different effects on the balance of payments of temporary compared with permanent changes in the rate of interest, Wicksell commented that 'the same procedure has precisely opposite consequences according as it is applied for a long or for a short period' and '[T]his seems a doubtful possibility' (1898: 99). As Pivetti (1991: 83) has pointed out, this criticism by Wicksell is curious given that Wicksell employed the same kind of distinction in his own monetary analysis.

16 Also see Tooke (1848b: (Q 5353–4) 417–18; 1848c: (Q 3044–5) 341), in which he argues that actual average levels of bullion reserves held by the Bank of England over the period 1832–1841 were considerably less than what he regarded as safe.

17 When asked by the 1848 Commons Committee on Commercial Distress over what period did the average reserve of bullion refer to, Tooke answered that it depended 'very much upon circumstances' (1848b: (Q 5361) 419); but, no doubt with the cycle of trade flows in mind, he indicated that it would be no more than five years (1848b: (Q 5370) 420).

18 However, elsewhere Tooke maintained this reflux of bullion could occur without any significant alteration in the foreign exchanges:

> there may be variations of international payments, in other words, of a balance of trade, without any grounds for inference of alterations in the value of the currencies of the countries from which or to which such balance may be due ... an occasional efflux of four or five or six millions would be followed at no distant period by a fully equal reflux. Such was the case in 1828–29 and 1831–32, when the treasure of the Bank having been reduced by five or six millions was replenished without the slightest operation of the Bank on the amount of its securities, or its rate of interest.
>
> (1844: 107)

19 Tooke believed the Bank of England proprietors were actually being short-sighted because in the long run 'their real interests are bound up with the permanence of the establishment, which can only be preserved in as far as it may be found to be conducive to the public interests' (1840a, III: 194).

20 Tooke also rejected the idea advanced by one witness before the 1848 Lords Committee on the Causes of Commercial Distress that independent 'Commissioners' be appointed by the government to the Court of Directors for fixed terms under an Act of Parliament (Tooke and Newmarch 1857, V: 607–13).

21 Provision was made in Tooke's proposal for the four ex-Directors to be eligible for a vacancy should it arise before the term of office of directors had ended.

22 As well as providing valuable assistance at times of crisis, Tooke argued a third governor would increase the weight of authority of the Governors in determination of Bank policy:

A third person in the discussion of difficult and delicate questions involving the consideration of a great variety of contingencies, is of great advantage both as moderator between two persons, [with] antagonistic opinions, and as, probably, suggesting additional facts and views which had not occurred to the other two. And there would be this further great advantage, that the proposal coming before the Committee of Treasury and the Directors, as the united judgement of three highly competent persons, would naturally carry much greater weight than if proceeding from two only.

(Tooke and Newmarch 1857, V: 629)

23 By this system of appointment Tooke contended 'there can hardly be a doubt that the services of persons of the highest order of ability, suited to the situations to be filled, might be secured' and

with Governors so eminently qualified; and with rules and regulations provided by the Directors as precautions against their own liability to crude discussion and hasty decision; the Bank of England would command an amount of confidence, both from the public and the Government, beyond any that it has enjoyed for many years past.

(1857, V: 632)

24 In the extraordinary case of an unreconciled difference of opinion between the Governors over a policy question, Tooke proposed it should be put in writing and 'the Committee [of Treasury] or the Court [of Directors] would have to decide upon that difference' (1857, V: 630).

25 In reference to his earlier approval of this extension of the circulation of Bank of England notes at the expense of country banknotes, Tooke stated to the 1848 Lords Committee on the Causes of Commercial Distress:

I am not sure that I should have given it so unreservedly ... had I been aware that it would be, as it has been occasionally, the Cause of a great deal of Confusion of reasoning as to the Character of the Bank of England Note [since] it seems to have had some Influence in investing, according to general Opinion, the Bank Note with some peculiar Properties which I do not think it is entitled to, that is, in distinguishing it from other Species of Paper Obligations.

(1848b: (Q 2989) 334).

26 This view by Tooke appears to lend support to the argument by Goodhart (1989b) that central banking owes its development to the natural advantages to a banking system of centralising reserves at one public institution. Also see Tooke (1840b: (Q 3797–9) 364, (Q 3845) 368–9; 1844: 58–9).

27 It is evident Tooke believed that at times of financial pressure the quantity of Bank of England notes actually tended to expand in response to the demand for liquidity, writing of the internal drain that occurred in the 1847 crisis: 'the gold was not wanted in exchange for Bank of England notes. These were equally in demand to supply the vacuum caused by the discredit, greater or less, of all other paper' (1848a, IV: 347–8).

28 Hence, in reference to the currency school's plan for separation of the Bank of England, Tooke wrote:

It does not appear to be a necessary, and hardly, perhaps, a probable, consequence of the proposed separation, that every action upon the bullion by the foreign exchanges should be attended with a simultaneous action upon the amount of the circulation; by which term of circulation I mean the amount of bank notes in the hands of the public.

(1840a, III: 254)

Also see Tooke (1840b: (Q 3716–19) 351–2).

29 This thinking stemmed from what Tooke (1857, V: 544–5) argued was the 'errone-ous' view of the currency school that, but for its note-issuing monopoly, the Bank of England was no different to other London private banks.

30 However, while Tooke (1857, V: 588n.) recognised the Bank of England's more com-petitive behaviour post-1844 was 'more profitable', he stopped short of concluding that it was an important reason why, when the 1844 Bank Act was first proposed by the Peel government, it obtained the 'cordial concurrence and co-operation of the Bank Directors' (1857, V: 527) who, later as witnesses before the 1848 parliamentary committees on the Causes of Commercial Distress, 'were uncompromising defenders of the Act of 1844' (1857, V: 499).

31 In particular, Tooke (1848b: (Q 5312–13) 411–12; 1848c: (Q 3041–2) 341) argued that provisions restricting the issue of banknotes in England and Wales under the 1844 Bank Act and in Scotland and Ireland under the companion 1845 Bank Act sig-nificantly exacerbated the position of the Bank of England by encouraging all other private banks in the United Kingdom to hold higher reserves of bullion and Bank of England notes. He estimated 'the treasure of the Bank [of England] in the autumn of 1846, was less £2,000,000 than it would have been but for those Acts" (1848b: (Q 5312) 411).

32 On his rebuttal of the currency school's defence on the grounds the 1847 crisis was largely the result of bad management by the Bank of England, see Tooke (1848a, IV: 348–96).

33 In support of this argument, Tooke pointed out that in 1847 'the lowest Amount of Bullion in the Two Departments [of the Bank of England] was £8,438,874' (1848c: (Q 3003) 336). He maintained that with an 'undivided' reserve the pressure on the Bank of England and the resulting variation in the rate of interest would have been no greater in 1847 than it was during the monetary pressures in 1836–1837 and 1839 (1848c: (Q 3006–10) 336–7).

34 The relatively low and stable interest rates over the period from mid-1848 to end-1852 was attributed by Tooke (1857, V: 597) to the large supplies of gold from Cali-fornia and Eastern Australia, which continually replenished the bullion reserve of the Bank of England. He indicated that but for these large gold supplies, interest rate instability in the 1850s would have been greater than it actually was (1857, V: 561–2, 576, 593).

35 From April 1847 to January 1848, Tooke ascertained the market rate of interest on short-term bills varied considerably more 'from 4 per cent. to 12, 15 and 20 per cent., [before having] fallen back to less than 4 per cent.' (1857, V: 400).

36 It is evident from his discussion of the currency principle that Tooke (1844: 1–6; 1848a, IV: 166–71) considered it a narrow version of the early-nineteenth-century classical economists' quantity theory of money because of its contention that price stability required 'the Bank notes in circulation should be made to conform to the gold, into which they are convertible, not only in value, but in amount' (1844: 2).

37 For example, an expansionary policy stance by the Bank of England which, as in the mid-1840s railway boom, facilitated speculative activity and heightened prices, will, according to Tooke, lead to a higher V_m than if it adopted a restrictive policy stance. On the other hand, the adoption of a restrictive monetary policy in circumstances of depression and low confidence is likely to be associated with a fall in VmY as a panic-stricken financial market scrambles for liquidity by selling off stocks, so forcing prices ever lower.

38 By contrast, the currency school maintained that, though initially caused by real factors, variations in the price level accommodated by changes in the quantity of cir-culating medium (i.e. M^* for given V_m^*), could only occur if there was accommodat-ing changes in Bank of England notes and coin (i.e. M). In this regard, an accommodating change in M was conceived to be of a smaller proportional magnitude than of M^* so that $1 > \Delta M^*/\Delta M$, associated with $V_m > V_n$, when $P_m > P_n$, and, with

$V_m < V_n$, when $P_m < P_n$, and, given $Y_m \approx Y_n$. In accord with the currency principle, price stability could be achieved by ensuring $M \approx M_n$ so that causally, $M^* \approx M_n^*$.

39 A speculative boom centred on the share market cannot be properly accounted for in the income-form of the monetary equations employed in the text. It could only be accounted for by the inclusion of asset prices into nominal income.

40 Hence, according to Tooke, the ratio M^*/M would tend to change in sympathy with changes in nominal income (and therefore the demand for money) as principally caused by price fluctuations.

41 This mechanism is most evident in Tooke's explanation for the significant rise in income (especially wages) and prices that occurred in the United Kingdom during the 1850s. Tooke and Newmarch (1857, VI: 204–13) largely attributed this development to strong growth in export income which, in turn, generated higher imports. The mechanism also clearly lies behind Tooke's early arguments for the British government to unilaterally adopt freer trade, as examined in Section 3.6. Also see Tooke (1819b: 171; 1857, V: 448–51, 483–5).

42 For the currency school's criticism of Tooke for inconsistency, see Torrens (1844: 1–2) and Clay (1844: 29–41).

43 That part of this passage which follows the first two sentences was quoted with approval by Tooke in the 'Preface' of volume IV of *History* (1848a: xi–xii).

44 They first appear in chapters IV and V of this volume which are devoted to controversies over the management of the currency by the Bank of England and included an examination of the proposals for the separation of the Bank by the currency school. Thus, in the preface, Tooke wrote:

> If the earlier [three] volumes of the present work be critically examined, there will be found in them some remains (chiefly, however, in the phraseology) of my former attachment to the currency theory, as it was generally received, before it had been caricatured by the modern school.
>
> (1848a, IV: x)

45 It is nevertheless significant that the period 1836–1840 is Tooke's most productive, writing the first three volumes of *History of Prices*. It is also during this period that the currency school emerged and their main policy proposal for dividing the note-issuing and banking functions of the Bank of England, which became the basis of the 1844 Bank Charter Act, gained influential support.

46 This is particularly evident in Section III, 'Upon the Regulation of the Bank Issues', of the *Considerations* (1826: 65–85). The *Considerations* is in fact important to the early development of Tooke's monetary thought because, as discussed in Smith (1996a: xl–xlvi), it represented his first attempt to systematically deal with monetary questions and to develop a distinct theoretical position. A different viewpoint is offered by both Fullarton (1845: 19), who believed the pamphlet could 'have been the production of Mr. Loyd and Mr. Norman', and Marx (1859: 186), who considered it 'could even be regarded as the first consistent exposition of the views which Overstone was to set forth later'.

47 In contradiction to Gregory's (1928: ix) view, quoted by Viner (1937: 218), that 'after 1832' monetary debate in Britain 'produced much heat and little light', we would argue that the development of banking school thought, principally by Tooke, but also by Fullarton (1845), as well as the contributions of J.S. Mill (1844), was *the light* stemming from *the heat* of the currency–banking school debates. However, this 'light' represents a repudiation of the classical economists' quantity theory approach.

8 Tooke's legacy

1 Economic historians who greatly benefited from Tooke's *History*, include Clapham (1959; 1963), Fetter (1965), Hilton (1977), King (1936) and Morgan (1965).

2 In particular, Overstone readily acknowledged his debt, frequently citing Tooke's pre-banking school writings to support his own views. In praise of him, Overstone wrote that Tooke was 'a writer, whose authority is entitled to the greatest weight, both on account of the extreme care which he balances conflicting considerations and the measured and cautious language in which his conclusions are stated' (1840a: 109). Also, see Torrens (1844: 44, 55).

3 In the currency–banking school debates Torrens was also highly critical of other banking school members, notably Fullarton, Wilson and J.S. Mill. Mainly based on a re-assertion of the currency school position, Torrens' criticisms were not particularly penetrating. However, for a sympathetic account of Torrens' critique of the banking school, see Robbins (1958: 121–43).

4 Another important progenitor who was not much influenced by Tooke is Irving Fisher.

5 In Mill's article there are no less than six references to Tooke's *Considerations* (see Mill 1826: 76–7, 86n.1, 92n., 97n., 109n., 111).

6 In a nutshell, Mill argued that '[S]upposing … the actual comforts of the labourer remain the same, profits will fall or rise, according as the population, or improvements in the production of food and other necessaries, advance fastest' (1844 [1874]: 106). He followed the Ricardian view that there was a tendency for the rate of profit to decline with the 'progress of society' because, with diminishing returns in agriculture, the growth in population would tend to raise the price of necessaries. On the other hand, Mill recognised that this tendency could be mitigated by technological 'improvements in agriculture, and in the production of those manufactured articles which the labourers consume' (1844 [1874]: 106).

7 A major change in the *Principles* was Mill's adoption of 'abstinence' as a determining factor of the minimum rate of profit:

> there is in every country some rate of profit, below which persons in general will not find sufficient motive to save for the mere purpose of growing richer, or of leaving others better off than themselves. Any accumulation, therefore, by which the general capital is increased, requires as its necessary condition a certain rate of profit; a rate which an average person will deem to be an equivalent for abstinence, with the addition of a sufficient insurance against risk.
>
> (1848 [1909]: 729)

It is well-known that Mill derived this notion from Senior (1836: 58–9).

8 In the *Principles*, Mill (1848 [1909]: 407, 637) divided gross profits into three parts: interest as the remuneration for 'abstinence', 'insurance' as the remuneration for risk and 'wages of superintendence' as the remuneration for 'exertion' or 'trouble'. It is evident Mill regarded the element of insurance to be determined independently of interest by the risks usually connected with the employment of capital in a particular line of business. He therefore conceived that profits less insurance resolved itself into interest and wages of superintendence.

9 This point about 'security of repayment' was later emphasised by Tooke in the *Inquiry* (1844: 80–1).

10 Under the influence of Tooke's early writings, this view had been taken up early on by Mill (1826).

11 See Mill (1848 [1909]: 521n., 533–5, 536n., 554, 648, 652–5, 665). There are also numerous references to Fullarton (1845) by Mill (1848 [1909]: 498, 500n., 537, 652–5, 668–70, 675).

12 An important aspect of Mill's articulation of the quantity theory is a clear restatement of the classical notion that in the long run the 'value of money' is determined by the 'cost of production' of gold so that the quantity theory only concerns short-run variations in the price level around its average level as fixed to the gold standard (1848 [1909]: 499–506). In this manner Mill makes it clear that his monetary analysis is

entirely consistent with the classical approach to value. With regard to his qualifica-tion of the quantity theory, Mill (1848 [1909]: 490–8, 524–5) maintained that an increase in the quantity of money would raise prices only if, other things being the same, it constituted an increase in the quantity of money *in circulation*, by which he meant that it facilitated an increase in spending on commodities. Mill's apparent apprehension about the quantity theory is likely to have emanated from concerns about the transmission mechanism, most prominently brought to his attention by the banking school writings of Tooke and Fullarton.

13 As Panico (1988: 47–9, 197n.1) has pointed out, these writings of Marx have in fact received very little attention in the literature.

14 According to the incomplete 'Name Index', there are twenty-four page references in this volume to Tooke and eleven to Fullarton. In other works by Marx, Tooke is cited on several occasions in *A Contribution to a Critique of Political Economy* (1859: 98, 178–9, 185–7) and, sporadically, in Parts I and II of *Theories of the Surplus Approach* (1861–1863). Though not generously acknowledged by Marx, J.S. Mill was also a major influence on the formulation of his monetary thought (see Marx 1859: 191–2; 1867: 125n.1; 1894: 389, 398, 519, 575, 878; also Panico 1988: 56–9, 96–7).

15 While there is an element of truth in Marx's criticism, it is evident Tooke was aware that banknotes were used to settle transactions between 'dealers and producers'. For example, Tooke (1844: 35) discusses how banknotes were still commonly used in much rural trade.

16 Marx (1894: 443–4) uses the example of money received in the form of banknotes and coin by retail merchants in payment for consumer products. This same money is revenue to the retail merchant, which is deposited in a bank and is used to pay for intermediate products (i.e. capital) by way of cheques drawn on the retailer's bank deposit.

17 While the evidence shows that the amplitude of fluctuations in the rate of interest defi-nitely increased, it does not support Marx's other contention that the rate of interest was 'on average' higher after the inception of the 1844 Bank Act than before it. It might be noted that the argument over the centralisation of bullion reserves under control of the Bank of England raged in England during the 1860s until settled by Bagehot (1873) (see Fetter 1965: 255–83).

18 On Mill's considerable influence on Marshall, see Groenewegen (1995: 145–9, 154–8).

19 On Marshall's monetary analysis and his explanation of the general level of prices, see Bridel (1987: 7–24) and Eshag (1963). On the possible influence of Marshall on Wicksell, it is evident Wicksell (1898 [1936]: 46, 76) closely studied much of Mar-shall's contributions on monetary questions to government inquiries. Thus, on the question of how the quantity of gold in the banks influences the level of prices, Wick-sell referred to Marshall's evidence to the Royal Commission on the Value of Gold and Silver (1887–1888) as '[B]y far the most valuable contribution towards a solution of this question' (1898: 76).

20 On fluctuations in trade and prices, Overstone (1840a: 87, 109; 'Appendix A' 147–8, 'Appendix D' 150–2) heavily cites the authority of Tooke's *History of Prices* (1838, I–II), of which Marshall would have been aware.

21 Nescience of this point has been a major source of unjust criticism of Tooke's posi-tion on the influence of the rate of interest on prices. Hence, it is significant that Wick-sell (1898: 88–92; 1906: 184–7) criticised Tooke for disputing the argument that a lowering of the rate of interest was an inducement to increased bank borrowing and increased monetary expenditure largely on the basis of his own marginal productivity theory of capital and investment (Pivetti 1991: 81–4). Following Wicksell, Gregory (1928: 22–31), Marget (1938: 189–205), Schumpeter (1954: 709n.11) and Humphrey (1979) have also committed the error of assessing Tooke's position from the stand-point of marginalist analysis.

22 It can be argued in classical economics that in the short run there is an inverse causal relationship running from changes in the money rate of interest to aggregate expenditure, but that this relationship is *non-functional* in that the causal effect is contingent on a set of other factors existing in the given situation. In consideration of investment spending, only long-lived investment in fixed capital (e.g. building construction) in which depreciation and technological obsolescence are not significant factors in the investment decision is likely to be sensitive to a temporary change in interest rates. Hence, for example, in the event of a temporary lowering of the money rate in relation to the long-run normal rate of profit it will be profitable for firms to take advantage of the lower cost of borrowing and increase capital expenditure on long-lived projects; whilst in the opposite case of a temporary increase in interest rates firms will tend to postpone long-lived investment spending. However, if the change in interest rates is considered lasting so that the long-run normal rate of return is expected to adjust accordingly, then no such effect on the inducement to long-lived investment will occur (Pivetti 1991: 43–5). In affluent societies in which a sizable proportion of households are home-mortgage holders and a significant proportion of consumption is financed by credit, the impact of interest rates on aggregate spending in the short run is in fact likely to work more reliably through its effect on consumption than through its effect on investment. Hence, for example, if household debt is relatively high, consumption spending is likely to be sensitive to a change in interest rates that affects the debt-servicing burden on households and, therefore, the level of disposable income in the short run. The sensitivity of consumption to interest rates is, however, likely to be less in societies in which household debt is not significant.

23 On the *non-functional* connection between the money rate of interest and spending in classical economics, see Caminati (1981) and Pivetti (1991: 41–51).

24 On the incorporation of Keynes's theory of output into classical analysis, see, in particular, Garegnani (1983a: 61–3), Kurz (1985), Vianello (1985) and Ciccone (1986).

25 Given that firms, for competitive purposes, normally maintain spare productive capacity, there is normally unutilised capacity in the economic system that can be exploited (Steindl 1952: 4–14). The additional production of capital goods associated with a utilisation of capacity above the normal utilisation will, in the long run, increase productive capacity itself and maintain planned spare capacity. By so allowing for persistent as well as temporary variations in the utilisation of productive capacity, long-run output has the elasticity to accommodate changes in aggregate demand free of steady-state conditions (Garegnani 1992).

26 This was the point of Keynes' (1937a: 206–11) 'revolving-fund' doctrine, whereby a flow of positive net investment in excess of *planned* saving is financed by newly created bank credit. Through the expenditure-multiplier process, an increased level of income will bring forth the necessary savings to service the higher stock of debt (or liabilities) of the private sector (and/or public sector) and restore equilibrium between planned investment and saving associated with ongoing capital formation. The crucial point is that the capacity of the banking system to make finance available for investment is not constrained (at least in the short run) by planned saving. On this issue, see Wray (1988; 1990: 155–92) and Terzi (1986–1987).

27 This argument can be represented in a simple model in which it is assumed that all transactions in the economy are performed by bank deposit transfers only. The balance sheet of the banking system can be expressed as $D = L + R$, where D is deposits, L is loans and R is bank reserves. Let us then suppose that bank reserves are determined on the basis of a reserve ratio, r, expressing the proportion between cash reserves and deposits liabilities: $R = r.D$. From $L = D - R$, can be obtained $L = D - r.D$ and, by re-arrangement, $D = L/(1 - r)$. In this latter equation, L is exogenously determined by the demand for finance which, given r, endogenously determines the volume of bank deposits, D. Furthermore, from the above quantitative relationships, $r.D$ can be expressed as $R = r.L/(1 - r)$, showing that the demand for bank reserves is derived

from the demand for credit and money. Hence, the volume of money created depends on the amount of bank loans demanded to finance monetary expenditure. In our example in the text, the endogenous increase in deposit money and reserves will therefore depend on an increased amount of bank credit, ΔL, necessary to finance the total increase in monetary expenditure initially stimulated by new investment, according to: $\Delta D = \Delta L/(1-r)$ and $\Delta R = r. \Delta L/(1-r)$.

28　On the notion that the 'necessary subsistence' wage can be explained by reference to social welfare, see Smith (1996b: 35–9) and also Aspromourgos and Groenewegen (1999: 198–200).

29　As Nuti (1971: 32) first pointed out in connection to Sraffa's suggested interest-rate closure of the system of prices and distribution, 'after Keynes we have to recognize that wage bargaining determines *money* wages, while the real wage rate is determined by the behavior of the price level'. On this point, also see Pivetti (1991: 33–7).

30　The major difference between this explanation of distribution in a gold-based monetary system and one in a fiat-based monetary system is that, for a given technique of production and rate of profit, the gold money wage cannot be given independently of the price–wage ratio and, hence, the real wage. This means that, for a given technique, a change in the gold money wage must be accommodated by an inverse change in the rate of profit. A major implication is that, unlike a fiat-based monetary system, any conflict over the distribution of income between capitalists and organised workers cannot result in wage–price inflation in a gold-based monetary system because the price level is approximately fixed by the gold standard for a given technique. On this difference, see Smith (1996b: 43–55).

31　This criticism was first made by Wicksell (1898: 99–100) from the theoretical standpoint of the marginal productivity theory of capital and distribution. As Laidler has argued, from this theoretical standpoint, Tooke's proposition would 'be true only were gold production less capital-intensive than some representative bundle of other goods' (1975: 226, n.14). By contrast, in classical analysis, whatever the capital intensity of producing gold in relation to all other commodities on the basis of the most profitable method of production, a permanent change in the rate of interest and, thereby, the normal rate of profit, will only affect relative prices in a gold-based monetary system because the general price level is approximately fixed by the gold standard (Smith 1996b: 43–4, 54–5).

32　As shown in Smith (1996b: 47, 53–5), in accordance with classical theory, the most plausible explanation of the Gibson Paradox in the era of the gold standard was that the nominal rate of interest tended to adjust to prior changes in the price level on the basis of wealth holders' desire to maintain a real inflation-adjusted rate of return on long-term financial securities.

33　After all, the discount policy of a central banking authority has long been regarded by economists as a major factor among the 'monetary forces' determining the rate of interest, albeit temporarily, in relation to the rate of profit. See, for example, Marshall (1923: 258), Wicksell (1898: 188–9; 1906: 109–15), Keynes (1930, II: 339–77), Hawtrey (1938) and Mises (1953: 357–64).

34　On the distinction between the nominal and real rate of interest in connection with the dynamics of price (wage) inflation, see Pivetti (1991: 52–8). From the standpoint of the monetary explanation of distribution in classical economics, this wage–interest–price inflationary process can be understood as part of a conflict over income distribution in which a significant supply shock to an economic system (e.g. a deterioration in the terms of trade) manifests itself in social groups (i.e. trade unions, firms and wealth holders) attempting to shift the burden of the resulting reduction in aggregate real income onto others through incompatible adjustments in their nominal income, compatible with a situation of high and rising unemployment (see Aspromourgos 1991; Stirati 2001). Clearly, this viewpoint has implications for the conduct of anti-inflationary monetary policy.

35 While Tooke advanced the notion that increases in the nominal interest rate is a causal factor of price inflation, his view that English wage-earners in the early nineteenth century did not have much power to respond to price increases means that he makes a limited contribution to an understanding of the dynamic process of wage–price inflation characteristic of modern economies. In this regard, it should be kept in mind that explaining persistent inflation by reference to distributional conflict (see note 34 above) relies on wage-earners, in particular, being able to exercise sufficient bargaining power to obtain cost of living adjustments in the money wage in response to a rising price level. The lack of bargaining power of workers supposed by Tooke helps explain why the high price inflation in Britain during the period of the French Wars was unstable which, according to the pattern of supply shocks, was characterised by alternations between rapidly accelerating inflation and disinflation (see Figure A3.1, p. 235).

36 A renewed interest in the notion of 'endogenous money' appears to have been sparked by Kaldor's (1970; 1982) response to 'monetarism'. For a survey account of post-Keynesian writers who have advocated the notion of endogenous money, see Rochon (1999).

37 In the marginalist approach, monetary forces can only exert an influence by causing the money rate of interest to deviate from the natural rate of interest (i.e. normal profit rate). Hence, from the standpoint of the quantity theory of money proposed in marginal theory, an exogenous change in the quantity of money, whether it is effected by bank lending as transmitted through a change in bank loan rates or effected more directly by financing an increase in government expenditure in excess of its revenue, can exert an influence on the economic system *only* by causing the money rate of interest to deviate from the natural rate, necessary to induce an alteration in aggregate expenditure in relation to full-employment output. In the classical approach, the issue is much less clear-cut because the normal rate of profit does not (except by accident) correspond with full-employment output and no functional relationship between changes in the money rate of interest in relation to the normal rate of profit and the level of monetary expenditure can be supposed to exist. The classical quantity theorists relied on Say's Law, with its assumption of a fixed level of aggregate output, to ensure money neutrality, at least in the short run. In absence of this assumption, long-run money neutrality can be assured in classical economics on the basis of (a) the money rate of interest is determined in the long run by real forces that determine the normal profitability on capital, and (b) that monetary forces *can only* transmit their influence by acting on the money rate of interest.

38 In the *General Theory* (1936: 203–4), Keynes proposed that because the rate of interest was a 'highly conventional phenomenon' its normal level was liable to be determined by the policy of the 'monetary authority'. Also see Keynes' (1945: 390–2) notes for meetings of the National Debt Enquiry proposing measures in support of a post-war cheap money policy.

39 The government's taxation and welfare policy will also play an important role in influencing the distribution of income among social classes and, thereby, will have an ongoing influence on aggregate consumption expenditure.

40 Twentieth-century history suggests that public capital expenditures (compared with recurrent expenditures) appear to be sensitive in the long run to interest rate changes so that at a permanently higher level of interest rates, and thereby, with a higher proportion of government (tax) revenue having to go to service public debt, government policy-makers come under pressure to reduce capital expenditures, especially those non-commercial public investments that do not generate a pecuniary return. There appears to be historical evidence to support the proposition that sustaining a persistently expansionary fiscal policy stance, entailing significant growth in public capital expenditures, depends on permanently low rates of interest. In addition, with regard to private investment expenditure, a persistently lower level of interest rates also appears

to support stronger growth in house building in those affluent countries in which private home ownership is an affordable aspiration for a large proportion of the population.

41 There appear to be several ways in which government expenditure can conceivably assist the inducement to private investment. One obvious way is through government financial support of research in the development of technical knowledge. This provides profitable opportunities for the development of new technologies in the form of more productive capital equipment and superior consumer products. In this regard, technical change is, at least partially, endogenous to capital expenditure. The best modern example of this phenomenon of national government support for technical change is the longstanding United States military expenditure program, including that related to financing scientific research (Pivetti 1989). Another, more straightforward, way that government expenditure can assist the inducement to private investment is by the provision of public infrastructure (e.g. transport, electronic communications, hospitals, dams with hydroelectric plants, etc.) that opens up new opportunities for profitable investment, perhaps by lowering the costs of producing and distributing products or, connectedly, by opening up new markets. It should be emphasised that this 'crowding in' effect, so to speak, cannot be properly considered in isolation from the wider structural features of a capitalistic economy. Indeed, under some circumstances, government expenditure may have little impact on private expenditure. Hence, proper consideration of the effect of government expenditure on private investment would essentially be part of an analysis of the role of the state in the economic development of a nation by reference to the historical concrete situation.

42 It follows from this argument that the long-run average level of interest rates that is seen to be the outcome of the long-standing interest-rate policy of the monetary authorities can influence the *growth rate of output* through its impact on those autonomous growth components of aggregate demand as well as on the 'social expenditure multiplier'. For the relevant demand-led growth theory, see Serrano (1995) and Trezzini (1995; 1998).

43 The only avenue by which monetary forces can exert a 'secondary' influence on real variables in the marginalist approach is through the effect of changes in the price level on the datum (especially the quantity of real capital) determining the natural rate of interest, of which the best example in the literature is 'forced saving'. On this remote theoretical possibility, see Pivetti (1991: 91–7).

References

Aftalion, F. (1927) *Monnaie Prix et Change* (being volume 1 of *La Valeur da la Monnaie dans l'économie contemporaine*), Paris: Sirey.

Arbuthnot, G. (1857) *Sir Robert Peel's Act of 1844, regulating the Issue of Bank Notes, Vindicated*, London: Longman, Brown, Green, Longmans and Roberts.

Arnon, A. (1990) 'What Thomas Tooke (and Ricardo) could have known had they constructed price indices', in D.E. Moggridge (ed.), *Perspectives on the History of Economic Thought: Selected Papers from the History of Economics Society Conference, 1988*, vol. IV, Aldershot: Edward Elgar: 1–19.

Arnon, A. (1991) *Thomas Tooke: Pioneer of Monetary Theory*, Aldershot: Edward Elgar.

Aspromourgos, T. (1991) 'Inflation in a Sraffa–Keynes framework', *Economies et Societes*, 11–12 (8): 107–26.

Aspromourgos, T. (1996) *On the Origins of Classical Economics: Distribution and Value from William Petty to Adam Smith*, London: Routledge.

Aspromourgos, T. (2009) *The Science of Wealth: Adam Smith and the Framing of Political Economy*, London: Routledge.

Aspromourgos, T. and Groenewegen, P. (1999) 'The notion of the subsistence wage in pre-Smithian classical political economy: some reflections inspired by the surplus approach', in G. Mongiovi and F. Petri (eds), *Value, Distribution and Capital: Essays in Honour of Pierangelo Garegnani*, London: Routledge: 181–203.

Bagehot, W. (1873) *Lombard Street: A Description of the Money Market*, reprint 1915, London: John Murray.

Bailey, S. (1825) *A Critical Dissertation on the Nature, Measure and Causes of Value*, reprint 1967, New Jersey: Augustus M. Kelley.

Bailey, S. (1837) *Money and its Vicissitudes in Value ...*, London: E. Wilson.

Barnes, D.G. (1930) *A History of the English Corn Laws from 1660–1846*, London: George Routledge.

Bharadwaj, K. (1989) 'Ricardian theory and Ricardianism', *Themes in Value and Distribution: Classical Theory Reappraised*, London: Unwin Hyman: 41–76.

Blake, W. (1823) *Observations on the Effects produced by the Expenditure of Government during the Restriction of Cash Payments*, London: John Murray.

Blaug, M. (1987) 'Classical economics', in J. Eatwell, M. Milgate and P. Newman (eds) (1987) *The New Palgrave Dictionary of Economics*, vols 1–4, London: Macmillan, vol. 1: 434–45.

Boase, H. (1804) *A Letter to the Right Hon. Lord King ...*, London: G. and W. Nicol.

Boase, H. (1811) *Remarks on the New Doctrine Concerning the Supposed Depreciation of Our Currency*, London: G. and W. Nicol.

Bortkiewicz, L. von (1906–1907 [1952]) 'Value and prices in the Marxian System', *International Economic Papers*, 2: 5–60. English translation of essays originally written in German in 1906–1907.

Bosanquet, C. (1810) *Practical Observations on the Report of the Bullion-Committee*, 2nd edn, London: J.M. Richardson.

Bosanquet, J.W. (1842) *Metallic, Paper, and Credit Currency* ..., London: Pelham Richardson.

Boyd, W. (1801) *A Letter to the Right Honourable William Pitt* ..., 2nd edn, London: J. Wright and J. Mawman.

Bridel, P. (1987) *Cambridge Monetary Thought: The Development of Saving–Investment Analysis from Marshall to Keynes*, London: Macmillan.

Bullion Committee (1810) Report together with Minutes of Evidence and Accounts from the Select Committee on the High Price of Gold Bullion, P.P. 1810 (349), III.

Burke, E. (1795 [1887]) 'Thoughts and details on scarcity', *The Works of the Right Honourable Edmund Burke* (1887), vol. 5, London: John C. Nimmo.

Caminati, M. (1981) 'The theory of interest in the classical economists', *Metroeconomica*, XXXIII (Feb.–Oct.): 79–104.

Cannan, E. (1925) *The Paper Pound of 1797–1821*, 2nd edn, London: P.S. King.

Ciccone, R. (1986) 'Accumulation and capacity utilization: some critical considerations on Joan Robinson's theory of distribution', *Political Economy: Studies in the Surplus Approach*, 2 (1): 17–36.

Clapham, J. (1944) *The Bank of England: A History, 1797–1914*, vol. II, Cambridge: Cambridge University Press.

Clapham, J. (1959) *An Economic History of Modern Britain: The Early Railway Age, 1820–1850*, 2nd. edn, Cambridge: Cambridge University Press.

Clapham, J. (1963) *An Economic History of Modern Britain: Free Trade and Steel, 1850–1886*, 2nd edn, Cambridge: Cambridge University Press.

Clark, G.K. (1951) 'The repeal of the Corn Laws and the politics of the Forties', *Economic History Review*, n.s., 4 (1): 1–13.

Clay, W.M. (1844) *Remarks on the Expediency of Restricting the Issue of Promissory Notes to a Single Issuing Body*, London: James Ridgway.

Creedy, J. (1986) 'On the King–Davenant "Law" of Demand', *The Scottish Journal of Political Economy*, 33 (3): 193–212.

Daugherty, M.R. (1942) 'The currency–banking controversy: Part I', *Southern Economic Journal*, 9: 140–55.

Daugherty, M.R. (1943) 'The currency–banking controversy: Part II', *Southern Economic Journal*, 9: 241–51.

Davenant, C. (1699) *An Essay upon the Probable Methods of Making People Gainers in the Balance of Trade*, in *The Political and Commercial Works of Charles Davenant LL.D.*, vol. II, as collected and revised by C. Whitworth, reprint 1967, London: Gregg Press.

De Vivo, G. (1984) *Ricardo and His Critics: A Study of Classical Theories of Value and Distribution*, Studi e ricerche dell'Instituto Economico, no. 23, Universita Studi di Modena.

Diewart, W.E. (1987) 'Index numbers', in J. Eatwell, M. Milgate and P. Newman (eds) (1987) *The New Palgrave Dictionary of Economics*, vols 1–4, London: Macmillan, vol. 2: 767–80.

Dmitriev, V.K. (1898–1904) *Economic Essays on Value, Competition and Utility*, English translation of essays originally published from 1898 to 1904 in Russian, edited by D.M. Nuti, 1974, Cambridge: Cambridge University Press.

Dobb, M. (1973) *Theories of Value and Distribution Since Adam Smith: Ideology and Economic Theory*, Cambridge: Cambridge University Press.

Dow, J.C.R. and Saville, I.D. (1988) *A Critique of Monetary Policy: Theory and British Experience*, Oxford: Clarendon Press.

Eatwell, J. (1982) 'Competition', in I. Bradley and M. Howard (eds), *Classical and Marxian Political Economy: Essays in Honour of Ronald L. Meek*, London: Macmillan: 203–28.

Eatwell, J. and Milgate, M. (eds) (1983) *Keynes's Economics and the Theory of Value and Distribution*, London: Duckworth.

Eatwell, J., Milgate, M. and Newman, P. (eds) (1987) *The New Palgrave Dictionary of Economics*, vols 1–4, London: Macmillan.

Eatwell, J., Milgate, M. and Newman, P. (eds) (1989) *The New Palgrave: Money*, London: Macmillan.

Eatwell, J., Milgate, M. and Newman, P. (eds) (1990) *The New Palgrave: Capital Theory*, London: Macmillan.

Ellis, H.S. (1934) *German Monetary Theory, 1905–1933*, Cambridge, MA: Harvard University Press.

Endres, T. (1987) 'The King–Davenant Law in classical economics', *History of Political Economy*, 19 (4): 621–38.

Eshag, E. (1963) *From Marshall to Keynes: an Essay on the Monetary Theory of the Cambridge School*, Oxford: Blackwell.

Fairlie, S. (1965) 'The nineteenth-century Corn Law reconsidered', *Economic History Review*, n.s., 18 (3): 562–75.

Fairlie, S. (1969) 'The Corn Laws and British wheat production, 1829–1876', *Economic History Review*, n.s., 22 (1): 88–116.

Fay, C.R. (1932) *The Corn Laws and Social England*, London: Cambridge University Press.

Fay, C.R. (1960) *The World of Adam Smith*, Cambridge: Heffer.

Feaveryear, A. (1931 [1963]) *The Pound Sterling: A History of English Money*, 2nd edn (as revised by E.V. Morgan), Oxford: Clarendon Press.

Fetter, F.W. (1942) 'The life and writings of John Wheatley', *Journal of Political Economy*, 50 (3): 357–76.

Fetter, F.W. (1954) 'The Bullion Report re-examined', in T.S. Ashton and R.S. Sayers (eds), *Papers in English Monetary History*, Oxford: Clarendon Press: 66–75.

Fetter, F.W. (1965) *Development of British Monetary Orthodoxy 1797–1875*, reprint 1978, New Jersey: Augustus M. Kelley.

Fetter, F.W. (1968) 'Thomas Tooke', in D.L. Still (ed.), *International Encyclopaedia of the Social Sciences*, vol. 16, London: Macmillan: 103–4.

Francis, J. (1851) *History of the English Railway 1820–1845*, reprint 1968, A.M. Kelley: New York.

Fullarton, J. (1845) *On the Regulation of Currencies*, 2nd edn, reprint 1969, New York: Augustus M. Kelley.

Garegnani, P. (1966) 'Switching of techniques', *Quarterly Journal of Economics*, 80: 554–67.

Garegnani, P. (1970) 'Heterogeneous capital, the production function and the theory of distribution', *Review of Economic Studies*, 37: 407–36.

Garegnani, P. (1983a) 'Notes on consumption, investment and effective demand', in J. Eatwell and M. Milgate (eds), *Keynes's Economics and the Theory of Value and Distribution*, London: Duckworth: 21–69.

Garegnani, P. (1983b) 'On a change in the notion of equilibrium in recent work on value and distribution', in J. Eatwell and M. Milgate (eds), *Keynes's Economics and the Theory of Value and Distribution*, London: Duckworth: 129–45.

Garegnani, P. (1984) 'Value and distribution in the classical economists and Marx', *Oxford Economic Papers, New Series*, 36 (2): 291–325.

Garegnani, P. (1987) 'Surplus approach to value and distribution', in J. Eatwell, M. Milgate and P. Newman (eds), *The New Palgrave Dictionary of Economics*, vols 1–4, London: Macmillan, vol. 4: 560–74.

Garegnani, P. (1990a) 'Sraffa: classical versus marginalist analysis', in K. Bharadwaj and B. Schefold (eds), *Essays on Piero Sraffa: Critical Perspectives on the Revival of Classical Theory*, London: Unwin Hyman: 112–41.

Garegnani, P. (1990b) 'Quantity of capital', in J. Eatwell, M. Milgate and P. Newman (eds), *The New Palgrave: Capital Theory*, London: Macmillan: 1–78.

Garegnani, P. (1992) 'Some notes for an analysis of accumulation', J. Halevi, D. Laibman and E.J. Nell (eds), *Beyond the Steady State*, London: Macmillan: 47–71.

Garegnani, P. (1998) 'Sraffa, Piero', in H.D. Kurz and N. Salvadori (eds), *The Elgar Companion to Classical Economics*, 2 volumes, Cheltenham: Edward Elgar, L–Z: 391–9.

Giffen, R. (1886) 'The depreciation of gold since 1848', *Essays in Finance: First Series*, 4th edn, London: George Bell: 82–106.

Gilbart, J.W. (1834) *The History and Principles of Banking*, London: Longman, Rees, Orme, Green and Longman.

Gilbart, J.W. (1841) *Currency and Banking* ..., London: H. Hooper.

Gilbart, J.W. (1849) *A Practical Treatise on Banking*, vols I and II, 5th edn, London: Longmans, Brown, Green and Longman.

Girton, L. and Roper, D. (1978) 'J. Lawrence Laughlin and the quantity theory of money', *Journal of Political Economy*, 86: 599–625.

Glyn, G.C. (1848) Evidence to the Lords Secret Committee Appointed to Inquire into the Causes of the Commercial Distress, P.P. 1847–1848 (565), VIII, Pt. III (Q 1645–1921): 197–224.

Gold and Silver Commission (1888) 'Final Report of the Royal Commission Appointed to Inquire into the Recent Changes in the Relative Prices of the Precious Metals with Minutes of Evidence and Appendixes', c.5512, P.P., XLV.285, 455.

Goodhart, C.A.E. (1989a) 'Monetary base', in J. Eatwell, M. Milgate and P. Newman (eds), *The New Palgrave: Money*, London: Macmillan: 206–11.

Goodhart, C.A.E. (1989b) 'Central banking', in J. Eatwell, M. Milgate and P. Newman (eds), *The New Palgrave: Money*, London: Macmillan: 88–92.

Gordon, B. (1979) *Economic Doctrine and Tory Liberals 1824–1830*, London: Macmillan.

Graham, J.R.G. (1826) *Corn and Currency: in an address to the land owners*, 2nd edn, London: J. Ridgeway.

Gregory, T.E. (1928) 'Introduction' to a reprint of Tooke's Six-Volume *A History of Prices and of the State of the Circulation from 1792 to 1856* (published in four enclosed volumes), vol. I, London: P.S. King and Son: 5–120.

Gregson, J. (1907) *The Australian Agricultural Company 1824–1875*, Sydney: Angus and Robertson.

Green, R. (1992) *Classical Theories of Money, Output and Inflation: A Study in Historical Economics*, London: St. Martin's Press.

Grenville, W.W. (Lord) (1828) *Essay on the Supposed Advantages of the Sinking Fund*, London: privately printed.

Groenewegen, P.D. (1995) *A Soaring Eagle: Alfred Marshall, 1842–1924*, Aldershot: Edward Elgar.

Harcourt, G.C. (1972) *Some Cambridge Controversies in the Theory of Capital*, Cambridge: Cambridge University Press.

Hawtrey, R.G. (1913) *Good and Bad Trade*, London: Longmans.

Hawtrey, R.G. (1938) *A Century of Bank Rate*, 2nd edn, reprint 1962, London: Frank Cass.

Hayek v., F.A. (ed.) (1939) *An Enquiry into the Nature and Effects of the Paper Credit of Great Britain (1802) by Henry Thornton ...*, reprint 1991, New Jersey: Augustus M. Kelley.

Heckscher, E.F. (1922) *The Continental System: An Economic Interpretation*, reprint 1964, Gloucester, MA: Peter Smith.

Henderson, J.P. (1983) 'The oral tradition in British economics: influential economists in the Political Economy Club of London', *History of Political Economy*, 15 (2): 154–69.

Herries, J.C. (1811) *A Review of the Controversy Respecting the High Price of Bullion ...*, London: J. Budd.

Higgs, H. (ed.) (1921) *Political Economy Club Centenary Volume: Minutes of Proceedings, 1899–1920; Roll of Members and Questions Discussed, 1821–1920*, vol. VI, London: Macmillan.

Hill, J. (1810) *An Inquiry into the Causes of the Present High Price of Gold Bullion in England ...*, London: Longman, Hurst, Rees, Orme and Brown.

Hilton, B. (1977) *Corn, Cash, Commerce: The Economic Policies of the Tory Government, 1815–30*, Oxford: Oxford University Press.

Homer, S. and Sylla, R. (1996) *A History of Interest Rates*, 3rd edn, revised, New Jersey: Rutgers University Press.

Horner, F. (1802) Review of Henry Thornton's 'An Enquiry into the Nature and Effects of the Paper Credit of Great Britain', *Edinburgh Review*, Oct.: 172–201.

Horner, F. (1803a) Review of Lord King's 'On the effects of the Bank restrictions', *Edinburgh Review*, 1: 402–21.

Horner, F. (1803b) Review of John Wheatley 'Remarks on currency and commerce', *Edinburgh Review*, 3: 231–52.

Horsefield, J.K. (1940) 'The Bank and its treasure', *Economica, New Series*, 7 (May): 161–78.

Horsefield, J.K. (1944) 'The origins of the Bank Charter Act, 1844', *Economica, New Series*, 11 (November): 180–9.

Hueckel, G. (1973) 'War and the British economy, 1793–1815: a general equilibrium analysis', *Explorations in Economic History*, 10 (4): 365–96.

Hume, J.D. (1834) *Letters on the Corn Laws and on the Rights of the Working Classes*, London: W. Clowes.

Humphrey, T.M. (1979) 'The interest cost–push controversy', *Federal Reserve Bank of Richmond Economic Review*, 65 (1) (Jan.–Feb.): 3–10.

Huskisson, W. (1810) *The Question Concerning the Depreciation of Our Currency Stated and Examined*, London: John Murray.

Inglis, B. (1972) *Poverty and Industrial Revolution*, London: Panther.

Jacob, W. (1828) *Tracts Relating to the Corn Trade and the Corn Laws ...*, London: J. Murray.

Jevons, S. (1863) *A Serious Fall in the Value of Gold Ascertained, and its social effects set forth*, in S. Jevons, *Investigations in Currency and Finance* (1884), edited by H.S. Foxwell, London: Macmillan: 12–118.

Jevons, S. (1865) 'The variations of prices and the value of the currency since 1782', *Journal of the Royal Statistical Society*, in *Investigations in Currency and Finance* (1884), edited by H.S. Foxwell, London: Macmillan: 119–50.

Jevons, S. (1869) 'The depreciation of gold', *Journal of the Royal Statistical Society*, 32: 445–9, in S. Jevons (1884) *Investigations in Currency and Finance*, edited by H.S. Foxwell, London: Macmillan: 151–9.

Jevons, S. (1884) *Investigations in Currency and Finance*, edited by H.S. Foxwell, London: Macmillan.

Johnson, A. (1856) *Currency Principles Versus Banking Principles* ..., London: Richardson Brothers.

Joplin, T. (1822) *On the General Principles and Present Practice of Banking in Scotland and England*, 3rd edn, Newcastle: Ridgway.

Joplin, T. (1823) *Outlines of a System of Political Economy*, London: Baldwin, Craddock and Joy.

Kaldor, N. (1970) 'The new monetarism', *Lloyds Bank Review*, X (July): 1–51.

Kaldor, N. (1982) *The Scourge of Monetarism*, London: Oxford University Press.

Keynes, J.M. (1930) *A Treatise on Money*, vols I and II, reprint 1934, London: Macmillan.

Keynes, J.M. (1936) *The General Theory of Employment, Interest and Money*, in Keynes (1971–1989), *The Collected Writings of John Maynard Keynes*, 30 vols, edited by D. Moggridge and E. Johnson, London: Macmillan for the Royal Economic Society, vol. VII.

Keynes, J.M. (1937a) 'Alternative theories of the rate of interest', in Keynes (1971–1989), *The Collected Writings of John Maynard Keynes*, 30 vols, edited by D. Moggridge and E. Johnson, London: Macmillan for the Royal Economic Society, vol. XIV: 201–23.

Keynes, J.M. (1937b) 'The general theory of employment', in Keynes (1971–1989), *The Collected Writings of John Maynard Keynes*, 30 vols, edited by D. Moggridge and E. Johnson, London: Macmillan for the Royal Economic Society, vol. XIV: 109–123.

Keynes, J.M. (1945) 'National debt enquiry: Lord Keynes' notes', in Keynes (1971–1989), *The Collected Writings of John Maynard Keynes*, 30 vols, edited by D. Moggridge and E. Johnson, London: Macmillan for the Royal Economic Society, vol. XXVIII: 388–96.

Keynes, J.M. (1971–1989) *The Collected Writings of John Maynard Keynes*, 30 vols, edited by D. Moggridge and E. Johnson, London: Macmillan for the Royal Economic Society.

King, Lord (1803) *Thoughts on the restriction of payments in specie at the Banks of England and Ireland*, London: Cadell and Davies.

King, W.T.C. (1936) *History of the Discount Market*, with an introduction by T.E. Gregory, London: George Routledge and Sons.

Kurz, H.D. (1985) 'Effective demand in a 'classical' model of value and distribution: the multiplier in a Sraffian framework', *The Manchester School*, June, 53 (2): 121–37.

Kurz, H.D. (1990) 'Factor price frontier', in J. Eatwell, M. Milgate and P. Newman (eds), *The New Palgrave: Capital Theory*, London: Macmillan: 155–60.

Kurz, H.D. and Salvadori, N. (1995) *Theory of Production: A Long Period Analysis*, New York: Cambridge University Press.

Kurz, H.D. and Salvadori, N. (eds) (1998a) *The Elgar Companion to Classical Economics*, 2 volumes, Cheltenham: Edward Elgar.

Kurz, H.D. and Salvadori, N. (1998b) 'Given quantities', in Kurz and Salvadori (eds) (1998a), *The Elgar Companion to Classical Economics*, 2 volumes, Cheltenham: Edward Elgar, A–K: 325–9.

Kurz, H.D. and Salvadori, N. (1998c) 'Classical political economy', in Kurz and Salvadori (eds) (1998a) *The Elgar Companion to Classical Economics*, 2 volumes, Cheltenham: Edward Elgar, A–K: 159–64.

Laidler, D. (1975) 'Thomas Tooke on monetary reform', *Essays on Money and Inflation*, Manchester: Manchester University Press: 211–27.

Laidler, D. (1991) *The Golden Age of the Quantity Theory: The Development of Neoclassical Monetary Economics 1870–1914*, New York: P. Allen.

Laughlin, J.L. (1886) *The History of Bimetallism in the United States*, New York: D. Appleton and Company.

Laughlin, J.L. (1903) *The Principles of Money*, London: John Murray.

Liverpool, Lord [Charles Jenkinson] (1805) *A Treatise on the Coins of the Realm, in a letter to the King ...*, Oxford: Cadell and Davies.

Longfield, M. (1834) *Lectures in Political Economy*, Series of Reprints of Scarce Tracts in Economic and Political Science, no. 8, 1931, London School of Economics and Political Science.

Lowe, J. (1823) *The Present State of England in Regard to Agriculture, Trade and Finance*, 2nd edn, London: Longman, Hurst, Rees, Orme and Brown.

McCulloch, J.R. (1824a) 'Standard of national prosperity – rise and fall of profits', *Edinburgh Review*, 79 (March): 1–31.

McCulloch, J.R. (1824b) 'Money', *Supplement to the Fourth, Fifth and Sixth Editions of the Encyclopaedia Britannica*, vol. 5, Edinburgh: Achibald Constable: 491–536.

McCulloch, J.R. (1830) *The Principles of Political Economy ...*, 2nd edn, London: Longman, Rees, Orme, Brown and Green.

McCulloch, J.R. (1845) *The Literature of Political Economy: A Classified Catalogue*, Series of Reprints of Scarce Works on Political Economy, no. 5, 1938, The London School and Economics and Political Science.

Malthus, T.R. (1800) *An Investigation of the Cause of the Present High Price of Provisions*, 2nd edn, London: Davis, Taylor and Wilks.

Malthus, T.R. (1811) 'Depreciation of paper currency', *The Edinburgh Review*, 17: 339–72.

Malthus, T.R. (1815) *An Inquiry into the Nature and Progress of Rent*, London: John Murray.

Malthus, T.R. (1820) *Principles of Political Economy ...*, London: John Murray.

Malthus, T.R. (1823) 'Tooke – on high and low prices', *The Quarterly Review*, vol. XXIX, April and July: 214–39, reprinted in C. Renwick (ed.) (1953) *Five Papers on Political Economy*, Series of Reprints of Works on Economics and Economic History, Faculty of Economics, University of Sydney.

Malthus, T.R. (1824) 'Political economy', *The Quarterly Review*, vol. XXX (Jan.): 297–334.

Malthus, T.R. (1836) *Principles of Political Economy ...*, 2nd edn, reprinted with an Introduction by M. Paglin (1986) New Jersey: Augustus M. Kelley.

Marget, A.W. (1938) *The Theory of Prices: A Re-Examination of the Central Problems of Monetary Theory*, New York: P.S. King and Sons.

Marshall, A. (1923) *Money, Credit and Commerce*, reprint 1991, New Jersey: Augustus M. Kelley.

Marshall, A. (1926) *Official Papers*, edited by J.M. Keynes, London: Macmillan.

Marshall, A. and Marshall, M.P. (1879) *The Economics of Industry*, London: Macmillan.

Marx, K. (1859) *A Contribution to the Critique of Political Economy*, with an Introduction by M. Dobb, reprint 1977, Moscow: Progress Publishers.

Marx, K. (1861–1863) *Theories of Surplus Value*, Parts I–III in three volumes, reprint 1975–1978, Moscow: Progress Press.

Marx, K. (1867) *Capital: A Critique of Political Economy*, vol. I, edited F. Engels, English first edition published in 1887, translated from the 1883 German third edition, reprint 1986, Moscow: Progress Press.

Marx, K. (1885) *Capital: A Critique of Political Economy*, vol. II, edited F. Engels, English first edition published in 1956, translated from the 1893 German second edition, reprint 1978, Moscow: Progress Press.

Marx, K. (1894) *Capital: A Critique of Political Economy*, vol. III, edited by F. Engels, English first edition published in 1959, reprint 1978, Moscow: Progress Press.

Marx, K. (1983) 'Letter to F. Engels, 5 March 1858', in K. Marx and F. Engels, *Collected Works*, vol. 40, London: Lawrence and Wishart: 282–4.

Milgate, M. (1982) *Capital and Employment: A Study of Keynes's Economics*, London: Academic Press.

Mill, J.S. (1826) 'Paper currency – commercial distress', *Parliamentary Review, Session of 1826*, in J.M. Robson (ed.) (1963) *Collected Works of John Stuart Mill*, vol. IV, University of Toronto: Routledge: 71–123.

Mill, J.S. (1844) Review of 'An Inquiry into the Currency Principle …', by Thomas Tooke, *Westminster Review*, LIX (2): 579–98.

Mill, J.S. (1844 [1874]) 'On profits and interest', *Essays on Some Unsettled Questions of Political Economy*, 2nd edn, reprint 1974, New Jersey: Augustus M. Kelley: 90–119.

Mill, J.S. (1848 [1909]) *Principles of Political Economy …*, 7th edn, edited with an Introduction by W. Ashley, reprint 1987, New Jersey: Augustus M. Kelly.

Mints, L.W. (1945) *A History of Banking Theory in Great Britain and the United States*, Chicago: Chicago University Press.

Mises, L. von (1953) *The Theory of Money and Credit*, new enlarged English edition, London: Jonathan Cape.

Mitchell, B.R. (1988) *British Historical Statistics*, Cambridge: Cambridge University Press.

Moore, B. (1988) *Horizontalists and Verticalists: The Macroeconomics of Credit Money*, Cambridge: Cambridge University Press.

Moore, P. (1995) *Robert Torrens: Controversial Colonel*, unpublished manuscript.

Morgan, E.V. (1965) *The Theory and Practice of Central Banking, 1797–1913*, London: Frank Cass.

Mushet, R. (1811) *An Inquiry into the Effects Produced on the National Currency and Rates of Exchange …*, 3rd edn, London: Baldwin.

Mushet, R. (1826) *An Attempt to Explain from Facts the Effect of the Issues of the Bank of England …*, London: Baldwin, Craddock and Joy.

Newmarch, W. (1853) *The New Supplies of Gold …*, revised edition with five additional chapters, London: Pelham Richardson.

Newmarch, W. (1857) Evidence to the Commons Select Committee on the Bank Acts, P.P. 1857 (220), X, Pts. I and II (Q 1554–2009): 140–76.

Newmarch, W. (1858) 'On the recent history of the credit mobilier', *Journal of the Royal Statistical Society*, XXI (Dec.): 444–53.

Nichols, J. (1812–1815 [1967]) *Literary Anecdotes of the Eighteenth Century*, edited by C. Clair, Fontwell: Centaur Press.

Norman, G.W. (1838) *Remarks Upon Some Errors, with Respect to Currency and Banking …*, London: Pelham Richardson.

Norman, G.W. (1841) *Letter to Charles Wood, Esq …*, London: Pelham Richardson.

Nuti, D.M. (1971) '"Vulgar economy" in the theory of income distribution', *Science and Society*, XXXV (1): 27–33.

O'Brien, D.P. (ed.) (1971) *The Correspondence of Lord Overstone*, in three volumes, Cambridge: Cambridge University Press.

O'Brien, D.P. (1975) *The Classical Economists*, Oxford: Clarendon Press.

O'Donnell, R. (1990) *Adam Smith's Theory of Value and Distribution: A Reappraisal*, New York: St. Martin's Press.

Overstone, Lord [Loyd, Samuel-Jones] (1837) *Reflections suggested by a perusal of Mr. J. Horsley Palmer's Pamphlet …*, in Overstone (1857) *Tracts and Other Publications on Metallic and Paper Currency*, compiled by J.R. McCulloch, reprint 1972, New York: Augustus M. Kelley: 1–40.

Overstone, Lord [Loyd, Samuel-Jones] (1840a) *Remarks on the Management of the Circulation and on the condition and conduct of the Bank of England and the Country Issuers …*, in Overstone (1857) *Tracts and Other Publications on Metallic and Paper Currency*, compiled by J.R. McCulloch, reprint 1972, New York: Augustus M. Kelley: 41–158.

Overstone, Lord [Loyd, Samuel-Jones] (1840b) Extracts from the Evidence of Samuel Jones Loyd to the Commons Select Committee on Banks of Issue, P.P. 1840 (602), IV (Q 2651–3260), in Overstone (1857) *Tracts and Other Publications on Metallic and Paper Currency*, compiled by J.R. McCulloch, reprint 1972, New York: Augustus M. Kelley: 339–486.

Overstone, Lord [Loyd, Samuel-Jones] (1844) *Thoughts on the Separation of the Departments of the Bank of England*, in Overstone (1857) *Tracts and Other Publications on Metallic and Paper Currency*, compiled by J.R. McCulloch, reprint 1972, New York: Augustus M. Kelley: 237–84.

Overstone, Lord [Loyd, Samuel-Jones] (1857) *Tracts and Other Publications on Metallic and Paper Currency*, compiled by J.R. McCulloch, reprint 1972, New York: Augustus M. Kelley.

Panico, C. (1988) *Interest and Profit in the Theories of Value and Distribution*, London: Macmillan.

Parnell, H. (Lord Congleton) (1827) *Observations on Paper Money, Banking, Overtrading*, London: J. Ridgway.

Parnell, H. (Lord Congleton) (1833) *A Plain Statement of the Power of the Bank of England and of the Use It Has Made of It*, London: James Ridgway.

Passinetti, L.L. (1966) 'Changes in the rate of profit and switches of technique', *Quarterly Journal of Economics*, 80: 503–17.

Passinetti, L.L. (1969) 'Switches of technique and the "rate of return" in capital theory', *Economic Journal*, 79: 508–31.

Passinetti, L.L. (1974) *Growth and Income Distribution*, Cambridge: Cambridge University Press.

Passinetti, L.L. (1977) *Lectures on the Theory of Production*, London: Macmillan.

Passinetti, L.L. (1981) *Structural Change and Economic Growth: A Theoretical Essay on the Dynamics of the Wealth of Nations*, Cambridge: Cambridge University Press.

Petri, F. (2004) *General Equilibrium, Capital and Macroeconomics*, Cheltenham: Edward Elgar.

Pickering, P.A. and Tyrrell, A. (2000) *The People's Bread: A History of the Anti-Corn Law League*. London: Leicester University Press.

Pigou, A.C. (1933) *The Theory of Unemployment*, London: Macmillan.

Pivetti, M. (1987) 'Interest and profit in Smith, Ricardo and Marx', *Political Economy: Studies in the Surplus Approach*, 3 (1): 63–74.

Pivetti, M. (1989) 'Military expenditure and economic analysis: a review article', *Contributions to Political Economy*, 8: 55–67.

Pivetti, M. (1990) 'Wicksell's theory of capital', in J. Eatwell, M. Milgate and P. Newman (eds), *The New Palgrave: Capital Theory*, London: Macmillan: 262–9.

Pivetti, M. (1991) *An Essay on Money and Distribution*, New York: St. Martin's Press.

Pivetti, M. (1998) 'Thomas Tooke and the influence of the rate of interest on prices: implications for distribution theory', *Contributions to Political Economy*, 17: 39–52.

Pivetti, M. (2001) 'Money endogeneity and money non-neutrality: a Sraffian perspective', in L.P. Rochon and M. Verengo (eds), *Credit, Interest and the Open Economy. Essays on Horizontalism*, London: Edward Elgar: 104–19.

Porter, G.R. (1838) *On the Progress of the Nation, in its various Social and Economic Relations, from the beginning of the nineteenth century*, vol. 2 (sections III and IV), London: C. Knight.

Reed, M.C. (1975) *Investment in Railways in Britain, 1820–1844: A Study in the Development of the Capital Market*, London: Oxford University Press.

Ricardo, D. (1811a) 'The high price of bullion, a proof of the depreciation of bank notes', in Ricardo (1951–1973) *The Works and Correspondence of David Ricardo*, 11 volumes, edited by P. Sraffa with the collaboration of M. Dobb, Cambridge: Cambridge University Press, vol. III: 47–157.

Ricardo, D. (1811b) 'Reply to Mr. Bosanquet's practical observations on the report of the Bullion Committee', in Ricardo (1951–1973) *The Works and Correspondence of David Ricardo*, 11 volumes, edited by P. Sraffa with the collaboration of M. Dobb, Cambridge: Cambridge University Press, vol. III: 157–256.

Ricardo, D. (1815) 'Essay on the influence of a low price of corn on the profits of stock', in Ricardo (1951–1973) *The Works and Correspondence of David Ricardo*, 11 volumes, edited by P. Sraffa with the collaboration of M. Dobb, Cambridge: Cambridge University Press, vol. IV: 1–41.

Ricardo, D. (1816) 'Proposals for an economical and secure currency', in Ricardo (1951–1973) *The Works and Correspondence of David Ricardo*, 11 volumes, edited by P. Sraffa with the collaboration of M. Dobb, Cambridge: Cambridge University Press, vol. IV: 43–200.

Ricardo, D. (1819a) Evidence to the Commons Secret Committee on the Expediency of the Bank Resuming Cash Payments, P.P. 1819 (202, 282) III, in Ricardo (1951–1973) *The Works and Correspondence of David Ricardo*, 11 volumes, edited by P. Sraffa with the collaboration of M. Dobb, Cambridge: Cambridge University Press, vol. V: 371–415.

Ricardo, D. (1819b) Evidence to the Lords Secret Committee to enquire into the State of the Bank of England, with respect to the Expediency of the Resumption of Cash Payments, P.P. 1819, (291) III, in Ricardo (1951–1973) *The Works and Correspondence of David Ricardo*, 11 volumes, edited by P. Sraffa with the collaboration of M. Dobb, Cambridge: Cambridge University Press, vol. V: 416–57.

Ricardo, D. (1819–1821) 'Letters 1819–June 1821', in Ricardo (1951–1973) *The Works and Correspondence of David Ricardo*, 11 volumes, edited by P. Sraffa with the collaboration of M. Dobb, Cambridge: Cambridge University Press, vol. VIII.

Ricardo, D. (1821) *On the Principles of Political Economy and Taxation*, in Ricardo (1951–1973) *The Works and Correspondence of David Ricardo*, 11 volumes, edited by P. Sraffa with the collaboration of M. Dobb, Cambridge: Cambridge University Press, vol. I.

Ricardo, D. (1821–1823) 'Letters, July 1821–1823', in Ricardo (1951–1973) *The Works and Correspondence of David Ricardo*, 11 volumes, edited by P. Sraffa with the collaboration of M. Dobb, Cambridge: Cambridge University Press, vol. IX.

Ricardo, D. (1822) 'On protection of agriculture', in Ricardo (1951–1973) *The Works and Correspondence of David Ricardo*, 11 volumes, edited by P. Sraffa with the collaboration of M. Dobb, Cambridge: Cambridge University Press, vol. IV: 201–70.

Ricardo, D. (1951–1973) *The Works and Correspondence of David Ricardo*, 11 volumes, edited by P. Sraffa with the collaboration of M. Dobb, Cambridge: Cambridge University Press.

Ricardo, S. (1838) *A National Bank. The Remedy for the Evils Attendant upon our Present System of Paper Currency*, London: P. Richardson.

Rist, C. (1940) *History of Monetary and Credit Theory: From John Law to the Present Day*, London: Allen and Unwin.

Robbins, L. (1958) *Robert Torrens and the Evolution of Classical Economics*, London: Macmillan.

Robinson, J.V. (1953–1954) 'The production function and the theory of capital', *Review of Economic Studies*, 21: 81–106.

Rochon, L.P. (1999) *Credit, Money and Production: an Alternative Post-Keynesian Approach*, Cheltenham: Edward Elgar.

Roncaglia, A. (1978) *Sraffa and the Theory of Prices*, English translation by J.A. Kregel, New York: Wiley.

Roncaglia, A. (1998) 'Sraffa, Piero, as an interpreter of the classical economists', in H.D. Kurz and N. Salvadori (eds), *The Elgar Companion to Classical Economics*, 2 volumes, Cheltenham: Edward Elgar, L–Z: 399–404.

Royal Society (1912) *The Record of the Royal Society of London*, 3rd edn, London: Oxford University Press.

Samuelson, P.A. (1966) 'A summing up', *Quarterly Journal of Economics*, 80: 568–83.

Say, J.B. (1821) *A Treatise on Political Economy or the Production, Distribution and Consumption of Wealth*, English translation from the French fourth edition by C.R. Prinsip, published as a 'New American Edition' in 1880, reprint 1971, New Jersey: Augustus M. Kelley.

Say, J.B. (1848) *Oeuvres Diverses*, 2nd edn, Paris: Guillaumin.

Sayers, R.S. (ed.) (1963) *Economic Writings of James Pennington*, Series of Reprints of Scarce Works on Political Economy, no. 17, London: London School of Economics and Political Science.

Schumpeter, J.A. (1954) *History of Economic Analysis*, edited from manuscript by E.B. Schumpeter, London: George Allen and Unwin.

Schwartz, A.J. (1989) 'Banking school, currency school, free banking school', in J. Eatwell, M. Milgate and P. Newman (eds), *The New Palgrave: Money*, London: Macmillan: 41–9.

Senior, N. (1830) *Three Lectures on the Cost of Obtaining Money ...*, delivered before the University of Oxford in Trinity Term, 1829, in Senior (1966) *Selected Writings on Economics: A Volume of Pamphlets 1927–1852*, reprint, New York: Augustus M. Kelley.

Senior, N. (1836) *An Outline of the Science of Political Economy*, reprint 1965, New York: Augustus M. Kelley.

Senior, N. (1840) *Three Lectures on the Value of Money*, delivered before the University of Oxford in 1829, in Senior (1966) *Selected Writings on Economics: A Volume of Pamphlets 1927–1852*, reprint, New York: Augustus M. Kelley.

Senior, N. (1966) *Selected Writings on Economics: A Volume of Pamphlets 1927–1852*, reprint, New York: Augustus M. Kelley.

Serrano, F. (1995) 'Long period effective demand and the Sraffian supermultiplier', *Contributions to Political Economy*, 14: 67–90.

Sherwig, J.M. (1969) *Guineas and Gunpowder: British Foreign Aid in the Wars with France 1793–1815*, Cambridge, MA: Harvard University Press.

Skaggs, N.T. (1995) 'The methodological roots of J. Lawrence Laughlin's anti-quantity theory of money and prices', *Journal of the History of Economic Thought*, 17: 1–20.

Smart, W. (1910) *Economic Annals of the Nineteenth Century, 1801–1820*, vol. I, London: Macmillan.

Smart, W. (1917) *Economic Annals of the Nineteenth Century 1821–1830*, vol. II, London: Macmillan.

Smith, A. (1776 [1976]) *An Inquiry into the Nature and Causes of the Wealth of Nations*, (Glasgow edition), 2 vols, edited by R.H. Campbell, A.S. Skinner and W.B. Todd, reprint 1979, Indianapolis: Liberty Classics.

Smith, M. (1996a) 'Introduction', in Tooke, *Considerations on the State of the Currency, A Variorum of the First and Second Editions*, edited by M. Smith with P.D. Groenewegen, *Reprints of Economic Classics*, Series 2, no. 8, The University of Sydney: vi–xlvi.

Smith, M. (1996b) 'A monetary explanation of distribution in a "gold money economy"', *Contributions to Political Economy*, 15: 33–61.

Smith, M. (2001) 'Endogenous money, interest and prices: Tooke's monetary thought revisited', *Contributions to Political Economy*, 20: 31–55.

Smith, M. (2003) 'On central banking "rules": Tooke's critique of the Bank Charter Act of 1844', *Journal of the History of Economic Thought*, 25 (1): 39–61.

Smith, M. (2008) 'Thomas Tooke on the bullionist controversies', *The European Journal of the History Economic Thought*, 15 (1): 49–84.

Smith, M. (2009) 'Thomas Tooke on the Corn Laws', *History of Political Economy*, 41 (2): 343–82.

Soetbeer, A.D. (1888) *Materials for the Illustration and Criticism of the Economic Relations of the Precious Metals and of the Currency Question*, 2nd edn, Appendix XVI, in Gold and Silver Commission, 'Final Report of the Royal Commission Appointed to Inquire into the Recent Changes in the Relative Prices of the Precious Metals with Minutes of Evidence and Appendixes', c.5512, P.P., XLV.285, 455: 139–244.

Sowell, T. (1974) *Classical Economics Reconsidered*, Princeton: Princeton University Press.

Spiegel, H.W. (1971) *The Growth of Economic Thought*, Durham: Duke University Press.

Sraffa, P. (1951) 'Introduction', in Ricardo (1951–1973) *The Works and Correspondence of David Ricardo*, 11 volumes, edited by P. Sraffa with the collaboration of M. Dobb, Cambridge: Cambridge University Press, vol. I: xiii–lxii.

Sraffa, P. (1952) 'Notes on the evidence on the resumption of cash payments', in Ricardo (1951–1973) *The Works and Correspondence of David Ricardo*, 11 volumes, edited by P. Sraffa with the collaboration of M. Dobb, Cambridge: Cambridge University Press, vol. V: 350–70.

Sraffa, P. (1960) *Production of Commodities by Means of Commodities: Prelude to a Critique of Economic Theory*, Cambridge: Cambridge University Press.

Steedman, I. (1998) 'Classical economics and marginalism', in H.D. Kurz and N. Salvadori (eds), *The Elgar Companion to Classical Economics*, 2 volumes, Cheltenham: Edward Elgar, A–K: 117–22.

Steindl, J. (1952) *Maturity and Stagnation in American Capitalism*, Oxford: Basil Blackwell.

Stephen, L. and Lee, S. (eds) (1885–1900) *Dictionary of National Biography: From Earliest Times to 1900*, vols. I–LXIII, London: Smith, Elder and Co.

Stirati, A. (2001) 'Inflation, unemployment and hysteresis: an alternative view', *Review of Political Economy*, 13 (4): 427–51.

Supple, B. (1970) *The Royal Exchange Assurance: A History of British Insurance 1720–1970*, Cambridge: Cambridge University Press.

Terzi, A. (1986–1987) 'The independence of finance from saving: a flow-of-funds interpretation', *Journal of Post-Keynesian Economics*, IX (2): 188–97.

Thomas, M.W. (1948) *Early Factory Legislation: A study in legislative and administrative evolution*, Leigh-on-Sea: Thames.

Thomas, S.E. (1934) *Rise and Growth of Joint Stock Banking: Britain to 1860*, vol. 1, London: Pitman and sons.

Thornton, H. (1802) *An Enquiry into the Nature and Effects of the Paper Credit of Great Britain*, as reprinted in Hayek (1939) *An Enquiry into the Nature and Effects of the Paper Credit of Great Britain (1802) by Henry Thornton …*, reprint 1991, New Jersey: Augustus M. Kelley: 65–276.

Thornton, H. (1811) 'Two speeches of Henry Thornton, Esq. on the Bullion Report, 7 May and 14 May, 1811', reprinted as Appendix III in Hayek (1939) *An Enquiry into the Nature and Effects of the Paper Credit of Great Britain (1802) by Henry Thornton …*, reprint 1991, New Jersey: Augustus M. Kelley: 323–61.

Tooke, T. (1819a) Evidence to the Commons Secret Committee on the Expediency of the Bank Resuming Cash Payments, P.P. 1819 (202, 282), III: 125–32.

Tooke, T. (1819b) Evidence to the Lords Secret Committee to enquire into the State of the Bank of England, with respect to the Expediency of the Resumption of Cash Payments, P.P. 1819, (291) III, (98 Q): 168–83.

Tooke, T. (1820) Evidence to the Lords Select Committee to Inquire into the Means of Extending and Securing the Foreign Trade of the Country [Relative to the Timber Trade], P.P. 1820, (269) III: 25–39.

Tooke, T. (1821a) Evidence to the Commons Select Committee to whom the Several Petitions Complaining of the Depressed State of the Agriculture of the United Kingdom were Referred, P.P. 1821 (668) IX: 224–40, 287–94, 295–8, 344–55.

Tooke, T. (1821b) Evidence to the Commons Select Committee Appointed to Consider the Means of Improving and Maintaining the Foreign Trade of the Country, P.P. 1821 (186), VI: 56–65.

Tooke, T. (1822) Evidence to the Commons Select Committee Appointed to Consider of the Means of Improving and Maintaining the Foreign Trade of the Country, P.P. 1823 (411), IV (West India Docks): 351–8.

Tooke, T. (1823) *Thoughts and Details of High and Low Prices of the Last Thirty Years, in Four Parts* (with Part i published in January and Parts ii–iv in July), London: John Murray.

Tooke, T. (1824) *Thoughts and Details of High and Low Prices of the Last Thirty Years, from 1793 to 1822, in Four Parts*, 2nd edn (Parts i–iv and Supplementary, iv.s.), London: John Murray.

Tooke, T. (1826) *Considerations on the State of the Currency*, 2nd edn, London: John Murray.

Tooke, T. (1829a) *A Letter to Lord Grenville on the Effects Ascribed to the Resumption of Cash Payments on the Value of the Currency*, London: Longman, Brown, Green and Longmans.

Tooke, T. (1829b) *A Second Letter to Lord Grenville: On the Currency in Connection* with the Corn Trade and on the Corn Laws, to which is added a Postscript on the *Present Commercial Stagnation*, London: Longman, Brown, Green and Longmans.

Tooke, T. (1832) Evidence to the Commons Committee of Secrecy on the expediency of renewing the Charter of the Bank of England ..., P.P. 1831–32 (722), VI: (Q 3809–4117) 269–304, (Q 5373–479) 432–43.

Tooke, T. (1838) *A History of Prices and of the State of the Circulation from 1793 to 1837; preceded by a brief sketch of the corn trade in the past two centuries*, vols I and II, 1928 reprint, London: P.S. King and Son.

Tooke, T. (1840a) *A History of Prices, and of the State of the Circulation in 1838 and 1839, with some remarks of the alterations proposed in our banking system*, vol. III, 1928 reprint, London: P.S. King and Son.

Tooke, T. (1840b) Evidence to the Commons Select Committee on Banks of Issue, P.P. 1840 (602), vol. IV: (Q 3261–306) 296–9, (Q 3615–859) 337–72.

Tooke, T. (1844) *An Inquiry into the Currency Principle, the Connection of the Currency with Prices and the Expediency of a Separation of Issue from Banking*, 2nd edn, in Series of Reprints of Scarce Works on Political Economy, No. 15, 1959, The London School of Economics and Political Science.

Tooke, T. (1848a) *A History of Prices, and of the State of the Circulation, from 1839 to 1847 inclusive: with a general review of the currency question, and remarks on the operation of the Act, 7 & 8 Vict. c32*, vol. IV, 1928 reprint, London: P.S. King and Son.

Tooke, T. (1848b) Evidence to the Commons Secret Committee on Commercial Distress, P.P. 1847–1848 (395), VIII, Pt. I: (Q 5301–493) 410–33.

Tooke, T. (1848c) Evidence to Lords Secret Committee Appointed to Inquire into the Causes of the Commercial Distress, P.P. 1847–1848 (565), VIII, Pt. III: (Q 2975–3158) 333–55.

Tooke, T. (1856) *On the Bank Charter Act of 1844, its Principles and Operation; with suggestions for an improved administration of the Bank of England*, London: Longman, Brown, Green and Longmans.

Tooke, T. (1996) *Considerations on the State of the Currency*, A Variorum of the First and Second Editions, edited by M. Smith with P.D. Groenewegen, *Reprints of Economic Classics*, Series 2, no. 8, University of Sydney.

Tooke, T. and Newmarch, W. (1857) *A History of Prices and of the State of the Circulation, during the Nine Years 1848–1856*, vols V and VI, 1928 reprint, London: P.S. King and Son.

Tooke, W. (ed.) (1798) *New and General Biographical Dictionary* ..., 15 vols, (editorship assisted by W. Beloe and R. Nares), London: G.G. and J. Robinson.

Tooke, W. (ed.) (1799) *View of the Russian Empire during the reign of Catherine II and to the close of the present Century*, 2nd edn, 3 vols, London: Longman, Rees and Debrett.

Tooke, W. (ed.) (1800) *History of Russia from the Foundation of the Monarchy by Rurik to the Accession of the Catherine the Second*, 2 vols, London: Longman and Rees.

Tooke, W. (the younger) (1855) *The Monarchy of France, its Rise, Progress, and Fall*, London: privately printed.

Torrens, R. (1829) *An Essay on the External Corn Trade* ..., 5th edn, reprint 1972, New York: Augustus M. Kelley.

Torrens, R. (1837) *A Letter to the Right Honourable Lord Viscount Melbourne*, 2nd edn, London: Longmans, Rees, Orme, Brown and Green.

Torrens, R. (1840) *A Letter to Thomas Tooke, esq., in Reply to his Objections against the* separation of the business of the Bank into a Department of Issue and Department of Deposit and Discount, London: Longman, Hurst, Orme and Brown.

Torrens, R. (1844) *An Inquiry into the practical working of the proposed arrangements for the Renewal of the Charter of the Bank of England and the Regulation of the Currency*, 2nd edn, London: Smith, Elder and Co.

Torrens, R. (1848) *The Principles and practical operations of Sir Robert Peel's bill of 1844 explained and defended against the objections of Tooke, Fullarton and Wilson*, London: Longman, Brown, Green and Longmans.

Torrens, R. (1858) *The Principles and Practical Operation of Sir Robert Peel's Act of 1844, Explained and Defended*, 3rd edn, London: Longmans and Ridgway.

Trezzini, A. (1995) 'Capacity utilisation in the long run and the autonomous components of aggregate demand', *Contributions to Political Economy*, 14: 33–66.

Trezzini, A. (1998) 'Capacity utilisation in the long run: some further considerations', *Contributions to Political Economy*, 17: 53–67.

Trotter, Coutts Sir (1810) *The Principles of Currency and Exchanges Applied to the Report the Select Committee of the House of Commons ...*, 2nd edn, London: Cadell and Davies.

Turgot, A.R.J. (1766) *Reflections on the Formation and Distribution of Wealth*, in P.D. Groenewegen (ed.) (1977) *The Economics of A.R.J. Turgot*, English translation with an introduction, The Hague: Martinus Nijhoff: 43–95.

Uhr, C.G. (1991) 'Knut Wicksell, neoclassicist and iconoclast', in B. Sandelin (ed.) *The History of Swedish Economic Thought*, New York: Routledge: 76–121.

Vansittart, N. (1811) *Substance of Two Speeches Made by the Right Hon. N. Vansittart on the Bullion Question (on the 7th and 13th May, 1811)*, London: J. Hatchard.

Vianello, F. (1985) 'The pace of accumulation', *Political Economy: Studies in the Surplus Approach*, 1 (1): 69–87.

Viner, J. (1937) *Studies in the Theory of International Trade*, reprint 1975, New Jersey: Augustus M. Kelley.

Wagner, A. (1857) *Beiträge zur Lehre von den Banken*, Leipzig: Voss.

West, E. (1815) *An Essay on the Application of Capital to Land*, London: T. Underwood.

Wheatley, J. (1803) *Remarks on Currency and Commerce*, London: T. Cadell and W. Davies.

Wheatley, J. (1807) *An Essay on the Theory of Money and Principles of Commerce*, vol. 1, London: T. Cadell and W. Davies.

White, L.H. (1984) *Free Banking in Britain: Theory, Experience, and Debate, 1800–1845*, New York: Cambridge University Press.

Wicksell, K. (1893) *Value, Capital and Rent*, English translation by S.W. Frowein with a Foreword by G.L.S. Shackle, 1954, reprint 1970, New Jersey: Augustus M. Kelley.

Wicksell, K. (1898) *Interest and Prices: A Study of the Causes Regulating the Value of Money*, English translation by R.F. Kahn with an introduction by B. Ohlin, 1936, reprint 1965, New Jersey: Augustus M. Kelley.

Wicksell, K. (1901) *Lectures on Political Economy*, vol. I, English translation by E. Classen and edited with an introduction by L. Robbins, 1935, reprint 1977, New Jersey: Augustus M. Kelley.

Wicksell, K. (1906) *Lectures on Political Economy*, vol. II, English translation by E. Classen and edited with an introduction by L. Robbins, 1935, reprint 1978, New Jersey: Augustus M. Kelley.

Wilson, J. (1847) *Capital, Currency and Banking ...*, Articles I–XIX, London: *The Economist* (cited as 1847, Article, page number).

Wood, E. (1939) *English Theories of Central Banking Control, 1819–1858*, Cambridge: Harvard University Press.

Wray, L.R. (1988) 'Profit expectations and the investment–saving relation', *Journal of Post-Keynesian Economics*, XI (1): 131–47.

Wray, L.R. (1990) *Money and Credit in Capitalist Economies: The Endogenous Money Approach*, Aldershot: Edward Elgar.

Young, A. (1801) *Annals of Agriculture and other useful Arts*, vol. 37, Bury, St. Edmonds: J. Rackham.

Young, A. (1812) *An Enquiry into the Progressive Value of Money in England, as marked by the Price of Agricultural Products*, London: B. McMillan.

Index

For Product Safety Concerns and Information please contact our
EU representative GPSR@taylorandfrancis.com Taylor & Francis
Verlag GmbH, Kaufingerstraße 24, 80331 München, Germany